Happy Boys
Happy!

A Rock History Of
THE SMALL FACES & HUMBLE PIE

featuring STEVE MARRIOTT, RONNIE LANE,
PETER FRAMPTON & ROD STEWART

Design: David Houghton
Printed by: Unwin Brothers Limited

Published by: Sanctuary Publishing Limited, The Colonnades, 82
Bishops Bridge Road, London W2 6BB

First edition (in German) published in 1993 by Sonnentanz-Verlag
© 1993 Sonnentanz-Verlag Roland Kron, Oblatterwallstrasse 30a,
D-86153 Augsburg
Translated from German by Uli Twelker

Copyright in this edition: Uli Twelker and Roland Schmitt, 1997

Photographs: John Hellier, Redferns, Pictorial Press, Ulli Kniep,
Rolling Stone, Klaus Witt, Pan Foto, Melody Maker, Helmut G Roos,
Hammersmith Pics

While the publishers have made every reasonable effort to trace the
copyright owners for any or all of the photographs in this book,
there may be some omissions of credits for which we apologise.

ISBN: 1-86074-197-5

Happy Boys
Happy!

A Rock History of
THE SMALL FACES & HUMBLE PIE

featuring STEVE MARRIOTT, RONNIE LANE,
PETER FRAMPTON & ROD STEWART

By Uli Twelker & Roland Schmitt

About The Authors

Uli Twelker: Born in Bielefeld, Germany, in 1953, Uli formed his first R&B band in 1968, as a schoolboy drumming through his English lessons. He has since played in various semi-pro bands, for instance with Mike Harrison's stand-in Danny Kreutzberger in the Anglo-German VIPs and Bielefeld rockers Thunderbirds. At the time of writing he's with the retro combo Witchwood. Uli encountered rock journalism during his years as a Londoner, meeting his hero Steve Marriott in 1978 as well as The Hollies' Bob Elliott, who would invite him to write an 'on the road' tour booklet in 1986. Numerous beat and R&B articles, interviews and reviews have appeared in German and British publications, including *Good Times*, German Saarland Radio/TV's *Pop Archive International*, *Musik Express/Sounds*, *Beat Goes On*, and *Hollies Carousel*. In his day job, Uli works as an English language teacher and translator. He lives in Gütersloh, Germany, with his wife Senta.

Roland Schmitt: Born of French-German stock in Mainz, Germany in 1953, Roland got interested in beat, R&B and rock while at school in Hockenheim near the famous race track. His first single was a present from his granny – it was supposed to be something by The Small Faces, but turned out to be 'Mama' by Heintje, Germany's answer to Little Jimmy Osmond! Fortunately his second single was 'Itchycoo Park'. Since 1982, Roland has been head of the library in the Saarland State Radio & TV Network (Saarländischer Rundfunk). As a side line, the amateur musician (on bass, guitar and harmonica) runs radio shows, mainly about folk and world music, but also including rock and blues. Roland writes for several music magazines and fanzines. His Small Faces newsletter, *Itchycoo*, has been issued regularly from 1985 and he has been publishing the *Pop Archive International* since 1989. This is a rock and pop encyclopedia, organised as a regularly up-dated loose-leaf subscription series which is also available via mail order. Roland lives in Eschringen near Saarbrücken on the German and French border.

Contents

Acknowledgments

We are indebted to the many people who helped us with research for this book. Several among them were invaluable in their assistance: primary among them is the late and very sadly missed Steve Marriott himself. He was aware that we were planning to write this book, he told us many a tale backstage and in pubs and would surely have cooperated much more had he lived to do so. Also Peter Frampton in Nashville, Tennessee, who spent many hours reminiscing with us. Klaus Witt and Detlef Mittmann we have to thank for discographic advice and rare illustrations. John Hellier (publisher of the Small Faces fanzine *Wapping Wharf*) and his predecessor Steve Chamberlain for keeping us supplied with numerous up-to-date details. Jim Leverton (who played bass and sang next to Steve Marriott, his and our dear friend, for almost fourteen years) for his charm and information. Alan 'Sticky' Wickett, Steve's last drummer and storyteller. Steve's widow, Toni Marriott, Toby Joe Marriott (his son with Pam), and Mick Eve, ex-Blue Fame and Steve's Eighties agent. Ulli Kniep (music journalist at ffn radio, Isernhagen, Germany) – quote hunter extraordinaire and an excellent photographer. Barbara Jacobs (a New York promoter), Ponty Bone and Scott Garber – for their contact with Ronnie Lane. Thanks also to Ian McLagan, Ronnie and Susan Lane who – via Barbara – related news about their lives and work. Thank you, Clem Clempson, for 1994's Colosseum time-out backstage, and Donal Gallagher for bringing Sanctuary Publishing and two Happy Boys together. Thanks are also due to Joe Vento of New York band The Out Of Bodies, for keeping us well informed about anecdotes, encounters and newspaper articles Stateside. Thanks too to Mechthild and Roland of Sonnentanz, and to Penny, Michelle, Eddy and Jeff at Sanctuary, for always being spot on.

On a personal note, where would we have been without our beloved wives? With tolerance, they endured our activities, our absence in spite of physical presence. Christa and Senta, we send our heartfelt thanks for your kind-hearted patience. And let's not forget the kids, who far too often had to make do without Daddy while he was stuck in front of his PC. On the subject of storing data, precious help with safe word processing was provided by Uli's brother, Erik Twelker.

Ta all,

Uli & Roland

Preface

The idea for a book about The Small Faces cannot entirely be claimed by ourselves. The well known British rock journalist John Pidgeon (his *Rod Stewart And The Changing Faces* was published as a paperback in 1976) had been in the process of preparing a lavish photo book-cum-portfolio, which was subsequently cancelled unceremoniously. Drummer Kenney Jones' confidante Terry Rawlings had also assembled sufficient material for a book but, back in 1982, Faces fan Paul Weller's tiny publishing company Riot Stories was apparently just able to finance a small volume called *All Our Yesterdays*, which is consequently limited to The Small Faces' Golden Era of 1965 to 1968. Since early 1992, Terry Rawlings has reportedly been assembling a book of Kenney Jones' illustrated memories, with Paul Weller as co-author. But this project, as well as his own Small Faces history *Quite Naturally*, has so far failed to attract the publishing industry's attention. At least a few welcome excerpts appeared in the October 1992 edition of the British magazine *Record Collector*.

Instead, the renowned music journalist Paolo Hewitt (also the author of Jam and Oasis biographies) presented a marvellous illustrated text about The Small Faces from 1964 to 1969. He aptly chose the sub-title *The Young Mods' Forgotten Story* (based on a song by Curtis Mayfield's Impressions).

Ever since he became an international superstar, there has been no shortage of Rod Stewart books, including detailed chapters on The Small Faces and Faces, as well as regular magazine/fanzine stories. Our project, though, appears to be the first publication to attempt a comprehensive history of the whole Small Faces family tree, including fringe bands and post-Faces solo careers. Apart from the quoted sources, we have utilised and consulted numerous British, American, German and French papers, magazines, fanzines, promo leaflets etc. Additionally, we made use of collected radio and TV interviews as well as many conversations we had with the individual musicians, especially during the last eight years. Problems appeared whenever these boys related incidents and stories with contradictions or even absurdities.

To a certain extent, these deviations came about because of fading memories (certainly in Ronnie Lane's case and to a lesser extent where Steve Marriott is concerned). But on the other hand we cannot rule out wilful misinformation which Steve Marriott – his tongue firmly in his cheek – was rather famous for. He loved telling 'fibs' – without batting an eye. Whenever we weren't sure about certain details, schedules or incidents in band history, we have tried to point these uncertainties out, rather than pretending insider status in every related passage. If in spite of that, incorrect details or 'genuine' mistakes appear, we will be grateful for comments setting the record straight.

Those who know The Small Faces' repertoire well enough will have guessed how we arrived at the title for this book. The song 'Happy Boys Happy' is not exactly a gem among the complete works of the band, but the phrase is meant to point out that in the face of many difficulties, they maintained a positive outlook on life, on and off stage, and were always open for fun and practical jokes.

Rather than restrict ourselves to one group or period, we have followed the often twisted and entangled solo ventures of the Faces, Small Faces and Humble Pie musicians from those successful years to the present day. While it would have been much simpler to tell a relatively continuous band story, the likes of which The Kinks, Hollies or The Who can claim, The Small Faces – unfortunately? – did not do us that particular favour. We could have focused on the most successful period of 1965 to 1975, but then we were curious why reunion attempts and solo projects either failed or met with only limited success. In the end we couldn't leave anything out.

INTRODUCTION
Shake

Who cares about The Small Faces these days? It's a good question, and one we had to contend with when we planned and indeed wrote most of this book in 1992. In Britain Steve Marriott and co were almost forgotten, at least as far as the media is concerned. For a number of years, back in the Swinging Sixties, they were a singles band, with a fair standing in the Mod scene, and Marriott was considered an above average singer. At least his sudden death in 1991 earned him a few decent obituaries.

But what else did they do in rock history? Given the nature of this book, and the fact that each chapter deals with virtually a separate career, it's worth taking an overview here. Humble Pie and The Faces, who had grown out of The Small Faces' bankrupt estate (with the fans as Official Receivers?), enjoyed considerable popularity in the United States and Europe but were far from well received back home. The solo careers of Ronnie Lane (with Slim Chance) in the Seventies and Steve Marriott (with Packet Of Three and other backing bands) in the Eighties were basically limited to clubs and pubs; and hardly anyone talked about Ian McLagan and Kenney Jones.

Steve managed to keep a dedicated pool of fans, especially on the continent. The big music papers didn't bother to acknowledge the history of The Small Faces or pursue it any further. That's why it comes as quite a revelation that to this day – with a massive avalanche called BritPop since 1994 – musicians and singers of different pop music eras quote the crucial influence that The Small Faces, especially Steve Marriott, had on them.

During the early stages of the band's career, their charismatic attraction for contemporary peers was necessarily limited – the boys were looking up to their own rhythm and blues and soul idols. But with growing success – they hit the Number One spot at the end of 1966 with 'All Or Nothing' – all that changed. As the flagship of the Mod movement, they exerted a remarkable influence on their regular audience: how they moved and acted on stage, on TV, during interviews, in photo stories etc, how they dressed (immensely important) – everything was analysed and copied. Marriott and Lane were soon in demand as songwriters, session musicians and producers for acts like PP Arnold, Billy Nichols, Twice As Much, Skip Bifferty, Art and many others, while Chris Farlowe became one of the first acts to cover a Small Faces song – 'My Way Of Giving', which had actually been written with him in mind in the first place. (Marriott's successor Rod Stewart would later try his luck at interpreting this ballad on his solo album *Gasoline Alley*.)

The charisma which made The Small Faces and their frontman Steve Marriott so unique has been described unashamedly by the British journalist Nik Cohn in the Mod chapter of his book *Pop From The Beginning*, 1969:

> More to my taste, though, were The Small Faces. Originally, the Faces came out of the East End, and they were ultimate Mods, small and neat and schnide, very spotty. In the first place, they were a muted echo of The Who, and they were small ravers, loud and brash and really a bit dire. Once they'd settled down, though, they turned out not to be dire at all.
>
> Their singer and lead guitarist, Steve Marriott, had once most suitably played the Artful Dodger in *Oliver!*. Now he looked like a teddy bear and showed a fine shamelessness, screaming himself purple and hurling himself at the mike as if he meant to swallow it whole. He sang well too, wild and strangled. Bopping up and back, his knees clamped tight and his eyes screwed up, he'd be berserk and he'd be good. He'd have everything it took.
>
> In many ways, the Faces have been the group that sums up all groups: they have that classic gift for self-delusion. They've thought themselves artists when they've only been loons, they've talked endlessly about getting themselves together and making masterpieces but, somehow, they've wound up in discotheques instead. They've jumped aboard every arty fad possible but they've never quite got the point

and, in the end, they've always made solid old-fashioned noises after all. Finally, none of that crap has mattered: they've meant fun and they've lasted. Little and fierce and pantomime, they've come to be one of my most favourite acts.

Thankfully, Cohn lets his sentiments run wild: he grossly generalises and exaggerates out of proportion, but somehow he's right on the button, and in a few bold sentences manages to catch the unique, special character of The Small Faces. When Cohn published his *Pop History* in 1969, he was barely twenty-two years old; as young as Marriott who had just left The Small Faces.

Of course, The Small Faces' impact wasn't limited to Britain. In Australia and New Zealand, the band – together with fellow Mods The Who – were more popular than The Beatles or The Rolling Stones. The Australian Valentines – whose singer Bon Scott would go on to front AC/DC – covered 'I Can't Dance With You', and when you heard Human Instinct from New Zealand with their 1968 opus 'Pink Dawn' you could easily spot their *Ogdens' Nut Gone Flake* inspiration. Even in Europe The Small Faces made their presence felt: French rock'n'roll legend Johnny Hallyday was so impressed with Marriott/Lane's 'My Way Of Giving' that he rendered it to his native French as 'J'en ai jamais rien demandé' and recorded it for his album *Johnny* in 1967.

In those days, Hallyday closely collaborated with a certain Micky Jones. This guitarist, originally from London, had passed through Paris on a French tour with a band called Nero And The Gladiators and had stayed, accepting the gig as backing musician and songwriter for Hallyday. Apparently he established contacts with Steve Marriott who, with Ronnie Lane and Peter Frampton, came to Paris in the late autumn of 1968.

There, with Mick Jones producing and Glyn Johns (of Olympic Studios, where The Small Faces used to record) twiddling the mixing knobs, he and Hallyday recorded a number of basic backing tracks. At least three songs carry the Marriott/Lane trademark; the number 'Amen', for instance, sounds suspiciously like 'That Man'. Obviously, no credits for this collaboration can be found on the finished Hallyday album, released by Philips in 1969. This would surely have caused trouble with Immediate Records. Incidentally, Jones' career soon flourished as guitarist for the similarly francophile Spooky Tooth before coming to public attention in 1976 as Foreigner's driving force and leader.

In Germany, The Small Faces were extremely popular, and for their spin-off Humble Pie, the land of the seedy Reeperbahn, castles and the Black Forest was second only to the United States. In 1968, according to the German trade paper *Musikmarkt*, The Small Faces were Number Four in the 'Beat Group' popularity charts: hot on the heels of The Bee Gees, Beatles and Manfred Mann, and beating The Rolling Stones! Many German beat and rock groups covered their material, and some numbers even managed to get recorded, though the results were rarely convincing (with the exception of Kin Ping Meh's version of 'Tin Soldier').

On the other hand, The Small Faces played only a small part in what was coined the British Invasion when, between 1963 and 1967, UK singers and groups cracked and dominated the US charts for the first time. In fact, only 'Itchycoo Park' managed to reach the stateside Top Twenty. For numerous reasons, an American tour had never materialised, but in insiders' circles, The Small Faces were highly appreciated, as documented later in a tribute by the exquisite underground fanzine *Bomp!*, famous today for having had such renowned journalists as Charlie Gillett and Greil Marcus among its contributors.

That Humble Pie and The Faces were household names in the US during the Seventies is a generally known fact. But interestingly, the split of both these Small Faces successors coincided with the rise of the punk rock movement in Great Britain around 1975-6. The media and even the public had, it seemed, forgotten Steve Marriott, Humble Pie and even The Faces had ever existed. Ironically, it was the young punks, of all people, who still cared about these "boring old farts". So it hurt even more when Steve Marriott was called just that by the British punk gutter press in 1978.

But The Sex Pistols, for instance, used to 'dig' the early Small Faces rockers and even recorded an extremely rough version of 'What'cha Gonna Do About It'. They also liked the early Faces, that "fun working-class blues-based rock band" (*Billboard*). 'Three Button Hand Me Down' counted as one of their favourite songs and they covered it live. When ex-Pistol bassman Glen Matlock started The Rich Kids with Midge Ure in 1978, a Small Faces number was compulsory: and so 'Here Come The Nice' appeared on the B-side of 'Marching Men'.

Elsewhere, Dead Boys frontman Stiv Bator (later to run Lords Of The

New Church) and Johnny Thunders (ex-New York Dolls) declared themselves fans of Steve Marriott's voice and charisma. At the same time The Small Faces were compared in the German edition of *Sounds* with a punk group ("The Damned of the Sixties").

It seems only natural then that, in the late Seventies, The Small Faces found new worshippers during the Mod revival, the musical progeny of punk. The darlings of Neo Mod Rock, The Jam, specifically called them their heroes and even released a lesser known Small Faces song – a live version of 'Get Yourself Together' – on a twelve-inch B-side (a demo studio recording can be found on their 1991 compilation of out-takes, *Extras*. Jam boss Paul Weller also made sure that the first Small Faces biography (by Terry Rawlings) was published – as mentioned – via his Riot Stories.

Other, less successful Neo Mod bands saw themselves in The Small Faces tradition as well: The Times, Lambrettas, Secret Affair or The Prisoners, who tried 'Don't Burst My Bubble', for instance), to name just a few.

In 1985, which was the year of Live Aid for African famine relief, many of these young musicians got themselves together and it was obvious which song was going to be chosen as a charity single: 'All Or Nothing' of course. On this new recording, the song's creator had to be part of the proceedings. And so Steve Marriott and a whole host of musical legends like PP Arnold, Chris Farlowe, Eddie Phillips of The Creation as well as an army of Neo Mod musicians got together with producer Kenny Lynch (the co-author of 'Sha-La-La-La-Lee'). The record's proceeds were donated in equal parts to the Band Aid Trust and Ronnie Lane's ARMS project.

The Mod revival may now be part of history, but a 'third generation' of young Mod bands, for instance The Clique, The Apemen (from Germany) and Los Flechazos (from Spain) are already coming through.

There is still 'rock', though, which is flourishing and has developed and split in numerous directions, including hard rock and heavy metal. Traditionally, Led Zeppelin or Deep Purple are seen as the godfathers of those genres, but these bands had idols, too, and listening to The Kinks' 'You Really Got Me', The Who's 'My Generation' or The Small Faces' 'E To D', you realise who had hit the chords really hard years before.

The Small Faces surely made one hell of a noise during their early days. This was followed by a more mellow period when they worked in folk and psychedelic styles, just about until the end of that group's first incarnation. But even then, hard hitting songs like 'Rollin' Over' or 'Wham Bam Thank You Mam' were part of the deal, and live they hit you like a thunderstorm.

Humble Pie's stylistic U-turn towards harder sounds became obvious with their 1971 *Rock On* album, after a less than successful – if attractive! – country and folk rock period. Marriott perfected a powerful, literally throat gripping singing style that was soon widely copied. To name but a few: Gary Holton of The Heavy Metal Kids, Foreigner's Lou Gramm and most recently Chris Robinson of The Black Crowes were, and to an extent still are, ardent followers.

On the other hand, the straight, unpretentious rock songs Marriott wrote for Humble Pie were all but ignored, with the notable exception of 'Thirty Days In The Hole', which was covered by Mr Big and Kick Axe. More often, hard rock and mainstream groups tried their luck with versions of classic Small Faces songs. But interesting, innovative interpretations were few and far between before a 1996 tribute, with only Great White's acoustic arrangement of 'Afterglow' or 'Rollin' Over' by guitar legend Brian May standing out. Most of the time, popular numbers like 'Tin Soldier' or 'All Or Nothing' are simply thrashed out no matter what.

The Faces' experiences with style versus success were similar to Humble Pie's. Ronnie Lane's mellow songs hardly stood a chance on stage, especially with big audiences. Bold rockers like 'Too Bad' or 'That's All You Need' were much better received. Most popular of all were the Stewart/Wood compositions which held a rather special charm for live audiences. Their melodies were plain and simple, so the fans could easily sing along to them. And as The Faces weren't exactly tee-totallers, and a pint of beer or bottle of wine was always at hand (several actually), their concerts were as high and happy as an all-night party. At the time, terms like 'Party Rock' or 'Sleaze Rock' had yet to be invented, but long since, bands like the (meanwhile disbanded) Georgia Satellites, Quireboys, Dogs D'Amour as well as The Black Crowes are likely to get branded with that trademark.

Even in the mid 1990s, The (Small) Faces don't seem to have been entirely forgotten by new musical trendsetters. Steve Marriott was delighted with the appreciation he got from the so-called 'rave' bands. US groups like The Screaming Trees, Gumball or Pontiac Brothers, who didn't baulk at weird or rough sounds, made no secret of their sympathy for the rough and ready noise made by The (Small) Faces. And over in the UK, where since 1994 a new phase called BritPop has emerged, young bands like Blur, Oasis, Ocean Colour Scene and Supergrass are all naming The Small Faces as their musical inspirations. To prove it wasn't mere media mouthing some of them documented their love for the band with a tribute album – a project which even had the go-ahead and drumming assistance of Kenney Jones.

It might seem odd now, but 'Who could give a monkey's about Steve Marriott these days?' was exactly what Steve asked himself from time to time throughout his career. Whether he was wondering – locked in his farm studio in 1974 – why nobody wanted those songs he'd developed during month long sessions, or whether he got depressed about the pitifully low fees he commanded – sitting in his transit on his way to a Manchester gig in early 1991 he asked: "What am I doing here, racing up the M1 for a bleedin' thousand quid?" His bass player, Jim Leverton, had answered, "Make albums, man!" but Steve could have answered the questions himself very well. He was both a full time musician and a twenty-four-hour connoisseur; he wanted to be creative and enjoy himself, preferably at the same time. And so it was difficult for him – most of the time – to just function. For many years during his career, he played the songs he fancied at the particular volume and length he wanted.

The little cockney lad had developed his instinct for musical as well as marijuanian hedonism during the prolific studio years of 1968 (Small Faces) and 1969 (Humble Pie), when he had vowed to act as creative catalyst, but never as a frontman for his new Pie project.

Backing the others with a joint hanging from his lips surely seemed far better than the demanding role of the spotlight kid. Nevertheless, after the nerve-wracking screaming girls of his Sixties Small Faces days, he did endure the American tour machinery from 1970-75 with Humble Pie. But this time he paid dearly for it – it cost him his health.

Marriott could have used the Eighties for reaping in a healthy retirement sum, the kind of bank account Mick Jagger and Rod Stewart became proud owners of ages ago. But the logistics of sophisticated tour schedules and night after night of Greatest Hits presentations weren't his kind of showbiz. Still, he was proud to be a hero for Mods, Bluesers and Ravers alike. These punters were really interested in him. "Most of those bands grew up on people like me, and I'm proud to be an influence. I love it. There's a lot of these youngsters in the audience. Of course, most of these people are now dead. I'm still alive: God knows how!" he laughed in Hannover DJ Ulli Kniep's face just a few weeks before his tragic death.

Some of Steve's fans – familiar with afternoon soundchecks – preferred the little shouter's soulful warm-up vocalising in dressing rooms to well-planned sets. Just like them, Marriott was aware of the dangers of simply rattling The Small Faces' hit repertoire off, as he told us in 1988:

"What we do is pick one song, otherwise it would be cabaret. I have to be very careful at my age not to be cabaret. So what we do is just one number from that era. And it is the anthem of that era: 'My Generation' and 'All Or Nothing' were the two anthems of that Sixties era, for the Mods anyway. So we do one, that's enough. The rest isn't enjoyable for me. If I had to play all those fucking old numbers..."

Of course he often did play more of these wonderful, "fucking" numbers. On his very last tour in January/February 1991, 'Itchycoo Park' was back in his set after a long absence. But Steve didn't want to feel obliged to do them and become a living jukebox: "Let them [other bands] play them. I'm glad they play them. I would hate to be someone like – for instance – Bo Diddley, having to play Bo Diddley every night. I would prefer to play what I felt inclined to play, and let all the other people play the old songs."

And that's why the hell music fans are still interested in Steve Marriott, because of his feeling. It was exactly this that made him unpredictable – he didn't guarantee a thing. But his name on a poster – up till the very last gig – stood for at least an hour's professional performance, sometimes more, but never less. If it went well, then it was really "all so beautiful" – like the chorus of 'Itchycoo Park' – which is to say it was inspired as well as so exciting.

CHAPTER ONE
From The Beginning
The Artful Dodger

S teve Marriott was the central Small Faces figure, not entirely due to his unmistakable, powerful voice. He had been musically active since his early childhood and – crucial in terms of his later stage presence – had been gathering acting experience for many years.

Stephen Marriott was born on 30 January, 1947 as the son of Bill and Kathleen Marriott, in Stepney, part of the British capital's East End, which the *Penguin Guide To London 1958* described as follows: "Stepney, once notorious as a congested and poverty-stricken borough, includes the greater part of the 'East End' of London, with a population partly employed in the neighbouring docks or other seafaring activities. Streets upon streets were completely devastated during the Second World War, and the slums have now been almost wholly replaced...The Highway (previously Ratcliff Highway) is a long street which formerly had an infamous reputation for its drinking dens for seamen." So there's your post-war cockney atmosphere, before it later became immortalised in the British TV soap *EastEnders*.

Thanks to his musically inclined family, Stephen grew up with the sounds of the music hall and folk taken for granted: "It was my dad, playing piano. He was a pub pianist, which meant that he got his drinks free, which is what it was about. And he used to be not hired so much for parties, but invited to parties, because he could play the piano and played about thirty songs right off the bat, that they could all sing to. So I'd go to sleep listening to it. I'd be the kid on the settee that had to be wrapped up, while they all stomped and danced. I couldn't stand it after a while, so I said 'For

Christ's sake, shut up!' even then. But yes, it did instill a certain...because everybody was so happy, 'cause they were so drunk. My father would be playing and [he hums madly] they would all be singing...so it instilled in me that music was happy, you see. That's what it did...

"I started out begging round bus queues – with a ukelele – when I was about seven years old, something like that, and I sort of subsidised my money, which was nothing. I got a four-string ukelele and used to go round the bus queues and just play. I suppose it was the novelty of seeing a little kid who had the balls to sort of do it. I used to get quite a lot of money, it was great... I used to play the ukelele, and my mother would play the washboard; my father had a tea-chest bass. They would play and my sister used to do the hand-jive. We would play at different little functions; you know, old people's homes, and that made them feel good, just a little bit of music. We did that, it was great, and we got paid for it, so therefore I suppose that's professional."

Apparently, little Stevie's talents were detected early by his ambitious mother. She had found an advert in the *Daily Mirror* offering acting parts for a stage version of the musical *Oliver!*. Steve wasn't too keen on taking part, but Mum had it her way, as was to be expected. The eleven-year-old set off for an audition with Lionel Bart, who had created the script based on Charles Dickens' novel *Oliver Twist*.

Bart immediately recognised tiny Steve. He had often spotted him at East End bus stops, busking for the waiting crowd with his ukelele. For his audition, Steve presented a skiffle version of the then popular Buddy Holly tune 'Oh Boy'. He must have been very convincing, for Bart offered him a contract on the spot for the part of the Artful Dodger. In 1960 Steve's recording career began when *Oliver!* was released as an album. It featured Steve's lead vocals on three songs – 'Consider Yourself', 'I'd Do Anything' and 'Be Back Soon' – as well as backing singing on the remaining, slower numbers. Of course, there's not an awful lot of the Marriott we know, for his voice had not even broken by that time.

Mother Kathy Marriott was quite pleased with her boy's

success and had him attend an acting school in Islington, North London. According to the creators of *Wapping Wharf* – one of two British Small Faces fanzines – there were other reasons for his change of education. Allegedly, Steve had messed around with fire at school and in the process set part of the building alight (thus giving us an early hint on his dramatic fascination with arson), upon which his mother took him off school. Indeed, Marriott himself remembered the incident in an interview with Capital Radio's Nicky Horne in 1985: "My mother still has the newspaper clips."

The Italia Conti Drama School didn't strike Steve as terribly exciting, though: "I never really acted the whole time I was there. All the parts were cockney kids, which is what I was anyway." He stayed in touch with acting, but had much more fun singing and playing.

Steve's first band was called The Moonlights. En vogue, they covered Shadows tunes, which meant there wasn't an awful lot of singing for Steve to do, and the group split up pretty soon. Landing on his feet, he was offered a deal with the Decca record label and, in March 1963, his first single 'Give Her My Regards' appeared, written by TV entertainer Kenny Lynch.

In the press promo clip, Steve readily admitted who he admired then: "I think Buddy Holly was the greatest. My voice resembles his, but I certainly don't try to copy his style." But as the record proved, he wasn't up to that promise. Anyway, the single was a flop: The Beatles were already popular in Britain, and Buddy Holly sounded dated even in comparison with the Fab Four's cover versions. (Steve himself would return to Buddy six years later, but that's another (Humble Pie) story.)

Steve, barely sixteen years old, duly returned to acting. On the basis of parts in TV productions like *Famous Five* and *Dixon Of Dock Green*, he got the chance to do two movies in 1963: *Heavens Above* with Peter Sellers and *Live It Up*, a music feature film portraying the up-and-coming beat scene. One of the main parts was played by Heinz Burt, who – like Steve – kept a day job as a postman. Heinz, as he also liked to be called in the world of showbiz, had also tried his luck with a 1963 single release – and hit the charts with his Eddie Cochran tribute 'Just like Eddie', featuring Ritchie Blackmore on lead guitar – and had been successful as The Tornados' bass player on their instrumental 'Telstar' during the previous year.

Live It Up tells the story of a beat group searching for a supposedly lost demo tape which they retrieve after the suitable number of adventures. Steve had the part of the drummer called Ricky, of all things. The soundtrack presented Gene Vincent, Kenny Ball's Jazzmen and Sounds Incorporated, produced – like The Tornados – by the legendary Joe Meek.

The success of *Live It Up* inspired a sequel – *Be My Guest* – the following year. This time, the plot worked around a stolen demo. Shel Talmy was responsible for the music – later to become famous as producer for The Who, The Kinks and The Creation, as well as engineering one song for The Small Faces Mk II in 1977. Jerry Lee Lewis and The Nashville Teens are just two acts who can be heard and seen in *Be My Guest* among the many lesser artists.

Being in a movie about the music business helped Steve make up his mind at long last. Nice as the acting scene might have been, it had to lose out to his first love. He had grown up with music; that was where he could express himself, messing about like he wanted. Following his heart, Steve found a job as harmonica player with The Andrew Oldham Orchestra – led by The Rolling Stones' manager of the time. The association would lead, in February 1965, to Oldham producing Steve's solo single 'Tell Me' – an ultra-rare record today.

Before that – around 1963-4 – Steve began getting interested in R&B, which in those days meant grooving to the sound that shattered the charts as soul music: Sam Cooke, Marvin Gaye, Booker T And The MGs and many more. His response was to start his own group, The Frantics, who after several shake-ups became The Moments. With their version of The Kinks' 'You Really Got Me' under their belt, they hoped at the end of 1964 to crack the American charts. They didn't.

In order to make ends meet, Steve was looking for a well-paying day job. He could not live off music and had fallen out with his parents after cancelling a major theatre touring engagement. Fortunately, Alexis Korner – 'The Father Of White Blues' – who Steve regarded as his mentor and stepfather, provided a welcome Moscow Road sofa at night (bringing back memories of Steve's childhood evenings on the settee listening to his dad).

Meanwhile, a certain Ronald Frederick Lane had established his band, The Pioneers, on a semi-professional basis. Born 1 April, 1946 in Plaistow, another East End suburb of London, Ronnie got into music during his school days. Unlike Steve's, his home was not musically orientated. His mother, Elsie, cared as little for music as his father Stanley, a lorry driver – and they certainly wouldn't touch that novelty American stuff with a barge pole.

Around 1963, Ronnie had started his first band, The Outcasts, with his friend Kenney Jones (born 16 September, 1948, in Stepney). They played mainly current chart material, but they really preferred what they thought of as R&B. Ronnie played the guitar and sang, Kenney sat behind the drums, Alan Hunt worked the bass, and a further guitarist as well as an organ player completed the line-up. But Ronnie was not completely happy with himself or the group. A new singer took over Ronnie's lead vocals, the second guitarist was swapped, and the organ player got the sack. The Pioneers were born.

During the day, Ronnie worked at Selmer's which, in the Sixties was a company with a world-wide reputation for amplifiers, loudspeakers and musical instruments. Ronnie: "There was a little soundproof room with a Fender Stratocaster and a Fender bass, and I was supposed to test the amps. Kenney Jones also worked there and installed the things. His amps I complained about on purpose. During that time, I really learnt to play, mainly during the lunch break. I used to really dig Booker T And The MGs and fancied myself as a bass player. But my father had just bought me a guitar on the never-never, and he wasn't at all keen on watching me change over to the bass.

"So I told him all about how much money there was in being a bass player, 'cause there were so few of them, and I offered to take over the installments for the guitar. In the end, my father agreed."

The very next Saturday, Ronnie and his dad set off to look around for a suitable bass guitar – in a shop renowned throughout the 'scene'. Little did they realise that the encounter would be fateful...

CHAPTER TWO
The Small Faces
White Rhythm & Blues

S teve Marriott worked on Saturdays as a sales assistant in the J60 Music Bar in High Street, Manor Park, London E12. The premises were a popular haunt for young musicians, who knew they were being assisted professionally. It wasn't long before Ronnie Lane appeared, accompanied by his father.

"That's where I met Ronnie – Ronnie Lane," Steve recalled. "I worked there weekends, 'cause it was great working in a music shop. You meet other musicians, and I had to go through the stock and point out the good ones. I always knew where the good guitars were. Even if they were cheap, some were better than the others. So if I saw someone I liked, I said, 'Don't buy that. Let me take you round the back and have a look at this!' And that's exactly what happened with me and Ronnie. He'd come in with his father to get a new bass guitar, and I told him about these harmony basses that had come out..." – which was what Ronnie wanted, and an expert talk ensued.

"We got on immediately, having seen each other before actually. He played in a group called The Outcasts. And I was in a group called The Moments. And so we kind of respected each other from a distance. He was singing and playing guitar at the time, not bass, and he was ever so good. And he liked what I did, and we went back to my house after the sale was agreed [at half price, by the way] and stayed up all night listening to blues records."

Ronnie was impressed and confirmed the story: "After he had sold me that bass, he took me home and played me all these amazing American R&B records he had, by James Brown and Otis Redding and all these great black singers."

Ronnie invited Steve to a jam session with The Pioneers in the

British Prince pub in Ilford. Steve had no commitments, his Moments having been disbanded a while ago. "So I went along to check out Ronnie's band, in which Kenney Jones played the drums. He was terrible at the time, and I'm sure he'd be the first to admit it. I had brought my harmonica along, and Ronnie and me started drinking whisky. We really chucked them down like mad, till we were completely pissed. As the final number we treated the audience to a wild Jerry Lee Lewis show, which ended with me destroying the piano. We got chucked out immediately and were banned from the pub. Ronnie's reputation there was ruined, because he had invited me. Anyway, I had already got on the lead singer's nerves – his name was George – having tried to take over his part, you know, stuff I just haven't got the nerve to miss out on. I'm the dominant type, and I've got to live with that. I got on his nerves so much the band broke up. So Kenney, Ronnie and me decided to start our own band, and I was supposed to learn how to play the guitar. With Ron on bass and Kenney on the drums, all we needed was a keyboard player".

Steve told his two new buddies of a guy who appeared at the J60 Music Bar from time to time. His name was Jimmy Langwith (born 20 April, 1945 in Stratford) and he was very sure of himself.

Jimmy's parents ran a pub named the Ruskin Arms in the same road where Steve lived at the time. Jimmy was the proud owner of an organ, and so the three duly invaded the pub to check out his rehearsal room. "Jimmy had his organ all right, but that was not the reason we asked him to join us. His playing was diabolical, but he had this old van, and that put things right back in the balance," Steve freely admitted.

After a few rehearsals they felt ready to face the public. That was in June 1965. The first gig they had to fulfil was a workingman's club in Sheffield, of all places. But the Geordie lads up there didn't feel like listening to their modern soul material. Steve recalled: "Our stuff just didn't seem right for them. We got paid after just three numbers." Fortunately, they had found the time to stroll along the streets of Sheffield after the gig. Finally they happened to pass the Mojo Club, where Joe Cocker also used to sing at the time. "It was damn fantastic, a little bit like *Ready Steady Go* – extremely wild and full of Mods. Two young brothers ran the place and told us we could have a gig there.

That's how we drove up there, played and went down like mad. We hung out up there for a few weeks and then returned to London to try our luck."

They played the Starlight Rooms in Oxford Street – which was where Elkie Brooks had heard them for the first time and – absolutely thrilled with Steve's voice – had raved on about the boys in front of Maurice King, the club's proprietor and manager. And of course, they also appeared at the Ruskin Arms – after Jimmy's parents had at long last sighed their defeated "yes". That was where the boys caught the attention of the owner of Leicester Square's Cavern Club who hired the young band on the spot. There was one condition, though: they had to appear under their own group name.

The choice was made with help from one of Jimmy's girlfriends, who – on being introduced to his three little friends – had called out quite spontaneously: "Cor! Ain't you got small faces." That was right on the button: 'Small' – obviously hinted at the boys' rather dwarfed appearance – while 'Face' was a crucial Mod term. As a face you're, well, "the face, ie the guy with a certain charisma". That's why The Who in their early High Numbers days had called their Mod-bandwagon single 'I'm The Face' – a hint to that 'honorary degree'.

The first Small Faces gig at the Cavern Club was so successful that they were booked for another five Saturday nights. Their repertoire was completely 'black': The Small Faces couldn't (yet) be bothered with British Beat. They would play James Brown's 'Please Please Please' and 'Night Train' (also covered by Georgie Fame), 'Baby What You Want Me To Do' by Jimmy Reed, Smokey Robinson's 'You Really Got A Hold On Me' (in The Beatles' set, too), 'Jump Back' by Rufus Thomas or Ben E King's 'Stand By Me'. They had little to offer yet on the original songs front, just 'Come On Children' and 'E To D'. As they didn't even have enough numbers for a complete programme by that time, they would start all over again and play the same set twice, which didn't seem to irritate their steadily growing number of fans at all.

It was during this formative era that Ronnie earned his nickname. Kenney's explanation, though, sounds more than a little peculiar: "We called him Plonk because he plonks [sic] instead of plinks his bass," he claimed in 1965. Ronnie's bass playing certainly did not correspond with usual standards. He followed the popular American style of freely varying between the different frets; a very rhythmic way of plonking, indeed.

Steve and Ronnie took up musical leadership inside the Small Faces camp very early on. And as they got on excellently, it's hardly surprising they were sharing a place pretty soon. In those days, they lived in a house in Loughton, owned by the Royal Air Force. Steve had lost his job at the J60 Music Bar ages ago, had gone on to star as a dish washer for a while, but now readily contributed to Ronnie's destiny of becoming jobless. He absolutely insisted on Ronnie organising equipment for him at Selmer's – gratis, of course. Plonk didn't budge, shouting at the top of his voice: "Free PA for Marriott, testing, testing, Free PA for Marriott." And before he knew, he was out in the streets with his papers. Subsequently, Ronnie tried his luck as a messenger in the Ministry of Defence (the abbreviation reads MOD, of course), a job he hated. During a meeting it was duly decided to go professional. Ronnie immediately managed to get something – anything – wrong at work and was presented with the sack.

During 1965, the year The Small Faces got together, the Mod subculture had had its breakthrough in the eyes of the British public. In the previous year, Mods had been recognised for the first time as they dared to stand up to the already established Rockers. The Mod movement had been growing quietly but steadily throughout 1962/3, mainly in and around London. Now they felt strong enough to fight it out with those despised dirty, long-haired Rockers. If Steve Marriott's claims are to be believed, he and Ronnie – as self-confessed Mods – got into fights themselves several times and got "pretty beat up" by Rockers.

The perfect hang-outs for those popular, grand style battles soon emerged – what better stage and background for breaking bones than the derelict charm of British seaside resorts? The negative press they got didn't deter the Mods in the slightest – the *Daily Mirror* for instance ran the headline "The Wild Ones are invading the Seaside". Mods bathed in self-confidence, they felt highly superior to the thick Rockers. This was despite the fact that Mods – like Rockers – mainly came from a working class background.

The Mods' mutual aim was to gain attention, to set themselves apart from other teens. That was why an up-to-date, fashionable appearance was deemed absolutely crucial – 'mod' as a short form of 'modern'. The Mods had short, well-cut hair styles. They wore exclusive Fred Perry shirts, measured suits – often with extreme colours – and the latest Italian shoes.

This outfit was matched by those obligatory Parkas, which they needed whenever they paraded with their typical kind of vehicle – the scooter. Their Vespas and Lambrettas were customised with numerous lights and mirrors – beautifully photographed for the booklet of The Who's Mod-Opera *Quadrophenia*. All Mods' savings went into these luxuries, though more often than not, their Fred Perry shirts had fallen off the back of a lorry.

All that counted for Mods was their peer group, the experiences as part of their 'crowd', or maybe their 'pack' (but only Rockers had 'gangs'). Whenever the crowd wasn't busy on the road on their scooters, discussing this and that with the Rockers, they met for raving all-nighters, parties where the newest soul and ska singles were danced into the ground. As Dave Marsh pointed out in *Before I Get Old*: "There was no Mod music – only music that Mods liked." But Mods were bored with white rock'n'roll or the bourgeois British skiffle. What they liked was black singers like James Brown, Otis Redding, Smokey Robinson or Laurel Aitken.

The first bands to come out of the Mod movement were The Action, The Birds (with Creation and Faces-man to be, Ron Wood) and – needless to say – The Small Faces. Other groups, like The Who and, later, The Creation, simply thrived on Mod euphoria and adjusted their own outfits, though they weren't really Mods themselves.

Kit Lambert, manager of The Who – who had a Tuesday residency in Soho's Marquee Club – recognised The Small Faces' popularity with ill feelings. His fears were that the Mod crowds might convert to these 'Ace Faces', as Superior Mods were called. On the other hand, he tried to get The Small Faces linked to him. But he hadn't counted on another smooth customer's finger in the pie: His competitor, Move manager Don Arden, had put his right hand, producer and songwriter Ian 'Sammy' Samwell, on The Small Faces' scent. And Samwell was out of his mind when he returned from a gig where

Steve and co had really delivered, advising Arden to strike immediately. The four youngsters, green as grass, had not wasted any thoughts on financial matters. Steve: "We thought, Sod it, we'll join whoever offers most of the readies."

Arden invited the group into his Carnaby Street office at the end of July 1965. After brief negotiations, the quartet went for a percentage rather than a set salary. Arden threw in some additional treats as bait to get his documents signed. Rather than a straight percentage, every band member was now offered twenty pounds weekly expenses – guaranteed – and accounts in Carnaby Street boutiques to get the right outfits. And so there was no question at all of Steve, Ronnie, Jimmy and Kenney duly signing the contract.

Now there had to be a record – and quickly, too. What they needed was a cracker of a song, preferably two. According to Arden, the group itself hadn't come up with anything suitable yet. This was why Ian 'Sammy' Samwell quickly offered one of his own titles, which was recorded right away.

Steve: "We went into IBC Studios and did a version of 'What'cha Gonna Do About It' with Ian Samwell producing. I loved that version, but it was never released. It was too raucous. We went into Pye and did it with a session tambourinist. I suppose they thought that was better... I've no idea if the first version still exists." It does, released on a French compilation in 1972 (see Discography).

'What'cha Gonna Do About It' is a full-throttle chunk of R&B – even the version with less balls – but a closer listen revealed that it was boldly pinched from Solomon Burke's own 'Everybody Needs Somebody To Love'. But that didn't really matter, because Steve belted his heart out and hit the chords like mad, Plonk tortured his bass, Kenney likewise his drums, while Jimmy tried ever so hard with the few organ licks Steve had taught him. The flipside, 'What's A Matter Baby', originally by Italian-American girl singer Timi Yuro, bears a striking resemblance to 'Stand By Me'; nevertheless Steve delivers this slow number with all his hair-raising intensity. The record was released on 6 August, 1965 – so the ink on the contracts was hardly dry – and for a debut single it did extremely well – reaching a respectable Number Fourteen in the British charts. For the next single though, one of the little Mods' own compositions was on the cards: about time.

Meanwhile, the group had to deal with a grave problem. The 'Shorties' couldn't stand Jimmy Winston's faults and antics anymore. He was by far the least accomplished musician, but the most pretentious prat with regard to the group's initial success (that's probably why his surname Langwith made way for the more easy to market, tobacco industry tested 'Winston'). During an appearance for the TV show *Thank Your Lucky Stars* Jimmy snubbed the band's unrivalled frontman intensely. It was mainly Steve then who was fed up and wanted Jimmy to jump in a lake: "When we came to the guitar solo, which I was very proud of, Jimmy started acting crazy in his corner, waving his arms and stuff, so that the cameras turned to him. It all got out of hand."

After Jimmy's tour van had had it, the other three rose to the occasion and duly told him to get lost. He accepted the sack reluctantly but realised that without the van he didn't have a real asset in the band anymore. Utterly convinced of his talent and charisma though, he went for a solo career – his backing group was suitably called His Reflection. He wanted to show his ex-buddies up, but that was wishful thinking. His first single, 'Sorry She's Mine' – which The Small Faces also recorded for their debut album – was released by Decca in June 1966, but bombed. The 1967 follow-up, 'Real Crazy Apartment', didn't fare any better, so Jimmy's attempts with his band Winston's Fumbs were in vain. But he didn't give up. Instead, he jumped on the psychedelic bandwagon with Snow White – again to no avail – before he remembered his notorious talent as an actor. In 1968 he got a part in the London stage production of the musical *Hair* and even appeared on the respective soundtrack album. Eventually Jimmy Winston disappeared from the limelight, only to return in 1976 with a weak single, 'Sun In The Morning'. Still, he can be proud of the fact that his recorded sensations are sought after collectors' items which fetch extremely high bids.

During this period of transition in the autumn of 1965, the hunt for a new, hopefully competent, keyboard player ensued – while the official Decca contract was already in the bag. By sheer coincidence, Steve had found the review of a Boz And The Boz People gig in *Melody Maker*. The writer raved primarily about the keyboard wizardry of their organ player, Ian McLagan, whose photograph appeared next to the article. The other two were also suitably impressed with McLagan's looks, and so Don Arden was asked to arrange a meeting with him. McLagan knew The Small Faces via the TV show *Ready Steady Go* and had followed their rocketing rise with interest. In a strange sequence of events, McLagan had only just left The Boz People when an acquaintance told him on their way home that The Small Faces had fired their keyboard player and needed a replacement urgently.

Back home, the phone rang. It was Don Arden, who asked McLagan for a meeting. Ian couldn't believe his ears, but followed the invitation and – once Ronnie, Steve and Kenney had impulsively accepted him with open arms – was hired on the spot. Ian, almost exactly as small as the other three, matched Steve's image of the perfect candidate to a tee: "I couldn't believe it. Here's a guy, standing right in front of us, who was already one of the boys. The chemistry between us was perfect, although he was bit shy at the time. His humour was perfect, his charisma was perfect – all I could do was hug him, because it was just like he was the missing part."

Ian McLagan, who his new colleagues soon called 'Mac' with affection, was born in Hounslow, West London on 12 May, 1945. From a middle class family, he had gone to university for a few terms, before deciding to earn his wages with music. He had even recorded a single, 'Back Door Man', with a band called The Muleskinners. Then Boz Burrell – later to become Bad Company's bass player – had enlisted him for Boz People, where Ian didn't feel at home. And now he'd arrived in The Small Faces, who at least enjoyed something of a reputation.

In terms of his outfit though, Mac did not match the strict Mod code yet. He was duly sent to an accepted hairdresser's – and of course to Carnaby Street, where he was fitted in style, with Arden footing the bill. During his brief probationary period, Mac earned more than the others, thirty pounds. After he had become a permanent member of the band, he insisted on getting wound down to the usual twenty which the rest of the band got. His new mates treated this gesture with deep respect, because Arden would have continued paying him the additional ten quid.

The first live appearance with the new line-up took place in the London Lyceum ballroom on 2 November, 1966. Mac now had the amusing task of having to promote the 'new' single, 'I've Got Mine', on which Jimmy Winston of all people had taken over the guitar duties. That was why Steve bought a brand new Fender guitar for Mac (see Guitarography). Marriott and Lane – with Jones and Winston still receiving official writing credits – had written 'I've Got Mine' exclusively for Jeremy Summer's movie *Dateline Diamonds*.

The Small Faces even appear in this confusing film about a pirate radio station – albeit with their old line-up – and they get to play two numbers after all. But the promotional effect the band had hoped for didn't materialise, because the film wasn't finished in time – appearing in British cinemas as late as April 1966. And so 'I've Got Mine' didn't even reach the charts, despite having a catchy melody, solid quality production and Steve Marriott in full passionate flight.

After the flop with a group composition, Don Arden again went for outside writers. British hitmakers Mort Shuman and Kenny Lynch – Kenny fancying himself as a beat singer, too, at the time – delivered the sing-along 'Sha-La-La-La-Lee', which The Small Faces recorded without much enthusiasm. But Arden was proved right again. Released towards the end of January, during a tour through Belgium, Holland, Denmark and Germany, this number – coupled with the instrumental 'Grow Your Own' (grass?) – did the trick and cracked the Top Ten of the British singles charts – Number Three in March 1966. The group's popularity rose by the minute, in response to numerous appearances in music-orientated TV shows in Britain and abroad, including Canada.

The follow-up, 'Hey Girl', became another hit (Number Ten) in May 1966. This was another Marriott/Lane composition: a substantially simple love song which gains a certain gospel feeling via the vocal call and response delivered by Steve and Ronnie. The B-side, 'Almost Grown' (grass?), was another instrumental, credited as a group effort.

Now the time had come to make an album, in spite of The Small Faces fancying themselves as singles artists – in accordance with their manager. The sessions for their longplaying debut, for Arden's tiny label and Contemporary Music publishing, had taken place under modest circumstances over only three days. The material for *The Small Faces* was a mixture of group as well as outside writing, but still mainly indebted to R&B.

The album opens, like their early gigs, with 'Shake', a Sam Cooke tribute and one of the few fast numbers sung by Ronnie. Steve the shouter returns for 'Come On Children', one of the first Marriott/Lane compositions. Extremely wild and rough, the song's structure was arranged suitably simple and rhythmic, with hand clapping typical for the era.

'You Better Believe It' follows, a memorable, soulful Marriott/Lane-number and B-side of 'I've Got Mine', then 'One Night Stand', a melancholic beat number with a beautiful melody. The version of 'What'cha Gonna Do About It' that appears is the polished single version (relegating the rougher alternative version to the French compilation *Small Faces* in 1972). This was Steve's set opener again from 1984 to 1991.

While the unspectacular Kenny Lynch composition, 'Sorry She's Mine', is nicely naive, with typical beat references, it seems positively complex preceding 'E To D', a dynamic, unrefined work consisting of just two chords (ie E to D). With snappy guitar riffs and Steve's almost shrieking voice, the song presents untypical, but contemporary words which hint at the later direction of 'All Or Nothing': "Sometimes I feel like a frustrated child/I've got everything I want/There's nothing that I need/I can't stop my brain from runnin' wild". It's hardly surprising that this number tends to appear under the title 'Running Wild' from time to time, especially on US compilations.

It takes the blues-orientated 'You Need Loving' to calm things down. Intriguingly, this Marriott/Lane 'original' was supposedly inspired by 'You Need Love', written by Muddy Waters' former bass player Willie Dixon and recorded by Muddy in 1962 for Chess Records. The Small Faces revamped the thing from scratch, and with Steve's treatment it developed into something of its own, so convincingly, in fact, that Led Zeppelin stole parts of it for their 'Whole Lotta Love'. Robert Plant went so far as to copy Steve's phrasing – for which he apologised during a backstage encounter in the Seventies. In 1987 Willie Dixon sued Led Zeppelin for plagiarism (they settled out of court) but interestingly enough, Marriott/Lane's 'You Need Loving' wasn't even mentioned.

By comparison, 'Don't Stop What You're Doing' is quite unexciting. It appeared on the album as the light weight counterpart to the Tamla-Motown standard 'Baby Don't Do It', which The Small Faces also had in their live set (and which Steve's Humble Pie Mark II re-recorded in 1980). More interesting is the instrumental band original 'Own Up' which features a classic blues chord sequence; hard-hitting, crashing guitar riffs combined with Mac's warm organ improvisations.

In the context of an album, the closer 'Sha-La-La-La-Lee' seems nothing but a beat period-piece – which The Small Faces, with Steve very much in command, manage to induce with quite a lot of fire. There was a rumour that Steve had managed to find out which shops were going to get interviewed for the charts for the crucial weekend – and sent his friends to buy copies of the song's single format accordingly: after 'Payola' here was 'Buyola'!

The album appeared on the market at the end of May 1966, just in time for their UK tour in June, reaching the respectable high of Number Three and stayed in the British charts for six months. In July, The Small Faces went on their first grand tour of Germany, with a gig in Hamburg's legendary Star-Club and a live appearance in *Beat Beat Beat* on Radio/TV Hesse (Hessischer Rundfunk) amongst other events.

On tour more or less permanently, Marriott and Lane still found time for writing songs together – which always seemed to come easy – for often spontaneous studio sessions as a quartet. On the other hand the strain of touring made itself felt during the summer of 1966: Steve collapsed during the production of another *Ready Steady Go*, but was still able to resume the UK tour, which in turn was interrupted by an appearance for French television. Kenney Jones remembers the trip to Paris quite accurately: "We went over there with The Herd, and Peter Frampton played with us. It was the first time we'd played with Pete, and I remember thinking what a great guitarist he was – he played his guitar like a flower opening, which was great."

After The Beatles had decided not to play any more concerts in order to concentrate fully on their studio work, and with The Rolling Stones and The Who taking long breaks from touring, The Small

Faces became Great Britain's Number One live attraction, even if The Hollies and The Kinks would hardly risk a bored yawn at this suggestion. Small Faces euphoria drifted towards its first big climax. Countless fans drifted to the foursome's house in Westmoreland Road, Pimlico, as if it was a place of pilgrimage. In reality, Kenney didn't even share, he lived in nearby Stepney – not fancying the mad trio's fly-by-night attitude: He needed his own bed and above all some peace and quiet.

On 5 August, 1966, 'All Or Nothing' was released, a classic song, which Steve later claimed to have written on his own, even if Ronnie was officially named as co-author. 'All Or Nothing' raced up the British charts just when The Small Faces were taking part in a package tour with Neil Christian and Crispian St Peters. Wherever The Small Faces appeared, they caused massed gatherings. On one occasion Ronnie Lane was pushed down – by accident – in front of a Glasgow Hotel, and later that day Mac was taken into custody – a mere precautionary move of course.

'All Or Nothing' reached the Number One spot in the British singles charts on 15 September, 1966 – three days before Kenney's eighteenth birthday – replacing The Beatles' double A-side seven inch 'Yellow Submarine/Eleanor Rigby'. The impact of 'All Or Nothing' as a Hymn of Adolescence, a Mod Anthem, could hardly have been predicted, but the song did indeed have certain qualities of which standards are made, including a chorus which contains a potentially symbolic hookline that everyone is infected by and can sing along to. Kenney confirms that the band itself were also more than pleased with the result: "It was getting us where we wanted to be musically. It wasn't as poppy as our other stuff, but it was still commercial and a better song than anything we had done so far. It broke us out of the pop system." The flip-side, 'Understanding', was another reflection of Steve Marriott and Ronnie Lane's growing competence as songwriters.

While other British groups had long since established themselves in the USA – as part of the ongoing British Invasion – The Small Faces' hunting ground had so far been restricted to Europe. But now they had a Number One smash on their CV, and Arden had in fact managed to organise a small promotional stateside visit which was scheduled to be followed by a full-scale US tour during December.

Unfortunately, it was leaked that Ian McLagan was facing a drug trial, and both US visits had to be cancelled. Disappointed, the band buried themselves in the studios for work on their second album. Bad luck was to stay with the four-piece for a while to come, because an up-and-coming attractive package tour with The Lovin' Spoonful and The Mamas And The Papas was also cancelled. A substitute autumn itinerary in October – with The Hollies and The Nashville Teens on the bill among others – developed into full scale chaos when the groups couldn't come to an agreement on who was to have headliner status.

Bobby Elliott, The Hollies' long serving drummer then as now, remembers: "The Small Faces – cocky Southerners that they were – must have thought that as flavour of the month they absolutely deserved headliner status, while in fact this was the tour of us Northern Hollies [the band members all came from Greater Manchester]. Don Arden even tried to make his point by using physical force, but Rod Shields [Hollies road and lighting manager since 1964] has so far put paid to every contender. On the other hand, Steve Marriott came over as a very nice lad backstage, almost subdued – you certainly couldn't sense his eccentric stage personality in the dressing room."

To make matters worse, relations with the media were cooling, as a team of producers for *Top Of The Pops* and several music journalists accused The Small Faces of letting their success go to their respective heads.

But the upheavals were soon forgotten when 'My Mind's Eye' – released on 11 November, 1966 – hit Number Four that Christmas. Whether it was clever planning on the part of the record company or a mere coincidence, the fact that the melody owes a striking resemblance to the carol 'Angels From The Realms Of Glory' meant it was perfectly timed. But The Small Faces were far from delighted with their new smash. Ronnie Lane recalls: "We were on the road in our van between gigs when 'Eye' appeared on the radio. It was a rough mix, done about four o'clock in the morning and duly sent to Arden's office in order to ram it down his throat that we were making full use of our studio time. Consequently, a huge row with the management developed out of this." Similarly unauthorised, the B-side, 'I Can't Dance With You', comes along as an average piece but gains momentum via Steve's powerful voice.

The band's relationship with Don Arden was now cooling down considerably. And this was not only due to the fact that Don insisted on an incredibly hectic, daily Small Faces gig-to-gig schedule and handed in tapes with unfinished recordings to Decca, either. On top of all this, the band were aware that their market value commanded about a thousand pounds a gig whereas Arden hadn't raised their weekly wages from the modest twenty quid per head.

It wasn't as if the boys actually lost any sleep over getting exploited like that. After all, whenever they felt like it, they could use the expense accounts Arden had organised in several boutiques. It was Steve, Ronnie, Kenney and Ian's parents who worried about the financial situation their celebrity kids had stumbled into and so they demanded a meeting with the Arden management. Mac remembers: "We only got wind of this when we returned to our house and all of us got phone calls from our mummies and daddies who wanted to know why we had never bothered to mention the state of things we had gotten into. They had gone straight to headquarters to enquire about our money, and Arden had told them we were all addicted – on the needle. You've got to imagine! Our mummies and daddies. It could have killed them. Of course they didn't realise it was a con, and they completely forgot to ask about the money. And we were left standing, looking stupid – absolutely innocent. That's how we came to leave Arden." The boys managed to make their parents believe they had nothing to do with hard drugs and, with the help of a solicitor and investigative financial accounting, they also attempted to get a clear picture of their economic situation, not least to escape trouble with the Inland Revenue concerning tax evasion.

Thus, on 17 November, 1966, The Small Faces signed a management contract with the Harold Davison agency. But if Don was the devil, then Harold certainly resembled the deep blue sea – proved by an ill-assembled package tour through the UK, where the band had to perform on the same bill with ballad singing Roy Orbison and the teen-twin-set of Paul & Barry Ryan. It was obvious to Steve that they played in front of the wrong audience: "I mean I can see their point. Those poor old darlings stroll in to listen to Roy Orbison, and after twelve bars of 'Shake' they're running out. Of course, they've had enough."

Due to their growing confidence, the four guys wouldn't go along with everything on offer. Thus, management hunting was resumed, along with looking for a more suitable record label. This was mainly because the staff at Decca were determined to categorise the group as a singles act, trying to shape them according to their idea of sales mechanisms – the law of the charts. No experiments with new sounds or styles – business as usual if you please. But meanwhile The Small Faces had a different perspective. Sure, they had their real fun (still) during the gigs, where they could really let go and the fans loved them the way they came over: rough and wild, but with their hearts in the right places. But on record...

In February 1967, The Small Faces announced their transfer to Andrew Oldham's agency and his newly established Immediate record label, the first crucial independent label of the Sixties. Oldham had achieved fame and fortune as one-time manager of The Rolling Stones, and Steve knew him from his early solo career. As a first move, Oldham increased the band's weekly wages to sixty pounds. In early March 1967, the last Decca single which was actually authorised by the group was released: 'I Can't Make It', a rocky beat number, not crammed with terribly original elements.

The single did neither badly nor fantastic: Number Twenty-Six in the UK. The flip-side, 'Just Passing', is more interesting, a miniature piece composed by Marriott/Lane and a certain O'Sullivan, running for a good sixty seconds. Still, the throwaway nursery rhyme type number, sung by Ronnie, made history by demonstrating their first sound experiments with car honking, echo and glockenspiel.

While the record company kept the band's profile alive, the members disappeared from the public eye for a while, at odds with several concert promoters and music journalists. According to Steve, these were only out to slam the band: "As far as the kids are concerned, they love us, but in the eyes of the press we're just dirty, boozing bastards. We were stereotyped as difficult – quite unfairly – because a clause in our contract demanded that 'the management has to supply soap and clean towels' for us. Is that asking too much?"

Things got to the point where even their precious live appearances didn't seem like fun anymore. Ronnie explains: "The reason for our tendency to our almost exclusive studio work was the fact that we were quite disillusioned with our live playing – we had not really worked on improving our stage act. There was no point. It was the same with all the screaming. For about two years [which is exaggerated, but then Ronnie was never good at approximating time] we literally couldn't even hear ourselves. We did not hear a note of what we were playing. It was just curtains up, wiggle your arse and a lot of screaming."

And so it seemed appropriate to put a distance between them and the hectic music scene, to fully enjoy their newly found studio freedom. Steve: "When we went to Immediate, the songs were shaped and played in a more disciplined way. What's more, we had all become better musicians and were also more creative. We managed to finish more things, we were allowed to stay in the studio as long as we liked. Contrary to Decca there was no time limit, and that was great."

The political, social and also musical changes of the last two or three years had not been without impact for The Small Faces. There was a different kind of feeling coming in from the USA – in every possible respect. Groups like The Byrds or The Lovin' Spoonful drew inspiration from their heritage of the American folksong, which the likes of Bob Dylan and Phil Ochs had paved the road for in the mid Sixties. Folk singer Dylan had dared to go electric, presenting his songs with amplified band backing and leaving his audience thinking. In the USA, topics like the Vietnam War and the Civil Rights and Black movements dominated the youth culture. A protest movement against the dormant, prudish, narrow-minded and bourgeois society fascinated many young people. Sex (uninhibited love) and drugs (marijuana, LSD, acid) and rock'n'roll had put the so-called hippies on the map. Those 'dangerous' ideas came to Europe via the song lyrics of a new generation of US bands, and of course for England, there was not even a language barrier to keep the hippy culture at bay.

The Mod movement – which had only made an impact in England's south anyway – lost momentum dramatically. The typical

Mod attitude of 'What do I care about how other people fare – all that counts is I'm okay, with enough readies for outfits and girls' suddenly seemed old hat. Reflecting on that period, Who leader Pete Townshend does not really rave with nostalgia: "The Mod thing was the rejection of everything one already had. You didn't want to know about the TV, you didn't want to know about politicians, you didn't want to know about the Vietnam War. If there had been a draft, there wouldn't have been Mods – the thing was that it was a sterile situation. It was perfect. You had to have short hair, enough money to buy a real smart suit, good shoes, good shirts. You had to be able to dance like a madman. You had to always be pilled up. You had to have a scooter covered in lamps. You had to have an army anorak to wear on the scooter. And that was being Mod."

While The Small Faces were immersed in their philosophical thoughts about the state of the new world, and busy writing new songs, Decca Records niftily shifted another single on 26 May, 1967. 'Patterns', which wasn't unlike Them's 'Gloria', was swiftly followed by *From The Beginning*, a compilation album featuring for the first time the hit singles 'My Mind's Eye', 'Hey Girl', 'All Or Nothing', 'What'cha Gonna Do About It' and a number of R&B standards. Quite surprisingly, the LP starts with the US mainstream smash 'Runaway' (which had been a 1961 hit for Del Shannon), a swinging warm-up number with a happy-go-lucky, aria-type intro, sung naively, probably straight-faced, by opera buff Don Arden. 'My Mind's Eye' was followed by two competent Marriott/Lane compositions, 'Yesterday Today And Tomorrow' and 'That Man', then there were the original versions of 'My Way Of Giving' – originally written for Chris Farlowe – and '(Tell Me) Have You Ever Seen Me' – composed to order for Apostolic Intervention.

Apart from 'All Or Nothing' there is also a rousing, precise cover of Don Covay's screaming 'Take This Hurt Off Me', and a hats-off-to-Marvin Gaye with 'Baby Don't Do It'. According to *Bomp!* reviewer Ken Barnes, this is "the best ever released rock'n'roll version, far better than The Who version, for instance". As mentioned, Steve had another go at this Holland/Dozier/Holland composition with Humble Pie II in 1980. The instrumental filler 'Plum Nellie' is followed by another soul gem, 'You've Really Got A Hold On Me' by Smokey

Robinson And The Miracles, superior to the original due to Steve's amazing voice. 'What'cha Gonna Do About It' closes this cash-in project. Still, Ken Barnes called it "one of the best British rhythm & blues-rock classics of the period".

Obviously, Steve and friends were far from happy with their old label's release and they counter-attacked in the best way they knew. The Decca products remained strictly non-promoted, whereas a mere week after 'Patterns' – on 2 June, 1967 – the first Immediate single appeared: 'Here Come The Nice', an unmasked reference to the golden age of Mod and the then popular period-drug Speed. This exciting Marriott/Lane song does not yet belong in their future category of sophisticated compositions, but it does have a great hookline and attractive arrangement with its acoustic guitar and deep Hammond organ sound, strangled at the end, on purpose.

'Here Come The Nice' achieved a respectable Number Twelve in the UK. Almost simultaneously with the single, the group's first album for Immediate was released – its not very original title *Small Faces* corresponding with their Decca debut. The name might be the same but the song material differs immensely. The previous criteria for British hit making were ignored completely. This time around the band made full use of studio technology and experimented liberally with instruments that to date had never – or hardly ever – been used in popular music. All the numbers – Marriott/Lane compositions bar one – are shorter than three minutes, some don't even last two minutes and, for the first and last time, Ronnie dominates as the group's lead singer.

The album starts with the controversial 'Have You Ever Seen Me', which had originally been ear-marked as the first Immediate single, but for legal reasons was shelved (their former label Decca would have intervened). As the sessions for the song were assisted by a hitherto unknown group called Apostolic Intervention (featuring future Pie Jerry Shirley, whose fellow musicians possibly did not play on the track), the single eventually came out credited to Apostolic Intervention (Immediate IM 043). With Steve's vocals, it certainly sounds like an original Small Faces creation. Its B-side, the instrumental 'Madame Garcia' has even more typical Small Faces trademarks, especially the intense organ licks that identify Mac's style of playing. But ultimately, the Apostolic tag was a mere con in order to escape Decca's legal action regarding a song which belonged to them.

More straightforward offerings follow, starting with 'Something I Want To Tell You' which, sung by Ronnie is reminiscent of The Beatles in its chord sequence with Mac's Hammond, and hints on Ronnie's later concept for The Faces. The short and sweet (1:31) 'Feeling Lonely' is sung by Steve and marks his debut on the harpsichord, while 'Happy Boys Happy' is a toe-tapping instrumental number with Mac's fat organ sound and over-the-top drumming courtesy of Kenney.

The keyboard sound – this time harpsichord, piano and organ –is just as impressive on 'Things Are Going To Get Better' which again features dominant acoustic guitar and powerful singing from Steve. 'My Way Of Giving' follows, a melancholic but still hard-hitting ballad, then 'Green Circles', a dreamy, psychedelic-tinged number with an attractive, hummable melody, sung by Ronnie. More than anywhere else, 'Green Circles' signposts the group's direction towards *Ogdens' Nut Gone Flake* territory. A slowed-down version, interpreted by Steve, can be found on the similarly-titled 1991 album (see Discography).

The quirky humour of The Small Faces comes through on 'Become Like You', an odd folk song with harpsichord, mellotron and dominant acoustic guitars. The Farfisa type organ is a bit nerve-wracking, as are the "oohs" and "ahs" in 'Get Yourself Together' which detract from Steve's irresistible hook. The sense of humour prevails in 'All Our Yesterdays' which Steve announces in his typical street market banter before handing over to Ronnie for the lead vocal.

The precise, jazzy horn section of the previous track is all but forgotten when 'Talk To You' kicks in. A rocking love song, sung by Steve with his customary power, it used to be the flipside to 'Here Come The Nice'.

This precedes 'Show Me The Way': not the Peter Frampton anthem but a melancholic song brought to life by Ronnie's bass and yet another appearance by his warm voice. By contrast, 'Up The Wooden Hills To Bedfordshire' marks Mac's long overdue debut as a singer and composer. The song's harmonic structure reminds the listener of Procol Harum, while acoustic guitars and layers of keyboards dominate throughout the track. After this interesting aberration it's back to business as usual with another Lane vocal, this time on the calypso pastiche 'Eddie's Dreaming'. Unusual Caribbean sounds characterise this fast and humorous number featuring flute, percussion and rich trumpet arrangements. In all, a fitting end to the album.

Small Faces reached Number Twelve in the album charts, five places ahead of the *From The Beginning* collection – which gave the group some re-assurance. Still, the fans had quite some difficulties getting to grips with the newish, not very hard-hitting or easily remembered songs. Obvious singles contenders were hardly detected. Ronnie and Steve, though, couldn't care less. They simply presented 'Green Circles' when they appeared on the renowned *Beat Club*, a TV show organised by the Northern German network Radio Bremen. What's more, they already had a new single up their sleeve.

The sound experiments which The Small Faces were allowed to indulge in courtesy of Immediate were fully employed for the most timeless song the band ever produced: 'Itchycoo Park'. "We had a number of brilliant ideas," Ronnie remembers, "but that didn't always go down well with the sound engineers. They thought we were smart-arses when we insisted on something, and when we didn't get our way and said, 'That's not how we want it!' they would reply categorically, 'No, you can't do it that way, it's not right, it does not work technically nor ethically, and it's certainly not in the manual.' Things like taking tracks for different sound effects out of synch with other tracks [ie phasing], I mean, today everybody does it." As we know, The Small Faces didn't budge, and for a distortion of Kenney's drum fills in 'Itchycoo Park' they did in the end make use of said phasing effect – with the assistance of sound engineer Glyn Johns.

The idea for the song goes back to Ronnie: "'Itchycoo Park' was a rip-off of a hymn called 'God Be In My Head'. It was set out in the form of a dialogue between an innocent, normal person and someone who was very hip, someone who had already been 'there'."

For a long time, rumour had it there really was a little park in London's East End which served as a hang-out for the hippies of that period. But Kenney Jones put this legend at rest in a conversation with Terry Rawlings in 1992: "'Itchycoo Park' wasn't really a park, it was an overgrown bombsite full of stinging nettles in Ilford, which ran down to the railway lines."

'Itchycoo Park' appeared on the market on 4 August, 1967, and really hit the spirit of the hippy-trippy late summertime spot-on. The first big open air festival had taken place in June in Northern California's Monterey, and the Flower Power movement hit its climax, mirrored in the charts: Scott McKenzie's stereotyped kaftan-jerker 'San Francisco' became Number One all over the world. In the event, The Small Faces could have predicted the obvious: smart-ass journalists were among the first to 'spot' hidden drug references in 'Itchycoo Park'. And there certainly was the odd line that invited speculation of that kind: "I feel inclined to blow my mind/Get hung up, feed the ducks on a bun/They all come out to groove about/Like mice that have fun in the sun".

The B-side, 'I'm Only Dreaming', was harmless in this respect. Unfortunately underrated, it remains a prime example of the more refined and sophisticated songwriting of Marriott and Lane. In a turmoil of emotions, Steve's singing swings between tender devotion and a slashing power which would suit a hard-hitting rocker. A Number Three position for 'Park' in the UK was almost taken for granted; on the other hand, the single's success as a Stateside Number Sixteen came as a complete surprise.

The band didn't waste any time preparing the next album. Inclined to escape the hippy tag early, the band returned to its R&B roots with a grand rock workout called 'Tin Soldier'. Originally, Steve had written it for Pat 'PP' Arnold, a former Ikette (backing vocalist for the Ike And Tina Turner Roadshow) with a solo deal at Immediate. Apparently, Pat was Steve's first love: "I had tried every goddamn trick in the book to lay her, so I wrote this song, and she married me. Anyway, we played it to PP, and she completely flipped, so much so that I thought I'm gonna keep it, it's got to be too good to give it away. So we wrote her another song called '(If You Think You're) Groovy'."

At least Pat got to sing undeniably gorgeous backing vocals on 'Tin Soldier'. Backed with 'I Feel Much Better', a potent rock song with a sweet kiddies' singalong feel, the single hit the shops on 2 December, 1967, reaching Number Nine in the UK in January 1968. In Germany, it was The Small Faces' first Top Ten success – Number Seven – considerably higher than the US hit list's rather modest Seventy-Three.

The session work between 'Itchycoo Park' and 'Tin Soldier' saw an additional two dozen songs and instrumental pieces recorded, as Kenney Jones confirmed in his conversation with Terry Rawlings. With a few exceptions, these still haven't been released and were left to gather dust in the archives, among them 'Love Is Here To Stay And Now You're Gone', 'Shimmer' and a cover version of The Ronettes' smash, 'Be My Baby', which had been projected for the up-coming album. (Steve later re-recorded the latter for an aborted 1974 solo album which appeared in 1991 as *Scrubbers*.)

Meanwhile, the band undertook a tour down under together with their mates, The Who, and Paul Jones, the former Manfred Mann lead singer. The boys, though, didn't get to grips with the tough regulations the Australians presented them with and there were clashes everywhere. Once, on 28 January, 1968, they were even kicked off a plane scheduled to get them to the next gig – for rioting.

It wasn't long before The Small Faces were fed up with live playing and were once again back in London – happily retreated to Olympic Sound Studios. But still another overseas tour was threatening on the horizon. The band's modest chart placing in the USA had encouraged Immediate Records to compile and release a Small Faces album for the North American market. In a rather hectic operation, the most impressive tracks from the most recent *Small Faces* album were thrown in with the two singles, 'Itchycoo Park' and 'Tin Soldier', complete with B-sides, and rush-released as *There Are But Four Small Faces*. But the American audience was not terribly interested. The album, released in April 1968, scraped to Number 178. For the moment, a US tour was no longer on the cards.

The plus side was that the four of them had plenty of time on their hands to concentrate on their next album, destined to eclipse everything that had gone before. A preview single, 'Lazy Sunday', had been released by Immediate in May 1968, much to Steve's frustration: "I wrote this whilst having 'difficulties' with my neighbours in Chiswick, West London. I suppose it was my way of getting all the hassles off my chest. It was never meant to be a single, just a track for *Ogdens'*, but Immediate released it without our knowledge!"

'Lazy Sunday' was a classic British goodtime song with pointed references to the vaudeville tradition in Steve's over the top Music Hall cockney singing, and with lots of sound effects – chirping birds, flutes, the roaring of the sea and, let's not forget, toilet flushing. In England, the single became their biggest success since 'All Or Nothing', and in Germany it achieved the highest position of all Small Faces releases – Number Two. Incidentally, a promotional clip was produced for the single, one of the first promos shot in colour, and its formal sequencing and cutting techniques even then seem similar to the video culture of the Eighties and Nineties.

In June 1968, the eagerly awaited album *Ogdens' Nut Gone Flake* caused quite a stir on the scene. It was the first LP to be packaged in a round, gatefold sleeve, adapted from a tobacco tin. The Small Faces' preferred tobacco brand for mixing their marijuana joints used to be Ogdens' Flake. As for the rest of the title, Kenney Jones revealed all in his 1991 article for *Rolling Stone*: "We called it *Nut Gone* because your nut's gone if you smoke the stuff."

The unusual packaging was also the band's idea, but apparently this stroke of genius annoyed a lot of record buyers because the album tended to roll off the shelves. The gatefold sleeve reveals a typical, psychedelically confused colour illustration by P Brown. There's also a photograph with the opened tobacco tin, and on its top we detect a packet of cigarette paper with the fantasy brand name 'SUS'. Kenney lets us into this secret as well: "That's because the whole box is 'sussed' – suspect. The suggestion, if you read between the lines, is to get yourself a little bit of *Ogdens' Nut Gone Flake*, roll a joint and put the album on – listen to it, get involved with it."

As the album is unfolded further, four jazzed-up black and white shots of the band appear. One of them shows Mac up front with a cat, behind him Ronnie 'Leafy' Lane is sitting with his banjo, Kenney is holding an ice wafer, while Steve is grinning as 'George the Cleaner', smoking a cigarette, a scrubber in his hand. Rock photographer Gered Mankovitz assembled the mad still life: "I asked them to bring various things from their homes which they liked, which were visually interesting. Steve Marriott forgot to bring anything, but decided to dress up in things we found in my studio, and he developed this guise of a manic lavatory cleaner." Later on, a similar shot was used for the sheet music of 'Lazy Sunday'.

While the first side of the LP presents more or less individual songs, most of the tracks on the other side are linked by the charming narration of the one and only veteran cockney comedian Stanley Unwin. He tells the tale of a certain 'Happiness Stan', who is looking for the missing half of the moon, accompanied by a gossiping giant fly. He meets the old and allegedly crazy hermit 'Mad John', and in the end he discovers 'Happydaystoytown'.

Before the narrative begins, the album starts with the purely instrumental title track. Massive use of strings, intense organ harmonies in the middle passage and a cutting guitar towards the end suggest a new arrangement of the basic 'My Mind's Eye' theme before the fun of the rest of the album kicks in with 'Afterglow'. One of Steve Marriott's favourite songs, this starts like a drunken crooner's lament (Dean Martin sends his regards) with pipes and soft vocal backing, only to erupt like a volcano. Kenney batters his drums, while Mac pounds away at his piano and organ. The song leads straight into the next track, necessitating that the single version be doctored later on – prolonged and faded out. The song in question, 'Long Agos And Worlds Apart' is another of the rare McLagan songs, again sung by him with his organ run through Leslie speakers.

A witty, folk-influenced Marriott/Lane composition falls next. From fairly straightforward origins, 'René' changes halfway through into a real sound kaleidoscope (with the cheeky East End reference that René is "the dockers' delight"). This is followed by the hard hitting rocker 'Song Of A Baker', featuring Steve's biting guitar alternating with Ronnie's bass runs, surely inspired by Jimi Hendrix. 'Lazy Sunday' brings side one to a majestic close.

The normal Small Faces album fare of the first half is soon lost to the conceptual second side of the record, kicking off with 'Happiness Stan', complete with introductory narration by Stanley Unwin, chirping harp sounds and a harpsichord. The writing duo of Marriott and McLagan supply the second track, the blistering 'Rollin' Over'. Slashing guitar riffs and honky tonk piano, fading out with a crafty horn section made this a popular live number (and B-side to 'Lazy Sunday').

Into its stride, the rock opera continues with 'The Hungry Intruder', another Marriott/Lane dreamy, psychedelic folk song, with flute and strings and Ronnie's lead vocals. Psychedelia is still present and correct in 'The Journey', which sees Mac's Leslie Hammond and Kenney's huge drum sound surround Ronnie's partly distorted voice and the filtered, glimmering guitar work.

Back to folk with 'Mad John', this time given ballad treatment with acoustic guitars, piano and gorgeous harpsichord lines. Sung by Steve, it was still obviously created by Ronnie. The single only came out in the US, while parts of the melody re-appeared later in 'Call It Something Nice', a possible studio out-take released on *The Autumn Stone*.

'Happydaystoytown' wraps up the band's finest moment so far in suitably joyous style with a fun fair, toe-tapping sing-along, written by Steve and Ronnie, armed with a suitable array of sounds like car horns, referees' whistles and hand-clapping.

For an amazing six weeks, *Ogdens'* sat triumphant atop the UK album charts. Of course, as befell The Beatles with *Sgt Pepper*, numerous fans now expected a live version of this masterpiece. The band didn't do it; only 'Rollin' Over' and 'Song Of A Baker' became part of the live set. This was a substantial mistake, as Steve would admit later: "We had spent an entire year in the studios, which was why our stage presentation had not been improved since the previous year. Meanwhile, our recording experience had developed in leaps and bounds. We were all keenly interested in the technical possibilities, in the art of recording.

"We let down a lot of people who wanted to hear *Ogdens'* played live. We were still sort of rough and ready, and in the end the audience became uninterested as far as our stage show was concerned. It was our own fault, because we would have sussed it all out if we had only used our brains. We could have taken Stanley Unwin on tour with us, maybe a string section as well, and it would have been okay. But we didn't do it, we stuck to the concept that had been successful for a long time, which is always the kiss of death."

Putting that behind them, in July 1968 a new single, 'The Universal', appeared, intended to be a taster for a new album with an entirely new direction. Steve was very optimistic about the song's impact: "I thought it had the best lyrics I ever wrote. I don't know why, just the word associations, the way I worked it out. I needed all of ten minutes for it. I was sitting in my garden, on a beautiful summer's morning, with a boiled egg." To get it down, Steve simply used a portable tape machine to capture his singing and guitar accompaniment, plus of course unintended ambient street sounds like a barking dog and a voice in the background. In the studio, the band added a clarinet, a trombone, electric guitar and a bass drum. Many critics who couldn't get to grips with 'The Universal' treated it as a joke. The fans were also irritated. Still, the single managed to get to a passable Number Sixteen in Britain – backed with the grotesque sound orgy 'Donkey Rides A Penny A Glass'.

All success is relative and for Steve this came as a huge disappointment: "It killed me at the time. I didn't think that anybody believed in what the song was, which was just a very sort of play-on-words type of song and, I thought, a very clever song. And the reviews said either it was a stroke of genius or a terrible mistake. And because it wasn't a hit in a big way, it was considered a terrible mistake. And it killed me – I didn't write again for a long, long time."

A strange, tense atmosphere took hold of the band now. Steve appeared nervous, distant, confused. The other three sensed that something was in the air. But they were all confident that their work in the studios and on stage would get them back together again as a tight unit.

On 5 October, 1968, The Small Faces started a new tour in London with The Who, The Crazy World Of Arthur Brown and Joe Cocker And The Grease Band. It was then that things took a turn for the worse. The young Herd guitarist Peter Frampton sat in with the band at one of the gigs, later prompting an excited Steve Marriott to ask his band to let Peter join The Small Faces. Their refusal would mark the beginning of the end for the band, although nobody realised it at the time and the real rift wasn't to come until New Year's Eve 1969. By the time Immediate Records released a double album of previously released songs, live recordings and half finished tracks, called *The Autumn Stone*, The Small Faces would be less a working band than four confused musicians issuing controversial statements and denials. And whether Ronnie, Mac and Kenney liked it or not, Spring 1969 was the time when Steve's new band was taking shape.

The scattered end of the little Mods really belongs to Humble Pie's birth, but whatever the future held, *The Autumn Stone* was all the fans of The Small Faces had and so it's worth taking a look at the original material (see Discography for complete rundown).

The title track is another melancholic ballad, with a simple, clear yet warm sound that already points to the first two Humble Pie albums, which took shape only a few weeks after these sessions. Steve's vocals get a slight echo, accompanied by accentuated yet subdued bass and drums and the flute solo sounds similar to the one on 'As Safe As Yesterday' on Pie's debut.

The band's fascination with fantastic names continues in 'Collibosher', where a guitar riff not unlike that of 'Rollin' Over' leads into a backing track without vocals. Yet its saxophone and trombone breaks and again a flute accompaniment make it sound complete and homogenous. Steve's guitar gets involved in a nice call and response interplay with the reeds and horns, taken over by Ian's Hammond organ.

Another fast number, 'Red Balloon' is acoustic, comparable in its outline again with 'Alabama 69' from the forthcoming *Safe As Yesterday* album. Acoustic and electric guitars are nicely combined, Kenney underlines the track with brushes, and the harmony vocals are a dream.

Unfortunately, the concert excerpts – 'Rollin' Over'/'If I Were A Carpenter'/'Every Little Bit Hurts'/'Tin Soldier'/'All Or Nothing' – are as shrill as they are flat. In particular, their cover of Tim Hardin's 'If I Were A Carpenter' and the more than six minutes long 'Hurts' both suffer from the screaming typical (still) of the era.

'Call It Something Nice' is half waltz, half twelve-bar blues, containing all the trademarks that a psychedelic ballad should: distorted guitar intro, acoustic guitars and Hammond sounds – the period's greetings ranging from Hendrix to The Hollies. They also pick up on the 'Mad John' theme from *Ogdens'* whereas on 'Wide-Eyed Girl On The Wall', it's The Who's 'Substitute' that is saluted in the tongue-in-cheek guitar intro.

By total contrast, the introductory riff to 'Wham Bam Thank You Mam' is as unique as a fingerprint. Although this rock number develops with dynamics and utter consistence until the break which follows the chorus, on this recording the song sounds neither bombastic nor clear enough. Six years later, this was rectified on the *Marriott* solo album.

Conclusion: the ingredients for the follow-up to *Ogdens'* could already be spotted, but Immediate had only used material for half an album. Strangely, the three tracks mentioned earlier which had already been recorded for the album didn't make it onto this double LP, namely '(If You Think You're) Groovy', which PP Arnold had covered under her mentors Steve Marriott and Ronnie Lane's guidance, plus 'Love Is Here To Stay And Now You're Gone' and The Ronettes' hit 'Be My Baby', which Steve would also record in his home studio five years later.

Splits, separations and divorces rarely occur overnight. The Small Faces felt their share of frustrations in spite of the huge success of *Ogdens' Nut Gone Flake* – or because of that – and they were determined to find solutions. Talking to *Melody Maker* early in 1969, Steve said: "A minor catastrophe was on the cards. For a while nothing was happening with us. But we have a new album in our heads. It's on tape, too, but we haven't had the chance to record it properly. Things have been frustrating, and on top of that we have to solve business problems. After our last album, this one has to be better. The last one had been a bit too clever and metallic, grown out of city life. Out here [in Steve's country cottage in Moreton, Essex] we'll write more country-influenced stuff with bottleneck and acoustic guitars. The last album was nice, and if people were fed up with the gag side of things, they could put on the other side on. Many tracks could have been singles. But the next album will be totally different."

The album's working title was *1864* for some reason, and the material Steve referred to probably included tracks like 'Autumn Stone' or 'Red Balloon' which had just been released – without the band's consent. But Steve's description also reads like a preview of *Town And Country*, an album by his future band with an entirely different team which would only be started months later. After their scandalous gig on New Year's Eve 1968, Steve and the other three were pretty much torn apart, but there was a background story to the shake-up. The Small Faces had been facing two giant problems: as Steve had mentioned to *Melody Maker*, there had to be a new direction in the studio; also, the band – at long last – had to find ways to present their more sophisticated material on stage, adequately as opposed to half-arsed. While The Beatles never bothered to present *Sgt Pepper* live, contenders like The Hollies or The Bee Gees went on tour with string and horn sections.

There had been a growing rift between the rough, rioting soul Mod band called Small Faces and those four little whizz-kid recording cats Steve, 'Plonk', Mac and Kenney. That great divide between studio skills and stage act could hardly get overlooked – ever since the hippy days of 1967 with 'Here Come The Nice' or 'Itchycoo Park'. As the quartet now played in front of more attentive audiences, they were suddenly able to hear themselves properly – and what they heard they did not like. Ironically, the lack of screaming seemed part of the problem, because bands' popularity was still judged by some according to this ecstasy factor. And this band had widened the studio-stage rift even further with "the man looking for the other half of the moon" – their *Ogdens'* album. Stanley Unwin, the moon-mad cockney comedian, may have made history as an honorary Small Face, yet he did not help his young friends' street credibility one bit.

With hindsight, tour plans with the funny old man might have given the lads a new lease of life, however, they never materialised. Apart from their renowned musical complexity and the new feel of not having to compete with fans' noises anymore, there might have been a third reason for the fatigue and frustration of the little ex-Mods, at least according to Ronnie Lane: "We worked things out in the studio just for fun – Steve wouldn't have done stuff like that on stage, he wouldn't make a fool of himself like that."

With this perspective, The Small Faces' swan song 'The Universal' had taken shape, being severely misunderstood in the process. After gems like 'Itchycoo Park' or 'Lazy Sunday' – the latter never even intended as a single but a smash anyway – this new little tongue-in-cheek veranda ditty just didn't seem to do.

Still, there were rescue attempts. The band had at least chosen the *Ogdens'* numbers 'Song Of A Baker' and 'Rollin' Over' for the stage set, and even hired guest musicians. Ronnie: "There was the half-arsed attempt to present Georgie Fame's brass section. [Ronnie Scott, Johnny Marshall and Tony Coe on saxes, Les Condon, Ian Hamer and Derek Healey on trumpets plus Morris Platt, trombone, documented on the album *The Autumn Stone*.] So we got into it all right, but this turned out to be so bloody expensive, and people were still screaming, so we gave that up." So the fans were still crying their heads off, as Immediate's stocking filler *Autumn Stone* would prove.

Steve Marriott of course had his own idea of improving and augmenting the live side: his suggestion – in vain – to include his young 'guitar hero' Peter Frampton of The Herd in the line-up. Steve rated the teenage George Benson and Wes Montgomery jazz expert as a subtle match to his own hard rocking guitar style, as he remembered in a 1981 interview with *Trouser Press*: "Yeah, it'd be great. He's a very talented guitar player, so I could drop the guitar, vocalise a bit more, and that'll rejuvenate us as a live band."

The young guitarist had sat in with The Small Faces during a gig at the Bubbles Club in Brentwood, Essex, playing lead guitar after having been introduced by Steve twenty minutes into the gig. Appearing in black leather jacket and tight blue jeans, Peter was a far cry from the *Rave* posters depicting him as a teen idol, and his contribution was utterly musical: taking exactly the lead guitar role Steve had wanted. In hindsight, the Brentwood gig did not turn out as an element of Small Faces history, but rather a slice of Humble Pie, before the band name was coined – with the band leaving out most of the hits in favour of tasteful, competent hard rock.

Peter and the band knew each other anyway: Ronnie and Steve had produced the last Herd single to feature Frampton: 'Sunshine Cottage', and in turn Peter had been sessioneering on another production project of The Small Faces, Skip Bifferty. But the most telling document of the metamorphosis in The Small Faces was Steve, Ronnie and Peter's Paris session with France's legendary rock'n'roller Johnny Hallyday.

On his album *That Man*, there's not only the Brit trio's

contribution to the title track as 'Amen', but two future Pie titles: 'What You Will' and 'Bang' – appearing here as 'Réclamations' with the English sub-title 'New Report', which was of course part of the Pie chorus "Your news report". Who would have predicted that nine months later, 'Bang' and 'What You Will' would turn up on Humble Pie's debut album *As Safe As Yesterday Is*? And who would have thought that The Small Faces would ever sound so much like Marriott's future band? According to Kenney Jones, Steve apparently didn't hear it: "He felt that we couldn't cross over from being a pop band into heavier music; he felt it was too difficult, which was wrong because we really had it all, and we were going that way naturally."

But the three other little faces were still not convinced at all that Peter's addition would work, in fact they bluntly denied Marriott's request. So the young Frampton asked his trusted friend Steve to put a future band together for him, as he was in the process of cutting his contractual ties to The Herd's mentor, Steve Rowland's Double-R Productions and his dreaded happy-go-lucky Dave Dee, Dozy, Beaky, Mick And Tich image. According to *Disc* and *Music Echo* dated 3 May 1969, he was under contract there till November 1971.

While a mutual Marriott-Frampton band did not seem possible, Steve had suggested a promising kid drummer for Peter: Jerry Shirley (born 4 February, 1952 in Wattenham Cross), who was with Apostolic Intervention, the heavy combo whose cover version of 'Have You Ever Seen Me' The Small Faces had backed in the studio. In the end nobody could remember whether Kenney or his young, meticulous style-copying admirer had drummed on the record. Kenney in October 1992: "We discovered little Jerry Shirley when he used to come and watch us as a kid in short trousers. We're all on that session, but it's hard to tell who's actually drumming, because Jerry would sit and scrutinise my drumming all the time, and copy it beat for beat."

Steve was thinking of calling Peter's future band The Nice, possibly because he himself always shouted 'Here Come The Nice' when, with Mods' notoriety, amphetamines and other refreshments reached the dressing room. But Andrew Loog Oldham reacted with disgust – "You can't use that name" – only to use the tag for PP Arnold's backing band, Keith Emerson's new Bach-torturing trio The Nice. "Andrew always steals with decorum – very Nice-ly." was how – with typical ease – Steve Marriott shrugged off such tactics.

Then, of course, in what seemed like a spontaneous eruption at the time, there was Marriott's spectacular stage exit at London's Alexandra Palace, making his friend and 'special guest' Alexis Korner – of all people – the one to rescue The Small Faces' encore. Steve: "It was all my fault. I take the blame. My friend Alexis Korner was there, with a bass player called Nick South. I said: 'Why don't you come and play on the last number?' So that's what they did. The sound in the Ally Pally was terrible. We tried to play 'Itchycoo Park' and 'Lazy Sunday', but it didn't work out. We should have had an orchestra and phasing machines to do it properly. But we played it half-heartedly and paid for it.

"The whole set was diabolical. It was New Year's Eve 1969. Alexis came on stage, and it got worse. It was my fault, but nobody was taking any notice of each other. They were all in their own little universe – it was a terrible mess, a nightmare. One of the gigs you dream of with your pants down. And as a frontman, I noticed the nightmare more than anybody else. So I put my guitar down."

Putting it down wouldn't have been so bad, but Steve threw his axe on the floor and stormed out – leaving his three team mates completely confused – and raced to the exit past Korner. As far as Steve was concerned, it was all over now baby blue, and the remaining Small Faces numbers were presented by Ronnie, Ian, Kenney and Alexis. The missing singer then spent the rest of New Year's Eve complaining about his band's rejection of Frampton to none other than Greg Ridley.

Greg, born 23 October, 1947 in Aspatria, Cumbria, was still Spooky Tooth's bass player and a convincing singer in his own right, but suffered equal frustration in his own band – standing in the shadow of lead singer Mike Harrison and his falsetto counterpart, keyboard player Gary Wright. That evening at the Ally Pally, Marriott and Ridley had wondered whether Greg would be the right man for the still incomplete Peter Frampton band. He certainly could be, but then Steve saw another angle: "I thought, Sod it! What am I doing?

I've got to do something else myself. Frampton's unhappiness made me feel I had to get out of the depressive rut I was getting into." So there – only an hour later he stormed out.

Apart from contractually binding tours of West Germany and the Channel Islands, all further Small Faces live commitments were cancelled – including an appearance at New York's brand new Fillmore East. For Steve, the reasons behind his New Year's Eve eruption were clear. As a frontman, he would continue to take the blame – for the discrepancy between studio and stage as much as the metamorphosis from Mod soul to psychedelic power, not to mention the challenge of the increasingly popular progressive and blues rock bands, like Cream, Savoy Brown, Bluesbreakers and other London blues acts. How could he match those trends as the star of an ex-teenbeat band?

Marriott was burning to play proper R&B again, but he felt tired of always playing little bigmouth in the limelight. But up to March 1969, he denied all rumours of leaving The Small Faces for good: "How could I ever exist outside the band?" he insisted in *New Musical Express*. "And," he added, "I'm not one for two timing." Frampton also refused to comment on a musical marriage, while at least he and Jerry Shirley 'officially' jammed at Peter's Essex country cottage and Jerry's parents' home. What was happening? Jerry Shirley: "Steve Marriott called me on New Year's Eve. He had just come back from a disastrous gig with The Small Faces at the Alexandra Palace and asked if he could join our band. My first reaction was, Oh dear, what about The Small Faces? because I was a huge fan, but Marriott was adamant. Then he said, 'By the way, I've got a bass player, Greg Ridley, who wants to come with me.' Needless to say, I was thrilled."

But Steve insists he had meant the band to be for Frampton in the first place: "It wasn't a planned thing. Greg said he wouldn't join unless I did, knowing I'd just left the Faces. It wasn't a planned thing. I'd literally formed the band for Peter. I wasn't involved beyond finding him the personnel. I thought it was gonna be a great band, so about two weeks later I rang Pete up and asked if I could join. I thought I'm fed up with being a front man, I'll just stand back, play some guitar, and let Peter be the front man... I should have known [him] a bit better, because when I said to him, 'Pete, do you mind if I join?' there was a long silence. He said, 'I'll have to think about it.' Fucking hell!"

Soon afterwards Immediate Records cheekily advertised that while they could neither confirm nor deny rumours of a Small Faces split they could release another *Ogdens'* song coupled with a brand new, hard rocking number ('Afterglow Of Your Love'/'Wham Bam Thank You Mam', double A-side). Steve meanwhile continued his interviews with ramblings of new, country-influenced album tracks of his band. Fans might have thought he was talking about *The Autumn Stone*, but he was thinking about 'Alabama 69'.

CHAPTER THREE
Humble Pie I
Life Outside The Small Faces

While Humble Pie had been developing for months as Peter Frampton's new trio, both The Small Faces and their manager Andrew Oldham's Immediate Record label did not want to believe that everything had come to an end. But as rehearsals took place in Steve's country cottage anyway, he couldn't resist the urge to join, even though Peter was torn between admiring the fellow veteran and fearing for his status of his band.

Stunned, surprised and overwhelmed, Frampton accepted Steve's addition to his band, and together with Greg Ridley and Jerry Shirley they experienced Spring 1969 full of tentative jams, recordings sessions as well as intensive rehearsals. Shirley recognised right away how well Peter and Steve complemented each other, as he reminisced in 1991: "Musically speaking [they were] like probably the most fabulous mix I've ever seen because one complemented the other so well and without either of them realising it they just did it: Peter's melodic sweet side compared to Steve's hard edged side – almost carbon copies of the parts of London they came from. Tremendous combination!"

Steve of course came from the rough East London suburb of the dockers, Stepney – "René, the Dockers' Delight" (*Ogdens'*) – and Peter from the equally working class but a little bit more sedate Beckenham with its hills and parks – near Catford, which was eternally romanticised in the Seventies by local band Squeeze with their kitchen sink storytelling. "And," added Jerry Shirley, "Steve and Peter personally got on very very well originally – in the beginning."

Far from having lost their music-making ideals in the jungles of cheap showbiz, the new group began to create new songs and sounds. They took their time letting numbers emerge not only from lengthy jams but from combining song fractions without letting their egos get in the way – stunningly exemplified in the title track for *As Safe As Yesterday Is*. So fruitful did these early sessions in Steve's cottage turn out that the prepared material was sufficient for two albums. The Pie sound ranged from hard rock in the style of the vintage 'stage' Small Faces to acoustic numbers reminiscent of *Autumn Stone*.

But this was by no means just Steve's new backing band. The harder stuff would often sport three strong lead singers who could all amazingly 'shout' in tune, whereas the quiet songs benefited from Peter's jazz guitar lines, sensitive percussion by Jerry and the fact that the four of them were multi-instrumentalists, each covering at least guitars, bass, drums and keyboards. On top of that, there were experiments like Steve learning to play the sitar, or Jerry's toying with harpsichord, for instance on Peter's 'I'll Go Alone'. This could be a lead to the influence of a fifth Pie member, recruited at short notice but tragically losing his life the day before rehearsals with him had been scheduled – Brian Jones of The Rolling Stones died before he could have joined Humble Pie.

Shirley was still new in the business, whereas for those three pop/rock veterans who worked in front of Jerry, star antics and image strategies were something they now wanted to get rid of – they'd had enough of the coloured spotlight. Even the band's chosen name was a consequence of that anti-stardom stance. 'To eat humble pie' was what they wanted to stand for: to be left in peace while they got their music together, away from the media whose headlines would only ruin it all.

But in spite of Steve's lip service to taking a back seat behind the bandleader who had accepted him in, Humble Pie's debut album did not reveal Peter Frampton as the front man. Sure, his voice is present in many of the songs' verses and choruses, and his guitar lines are inventive and prominent, but he is certainly not the focus. Only two tracks were written by Pete, compared with five Marriott compositions – while they collaborated on the title track.

And incidentally, those who wondered whether it was Steve or Peter who played that Ian McLagan-type Hammond organ in the studio probably didn't realise that Ian played a humble part in the beginning of Pie history. Possibly without Laney or Kenney being aware of this, he rehearsed with the band for a while, and some of his contributions found their way onto the tapes of Olympic Sound Studios, where Andrew Johns worked with the band (his brother Glyn was taking care of The Rolling Stones' *Let It Bleed* sessions).

For all the songwriting talent amassed for the resulting album, *As Safe As Yesterday Is*, it came as a surprise when the first track turned out to be a cover of Steppenwolf's 'Desperation'. This beautiful blues, about a girl who wants to be taken by the hand, was written by the LA-based band's German/Canadian lead singer John Kay. (Glimpse into the future: Steppenwolf's keyboarder at the time, Goldy McJohn, would play in a Humble Pie edition in 1982.) 'Desperation' was more than six minutes long and certainly served its purpose of a calling card: showing off Pie's potential. Marriott's Hammond leads into the theme, remaining between The Small Faces' Ian McLagan and Spooky Tooth's Gary Wright in terms of sound. Frampton's already self-reliant lead guitar fits in well, Marriott's rhythm chops assist with team spirit, but all this really takes shape with the energetically active, shit-tight rhythm section of Ridley and Shirley. Marriott sings the first verse, during the second and third section Steve, Peter and Greg often take turns in mid sentence. This would become Pie's trademark which no other rock group has ever attempted – let alone perfected – in this way.

'Stick Shift' is the first Frampton number to be heard. A rocker about a working lad whose wife found her way back to him and is now expecting, the number takes its strength from the contrast between Steve's slide guitar dominating the verses and a harder style for the chorus. 'Put me on the stick shift' is American slang for 'Let me take the tougher part of the job' – derived from the middle class family quarrels on who's to take the newer, automatic gear shift car, and who is left with the second hand 'stick shift' motor.

'Buttermilk Boy' starts as fast rock'n'roll, but then a beautiful Frampton lead guitar carries it mid tempo. Those changes continue during the whole song, a mild micky-take on a farmer's boy who wants to get married to an upper class high-brow girl. The three front men again thrive on their mid line vocal take-overs. Before they wail into the final instrumental passage, you can hear Steve's relishing "Let me hear some of that strong-armed music." before the band, led by Jerry Shirley get into full gear once more.

'Growing Closer', known as Mac's number, features acoustic guitar chords by Pete, harmonica and tablas courtesy of Steve and flute by guest Lyn Dobson, who used to play for Georgie Fame and Ian Matthews. The additional title points to McLagan as composer (as well as a player?), and in fact this song would not sound out of place on *The Autumn Stone*.

'As Safe As Yesterday' shines as the colossal title track made up of separate songs by Steve and Peter, combined Lennon and McCartney - style in sessions. Jerry: "It began as a song Frampton had, a part of which ultimately became the first section. Marriott then added the middle part from one of his unfinished songs, and the ending came from a jam we had done in the studio. Then we pieced it together and recorded it again as one song." 'Safe' starts as a gorgeous orgy of sound, its heavy 4/4 rhythm stressed by acoustic piano and organ. These keyboard walls have a more dramatic effect than the complete 1990s sample options. A dreamy section follows with tablas and acoustic guitars, which remain both present and transparent during the loud finale.

'Bang!' is another straight rocker, not unlike 'Stick Shift', with Ridley's typically rolling bass lines. The mighty chorus appears courtesy of the three front singers. Note the attractive guitar riffs during the breaks. The electric Fender Rhodes piano again reminds us of Mac, during the middle section Steve and Greg take turns. The whole quartet again injects all their energy into this recording.

'Alabama 69' is the acoustic log-fire number which the foursome celebrated with joy in the TV studios of German Radio Bremen's *Beat Club* – sitting in a doped semi-circle. Surely, the show's host, Uschi Nehrke, still smelled of Black Afghan on her way home. For the studio recording, acoustic guitars, blues harp, hi-hat and bass are complemented by Lyn Dobson's sitar and flute. Note for vinyl lovers: according to the actual track grooves on plastic, the Lyn Dobson dominated instrumental passage is not part of 'Alabama' – as the liner notes on the *Repertoire* CD release claim, but actually belong to the next track, 'I'll Go Alone'. This is another more dramatic mid tempo composition by Frampton. Again, Greg's rolling bass forms the basis for organ and piano. The song's highlight is Pete's guitar solo, which he manages to make as frenetic as he does melodic.

Maintaining his fascination with C&W, Steve wrote 'A Nifty Little

Number Like You' as a revenge with a certain country girl who used to "smell like a field of cow shit in midsummer sun". Perhaps this experience was due to the country atmosphere round Steve's cottage, like 'Buttermilk Boy'. Some great instrumental leads follow with expertly geared rhythm guitars.

Finally the album wraps up with 'What You Will' which sees the four of them again letting all their collective energy flow, piled up perhaps by waiting for live gigs. Shirley leaves an excellent impression with a short drum solo, which must have been a demonstration gem for late Sixties hi-fi dealers, bouncing as it did from the left stereo channel to the right and back again. Traditionally, vinyl grooves put the drum solo at the end of 'What You Will' (7:01), while Repertoire Records programmed it before 'Nifty' on their CDs. The drums are followed by Steve's beautiful, romantic ballad about someone whom life has disappointed and depressed. Another exciting drum break which consists entirely of double shots leads into a magic Spector-esque wall-of-sound finale, again over-dubbed by acoustic guitars.

Some critics called this album the most Small Faces-type set by the Pie. Surely there are certain elements and parallels, for instance to *Autumn Stone* tracks, but at the same time Steve, Peter, Greg and Jerry were determined to reach their musical limits – trying to appeal to more eclectic, fringe tastes as much as to rock's mainstream. Even before *As Safe As Yesterday Is* was released, Humble Pie had resumed work on more tracks, and while not one single live concert had been played, the new sessions with Andrew Johns, this time at Morgan Studios, had produced an entire second album.

Steve: "We were in the studio for about six months. We did *As Safe As Yesterday Is* and *Town And Country* before the first was released. Delays, delays – I don't know why. Andrew [Loog Oldham] had all these concepts for the album cover of *Yesterday*, and I said, 'Fuck it, put it out in a brown paper bag and write 'Humble Pie' on it with a pen.' So they did that and photographed it and that was the cover."

Andy Johns' part in the 1969 recording sessions can hardly be underestimated. Like his brother Glyn, he would also work intensively with The Rolling Stones. With all respect to later engineering and mixing masters like Eddie Kramer in the States or Steve Marriott himself – apart from Andy's big brother Glyn's studio work with Pie –

none of the others would reach the utter brilliance of those early Johns productions.

With all their bursting energy intact and armed with inspiration for various musical styles, Humble Pie seemed truly stunning at the time. While they were immediately billed as a 'supergroup' – along the lines of Blind Faith, with Eric Clapton and Steve's namesake and soul mate Steve Winwood – they could not release a thing. With legal wrangles also preventing live gigs, they had neither a live nor record audience as a feedback and indication of the popularity of what they had been working on. The speed of their 1969 recordings was based on two factors. The band's aim had been right from the start to find a number of musical styles and outlets; on the other hand they wanted to find out how far their collected skills would take them in the craft of creating new sounds while still remaining a down-to-earth rock group.

A sensationalist tag by the press was all Humble Pie needed at a time of slow musical growth. Steve: "You're supposed to be amazing the day you come out, but you need time. There was so much pressure, I was really at the point of mental breakdown. It drives you into being a recluse, instead of the extrovert you're known as. We wanted to come in the back door but the media wouldn't let us." On top of that, the band were surely working against a timebomb – ie Immediate's financial situation – which was ticking louder and louder.

As late as August 1969, the British music press announced that Peter Frampton had been bought out of his contract with Steve Rowland's Double-R-Productions and now the band's career could speed up at last. With a rocking debut single, 'Natural Born Bugie', Pie played it safe on Oldham's suggestion. While The Beatles had shamelessly milked Chuck Berry's 'You Can't Catch Me' for 'Come Together' on the just released *Abbey Road* album, the Pie pinched the 'Little Queenie' riff from the same St Louis-based legend. The debut album's trademark – three lead singers taking turns – reached an audience for the first time and managed Number Four in the British singles charts. The B-side, 'Wrist Job', is a dramatically melancholic ballad where a Hammond organ fed through rotating Leslie speakers creates even more energy than the guitars on the actual hit.

Compared to the rough and not always ready 'late' Small Faces stage presence, Humble Pie lived up to the demands of popular blues rock and played a more than solid club date in August 1969 for 'rock business people' at London's renowned Ronnie Scott's (on whose top floor Marriott's future agent Michael Eve would reside twenty years later). After their debut, their concerts would often last two or three hours. "We lived up to the demands of Bruce Springsteen, or the 'Unplugged' era, even then," a quite amused Peter Frampton mused in 1994, and indeed, a sit-down acoustic set (see Guitarography in the appendix) preceded the rockier second half of Pie shows, maybe as a reaction to the despised supergroup tag. "They wouldn't give us time to grow," Steve had sighed – there was no chance of eating humble pie. And so, after initially using their waiting time for preparing their recording sessions, they now stole their time on stage.

Blues harp, tablas, bongos and a sparse bass-drums pattern used to round off their countrified sound, with straight, often quite heavy rock songs as a considerable contrast – welcomed by the open-minded late Sixties audiences, for example during their rainy touring debut on a Belgian pop festival or an appearance in Amsterdam's Paradiso, the legendary dope mecca. But the general European feedback was subdued as long as Steve Marriott held back his raving stage personality. The Hamburg-based group Frumpy, hired as support act, claimed in German magazines *Bravo* and *Musik Express* to have reluctantly stolen the supergroup's show.

By the time Humble Pie announced a British tour of nine cities in September 1969, *As Safe As Yesterday Is* had followed their single into the charts, even if it only peaked at Number Thirty-Two for one week. Their supports this time were Dave Edmunds' Love Sculpture and David Bowie, Peter Frampton's old school tie from Beckenham Grammar, whom he would assist musically some eighteen years later.

At the end of the year, the second album *Town And Country* – recorded all through early summer – appeared as one of the last releases of Immediate Records, whose bankruptcy had been rumoured for several months. Those who remembered Steve Marriott and Peter Frampton's claims in press statements about growth and being taken seriously, were in for impressive musical evidence. Far beyond commercial considerations, one of the most versatile albums of the Woodstock era had taken shape. Here, four multi-instrumentalists – among them three individually and mutually brilliant singers – had

67

staged rock styles ranging from Crosby, Stills And Nash to Led Zeppelin, without evoking comparisons, but also without shying away from them. Steve Marriott later seemed reluctant about accepting that praise: "On the first two LPs we were confused as to what to do. I can write lots of different types of songs – so can Pete, though they were mainly my songs at the time. I had all this country stuff and all this rock stuff; we wound up doing more quiet stuff than people expected."

The hazardous business ignorance of both Humble Pie and Andrew Oldham also shows in the second album's cover art. Neither the band's name nor the title *Town And Country* appeared on the front sleeve – well, only on its small rim, in good company with other 1969 releases like The Beatles' *Abbey Road* and Georgie Fame's *Seventh Son*, but Pie's album presented a still new act. And so, on the front cover, Peter and Greg pose as early Yuppies in a London luxury flat, whereas the back cover seems to portrait Sherwood Forest near Nottingham – but Barnes by the Thames or Marriott's Moreton seem more likely. We spot Steve sitting in a tree as Robin Hood armed with a bow and arrow, while Jerry as his Little John is seen quietly squatting by a brook. And while both The Beatles and Georgie Fame had made sure that their name was prominent on their back sleeves, Humble Pie's anonymous concept was only copied two years later on Led Zeppelin's fourth album, *Four Symbols*.

While the cover might have been anonymous, the music couldn't have been anyone else, especially since *Town And Country* would be the only Humble Pie album not to use any guest musicians. Peter Frampton opens the album with the country sounding 'Take Me Back' (more Moreton/Essex than Nashville/Tennessee). Over some subdued percussive assistance by the others, the would-be band-leader presents a romantic ballad which not only confirms his strength as a matured, sensitive singer but also – after 'Safe''s more powerful soloing – as a serious master of the acoustic guitar.

Marriott's contributions begin with 'The Sad Bag Of Shaky Jake', a colourful cowboy story leading us into US Western territory. The dynamic slow rock is characterised by solid guitar and drum work behind Steve's blues harp and harmony chorus. As their second single, it would have needed major promotion of the type Immediate was not able to deliver anymore. Steve's Eighties bass player Jim Leverton still features the gem in his mid Nineties stage set.

Putting C&W aside for a moment, 'The Light Of Love' draws influences from The Beatles and Byrds with sitar sounds courtesy of Steve. Pete's guitar lead into an acoustic ballad is dominated by Greg Ridley's smokey voice, accelerated by harmony vocals and Jerry's change from tablas to drums.

The rhythm becomes faster on 'Cold Lady' where Steve treats Jerry's cool girl lament as an R&B crooner torn between tenderness and suffering, gathering momentum in the chorus. Shirley's Wurlitzer piano adds an attractive additional touch to the overall sound.

'Down Home Again' is the 'Town' rocker with all those melodic metal ingredients of the future US-shaking Pie. The band sings about the limitless joys of returning home after gigs: "Well, the show's all over, I just pack my guitar..." With such energy and compact catchiness, Humble Pie would surely have been able to chart following up 'Bugie' and the failed 'Shaky Jake'.

As was the Sixties craze, 'Ollie Ollie' is a noisy party orgy, meant as some sort of gap filler at the vinyl end of part one before 'Every Mother's Son' commences round two. As a counterpart to Peter's 'Take Me Back' Steve begins with another acoustic ballad about a rock artist's lost love, reminding us that at least in the studio this direction was as dear to his heart as to Peter's, who responds to Steve's chords with sensitive and dramatic solo fills.

According to their own admittedly young standards, it wouldn't be a Pie album without a cover version. This time round it was 'Heartbeat', Buddy Holly's tear jerker here transformed into a happy-go-lucky, rousing rocker which had the crowd on its feet during Pie's debut at Ronnie Scott's club in London.

Back with the original material, 'Only You Can See' is a dynamic, resonant soft rock by Peter, recorded here as a trio: with Greg's floating bass and Steve on drums helping Frampton's multi-layered vocals, guitar and E-piano. Next, 'Silver Tongue' sees Steve's Leslie speaker-fed guitar, echoey vocal and time changes which form a pleasant reminder of 'Tin Soldier'. But this still holds its own as a composition, receiving one early Pie trademark in Peter's rousing solo.

Clocking in at six minutes, the grand finale of the album, 'Home And Away' combines the 'Town' ingredients – electric piano, bass and drums – with the 'Country' elements – like acoustic guitars and harmony singing. This album stands as nothing less than a parallel to The Band's *Music From Big Pink*.

Humble Pie's artistic and commercial status couldn't have been further apart in the late autumn of 1969. For months on end, they had put bursts of studio creativity against the fans and the media's superstar expectations – and with Peter Frampton in contract limbo. And now – after the British October tour – Immediate were not even able to assist their subsequently scheduled first US trip financially or even with some product to flog.

Town And Country had reached British shops on the run from the official receivers, but could not be released in the States at all. So they went to America, supporting The Moody Blues instead of having their own album in the shops. To make matters worse, US audiences did not rave as much over their marathon gigs as the Pie would have wished. Jerry: "You could say we were twenty-five years ahead of our time, because we would perform unplugged for the first twenty minutes of our set. This didn't go down too well in America." Humble Pie's return to England was therefore less than ecstatic, and the bad news hadn't even started.

Andrew Loog Oldham saw no way of rescuing his ailing label, so the band was in fact without a recording deal – and, come to that, without a managing contract. Steve remembers: "He said, 'You've gotta leave now 'cause we're going under', and suggested ways of getting a record deal, which was really nice 'cause I'd had no idea. We could have gone with the company and wound up as assets to the liquidator. So we went to A&M [the company founded by the Tijuana trumpeter Herb Alpert with agent Jerry Moss], told 'em what we wanted and they gave it to us."

So the supergroup almost stranded soon after its inception. It was Pie's roadie Danny Farnham – who, as Spooky Tooth's handy man was the only one apart from Greg Ridley with American experience – who suggested fat Dee Anthony, an American agent with rock pedigree, as their new manager. "There's this great rock'n'roll manager in America; want us to put in the good word for you?" Dee was indeed interested in the band, and Steve "thought he was just the type of strong guy we wanted". As early as November, Dee flew the band back to America again, still with support status, but it was still like a fresh start, opening for the Butterfield Blues Band and Santana.

Steve Marriott reminisced in an interview in 1985: "It was hard work. We didn't get there on the crest of a wave, we came in the back door, and we had to work our way up – like third on the bill, little dives – but watching great acts, it was worth it: like Santana when they first formed and Johnny Winter when he was first having a go. It's the best way we could have done it. We were being called a supergroup at the time and we'd had one hit, 'Natural Born What's Name?', and we thought, if we carry on like this, there's only one way for us to go and that's down. Because we didn't have to work our way up – and we all know how long that lasts. So we literally went to America to break our bones and become a band."

Svengali Dee Anthony surely helped breaking bones, working the band on his own terms. Whether Humble Pie were supporting or a headlining act, the country set – Peter's favourite – had to go. Jerry Shirley seemed to understand at the time, as he remembered for Pie's 1994 retrospective *Hot'N'Nasty*: "It had been working in England, but we soon realised that you had to do some serious rocking and rolling to get across in America. We dumped the unplugged bit and got down to business." So the two-and-a-half-hour gigs in hippy fashion became a straight ninety minutes of town rock.

Steve: "On stage we used to come out and sit down and play acoustic. He told us to kick that out for a start, 'cause until you're in a position to do that – until they want you to do that – they're going to boo you at the Fillmore and throw their popcorn. He wasn't wrong; it just hadn't dawned on me, 'cause I was still too busy smoking hash and being introverted."

But the band gained confidence: Peter took the change in his stride and replaced his filigree jazz runs by more aggressive, yet still stunningly melodic, rock soloing, which quickly catapulted him into the top league of lead guitarists in the industry, whereas Steve grew onto his natural role as a band's focus, as the raver challenging his audience. The streamlined repertoire sounded exciting, while it became more relaxed and increasingly improvised at the same time. The band developed cover versions like 'I Walk On Guilded Splinters' to epic length and so could get away with less than a dozen songs per set – putting quality before quantity.

When Humble Pie returned to the United Kingdom from their second US tour, they realised Oldham had been right. Inland Revenue seals stuck to the Immediate office doors. So A&M had come to their rescue just in time, and they would guarantee the band all the freedom they wanted. Marriott: "Jerry Moss helped us in any way he could." They returned to Olympic Studios, hiring Andy Johns' brother Glyn this time to put into shape the jams and song ideas Pie had developed during the American sojourns.

On their A&M debut LP, simply called *Humble Pie*, the development from "eclectic rock artists" – as *Melody Maker* had put it – to stage trained pros was apparent. Steve: "By our third album we were starting to mix everything in, including some of the heavy stuff we later moved into."

Their more melodic hard rock had been limited to 'Heartbeat' and 'Down Home Again' on *Town And Country*. Now half of the numbers were tough rockers, with Jerry, Peter, Steve and Greg each – in that order – supplying one acoustic ballad. Humble Pie's 1970 summer single, which just scraped the UK Top Thirty, also combines town and country: on the A-side, 'Big Black Dog', Steve – with Peter and Greg's assistance – recalls his adventure with a stubborn sheep dog in a hard rock setting with Jerry's cow bell breaks; while on the B-side, Shirley uses a country waltz to sing about the (Pie) pleasures of smoking marijuana in 'Only A Roach'.

The careful balance of the single is continued on the first track of the new album. 'Live With Me', by far the longest piece of work on their new collection at almost eight minutes, was written by the whole band taking a verse each. The result showed how Pie had grown in America and, matured out of jamming experience, Glyn Johns captured their fascinating ensemble work. Rarely has a group managed to develop such fire from initially warm Hammond sounds and tender cymbal work. Organ, guitar and E-piano sections follow each other as coherently as the three singers. Glyn's production is as compact as it's transparent, and after two and a half decades this has lost nothing of its dark fascination.

The B-side to the first single, 'Only A Roach' ("won't keep us from 'grass' in the ocean"), witnesses Jerry's dope rhyming leading his frontmen into temptation with this soft-drug country waltz. Pie get atmospheric help from pedal steel expert and Glyn Johns house musician BJ Cole, while pub piano courtesy of Steve helps the overall impact.

From an illicit pleasure to a more socially accepted one, 'One-Eyed Trouser Snake Rumba' includes the cheeky euphemism for a man's most treasured organ in this hot R&B, with Steve, Peter and Greg again singing in turns: true trademark fashion, before they scream their "Give me more" chorus together. The 'rumba' guitar/bass/drum basis is exemplary in terms of precise playing and crisp recording.

'Earth And Water Song' starts out as a coy, reserved but tender love song of Peter's which grows on the listener with repeated plays – revealing a surprisingly dynamic rise to its climax. Initially carried only by Peter's acoustic and Greg's bass, his electric guitar solo spot is assisted by Steve's lead and rhythm guitar chops. A kind of follow-up to 'Home And Away'.

The band's trend for cover songs continues of a fashion with 'I'm Ready', a track which is much less faithful to Chicago blues godfather Willie Dixon's original than, for instance, Frankie Miller's 1972 version. Here, Pie present their first arrangement of many black R&B standards which they would delve into more and more. There was never a shortage of original material, but especially Steve derived as much pleasure from interpreting other people's work as writing his own (as he confirmed in a conversation with the Hannover-based DJ Ulli Kniep in one of his last interviews in January 1991). Jerry's drum intro would electrify audiences into motion, demonstrated on the *Performance* concert version (see Fillmore chapter). A similar intro would be used on the also live 'Honky Tonk Woman'.

Looking back at their lucky escape with a smile, 'Theme From Skint – See You Later Liquidator' recounts Humble Pie's narrow escape from the official Immediate receiver. Steve verbally indulges in his indifference and insecurity in terms of money matters, accompanied by acoustic guitars and again BJ Cole's pedal steel: "Whosoever whatsoever it's for, the slogan's on the door, we shall overdraw." On top of that, "Mr Ridley" has already "bought a Bentley". And on business people's nasty habit of interfering with the artistic, creative side of things, Steve adds "Oh, Mr Banker, won't you write a song for us", not forgetting to give a big thanks to his audience: "We'd like to thank you people, for listening to our song, we hope you get to hear the rest of the record, before they drop their form."

Satire aside, the album concludes with two 'normal' Pie tracks. The first is 'Red Light Mama Red Hot', another hard-hitting Pie stage-orientated R&B production with walls of guitars. Steve's unmistakable blues harp as well as Jerry and Greg's solid rhythm base expose why they would be hired by BB King only weeks later. Finally, the record winds up with the acoustic 'Sucking On The Sweet Wine'. Mr Ridley cannot even find solace in his new Bentley, but has to succumb to lots of 'plonk' to forget his latest love, revealed in his smokey rasp and incredibly sweet and sour bass lines. Again he is assisted by BJ Cole's Hawaii sounds behind Peter and Steve's acoustic guitar duets, until they all speed up following Jerry's drum signal. For the outro, Frampton presents another of his jazz solos which George Benson would have been proud of.

Probably as a sign for resuming their career without the hassles of the past, Humble Pie's A&M debut did not receive a specific album title, but simply presented Jerry's attractive bass drum logo on the front cover. The English, Brighton-based artist Aubrey Beardsley had created this motif in 1894 as part of a series for the illustration of Oscar Wilde's *Salomé*. The inner gatefold shows the band in a Spaghetti Western setting, Marriott sporting a Bronson moustache and his band wearing full beards, even 'the Face of 68' – Peter Frampton. The back cover presents another artistic highlight: 'Hope' is an 1886 oil painting taken from the *House Of Lige* range by George Frederic Watts (1817-1904) and his assistants. Humble Pie couldn't have chosen a more fitting symbol for the current state of their career: 'Hope' is sitting on the globe with bandaged eyes, picking on a lyre with all but one of its strings broken, still listening with intent. Pie fans have the chance to admire the original painting in London's Tate Gallery.

The album was at least a critical success for the band, it became a slow but increasingly steady seller. According to Steve, A&M boss Jerry Moss saw the album's commercial potential with astute realism: "He turned round at one point and said, 'You're about three albums away', which upset me. 'Don't you believe this one will do it?' But he was right on the money. That third album was – the Fillmore album. Jerry was a guy with a bit of longevity. He wasn't talking about 'This album's gotta go platinum or we'll drop you', he was talking strictly long term…he's a wonderful man!" But for now, it was Kinks leader Ray Davies of all people who decided to make *Salomé/Pie III* his 'Album of the Week' – in Germany's *Bravo* pop magazine.

Meanwhile, Humble Pie were back in the United States once again, where they were spending more time touring now than they did recording in the United Kingdom. Usually based in New York City, the band were able to build their reputation of an excellent live act on solid economic ground. Apart from support slots, where they became renowned for more than occasionally stealing the show, Pie headlined in increasing numbers of clubs and smaller halls and theatres. Their highly developed stage coherence during the summer of 1970 is well documented on the live-in-the-studio sessions they did for BBC Radio, for example 'Natural Born Bugie', 'Big Black Dog' and Muddy Waters' 'Rolling Stone' – their extended version complete with rousing boogie part had become a focal point of their gigs and would also find its way on their forth album.

Jerry Shirley on the more balanced and focused sound identity on the third and forth albums: "[That was] because we'd been on the road, unlike the first two records when we hadn't been on the road when we made them, and that's the simple difference. That's my personal feeling about it. A lot of the material in fact that went on the first two A&M records (*Humble Pie, Rock On*) cut its teeth live before it was actually recorded in the studio."

And so, from numerous American soundcheck and session afternoons as well as solid gigging, the band had enough material to join Glyn Johns at the end of 1970 in Olympic Studios Barnes. Serious recording resumed in January. Apart from the stage-tested songs, Humble Pie saw the fourth album as a kind of studio party, with numerous guests from the world of blues and soul, whose skills mirrored all of the band's stylistic range amazingly well. Too many cooks didn't spoil the 'soul stew' here but were most effectively combined once again by Glyn's powerful engineering and production.

Steve Marriott: "*Rock On* was the first sixteen-track (or was it twenty-four?) album we'd done; it had extra backing vocals and sax and all that shit. It was a further combination of elements, but mostly harder rock with a bit of soul in there. The first Small Faces albums consisted of our going in and doing our stage act, but in the Pie we started going in and *creating* the stage act – getting the songs down that we wanted in the set, instead of coming out scared thinking, Oh shit, how we gonna play that motherfucker?"

Not quite Jerry Shirley's version, but at least the band saw enough connections between stage and studio to prevent the disaster of the *Ogdens'* aftermath in 1968-69.

The band's familiarity with the material eventually recorded for *Rock On* comes across well. 'Shine On' sees a George Harrison-type phased *Abbey Road* guitar lead into Peter Frampton's mid tempo rocker, recreated on stage via Steve's Hammond (and subsequently presented by Peter on his *Frampton Comes Alive* five years later). Unusually, three female soul voices support the chorus: old friend PP Arnold was one, of course. Another American black girl, Doris Troy was the second; she had an early Sixties US hit with her self-composed 'Just One Look' – covered successfully by The Hollies – and had recently enjoyed a comeback via an Apple recording contract. She also guested on Pink Floyd albums – and in turn for her work on Humble Pie's album, Peter Frampton played lead guitar on her single 'Ain't That Cute' and also on an album track. The two "black chicks" (Marriott) Pat and Doris were complemented by Claudia Lennear, who had sung backing for Gene Clark, Joe Cocker, Freddie King and Taj Mahal.

Track two, 'Sour Grain', keeps 'Shine''s tempo and atmosphere, but this time with vocals delivered just by Steve and Peter on their joint composition. Stones-type guitar riffs feed its power, interrupted by delicate steel guitar breaks, which would have been the only ingredient missing on a live rendition.

Next comes 'Seventy-Ninth And Sunset', Steve's hymn to some of Pie's infamous red light spots – The corner of Hollywood's Sunset Boulevard and also on Seventy-Ninth Street in New York City – which seems an attempt at attracting an 'eighteen' certificate. Steve: "It's about these very organised tarts...in those days they were a union." Jerry: "They looked after you, they treated you like royalty. I was only seventeen in 1969..." Lines about "nut-cracking boobs" and the fact that "She's young, she's wealthy, she's far from healthy...got a pill to bend your will", are delivered with Steve's own pub piano backing.

Built on acoustic guitar and subdued rhythm and bass, there's an inventive, lively guitar solo by Peter. The alternative version on Repertoire Records' *Town And Country* CD, called 'Seventy-Ninth Street Blues' contains an even more attractive vocal doo-wop arrangement (see Discography).

Hard rock and Louisiana blues were so prevalent in their live act that 'Stone Cold Fever' and 'Rolling Stone' were lifted directly from their stage set and were put down on on sixteen – or twenty-four! – track without any guests or overdubs. There is hardly a difference between this version and the Pie-Muddy Waters standard performed for the BBC sessions in the summer of 1970.

'A Song For Jenny' interrupts the party line and leads back to the *Town And Country* period with the help of BJ Cole's pedal steel Hawaiian sounds. Steve wrote this little love song for his wife, Jenny, who suffered as much from the long, tour-inflicted separations as Steve did. 'The Light', however, is Frampton's showcase for rocking out. Featuring inventive rhythm and lead guitar work by Steve and Peter respectively, apart from a more lyrical soloing and mild Fender Rhodes piano, the number's drum pattern shows that both 'camps' loved rock'n'roll. It was just that Peter wanted certain subtle treats included which would get lost on the way to Steve's insistence on power boogies.

Away from the two guitarists' rivalry, bassman Greg Ridley was busy with his own material. 'Big George' is a hard and happy rocker, once more with Pie's guitar combinations (in true Keith Richards style but more sophisticated), rhythm changes and a wild saxophone solo by the Stones' Bobby Keys.

From Keith Richards' to Ray Charles' style, on 'Strange Days' Steve's (or Alexis Korner's) piano is coupled with delicate jazz guitar lines, soft bass drums and exciting percussion, all building up to fantastic gospel heights. The acting artists get in the groove for several minutes before a kind of 'Iljushin' jet effect from The Beatles' 'Back In The USSR' leads to the slower section and Steve's echo-filtered vocals and his Hammond organ add to the overall sound. Piano and jazz guitar share themes in such a subtle way that the number could last for hours without boring the musicians, or the listeners.

To round off the album in typical Pie fashion, the piano is carried from the church directly to the pub, where the gang rave on in the same line-up on 'Red Neck Jump'. Greg and Alexis Korner's doo-wop vocals from the days of Fifties rock'n'roll assist Steve's cheeky ramblings about cowboy bars in the Deep South with Lana Turner pin-up posters.

As mentioned, five of the *Rock On* session artists went on to take part in recordings for BB King on his *In London* album: Pie's Steve, Greg and Jerry, sax player Bobby Keys and Alexis Korner, immortalised on 'Alexis' Boogie', shared the booths with Ringo Starr, Hollies keyboarder, Chipping Norton studio producer and Freddie King collaborator Pete Wingfield, as well as Dr John, the Floyd's Rick Wright and Spooky Tooth's Gary Wright. Jerry and Greg quite rightly had a reputation as 'shit tight rhythm section'.

The 'track by track' outline of *Rock On* shows that studio work – in spite of good intentions in terms of catching the stage sound on master tape – tends to develop its own dynamics. New gadgets get checked out, guests have to be integrated, and the chosen songs must capture the band's whole range on repeated listening in the intimacy of the fans' own homes. So the rules are quite different from successful 'In Concert' presentations. 'Song For Jenny', for instance would have been cut out by set censor Dee Anthony. In order to combine both aspects of the band's work, Humble Pie saw the possibilities of a live album. Jerry: "I think that the two aspects are probably the whole reason why we finally made the decision to do a live album: because we were at that time far better live. Our forte was – without wanting to sound big-time – we were one of the best live acts at that time on the road."

By May 1971, Humble Pie were really cooking all over the United States. They seemed absolutely confident of their impact, so getting this 'in the can' was a challenge and had to be just right. Jerry Shirley: "We had developed into a strong live act, but our record sales weren't enjoying the same kind of success. It was decided that what we needed to do was to capture what we were doing on stage and release that." There were sound arguments for recording the live album in Bill Graham's Fillmore East auditorium in New York City, as other artists had found out before Humble Pie.

Jerry Shirley remembers the scene: "There's one simple reason why everybody wanted to play there other than it being the cool place to play. The sound of the room was the best sounding live room I personally ever remember playing, and I think if you ran that question by just about any musician that played the room they would all say the same. That theory is held up by comparing the live albums that were recorded at the Fillmore by bands as diverse as John Mayall acoustically, Humble Pie and The Allman Brothers or Frank Zappa – all their live albums recorded there all sound similar in that there is a presence to the liveness of that room."

Peter Frampton confirmed the crucial sound advantages in an early Nineties interview: "I think that the ambient sound of the room in the Fillmore is not too big. Therefore you can bring it up and not only can you hear the audience well, it adds a special room sound, a theatre sound to the instruments and it makes you feel more like you're there. The quality of the recording is down to Eddie Kramer of course. He definitely miked the room as well as he miked the stage, the amplifiers and the voices. If it had been Madison Square Garden, you wouldn't have been able to utilise the room mikes as much because you would have lost the sound of the band. Therefore you lose the feedback of the audience a bit, too. Because let's face it: when you're in Madison Square Garden and you hear the roar of the crowd, there's nothing like it, 'cause it's thunderous. In the Fillmore it's a much more controlled environment as far as sound is concerned, much more intimate. So I think that definitely helped the sound of the record."

Apart from this sterling reputation, the place had a very special significance for Pie in those early years of working far away from home for months on end. Since autumn 1969, Humble Pie had rocked the place more than twenty times, as Peter Frampton remembers fondly: "It had this aura about it because so many great people had seemed to come from there, and it was a legendary place. Because we were based in New York when we were touring, if Bill Graham had a cancellation or something, we would be called immediately because we had such a good following. So it was sort of our local. I mean we played there so many times I can't remember. It was a lot of times, and often on a moment's notice as well. It was a lot more easy-going and freer in that period."

With sound and atmosphere taken care of, what about material? Most live albums become greatest hits collections with only minor alterations to the studio arrangements. Humble Pie were different. The wealth of material recorded for their first four studio albums had developed in lengthy cottage and studio jams, so vice versa, these versions tended to be taken as rough prototypes for much looser, longer arrangements in the stage show.

Four sold-out shows were recorded, two each on 28 and 29 May, only weeks after The Allman Brothers had canned their concert. Like the Allmans, Pie secured enough material for *Performance – Rockin' The Fillmore*, a double album – without even touching their Immediate material and with only three titles from their two recent A&M albums. Steve recalled how this came about: "There were lots of R&B tunes and cover versions in *Performance*. By the time we did that album, the audience was familiar with us and we knew what they wanted, which was hard hitting rock – so okay, let's give it to them. It's not as if I'd stopped writing other stuff; it's just that there's a time and place for it. It's also that I started coming out more. I was still introverted to a point. Dee Anthony would take me into a corner and give me a big lecture: 'You've got to come out, they want you. You're a front man, now b e a front man.'"

'Four Day Creep' (called 'I Want You To Love Me' in Muddy Waters' repertoire, and also on a Pie bootleg) sees Steve really getting the audience going with hot boogie and guitar breaks. As Jerry Shirley points out, "Again, we had been jamming when Marriott heard something and said, 'Wait, we can apply this approach to Ida Cox's "Four Day Creep"'. It became the opening number of our live set and, save for the version on the live album, was never recorded in the studio."

'Creep' was followed by the old Willie Dixon standard from *Humble Pie III*. Jerry again: "That came about during the taping of a television show in Europe. We were messing with the riff itself when Marriott – who was extremely good at this – added, 'We can take the old blues tune "I'm Ready" and put it on top of this riff.' Then it developed from there, finally to the point on the live record where it was three times as long and ten times as heavy."

'Stone Cold Fever' from *Rock On* was next, and then two epic numbers would cover an entire LP side each – with twenty-three and sixteen minutes respectively: Dr John's 'I Walk On Guilded Splinters' presents very lyrical passages, in which Steve and Peter's guitar work reflect the twin-lead trademark of Wishbone Ash, a bit drawn-out if there's no roach at hand, in spite of a few dramatic climaxes.

On the other hand, 'Rolling Stone' consequently builds on the studio version and ends with a rousing boogie finale. Frampton follows with the more lightweight, but attractive 'Hallelujah I Love Her So', proving he was also open for black influences. The story of how 'I Don't Need No Doctor', the energetic final number came about, is so exciting that it should be left to an eye witness.

Peter Frampton, December 1970: "The story that goes behind that is probably the greatest story about the way we arranged a number. We were supporting Grand Funk a lot, and one day it was Madison Square Garden. It was the first time any of us had ever played there or, I believe, been there. I don't think I'd ever been there before, and never seen anywhere indoors quite that big. So Jerry's drums were set up and my amplifier was set up. Jerry was fiddling around with something and I just played. Nothing was miked or anything, nothing was going through the PA at this point, and I just put on my guitar and just hit this chord, this E minor chord and then stopped it. Then I listened to it reverberate around Madison Square Garden.

"And I got so inspired from the enormity of this building – which is a pretty legendary place, to say the least – and I just did the first three chords of what was then to be 'Doctor' – dum dum dum – and Jerry came in immediately. And I saw Steve at the mixing board telling the guy to turn the PA on. Then he ran down with Greg. We kept playing those chords over and over again. So Greg joined in and then Steve got up. He didn't even have a guitar on at this point, I don't even think his amp was working. We just held on an E chord for a while and he started singing 'I Don't Need No Doctor' and we all went, 'Oh God, this is great.' We then arranged it right there and then, on the spot, Steve got his amp working…and I believe, I believe we did it that night." Consequently, A&M used an edited version as their – quite successful – autumn single.

So what made the album so special? Live albums had been around for decades, but they could be either sloppily played – not a problem for Pie – or too sterile. Jerry Shirley can recall nearly falling into trap two: "We tried to mix it ourselves in England, and we forgot the audience, we forgot the ambient mikes. We treated it as if it was a studio album and the powers that be at the time heard it and went, 'Well this is all very well, but where is all that atmosphere?' and we said, 'Oh, I think we ought to push the ambient mikes up.' and bring the audience – as it is such an important part of the record – into it."

Still, with such a fantastic live sound, which even the grunge generation should acknowledge as a role model, the old question remains whether any overdubs were used to dress the album's sound up – after all, Keith Richards once chuckled that The Rolling Stones needed as much time for live albums as for studio projects. So did Humble Pie succumb to the temptation of using studio re-runs?

Peter Frampton insists: "None – it's completely live. Nothing was redone on that at all. Out of the two nights we just chose the best thing. If you really want to have a giggle, there's a really terribly green note that I sing on 'I Don't Need No Doctor'. It's an answer to one of Steve's ad libs, and I do an ad lib. I don't know, I just didn't get to the mike in time or something, but it's in another world, it's not even in the same key. When this thing came over full blast when we played it back, we were on the floor in stitches laughing, because this was so horrendous. It was green. At the time I just ditched that track, but you can still hear it in the audience mikes. So when it goes down to just bass and drums and Steve is doing a bit of ad lib singing, you listen for it. And that's very nice of me to tell you by the way."

With all the fun on stage and during the mixing-sessions in the studio, Frampton must have realised that his music as well as his personality looked second league compared to Steve's dominance. Still, during the summer, Peter was able to enjoy the biggest successes of the band which, after all, he had started in the first place. Two years after Blind Faith and The Rolling Stones, Humble Pie really triumphed in London's Hyde Park – as a genuine supergroup, no hype necessary – and the press exploded with rave reviews.

But even at their highest point, Greg and Jerry could feel the rift between Steve and Peter clearly. Greg: "Personally they were like chalk and cheese... I guess Steve's harder side maybe sometimes didn't gel with Peter's more gentle side, but they were dear friends really." Be that as it may, they both had a career to follow, and a few days before *Fillmore* was released, Frampton left the band to start a solo career (See the Peter Frampton chapter).

Meanwhile, *Rockin' The Fillmore* stormed up the American *Billboard* charts to Number Twenty-One and enjoyed long term popularity. What's more, the double album sucked *Rock On* up the listings in the process, so Humble Pie were awarded gold albums for both releases before 1971 was over. The implications were obvious: more touring, more "hard slog", as Marriott liked to call it – and didn't that depend on finding a lead guitarist as inventive and credible as Peter?

"As a three-piece we can really play what we like – and we'll just call ourselves The Pie!" Steve Marriott claimed on the release of *Rockin' The Fillmore*. In a trio he'd have things his way was probably more to the point. But after a number of sessions for the preparation of a new album, started in autumn 1971 in good tradition at Olympic Studios, Marriott found out that – with all their undoubted harmony – the trio wouldn't work so well on its own: a certain excitement and versatility was missing. Then he heard the album *Colosseum Live* at a party – and Dave Clempson's guitar sound immediately got to him. Whatever commitments he had, they had to try him out – and invited him round to Olympic in Barnes.

Steve on the imminent *Smokin'* album: "That's the album where we really got into hard rock, and the soul influence started coming out. I was leaning that way; hell, I started out that way in The Moments. Dave 'Clem' Clempson had joined after we'd done most of it. He wasn't on a lot of the backing tracks and wasn't in on the working-up of any of them. I don't think I would've liked being in a three-piece; I'm not a good enough guitar player. I like to be able to stop playing at any point and concentrate on singing, and that was hard enough in The Small Faces where at least we had a keyboard. We got Clem in the band, put him straight into the studio and said, 'Here, overdub on this and this.'"

Equally matter-of-factly, Steve, Greg and Jerry threw their new man on stage. Passers-by standing in front of Düsseldorf's Philips

Halle in Germany in late November, could listen to the rehearsals with the newcomer taking place inside. The stops and starts were far more concentrated than a usual soundcheck called for. But as it turned out during the night's happy-go-lucky Fillmore-based concert Humble Pie could let their fresh axeman Clem loose during his solo guitar sections, even if he had to peep towards Steve's fretboard occasionally for the right chords. Eddie Cochran's 'C'Mon Everybody' was new to their set and enhanced curiosity for the up-coming album with the altered line-up.

Dave 'Clem' Clempson had made the headlines when he left drummer Jon Hiseman's Colosseum for Pie, but his career move had in fact not broken up the band. As their sax player Dick Heckstall-Smith recalled in his biography, *The Safest Place In The World*, the band had been in disarray anyway because working live non-stop had prevented them from writing enough for their future. And then: "In the first days of November Clem visited Jon Hiseman at his home to say that he'd had an offer of twenty-six thousand pounds, plus the use of a Bentley [Greg's in 'Theme From Skint'?!], to leave Colosseum and play with Steve Marriott. He asked Jon what Jon felt he should do. Jon said he thought he would be mad not to take it, upon which Clem asked what Colosseum would do. Jon said he doubted if Colosseum would bother to replace Clem at all. 'What does that mean?' asked Clem. 'I doubt if the band has a future,' said Jon. He felt that, rather than struggle at such panic-stricken short notice to find another guitarist of equal stature for the American tour, the band should fold."

Clem joined Humble Pie during a period in their career when they were on the up commercially, but were about to change dramatically in terms of production and musical direction – focused now on their unchallenged leader Steve. Jerry, on the other hand puts the apparent love of soul and blues down to the complete band's taste in a 1992 interview, and he doesn't even exclude the deserted Peter Frampton from this:

"Well, the obvious source – because of his voice – would be Steve, but it was a collective really because we all had our honest to goodness roots in soul and blues music more than anything else. For instance, my favourite singer in the entire world – other than Steve himself of course – is Ray Charles. Ever since I was a young lad of three or four, my mum played him to me: 'Here, listen to this.' Peter was a huge black jazz guitar fanatic. Greg was a huge Little Richard fanatic." And didn't the Frampton-Pie choose Ray Charles' 'Hallelujah I Love Her So' for the *Fillmore* album?

Anyway, at the time when Steve was – visually and stylistically – the focus of the band, he also took over responsibility for proceedings behind the massive double-glazing in the studio, and for the first time, album production took place without the helping hands of Glyn or Andy Johns. Engineers Alan O'Duffy and the late Stones assistant Keith Harwood were both tremendously experienced, but Steve ruled. He wanted to face the challenge of running a compact R&Blues sound to the rules of a high-tech twenty-four-track mixing board, and he paid this ambition dearly, when he collapsed at the end of February: "Following intense recording sessions with Humble Pie, Steve Marriott collapsed with nervous exhaustion and doctors told him to rest," reported the *New Musical Express*.

The resulting album excelled as an impressive 'calling sound card' by a self-contained band. But in spite of great songs and thrilling excitement via voices and instruments, the overall sound was still less compact than on the other, Johns-produced albums. The CD mix was able to restore some of the desired clarity, but on vinyl several spell-binding sounds – drum tracks for instance – seemed to be running in separate grooves, whereas masterpieces like 'Live With Me' or 'Strange Days' had presented complete dynamic sound patterns.

One year after the *Rock On* sessions, blues daddy Alexis Korner and Apple soul sister Doris Troy were once again part of proceedings, assisted this time by Blue Mink, jazz and soul singer Madeline Bell, who remembered Marriott well when we interviewed her in 1994. She sang 'Thirty Days In The Hole' on the spot in her dressing room, reminiscing: "Steve was a bit of a nutter, but weren't we all in those days?"

Also, Cochise bass player Ricky Wills returned Steve's help on his band's 'Why I Sing The Blues', and none other than CSN's Stephen Stills took part in the sessions as well. After his contemporary split from C&N, he had bought his Brookfield House in London from Peter Sellers (including Sellers' gardener – immortalised on his 'Johnny's Garden') and loved to jam in between recording his own solo stuff.

The first thing fans heard of Stills' involvement was on the new single, and first track on *Smokin'*, 'Hot'N'Nasty', a slow burning, then dynamic R&B number, and an exemplary showcase for the new line-up. Apart from Steve's soulful vocals and his piano and organ work, it manages to point to Clem's lead guitar tricks as Pie's added asset. The backing vocals were overdubbed one night by the two Steves – Marriott and Stills – after the Latin American hippy had strolled in again from his own sessions next door, for some fun and working liquid supper.

The second track on the album, 'The Fixer', was more likely to appeal to Led Zeppelin than CSN. A killer riff, tough rhythm work and Clem's dominant wah-wah pedal tricks create lively metal which would have done Marriott-copyist Robert Plant proud. Hard to believe, the track was filled with new life during Steve's Eighties live shows.

'You're So Good For Me' seems to lead Greg, assisted by Steve, back to *Town And Country* territory, but the chorus with Madeline Bell and Doris Troy shows that this is a trip into the Soul sounds of America's Deep South: delivered with gospel credibility and – in this case – crisply recorded. A brilliant showcase for Ridley, who remained underrated through his career.

Fans at the first gigs with Clempson now were offered a vinyl memento of 'C'Mon Everybody', recorded here in true 'Fillmore' tradition. The band's coherence is again impressive, as are the ecstatic vocal harmony chorus breaks and the twin lead guitar sections which lead into Clem's solo.

Leaving the Wishbone Ash tributes aside, 'Old Time Feelin'' offers another break from *Smokin'* rock with country blues, barrelhouse piano, bottleneck guitar and blues harp. Steve takes a vocal back seat behind Greg, and Alexis Korner, the bluesman with the funny dungarees (long before Steve took up that craze), contributes a solo on his mandolin-type Martin Tipple guitar. This creates a log-fire atmosphere reminiscent of 'Alabama 69' from the first album. There still seems to be a time and a place for rural country blues sounds, at least in the studio.

'Thirty Days In The Hole' begins the vinyl side two with finger snapping and Steve's amused vocal training with his Soul Sisters. Before long, Steve was to introduce three other "chicks" as permanent band members for studio and stage. The a cappella introduction is followed by a truly roaring sound attack: one of the most exciting stage gems – for this band as well as Steve's Eighties Pie and Packet Of Three.

The mood continues with 'Road Runner'/ 'Road Runner's 'G' Jam' where, for the first time, a song title is a nod to the band's working habit of developing numbers out of jam sessions. Here, 'Road Runner' by Junior Walker and The All Stars (who Steve would soon mention as a role model) is a mid tempo groove number with amazingly dirty Hammond sounds and the legendary ensemble interplay of the band, grown tight on gruelling tours, with Clem fitting in perfectly.

The quiet before the storm as the album draws to a close is 'I Wonder', a slow blues, with Steve singing as sensitively as he's shouting madly, backed admirably but presented in a weak mix. Greg's surely brilliant bass is far too dominant in the overall picture, Steve's vocals and guitar licks appear way back initially, although by the time of Clem's solo the balance is about right. The climax that follows, 'Sweet Peace In Time', again stresses the hard rock strength of the band, and especially their solid rhythm section. A simple yet effective drum intro by Jerry opens a vocal fight between Steve and Greg, with murderous Fender lines by the bass veteran.

Away from the studio, Humble Pie always had headliner status during their tours, with occasional bill sharing. In July 1972, tour posters announced a memorable encounter: Humble Pie and Steve's old friends, The Faces, rocking out together at the Mount Pocono Festival in Long Pond, Pennsylvania. But it was another combination of supporting acts that would soon have far-reaching musical consequences. During the same year, avant-garde art rockers King Crimson opened Humble Pie's US shows along with Steve's mentor Alexis Korner, taking a break from his Collective Consciousness Society studio big band in order to present a duo with Danish blues champion Peter Thorup. Alexis had introduced Thorup to his New Church line-up during a tour of Denmark with Peter's Beefeaters. (Footnote: Rolling Stone Brian Jones had planned to join New Church prior to his swimming pool death in July 1969.)

Back to America 1972 and the 'packet of three': Alexis Korner and Peter Thorup, King Crimson and Humble Pie touring together. Crimson drummer Ian Wallace, tired of syncopations in his sophisticated – and therefore complicated – combo, was quite impressed with Korner and Thorup's simple yet fun-loving blues pieces. So one evening in Roanoke, Virginia, he joined in. Crimson bass player Boz Burrell and sax player Mel Collins got ideas watching the fun – and after the King Crimson part of the tour ended in Birmingham, Alabama, the drum/bass/sax trio deserted Crimson king Robert Fripp and joined the grand old man from the Ealing Blues Club, with Steve Marriott frequently playing his part in the happy openers' sets.

So Alexis Korner had a new working band – named Snape (Something Nasty 'Appens Practically Every (day)). In San Francisco, the first demos took shape while on tour, and on returning to England, a record deal would be signed with the small folk label Transatlantic Records. Steve and veteran keyboarders Zoot Money and Tim Hinkley helped with more sessions held in London. Here, in Island Studios, seeds were sown for another accidental band two years later. During Steve's session marathons in 1974, the three Crimson/Snape members Boz, Mel and Ian as well as Tim Hinkley would become Marriott's studio band.

But for the time being, Humble Pie were on the crest of a successful wave, and after more US touring, Steve had ambitious plans for his band's line-up. Inspired by *Smokin'* songs like 'Thirty Days In The Hole', he wanted to augment the group to a complete soul revue. His dream came about by remembering the Ike And Tina Turner Show of the early Sixties, which had featured the lively female vocal backing trio known as The Ikettes – among their ever revolving members, the future Small Faces and Humble Pie soul sister PP Arnold. As original Ikette Venetta Fields reminisced in autumn 1973: "Steve had remembered me from the Ike and Tina days. Somehow, he managed to contact me in California and asked me to get some girls together to do some shows with the Pie...we've done two complete tours with Steve."

Marriott had worked out a complete presentation concept: "We used The Blackberries – Venetta Fields, Billie Barnum and Clydie King – on backing vocals. They were a great influence on me; great singers, all of 'em. I thought the black backing vocals would be good for the vocal side of the band. The instrumental side was virtually tied up at that point, but I thought we needed something else. As soon as I find a formula, I want to break it. What I was originally going for, which the rest of the band objected to (although I don't blame 'em), was a 'revue' format, like the old Ike and Tina Turner shows, which rock audiences hadn't really seen. I wanted to get Junior Walker to tour with us. He'd step out – we'd back him up – and do, say, 'Shotgun', and we could do a couple of our numbers, and The Blackberries could step out and do a couple of the old Ikettes things, 'Peaches And Cream' and stuff."

Instead of Junior Walker, Humble Pie took the renowned sax player Sidney George on tour through America in Spring 1973. Sid was an obvious choice for Steve: he had been recommended by Clydie King – The Blackberries had just worked with him on singer/guitarist Vince Martin's album – and also by *Smokin'*'s studio guest Stephen Stills, who had used George on both his solo LPs and his two Manassas albums. Sidney had also been on the hand-picked studio shortlist for Dr John's *Gumbo* LP, which all of Pie loved.

The Blackberries enjoyed the shows immensely, building on their past experiences. Venetta Fields: "You have to blend with whatever's going on. It's different working with the Stones or Pie than working with, say, Diana Ross or Aretha Franklin...But all the time you're expanding your understanding of different kinds of music."

For the next Humble Pie album, Marriott had even more colossal plans. Surely, the soul revue concept would be considered, but for him even that wasn't versatile enough: "I thought, Heck, maybe now's the time to blend in the quieter country stuff and the soulful stuff with the rock'n'roll; I had all these songs hanging out. So one side of the album was rock tunes and one side country-type, plus a side of old soul numbers and a live side."

That was the plan, and Steve roughly managed to get this on Humble Pie's new double LP, with the rock side having a definite soul stamp. The album was called *Eat It* – in terms of 'dig it' – and Steve cooked it almost single-handedly, maybe because he could have a go anytime he wanted – the sessions were the first to be held in his new home studios, which were still under construction, built from hard-earned touring money near his Essex cottage. Apart from the four covered soul standards, all the remaining material was entirely written by him. Steve again: "Maybe the others had dried up as far as songwriting; they weren't forthcoming, so all I had was my own stuff…"

Four Marriott compositions on the vinyl A-side of this double album present the aforementioned rock material: Marriott's Hammond organ, The Blackberries' background voices and a way too dominant tambourine characterise the first of them, 'Get Down To It', a rock and soul shuffle whose guitar riff and vocals remain too far in the background. The result is relaxed but ultimately unspectacular.

The next track sounds like Pie's on-the-road motto: 'Good Booze And Bad Women'. Straight rock in a 'Little Queenie'/'Natural Born Woman' rhythm, with an interesting call and response gospel arrangement, solid blues harp and great guitar licks by Clem, but again it's thinly produced, without the compact sounds always achieved before by the Johns brothers. Strangely, the production for 'Is If For Love' is adequate, apart from Steve's voice, which again comes over as feeble. The song is a soft soul ballad with wonderful chorus lines by The Blackberries.

By far the most interesting composition on this A-side, 'Drugstore Cowboy' features tender lead work by both guitarists opening a standard Chuck Berry rock'n'roll theme, then it's down to half the original tempo for catchy riffs and Steve's almost talking vocals. Next, the song develops quite dynamically towards the chorus, with Marriott acting convincingly in front of his gospel girls. The Marriott Soul Revue can't be far away…

…and on 'Black Coffee' it begins with two gospel-soul classics, on which Steve and his charming harem beat even their own high standards with their vocal call and response acrobatics. Ike and Tina's hymn to the joys of a good cup of black coffee sounded so convincing in this slow funk setting that this arrangement re-appeared on a Nescafé TV commercial at the end of the Eighties – supplied by Marriott and Clempson.

Following swiftly, 'I Believe To My Soul', by Ray Charles, repeats the gospel feeling even more faithfully, having been successfully road tested by the eight-piece Pie. Venetta Fields: "We get to play in front of so many people and everyone seems to really enjoy themselves and in a kind of way, it's like what happens in church – with a great feeling of togetherness and coming together." This one has a blues rhythm and risky breaks by crooner Steve, saxman Sidney George and Clem – working his wah-wah guitar in true Hendrix tradition.

US soulmates Edwin Starr and Johnny Bristol contribute the track 'Shut Up And Don't Interrupt Me', which marks a return to up-tempo proceedings. Soul elements like saxophone and gospel chorus are combined with the Pie quartet's driving guitar-bass-drums basis. Greg Ridley and his dearly missed rough voice get their chance at long last. His bass lines are again exemplary on the whole album and dominate *Eat It*'s sound quite rightly, but they could have been better produced.

The covers corner continues with 'That's How Strong My Love Is' in which Humble Pie deliver the fourth European record version of the gospel classic, after The Rolling Stones, The Hollies (both 1965) and also Georgie Fame and Alan Price (together in 1971). Still, Steve's duet with Venetta Fields has a much blacker touch than all the other British versions.

A complete change of scene arrives for the 'Country Pie' C-side of the double album. 'Say No More' begins proceedings with light guitar picks and tambourine – Steve sings in an unbelievable transformation from downtown Memphis towards rural Alabama. A tender love song, short but with tons of charm. 'Oh Bella (All That's Hers)' follows, a dynamic ballad in best Immediate tradition with pronounced but still subdued bass and drums underlining acoustic guitars. Back again is BJ Cole's pedal steel, rescued for the sessions in spite of the soul age.

'Summer Song' is next, again completely 'unplugged' and played on Steve's treasured Crispian Mellor Custom, made especially for him by the renowned London guitar manufacturer (see Guitarography). Assisted by his harmonica and sparse percussion, Steve's guitar sounds unpretentiously bluesy as the track sets the stage for 'Beckton Dumps', a return of sorts to the melodic rock days of Pie's *Rock On* days. The song initially reminds us of 'The Light', before taking on a psychedelic dimension during the middle eight section via Steve's echo chamber vocals. In songs like this, Clem Clempson comes over much more relaxed and lively while still excelling with valuable ideas and sounds for those soul numbers.

Which leaves us with the final live D-side: 'Up Our Sleeve' was 1973's new opener, replacing 'Four Day Creep'. This rock'n'roller is a pure demonstration of unharmed Pie energy, and Clem's own wah-wah display of treasuring the Hendrix heritage next to Robin Trower. But neither Steve's screaming nor the weak chorus are very convincing.

Just to prove Marriott didn't only cover soul standards, next up is the Stones' 'Honky Tonk Woman'. Jerry's drum intro could be called solid, but his subsequent cymbal work sounds completely over the top. Steve's voice sounds strained and less powerful than usual, suggesting he needs his Blackberries desperately here. The version on *Live In San Francisco 1973* is more convincing (see Discography).

Finally, '(I'm A) Road Runner' sees the Pie quartet rock itself into a more than solid groove amidst its wild, rousing audience in Glasgow's Green's Playhouse, but without ever reaching the magic of the Fillmore recordings. The band does play with inspiration, the blues harp solo delivered by Steve is a treat and the fans play their part, but the spark of New York's legendary rock theatre is still missing.

Staying with the Fillmore, it is more than dubious whether these twenty-two minutes of live tapes – only eighteen months after the live album – justified the release of another double album. The remaining twelve studio tracks would have made up a single album of *Smokin'*'s duration (forty-four minutes), which via a much lower price could have cracked the American Top Ten with Humble Pie's popularity at the time. But as it was, the expectations – at least at A&M – had to be disappointed.

Steve commented with irony: "It was considered a failure 'cause it only got to Number Twelve in the US. What a pity!" As far as he was concerned, the unusual mixture of styles was to blame for the more modest success, but he didn't regret a thing: "Maybe it wasn't the right time. But fuck it, I'll own up to that: it was my fault – if you can call it 'fault' – and I really enjoyed doing it!"

On stage, Steve also seemed to be the one getting the most fun out of the revue, apart from The Blackberries themselves, who, with Marriott's assistance, even recorded their own album at the time. Venetta Fields: "I have to say that Steve Marriott is the one who really gave us the most encouragement to do something of our own. We did actually cut a single for A&M, 'Twist And Shout', but it didn't do too much." The album was cut with the help of Humble Pie – mostly Steve, in his new home studios – as well as Billy Preston, who took over finally, with exciting tracks like 'Nobody Belongs To Me', but sadly it hasn't come out to this day. In the end Billy Preston produced, and mixed the masters, but, according to Steve in August 1975's *NME*: "I heard the results but they weren't very good."

While The Blackberries were retained for the autumn 1973 US tour – Venetta Fields' friend Billie Barnum replacing the solo-bound Clydie King – the band's line-up was cut back with losing Sidney George. More soul standards like 'Higher And Higher' – which became a medley with 'Thirty Days In The Hole', for instance – were integrated into Pie's set of original songs. But Greg, Jerry and especially Clem began to long for a more compact rock sound. After the tour and during resumed studio sessions, again in Marriott's own Clear Sound home studios in Moreton, the band leader began to feel the pressure more and more. Then he complained in public: "I remember Clem saying, 'Look, we've gotta make a rock'n'roll album.' I didn't understand that kind of logic. What the hell is rock'n'roll? Is it Black Sabbath? Chuck Berry? Yes? Or just what people say you are when you do it?"

With his examples, Steve was not completely off track, because the new album Pie released in the spring of 1974, *Thunderbox*, contained sounds tough enough for the aforementioned doomsday priests from Birmingham, as well as a cover version from the St Louis rocker's repertoire.

The Blackberries still made their attractive vocal presence felt. During the recording, Steve seemed to regain his balance a bit: "It (*Thunderbox*) may seem like a turnaround, but then I think it could be an advance because the band are that much more mature." *Thunderbox* would not be the last time Steve would use black vocal backing; only two years later there would be another opportunity, but for now he summed up his feelings:

"Working with The Blackberries was great but it couldn't work as a permanent thing. They've got their own things to do and we've got ours. It was great while it lasted. In fact I was almost a bit overwhelmed by them – it made me feel a bit paranoid at times because they were so good. I really dug it, because I was always into black music. The chicks used to call me 'nigger', in fact." While these comments sounded fairly diplomatic, Steve wasn't quite so understanding a year later, when he revealed: "I thought that was the best period of the band. But they were asked to leave" – apparently by Shirley and Clempson, putting their foot down in open rebellion.

Before their exit, The Blackberries were well utilised on *Thunderbox*, especially on the title track. But their contribution aside, the title track is a return to *Smokin'* days, reminiscent of 'Thirty Days In The Hole' in terms of rhythm and riff structure. While the playing is pure dynamite – Steve's blues harp is hair raising – guitars and vocals seem too trebly and shrill in the mix. And in general, engineer Alan O'Duffy and assistant Marriott delivered tapes with such a lot of hiss that even Japanese digital clean-up buffs couldn't get rid of the noise in the Eighties.

The title of the next track, 'Groovin' With Jesus' again points to gospel and indeed it could be a funky follow-up to the soul revue songs like 'Black Coffee', but with a more limited theme. The black tribute continues on the stand-out 'I Can't Stand The Rain' where Steve gets the chance to show off his unique vocal power and piano routine. Accidental band Snape's saxman Mel Collins demonstrates his 'kick horn' skills (he would play his part not only on a further Pie album, but also in Marriott's own marathon studio sessions only weeks later). American soul lady Ann Peebles co-wrote this thrilling groove number and had the hit long before Tina Turner or The Commitments movie group, but Humble Pie came second in 1974.

Another cover, 'Anna (Go To Him)' by the late country-soul bard Arthur Alexander, had caught The Beatles' attention for a tender rendition a decade earlier. By the time Pie did their thing, Arthur was a poor bus driver in Memphis, but he would surely have loved listening to Steve injecting so much power and emotion into it that The Blackberries could hardly keep him on the ground.

More 'Black Coffee' is served up in 'No Way' – along with more production problems. An exciting and strong funk groove loses most of its impact with a thin guitar sound and a bass drum without bass frequence. Fortunately, 'Rally With Ali' fares better with a memorable riff typical of R&B-style Pie, and a kind of metal call and response. Pie handle all vocals themselves; Clem Clempson grabs an opportunity to cut loose, and Mel Collins acts out his own complete brass section.

The hard edge is put aside very quickly as 'Don't Worry Be Happy' turns the mood back to soul funk once again. Hammond organ and hand-clapping inject the well-worn formula with irresistible drive, before the sound of 'Ninety-Nine Pounds' returns things to more mainstream hard rock. Combining solid arrangement with a compact production, given enough promotion and airplay this single could have been the umpteenth successor of Humble Pie's first and only chart hit – there's even the hint in the lyrics: "Ninety-nine pounds of natural pureness" sounds like "Ninety-nine pounds of Natural Born Bugies". Steve adds "Ninety-nine pounds of soul", forgetting maybe that his band don't dig soul anymore. (This song was covered in 1993 by German R&B band Panama Jack.)

From the sublime to the ridiculous, 'Every Single Day' seems almost Pie parody – a tired 4/4 riff. Steve sounds convincing in his plea that a band's road life can ruin many a relationship, but apart from Clem's truly magnificent slide guitar work, Pie sound for once a bit strained.

You can't keep a good band down for long, and the other musical highlight in this collection quickly follows. 'No Money

Down' is Chuck Berry's incredibly witty demand for many special fittings in his convertible. We can imagine Steve re-living the scene in London with the ruthless second hand TV car dealer Arthur Daley, and this is proof that there's a lot of rock'n'roll left in Humble Pie. So in the end Clem was right, too.

Greg Ridley hadn't got his fair share on *Eat It* either, so 'Drift Away' marks his big comeback 'comeback'. He covers this soft, reflective Mentor Williams hit quite conventionally and – quite rightly – lets his great voice do the talking. Greg possibly had another role model – his old chums Spooky Tooth did the standard in 1970 and singing in competition with their Mike Harrison takes some courage.

Finally, as a fitting end to the band's relationship with The Blackberries, 'Oh La-Dee Da' sees driving guitar rock with Steve and his backing singers once again in full swing, delivering ninety-nine pounds from each side of the Pie coin. But for a successful single, only the recipe and the ingredients looked good: the finished Pie was a badly mixed mash, with the fun that was surely had in the studio not translating too well on home stereos.

This most versatile album was presented in attractive outer and inner sleeves. On the back cover painting, a turn-of-the-century *Salomé*-style nude girl stands on a monument, held by her lover and holding a guitar – an attractive design re-employed by A&M for 1994's *Hot'N'Nasty* anthology. Around it you spot the four Pie members. Clem looks in good shape, Greg even better (trouser snake rumba!) and Jerry and Steve a bit overweight, maybe as a result of hustling Guinness Stout brew in the liner notes. Through the 'wooden' front cover's keyhole you peep into bathrooms on the inner sleeve, one side sporting an under-age 'chick' on the Thunderbox Zappa-style for dirty old men, while on the back more naked girls chat by a bath tub. This was the age of the twelve inch cover, but it's nicely reproduced for CD.

With the slightly chaotic, but still desirable studio work in tow, Marriott remembered his stage raver qualities and went back to work with a vengeance. All over Europe, whether it was London's Rainbow Theatre or Dortmund's Westfalen Halle, thousands of fans witnessed a hot, compact Humble Pie quartet recalling the golden

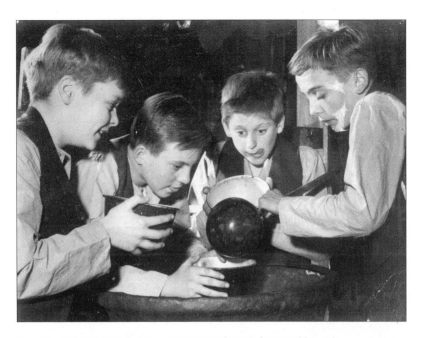

Steve Marriott as the Artful Dodger in Lionel Bart's *Oliver!*, 1960 (second from left)

CA RECORDING ARTISTES
STEVE MARRIOTT AND THE FRANTIKS

An advert for Steve's second band, from a
1963 *Melody Maker*

Steve Marriott on drums in the film *Live It Up*,
1963

"The sweat on their faces tells the whole story" – The Small Faces at the legendary Star-Club, Hamburg, Germany, in July 1966

"It's all so beautiful" – television becomes crucial. The Small Faces on TV in 1967 (l-r: Ronnie Lane, Steve and Ian McLagan with Kenney Jones on drums)

The Small Faces, 1966, doing the rounds for the teenage papers (l-r: Ronnie, Kenney, Mac and Steve)

Steve Marriott at home with his dog Seamus (who inspired the Pink Floyd track of the same name on *Meddle*)

Ronnie Lane and Kenney Jones, dressed for court in 1968

The (Small) Faces, 1969 (l-r: Kenney, Ron Wood, Rod Stewart, Ronnie and Mac)

The up-front Faces, 1972 (l-r: Woody, Ronnie and Rod)

The original Humble Pie (l-r: Steve Marriott, Greg Ridley, Jerry Shirley and Peter Frampton) on one of their early US tours, late 1969

Humble Pie on stage in 1973 (l-r: Steve, Greg and Dave 'Clem' Clempson who had replaced Peter Frampton)

The Faces, around 1972

Rod Stewart (with The Faces) live in
Hamburg, Germany, 1974

The never-ending *Comes Alive* tour. A pretty, but pretty exhausted, Peter Frampton on stage in the US, 1976

days of the Fillmore in the summer of 1974. A delighted Steve would duck-walk to the stage-curtains Chuck Berry-style during a Clem Clempson solo, only to kick his fat 'Colonel' Dee Anthony in the backside without missing a single power chord. "I'm a performer first – musician second. Every night I want to leave a bit of blood on the stage, cut my fingers a bit, sweat and scream. The whole band loves that feeling you get off a crowd, the loudness of the amps, the roar," Steve would stress after the Rainbow concert. Asked about his reaction to the British fans' welcoming noises, he was almost in tears with joy.

After another long and gruelling tour of the States, 1974 ended with ambitious plans. Ever since the summer, Steve had spent all his off-road time in the less than sophisticated Clear Sounds studio in his cottage: "I blew all my money on a studio," he told the *NME*, "but that was a good investment because it's there forever. It's a way of making music. Period. That cost a lot of money, you know. I suppose that's why I'm skint. I bought me parents a house. That's probably why I'm skint…I'd hate to lose the studio, because that's what I worked for – for seven years."

During that last winter and spring, Humble Pie's *Thunderbox* had been done there – partly under chaotic circumstances: Steve the engineer still coming to grips with it. And right now Pie didn't get on as well as they used to in the beginning. After all the fun and the strain on their tours they regularly fell into adrenalin-free holes back home in England. And these could not always be filled with creativity.

What's more, while on the road everything was paid for. At home they didn't exactly feel like the well-off rock stars they were supposed to be. Come 1975, they had done twenty-one tours and surely there was money in the bank, but according to Steve: "No. Most of it is invested in Nassau [Bahamas] in land. I've asked our manager [still Dee Anthony], to sell it for me cause I don't need it. I certainly couldn't afford to go there." And some actual readies – notes in cash – apparently weren't forthcoming: "It's like sending packages to the Zulus" was how Steve Marriott sarcastically reacted to the *NME*'s questions about regular retainers from Fat Dee, but when he still insisted that Anthony didn't rip them off, Greg Ridley would comment: "You couldn't say it even if he had. You can't say

97

things like that to a paper."

According to 'witnesses' the working atmosphere in Clear Sounds was more than relaxed, with a lot of 'Lazy Sunday' consciousness and more than the odd 'refreshment' being delivered. That didn't leave much money or time: A&M demanded a new studio album by Humble Pie, whereas Steve wanted to do a solo LP plus a duo project with Greg Ridley.

So while tracks for those three albums were laboured on in Essex, Steve hardly ever showed up in London – where in Olympic Sound more work on Humble Pie tracks continued, too: "I'd backed out by then and would just show my face every now and then to do a vocal and split, because I was fed up with the whole situation."

A&M were not too keen on the musical adventures which took place without a detectable commercial focus. They wanted a product for the American market, while Steve was less than cooperative, and didn't even feel like another Atlantic crossing. Neither did he want to match Rod Stewart's ultra-hot and accessible song collection of the same name, nor did he want to go on the road in the US: "We'd been on tour for about four years and we were just very tired." But A&M as well as Dee Anthony could afford to insist; in fact, couldn't afford to give in. The reason was obvious in the small print: Humble Pie were contracted to do another tour. And without a new album this would have been unwise.

Come early 1975, the record company got so restless waiting for a *Thunderbox* follow-up that they secured – almost confiscated – some of the tracks recorded at Clear Sounds, some of them never meant for Pie of course. The other members had not seen a lot of progress anyway, neither at Olympic nor in Steve's Clear Sounds, and – trying to make the best of the 'stolen tapes' situation – decided: "Let's bring in a producer!" Steve in 1982: "If we must, let's bring in Andrew Oldham; he formed the band, blah blah blah. Andrew put homemade things in some cuts and took them to America to make them metally, which I think was a silly move. I guess he had to do it – he was under pressure from A&M – but the whole thing was disgusting."

But a few months after the album was released, in the summer of 1975, Steve's verdict was more vague: "I was tired of having the responsibility of producing our albums. We didn't want Andrew to produce anything. We just wanted him around. He was so nice. He thought he had a job to do though. *Street Rats* (that was the album's A&M-chosen title) was disastrous. I had nothing to do with the fucking thing! Andrew used the wrong vocal track on the title track and that wasn't intended to be on the album anyway." Accompanied by Steve's public outrage, eleven tracks had finally been assembled. Company colleague Joan Armatrading suffered a similar fate in 1979/80; she had to make amends in the end and – like Marriott – stayed with A&M for quite a while. (And this was pre-Sony/George Michael days!)

Greg Ridley's and Clem Clempson's comments on the album weren't much friendlier. Greg hinted as much: "The last LP, *Street Rats*, was terrible. They had a different one out in the States y'know. It had different numbers [one actually] and different mixes [true]." Clem confirmed this in more detail: "The mixes were done by somebody outside the band [the name's Oldham, Clem] and when we heard it, we were horrified. We just got the tape, in time, and substituted our own mixes and material. But when I got to England and saw *Street Rats* in a shop, it had all the old numbers on it we had rejected. And that sold five thousand copies."

Funnily enough, their little rebellion got them additional US mixing credits. On the American album, "Produced by Andrew Oldham" is complemented by "and Steve Marriot" (*sic*). A&M cover designers did not even seem able to spell the name of the alleged producer who denies all responsibility...

Despite everything, the album is still worth looking at in detail, notably for the transatlantic differences. The title track is most interesting in that it is not really Humble Pie at all (just like 'It's Only Rock'N'Roll' wasn't really the Stones because The Faces' Ronnie Wood and Kenney Jones replaced old Wyman and Watts). Still, 'Rat' was quite rightly selected as Pie-related in style and character – in spite of the line-up. Steve in 1975: "'Street Rats' was a track with me, Ian Wallace and Tim Hinkley playing piano. It was nothing to do with Humble Pie. Somebody stole the sixteen-track mix and put it on Humble Pie's album. It was intended as the title track of my album." The line-up had 'shrunk' by 1982's look-back:

"It was just musicians up in my studio. 'Street Rats' was just me and a drummer friend, Ian Wallace – nobody else on it – messing around in my studio."

The UK version features a precise drum beat and Steve on distorted guitar. Rock'n'roll piano and bass transport energy in spite of echoey vocals. In the US there was an additional bass line, the vocals track was the correct one chosen by Steve as superior, with the unmentioned above Greg Ridley on backing vocals.

'Rock'N'Roll Music', the indestructible if over covered Chuck Berry standard, features a powerful Greg Ridley vocal and was possibly meant for his album with Steve. UK version: the slow but still sharply driving beat has Tim Hinkley repeat his 'Street Rat' rock'n'roll piano in a more relaxed way. Thundering drum breaks off-set this pattern without coming over too session-like; it's pre-arranged stuff this time. US: Clem and Greg chose this version with additional rhythm guitar over the distorted one. There is a different drum track and Steve's second voice. The song gets faded out and in again at the end.

An even slower early morning number is 'We Can Work It Out'. Here, Pie don't use much more than Lennon/McCartney's lyrics, but the lovely chord sequences are their own. UK: like Phil Spector and The Beatles' *Let It Be* album, Andrew Oldham put his strings and oboes on this one, paired with sparse lead guitar and Tim's Fender Rhodes electric piano, so that the group's identity is kept intact. US: Greg and Clem did not accept the Oldham strings – instead, a drum break leads into a clear sound picture with Clempson's well-chosen blues guitar licks, Hammond and Rhodes E-piano. Marriott's singing is more relaxed here.

'Scored Out' is sort of 'Street Rat''s groovy brother. Passages at half the song's usual speed vary the number but next to the title track it's no more than a filler, despite a good Marriott Hammond sound courtesy of Steve at the end. UK: Additional hand-clapping. US: Ridley and Clempson chose a different vocal track, the piano is more dominant, there's no hand-clapping. There is severe tape hiss even on the Japanese CD of the US mix.

"I've been through a bad spell," Marriott tells his audience in 'Road Hog', almost talking over a slow rhythm and his attractive

Ovation acoustic guitar, with added slide by Clem. Piano and harmonica back the melancholic atmosphere. For the US version, congas and more blues harp were added.

Yet another Beatles number is next. In the UK fans hear a distorted guitar chord, wah-wah sounds and again a slightly dragging rhythm. For the verses, Steve and Greg take turns like they did in the old days, Clydie King and Venetta Fields become The Blackberries again (their unreleased solo album was recorded in Clear Sounds at the same time as this track), and Clem's electric solo is inspired. US: the three-part guitar riff on the chorus is wiped, instead Clem adds rhythm guitar chords which seem directly taken off The Rolling Stones' 'Salt Of The Earth' from *Beggar's Banquet*. The Blackberries sound more dominant in this mix.

With these six tracks, side one is by no means the catastrophe the band would have had us believe. For all its shortcomings, so far it is certainly more varied and better produced than *Thunderbox*.

Side two features the UK-only 'Funky To The Bone'. More like a jam session than a straight song, this is by no means the 'funk' as popularised by the British groups of the mid Seventies, like Average White Band or Kokomo. Punters who took those as too slick will smile at the never-ending mock Memphis soul guitar groove here, with numerous breaks and Mel's powerful sax. But ultimately the whole is not too exciting.

Steve: "'Funky To The Bone' had nothing to do with Humble Pie, it was just musicians up in my studio!" Clem and Greg therefore removed it from other editions.

After the mock soul on the previous track, 'There 'Tis' offers real funk which would have suited *Eat It*. Steve tells his story aided by rhythm guitar, his two Blackberries assist adoringly and Mel Collins adds great brass riffs and a lively tenor saxophone solo.

'Let Me Be Your Lovemaker', with its slow burning drum intro, is a continuation of 'Waiting For The Wind' from Greg Ridley's days in Spooky Tooth. The breaks here remind us of 'Fire And Water' by Free. In year one of punk, such an endless riff number might have seemed old hat, but this one stays inspired and varied throughout. US version: the track has a more rounded sound here, with E-piano and a hot, inventive guitar solo (possibly by Clem).

Far from inspired is 'Countryman Stomp', the most chaotic, incoherent piece of work on this album. Quite unnecessarily, Greg blasts, breezes, then sings over a turmoil of, in themselves, quite interesting piano, guitar and rhythm tracks – but if the boys had fun with this, there's only a slight hint of pleasure for the listener. UK and US versions are almost identical.

'Drive My Car' closes Pie's Liverpool trilogy, dominated by Greg Ridley, a professional who sadly remained an underrated singer for his entire career (from 1966's VIPs to 1975's Marriott All Stars). He would have deserved at least one solo album. His interesting variations over this *Rubber Soul* classic by The Beatles are again underlined by Oldham's string section, usually an acquired taste, but very effective in this case.

The combination with BJ Cole's pedal steel guitar evokes associations with Andy Fairweather-Low's 'Wide-Eyed And Legless' which was released at the same time. This time Greg and Clem decided to accept the strings, so the UK and US versions sound almost identical; Stateside the pedal steel is slightly more dominant.

Coming at the end, 'Queens And Nuns' is a relief from all the drama. It sounds more like a Marriott solo track (which he may well have wanted for his album; he couldn't remember). Steve's tongue-in-cheek dirty girly story is in marked contrast to the basically melancholic tone of the album, and his voice is more than welcome after four tracks by Greg, whose singing is fine in its own right but not typical of what people expected from Pie. With its faster rhythm and a clarinet, it's another reminder of 'The Universal'. Towards the fade-out, Steve hollers: "Andrew, don't put me on records again, just because I'm the oldest this week, according to to the itinerary! You should have hurt the public, not me, and put John, Paul, George and Ringo, or Linda, or Yoko all on this record in the first place!" UK and US version are identical.

Most obviously, Steve and Greg's various solo and duo projects (which finally became *Scrubbers* in 1991, see Chapter 6) had been plucked by A&M. Greg has the last word regarding this album: "Humble Pie were capable of better than that, but we were not really consulted."

According to Marriott, the decision to dissolve the band did not come from him but from Jerry Shirley and Clem Clempson, though he had considered leaving when the others rejected his beloved Blackberries during 1974. Shirley called Steve and wanted out, just one day after peaceful talks about royalties and publishing rights as if nothing was up. Steve: "Nobody really left, exactly; a roadie came round to tell me my band was breaking up," – probably while Greg and Clem rehearsed with a very muscular, Jeff Beck Group-trained drummer, Chapter 6).

Steve asked: "'Why are you telling me this?' It made me a bit sick. I'd said I hadn't wanted to tour, but we were contracted to do one more. We actually enjoyed it, 'cause we knew it was a farewell tour and no more bullshit. We probably became closer on that tour than we'd been for the past eighteen months; we'd been splitting up personally and professionally, my wife had left me – it was a nasty period. We talked about it, why we were splitting up, and it was a big own-up all round."

In another interview, Marriott became even more specific in calling long tours "good marriage breakers". His 1971 'Song For Jenny' had obviously not done the trick of keeping his relationship intact over thousands of miles and many months apart each year.

Greg remembers these times as hard work, badly planned in terms of effective career moves and almost purely done to profit Dee Anthony's management. He is in good company with his ex-mate Peter Frampton, who also felt exploited by Dee (see Chapter 5). Greg looking back on Humble Pie's life in the road: "We did about twenty tours of America [twenty-two in the end]. Some of them were six months at a time, then we got it down to five or six weeks, working five nights a week.

"I never felt like quitting, but sometimes you get pissed off at the situation and I was disappointed it didn't improve with our growing status. Like the gig at Hyde Park [in 1971] and at Charlton [football ground] last year, which was like the Cup Final. But we were managed from the States and we had to work there, and make hay, for some of us I suppose."

On their last American tour, the band – as a five-piece with 'Street Rat' Tim Hinkley on keyboards – did make more hay for Dee, but also got excited reviews: "Humble Pie played their last New York concert, the first of their 'farewell tour', in New York's Academy of Music last week, to thundering applause. Their set, which brought music from the *Fillmore* and *Smokin'* albums, lasted almost two and a half hours and was as explosive as it was emotional." So the times of rifts – over musical direction – between Steve's Blackberries camp and Clem's rock gang were all but forgotten?

Marriott's moving intro, or rather outro, to 'I Don't Need No Doctor' during the final tour gig in Philadelphia, said it all: "Before we disappear into the depths of rock has-beens, we would just like to say we've always had a very special spot for Philadelphia and you know it! So listen: thank you for making us proud and popular. Nice people! Nice people!"

You could hear the lump in Steve's throat on this emotional moment, of which there were many on this tour. With all the arguments, new plans and departures, Humble Pie felt their hearts sinking as they said goodbye to a golden era.

CHAPTER FOUR
The Faces
Had Me A Real Good Time

Steve Marriott's decision to leave The Small Faces hit Ronnie, Mac and Kenney like a flying mallet! Still, they knew too well that they would not be able to persuade their frontman to return. Over the second half of 1968, the atmosphere in the band quarters had deteriorated rapidly. Their studio work had practically come to a standstill, and musical differences, especially between Ronnie and Steve, documented the lack of direction in the quartet. They had sensed that something was in the air, and Steve had been the one who was brave enough to draw the consequences out of this turmoil.

The remaining trio decided to stay together for the time being, and to look for solutions to keep the band afloat. Ronnie Lane took charge and encouraged the two others to keep playing till a replacement had been found. At the same time, Ronnie had started to think about not simply continuing with The Small Faces, but forming a new band reflecting his own musical intentions – which shot in the direction of folk, blues and country rock.

Meanwhile, the band received the first offers of backing work. Donovan of all people showed an interest, but they declined, although in the past they had worked with the singer/songwriter sporadically. Ron, Mac and Kenney wanted a genuine group of three equally represented members,not a mere backing band for somebody else. Apparently Ian McLagan did not have a lot of trust in the band's future – which he kept quiet about of course – and he stayed in loose contact with Steve Marriott and Humble Pie. He even rehearsed with the band – at least for one day, and if Greg Ridley had not vetoed his inclusion, he might have joined the band.

At the same time, during spring 1969, the band had got in touch with the bass player in the Jeff Beck group, Ronnie Wood, a link which ironically had been established by none other than Steve Marriott. Ron Wood remembers: "As soon as I'd got fired I went to Steve Marriott." And indeed, the eccentric rock guitarist's new band – formed in March 1969 – broke up only three months later. And so Woody, as everyone now called, was finally a free man and could try his luck with The Small Faces.

Ron Wood was born on 1 June, 1947 in Hillingdon, Middlesex. He came from a music-loving family, and in beat and rock circles he was far from an unknown entity. His older brothers, Art and Ted, had put him in touch with blues and skiffle right from day one: Art Wood used to sing in Alexis Korner's Blues Incorporated and had subsequently formed The Artwoods (featuring Purple Jon Lord and Keef Hartley among others). Ted Wood preferred trad jazz, and he had played with Temperance Seven. Little Ronald started out by learning the clarinet and sax, dabbling in drums and percussion, but then he developed his love of the guitar.

In 1964 – with a daytime career as an artist in mind – Ronnie formed the semi-pro, R&B-orientated Mod band The Birds. After several singles, the quintet gave up in November 1966, in spite of hard earned popularity on the London club scene.

A few months later, Woody found a job as a second guitarist with ex-Yardbird Jeff Beck, who would soon sentence him to the bass, which used to be the instrument of frustrated guitar players in those days. The Jeff Beck Group had tremendous musical potential and enjoyed a high profile (not only) in critics' circles, but it was always dogged by the unpredictable escapades of their boss, and further handicapped by frequent line-up changes. During this time, Ron Wood became friendly with the group's singer, Rod Stewart.

For a while – March till June 1968 – Woody had played for The Creation, a Mod band mainly popular in Germany, producing three singles with them. He then returned to Jeff Beck, who fired him for good in June 1969.

During the early summer of 1969, everything started to snowball: Ronnie Wood started to rehearse with Ronnie Lane, Ian McLagan and Kenney Jones – The Small Faces. The Rolling Stones' rehearsal room in Bermondsey was at their disposal without any cost. Ronnie had already started working on new songs, and they jammed with ease and motivation. It was a nice and relaxed period, but the four of them realised that a certain ingredient was missing in the band. Kenney confirms this: "Ronnie had a good voice, but in my opinion it wasn't powerful enough, especially after a singer like Steve Marriott, and the backing vocals from Woody and Mac were making me laugh. We had a crack at it, but I kept thinking how Woody, Ronnie and Mac would make a really good vocals team. I wasn't trying to knock Ronnie, because I knew he was a good singer, but I could see it being even better."

Ron Wood took the initiative and called his friend Rod Stewart, who had also had trouble with Jeff Beck and was looking for new projects. Woody invited him to be his guest at rehearsals, without any commitments. And Rod agreed immediately: "I'd listen at the top of the stairs to them rehearsing, and I thought they sounded good, but there was no one singing. And they knew that as well. Ronnie Lane knew that. So it was only a matter of time before they asked me to join."

Rod made a habit of turning up at rehearsals and would take the odd vocal. Mac and especially Ronnie had their reservations with regard to the singer's relative popularity, but on the other hand he was blessed with the powerful, striking voice they needed. They agreed to collaborate loosely, without any obligations.

Their first, tentative gig was in late June 1969 at the Cambridge University end of term party. Spontaneously, they had named themselves Quiet Melon (no relation to the popular US band of the mid Nineties). Woody had hired his well-known older brother Art as provisional singer, and as there was not enough time for rehearsals, they simply played a few R&B standards like 'What I'd Say', 'I Got My Mojo Working' or 'Hoochie Coochie Man'. Then Rod also joined them on stage and contributed a few numbers. The whole thing probably didn't sound too good, but the audience seemed to love them anyway, because they played loud and fast.

During a second college date in Surrey, the band met Long John Baldry with his composer and arranger Jimmy Horowitz (who would stay with LJB up until the 1980s). Subsequently, Art Wood lured the whole entourage – except for Rodney – to studio sessions.

The resulting recordings for the Philips label would not see the light of day for some twenty-six years – till the end of 1995, and even then, only three tracks got released, featuring Kim Gardner (ex-Birds and ex-Creation)on bass, replacing the absent Ronnie Lane.

The positive experience with the Quiet Melon project encouraged the boys to give the band some solid framework. They saw an actual chance to get established in the British rock scene. And then Ron Wood would almost have left the band – had he only known of a most lucrative offer from another group! At the end of June, Ian 'Stu' Stewart, pianist, roadie and minder of The Rolling Stones, had called at the rehearsal room to suggest that Ronnie should take the place of Brian Jones as lead guitarist. Brian and the Stones had recently 'parted company', accompanied by as much noise in the media as Steve Marriott's recent departure. So Stu called, but he got Ronnie Lane at the other end of the line, who declined the enquiry in most nonchalant shrugs: "No thanks, I think he's quite happy where he is." And thus the matter was settled. Ron Wood only got wind of this conversation five years later.

With that friendly takeover prevented, what the band needed most now was a capable manager. Jimmy Horowitz finally established contacts with Irishman Billy Gaff, who up till then had mainly worked for Polydor. Gaff agreed to help especially with the difficult contractual negotiations. Officially, The Small Faces were still tied to Immediate, while Stewart – on his own – had signed a solo recording deal with producer Lou Reizner as early as 1968, which had been taken over by Mercury: also during that fateful June 1969. Ian McLagan and Ronnie Lane were still sceptical about asking Rod into the band officially. They wondered which label would be interested in getting their hands on a shaky band with a front man making solo albums.

Gaff hustled the group on every business doorstep and got no-nos all round. Track and Apple seemed keen enough in the beginning, but backed off as soon as the legal situation became apparent. To make matters worse, Polydor fired Gaff cause The Small Faces took up all his office hours and other deals suffered. But thanks to his stamina and his persuasive negotiating skills, he eventually scored a contract – with Warner Brothers. Conditions for the group were not favourable, though. On top of that, the label insisted on keeping the well-established band name. In discussions for new trademarks, Ronnie had initially suggested Slim Chance. This name was destined to close The Small Faces chapter, but had been rejected by the others. Quiet Melon was seen as a temporary solution anyway, but in the end with the prospect of a recording contract, the band members agreed on a compromise: they'd drop the tag 'Small' – Rod and Woody being taller than the miniature trio,and everybody seemed fairly happy with the shortened name Faces.

Next, they had to resolve 'the Rod Stewart problem'. With Rodney already at work with his first solo album, Kenney Jones gathered all his strength and met his singer before an evening rehearsal in a pub called The Spaniard. Kenney asked Rod to join the band – at long last: Stewart had waited for this vote of confidence for quite a time. Together they went to the sessions, where the other members agreed with procedures. On 18 September (other sources insist on October) Rod officially joined The Faces.

More history is called for: Roderick David Stewart was born on 10 January, 1945 in London, as the son of Scottish middle-class parents. As a youngster, he showed more interest in soccer than in his music hobby. He even dared to step into semi-professional football at the age of sixteen – by joining a Second Division club, Brentford, which he soon left disillusioned. Rod's love of music prevailed, although initially he was not so much into rock'n'roll or R&B but thrived on folk. Armed with a guitar and harmonica, he hitch-hiked all over Europe, much like his future friend Baldry had done in the late Fifties. Rod earned his modest upkeep with odd jobs and the pitiful busking cash. He quickly managed to find his way into the London R&B scene during 1963 and took part in many sessions as a harmonica player.

Rod subsequently joined several bands, like Jimmy Powell's Five Dimensions (one single for Pye Records), then in 1964 Long John Baldry's Hoochie Coochie Men, after the lanky loony with the deep voice had met Rod waiting for a train at West London's Twickenham Station. Rod's first solo single, 'Good Morning Little Schoolgirl' was performed on the *Ready Steady Go* TV show with the Hoochie

Coochies, flopped, and Rod joined The Soul Agents before reuniting with Baldry in Steampacket, where he met with a pianist called Reg Dwight, later to become one Elton John. Via Shotgun Express, featuring Julie Driscoll and organ player Brian Auger, he arrived in The Jeff Beck Group in 1967 with Shotgun's drummer Mickey Waller. Before Beck, Rod had recorded his second single, 'The Day Will Come', in 1965, but like 'Schoolgirl', the performance was a far cry from his now characteristic sandpaper voice. That same year, Stewart appeared in the TV documentary *Rod The Mod*, a thirty-minute portrait of a typical – well – Mod. In The Jeff Beck Group, Rodney had met up with Ron Wood, together they were destined to fill the huge gap Steve Marriott had left in The Small Faces. As Rod recalls: "Woody joined The Faces and so did I!"

With Rod on board the first demo tapes were recorded and the band duly played them to Glyn Johns, whose brother Andy was now working on Humble Pie's second album *Town And Country*. Glyn was quite taken with what he heard from the new quintet and he invited the boys for more sessions at Olympic Sound Studios. There, by the Thames, they managed to record six tracks during a single evening, and these proved good enough to persuade the powers that be at their record label.

On 1 November, 1969, The Faces – featuring Rod – signed the agreed contract with Warner Brothers. A few weeks later, Stewart's solo album *An Old Raincoat Won't Never Let You Down* was released, with collaborations by Ronnie Wood, Ian McLagan as well as Beck Group cohort Mickey Waller. It was hardly recognised in England, but when it appeared in the States as *The Rod Stewart Album*, critics rated it enthusiastically.

The Faces' debut album, recorded during December 1969, appeared in Great Britain on 21 March, 1970 and was aptly titled *First Step*. The Faces had been their own producers with assistance by sound engineer Martin Birch (Deep Purple), after their original candidate Glyn Johns had come out with quite imaginative royalty conditions. Reactions to *First Step* in the music press seemed acceptable: they weren't euphoric, but they did not slam the album either. In the UK Charts it reached a respectable Number Forty-Five, while in the US they had to be content with the one hundred and nineteenth position. A US tour supporting Savoy Brown went down better, but didn't influence record sales. The single, 'Flying', had already flopped completely in the UK during February, in spite of the band's enthusiasm.

The album begins with 'Wicked Messenger', a lesser known Bob Dylan number, from his 1968 LP *John Wesley Harding*, and with the very first step leads the band in the direction of blues and country rock, dominated by Mac's fat Hammond organ sound. Rod's vocals sound subdued and cool as they do on 'Devotion', here backed by Ronnie Lane on his own bluesy composition. An ace lead guitar courtesy of Woody and once again Mac's full organ passages are highlights of a song that was part of The Faces' live set in 1971.

The fledgling Wood/Lane writing team are responsible for 'Shake Shudder Shiver', a powerful blues rocker that is the only title on this long player clocking in at less than four minutes. The song title is a reference to the ice cold bathroom at Ronnie Lane's little dive in West London's Who suburb of Shepherd's Bush.

For 'Stone', a typical Lane song, with finger-snapping country folk touches, Ronnie sings and plays the guitar, Rod picks his banjo and supplies backing vocals, while Woody excels on the blues harp and Mac tinkles on a Honky Tonk piano. Ronnie presented the same song on Pete Townshend's first solo album – *Who Came First* – titled 'Evolution', and later re-recorded it with Slim Chance.

A leftover from the Beck era, 'Around The Plynth' sees a new treatment of a Stewart/Wood standard which showcases Woody's inimitable slide guitar work and Rod's rough vocal shots. The same writing team, this time with Lane, were responsible for the seven-inch failure, 'Flying'. This strong ballad had actually begun to take shape during the Melon days.

And speaking of fruit, 'Pineapple And The Monkey' which follows, is an instrumental by Wood that is characterised less by his guitar work than by Mac's Hammond organ. The result is filler material, the likes of which can be found better placed on several single B-sides.

Back on form, 'Nobody Knows' is another sad Lane number with a typical country atmosphere, featuring Rod's strong second harmonising voice and Woody's assortment of slide and acoustic

guitars. Based on a truly dynamic rhythm foundation laid down by
Ronnie, Kenney and Mac, Woody comes up with more impressive
guitar improvisations on 'Looking Out The Window', another blues
rock instrumental.

The next track, 'Three Button Hand Me Down', goes down as the
prototype for the future success story of Faces-type party rock. Rod:
"All I really learnt from The Faces was drinking!" The catchy melody
is a direct quote from 'Some Kinda Wonderful' – a standard which
Steve Marriott and his Official Receivers later covered under its
correct title – and it stands as a preview to Status Quo's boogie-on-
down philosophy. A popular live-number where the fans can join in
instantly.

True to its title, the album presented the 'first step' in the right
direction: stylistically unbalanced perhaps, but instead presenting
the necessary rough edges – an unpolished diamond.

In order to promote their debut, The Faces toured the UK non-
stop and full of energy. But the audience appeared stoic. Rod
remembers: "We worked bloody hard in those days. In the first six
months I don't think we played to more than a hundred people at
each concert. When we first started, nobody wanted to listen to us
and nobody was taking us very seriously, and we decided to go
round the pub beforehand. Call it Dutch courage if you want, but
that's what it was down to. We were just lacking confidence, and I
think all the boys enjoyed a drink more than anything else."

Of course, they still carried the additional burden of being
announced as 'The Small Faces', especially by concert promoters.
And the audience did not only want to hear new songs, they
requested the old hits. There were typical shouts for 'Tin Soldier'
during one legendary gig at London's Marquee Club on 7 December,
1970 (which in those days was still situated in Soho's Wardour Street
but has moved to Charing Cross Road in the early Nineties). Still,
even on this occasion the band stayed true to its principle of only
playing their new material.

At the end of March 1970 The Faces flew over for their first
genuine North American tour, which opened with a date in Toronto,
Canada, on a bill with MC 5 and Canned Heat. After the British
experience they were surprised about the big halls they had to play.

Following twenty-eight appearances in the United States and Canada, the band returned home in June 1970 justifiably pleased with themselves. For the majority of those gigs, The Faces had been presented as headliners and had still been able to meet the high anticipation of the audience.

Subsequent gigs in Britain brought the band back to square one with a vengeance. They still couldn't win back home and had to appear in small clubs or half empty halls. Rod was also working on his second solo album, *Gasoline Alley*, with Ron Wood and Ian McLagan helping him out again. Two songs on the LP actually featured the entire Faces line-up exclusively: 'You're My Girl' and The Small Faces ballad 'My Way Of Giving'. And four further tracks from it, namely the Stewart/Wood title song, Womack's 'It's All Over Now', 'Country Comfort' by Rod's Steampacket mate Elton John as well as Eddie Cochran's hit 'Cut Across Shorty' became part of The Faces' live repertoire.

Gasoline Alley appeared on the market in September 1970 and took a respectable position in the US charts – Number Twenty-Seven – paving the way for their third tour there in a single year, starting at the beginning of October. Again, The Faces travelled with Savoy Brown, a down to earth British blues rock band popular with American audiences but soon reduced to supporting status as the tour got underway. The concert arenas got bigger all the time – till at the Los Angeles Forum they played in front of almost twenty thousand people. Slowly but surely word had got round that The Faces were one of the hottest live acts of the period.

During the winter of 1970/71, the group produced their second album, *Long Player*, in London's Morgan Sound Studios (where during 1969 Humble Pie had finished *Town And Country*) and via the Rolling Stones Mobile Recording Unit. It was released during March 1971, simultaneously with its single 'Had Me A Real Good Time'.

A new writing team begins the new album. 'Bad'N'Ruin' is an energetic Stewart/McLagan composition featuring Mac's keyboard sounds on organ and electric piano, Woody's brilliant lead guitar and precise ground work by their rhythm section; a popular sing-along live number. The Lane pen came up with track two, 'Tell Everyone', a heart breaking ballad adequately delivered by Rod. Mac's organ sequences towards the end are reminiscent of Joe Cocker's 'With A Little Help From My Friends'. Pleased with the song, Ronnie tried his luck with it again on his solo debut *Anymore For Anymore* in 1974.

Track three and the third writing credit for 'Sweet Lad Mary'. Written by Stewart/Wood/Lane the song works as an enticing country rock ballad with religious elements, and featured versatile guitar work courtesy of Woody: apart from his acoustic guitars, electric lead and a fine pedal steel appear.

'Richmond' is oozing with that homesickness which caused Ronnie Lane to write this number during a US tour. Woody's on slide and Ronnie sings and plays acoustic guitar. An absolute counterpoint to The Faces' party rockers it was therefore unsuitable for the band's live set – unfortunately!

After Humble Pie's spate of Beatles covers it's refreshing that the next track is only by one member of that band. But having said that, Paul McCartney must have been stunned about the effect one of his more average songs – 'Maybe I'm Amazed' – can achieve when played by the right band. Heavy organ harmonies, Woody's lead guitar and the dynamic rhythm section are now taken for granted; Ronnie sings the first verse, then Rod rasps in his inimitable style. This is an exciting live recording from New York's Fillmore East – the slightly antiseptic studio version also became a single – albeit only in Germany.

'Had Me A Real Good Time' is a prime example of the kind of party rock the fans wanted from The Faces. The song appears in two parts. Woody's rock guitar and Mac's honky tonk piano supply the framework for Rod's shouter's delight. During the second, mainly instrumental part, Bobby Keys on saxophone (Stones) and Harry Beckett (Georgie Fame) on trumpet let go. For reasons beyond comprehension, the seven-inch was abbreviated quite substantially.

Three distinctly different tracks follow to end the album. 'On The Beach' is a peculiar, odd folk number with slide guitar, acoustic guitars and more honky tonk tinkling, sung by Ron Wood and Ronnie Lane. In parts, this sounds off-key, but that's all part of the song's charm. Next, 'I Feel So Good', by blues legend Willie 'Big Bill' Broonzy is the second number from the Fillmore East and further proof of The Faces' live impact. Finally, Ronnie's bottleneck-based instrumental 'Jerusalem', a version of William Blake's hymn, sounds like a filler on first encounter and closes the album a little bit abruptly.

Listening to the album, the general feeling prevailed that the five-piece managed to grow together more and more. In spite of the different composers' contributions, the *Long Player* album appears more substantial and mature than The Faces' debut, with Woody's guitar riffs taking more of the limelight right now. In the US, *Long Player* managed to crack the Top Thirty of the LP charts (Twenty-Nine), and in Britain the band were apparently taken more seriously now (Thirty-One). The revealing single title 'Had Me A Real Good Time' became another flop, but still managed to become a compulsory ingredient of all future concerts.

While British audiences 'discovered' The Faces at long last for their own pleasure, the local rock journalists and radio DJs remained sceptical. One of the few media personalities who liked the band and even became friends with them was BBC DJ John Peel.

"I was a very serious hippy when I met The Faces for the first time," he recalls, "backstage during one of their concerts. I felt absolutely shocked – sober and precious as I was – when they stumbled out of their dressing room, loud, vulgar and very cockney. 'Ahm, no thanks. No, really,' I mumbled nervously when they called after me, something that sounded like 'Come on, John – old sod, we'll have a drink!' While they stormed down the hall and disappeared, I realised that The Faces were having a lot more fun in life than I had. Next time they invited me I went along. And the other times, too. The Faces and their lead singer Rod Stewart changed my life. During one of their gigs I'm supposed to have danced with a bottle of Blue Nun in my arm. And I'm a person who never ever dances. Never, never, never."

The Faces may have been happy and boisterous in public, whether they appeared in concert, for press conferences or elsewhere, but still, the seed of uneasiness inside the group began to develop slowly but surely. Ronnie Lane began to sense more than anybody else that Rod Stewart had moved into the band focus over the last twelve months. The media lost interest in the band's fate just as rapidly as they began to court their frontman and solo singer. While The Faces were still on their fourth – and triumphant – US tour during the summer of 1971,

Rod's third solo album *Every Picture Tells A Story* was released. Once again, Ian McLagan and Ron Wood had been among the studio crew, Wood had also co-written the title song. The album's new treatment of The Temptations' '(I Know) I'm Losing You' was, in fairness, a Faces production separate from the album sessions, a fact that wasn't even mentioned on the back cover. At least he pays polite thanks to his mates on the sleeve with: "Also I'd like to drink a toast to my old associates and colleagues The Faces (Jones, McLagan, Lane and Wood) (and their persons) for being patient in giving me the time to make this recording and for the musical development on losing you."

The song's arrangement owed practically everything to the version supplied by the white Detroit-based Motown band Rare Earth. Asked about this uncredited idea transfer in 1993, Gil Bridges, Earth boss then and now, shrugged it off: "It just made us proud, believe it or not!"

In October 1971, Rod Stewart's solo single 'Maggie May' – which had oddly started life as the B-side of his Tim Hardin cover 'Reason To Believe' – rocketed up the international charts and drew the accompanying album *Every Picture Tells A Story* in its wake. A few weeks later Rod watched with amazement as both single and album blocked the Number One spots in Britain and the United States. This was unheard of to date (and still is!) in the world of pop music.

Suddenly, Rod wasn't just the lead singer of a rated live rock group – he was a pop star: and that meant solo artist, of course! Music magazines, TV and radio stations couldn't get enough of him – just him. Rod was supposed to hustle his ballad of 'Maggie May' – a lady with a lot of experience in love and life – and the other Faces were expected to perform as his backing band. Unfortunately the boys were bitter about playing this silly game of miming to Big Rod's playback tapes. In fact, Woody was the only one to understand – which was hardly surprising with half of the title song's royalties heading for his bank account. The old trio had to be dragged along because, if they had not relented, a split would have been inevitable even then. In the crucial appearance for *Top Of The Pops*, they were duly billed as Rod Stewart And The Faces – with an additional member as their biggest fan, DJ John Peel, pretended to play the mandolin. A short, chaotic soccer spot couldn't hide the fact that vibes in The Faces camp were not pleasant.

17 November, 1971 saw the British release of *A Nod's As Good As A Wink...To A Blind Horse*, generally regarded as the best Faces album. As their co-producer, the band had finally been able to hire Glyn Johns. The ways in which he assisted them in the studio are documented in a little credit on the included giant poster: "We thank you, Glyn, you made all the difference."

The album gets off to a quality start with 'Miss Judy's Farm', a simple riff song based on just one chord, perfectly suited for improvisation. Not surprisingly, the song was also the driving force during many concerts.

Heavy duty boogie with tongue-in-cheek lyrics follows in 'You're So Rude'. A McLagan/Lane composition it tells of how the parents have gone visiting Aunt Renee, and the teenage couple take advantage of the home love nest – until mum and dad return early...

From adolescent fumblings to adult passions in the next two songs. First up is 'Love Lived Here', a melancholic ballad – not about lost love in this case, but memories of popular hang-outs like snooker clubs or pubs which have been demolished since. The text, with its unusual comments on a political matter, was written by Ronnie Lane, while Woody and Rod supplied the music. Similarly, 'Last Orders Please' celebrates the institution of the British pub, composed and sung, with Dobro accompaniment, by Laney. Woody does not only contribute lead guitar, but makes an appearance on double bass.

The crisp riff rocker that follows would result in the long overdue hit single for The Faces. By Wood and Stewart, the words to 'Stay With Me' are rude, relating Rod's adventures with more 'horizontal' concerns than pub frequenting. The start is decidedly mid tempo. while Rod and co rev up in the wild finale with Kenney shining. The song is everything its B-side, and next track on the album, isn't, in fact. 'Debris', the song in question, is Ronnie Lane's homage to his Dad, a tender, somehow fragile song, with Rod helping out with second vocals and harmonies during the higher passages. Ronnie plays Dobro again, and now it's him who picks the double bass; a rare occasion.

Another tribute falls next, this time taking the form of a cover version. Chuck Berry's rock'n'roll classic 'Memphis Tennessee' gets

The Faces treatment – as 'Memphis' – with Woody trying out a few effects on his electric guitar. Otherwise this is filler material – which means it went down a storm in live shows, of course, like 'Too Bad' another highlight from The Faces' live repertoire. Straightforward, uncompromising rock, it's obviously written by the team Wood and Stewart.

To wrap things up, 'That's All You Need' uses an intro reminiscent of 'Plynth', but it cannot hide the fact that this is average riff rock, just about rescued by Woody's slide guitar showcase in the middle section. For the final onslaught, steel drums courtesy of Harry Fowler are added to the full-blown band.

As usual the good outweighed the bad and with *A Nod's As Good As A Wink...To A Blind Horse*, The Faces achieved their biggest success to date: Number Two in the British hit lists and the sixth position in the American charts. A new US tour became another huge smash, resulting in an entry in the *Guinness Book Of Records* when, on 26 November, 1971, New York's Madison Square Garden sold out quicker than ever before.

The chosen single, 'Stay With Me', took a long time coming but reached Number Six in the UK, and scored a respectable Seventeen one month later in the US, where their three month trek began in June. One of its highlights was 8 July, 1972. Among others, Steve Marriott's Humble Pie shared the bill of a huge open air festival on the premises of the Pocono race track near Long Pond in Pennsylvania. They played to the biggest crowd since Woodstock – with more than two hundred thousand fans turning up. Other landmarks were concerts in the Cotton Bowl in Dallas, Texas in front of forty thousand people, LA's Hollywood Bowl where the band appeared for a solid week, and Madison Square Garden on 12 September, where The Faces surprised their audience with a Dixieland band, a bagpipe player and Charleston tap dancers.

During this glamorous journey, Rod Stewart's fourth solo album, *Never A Dull Moment*, came out world-wide reaching Number One in numerous charts and issuing two hit singles: 'You Wear It Well' and the Jimi Hendrix ballad 'Angel'. It's hardly surprising that *Never A Dull Moment* is the Stewart album with the most obvious Faces sound. Three songs were supplied by the Stewart/Wood team, most notably 'True Blue' which is also a complete band recording. Ronnie Lane, Ian Mc Lagan and Ronnie Wood assist with three further titles: 'Angel', Sam Cooke's 'Twisting The Night Away' and Etta James' 'I'd Rather Go Blind'. All the songs mentioned here now became part of The Faces' live repertoire.

After their UK tour in December 1972, The Faces were scheduled to enter the studios to tackle yet another studio album. Work dragged on slowly, Rod had little time to spare due to his solo commitments and seemed hardly inspired. At least, the single hit 'Cindy Incidentally' resulted from the sessions, released during February 1973 and in fact their biggest success in the UK charts at Number Two. But the LP wasn't really forthcoming. Mac: "It was a shame, because it had started promisingly, and it could have been our fastest and best album."

Warner Brothers' marketing experts had hired renowned designer Jim Ladwig for the album's artwork. But as neither the songs nor any hints of the record's lyrical content existed yet, Ladwig designed a quite general, flexible sketch which bore a suitable connection to The Faces' humoristic aura. Jim, as a collector of historical press items, stumbled upon an old newspaper advert of the 1930s. The then popular American radio entertainer Fred Allen was seen advertising a toothpaste. The gimmick of this ad was that by pulling a marked paper clip, you could move Allen's eyes and mouth. Ladwig went on to assemble an LP-sized model of this commercial gimmick and presented this amusing record sleeve to Stewart and Wood, the latter spontaneously uttering the words "Ooh La La", also hinting on a song he had just finished writing with Ronnie Lane. Why not use this Francophile term of surprise and admiration for the album title?

That was what the creative trio were thinking, and when the remaining Faces had given their consent, Ladwig got the outline in shape for publishing. Instead of Allen's features he used the portrait of an unknown bohemian wearing a bowler hat. By pressing the rim of the LP sleeve, you got the same effect that characterised the vintage ad: mouth and eyes got moving, and the guy's well developed set of teeth duly appeared.

The inner sleeve of this gatefold album was also designed with

119

regard to a line in the song 'Ooh La La'. The photomontage showed five grinning Faces peeping under a Can-Can dancer's skirt! On the back cover, hand coloured photo portraits of the five are presented – looking peculiarly wary and frustrated, except for a genuinely laughing Ronnie: maybe a hint of his imminent departure?

Anyway, in April 1973, *Ooh La La* was released at long last, with 'Silicone Grown' starting proceedings. A rocky opener fulfilling a typical Faces fan's expectations, it was written about hot performances by Stewart and Wood and culminates in cheeky remarks on busty females who have not only mother nature to thank for their opulent bra sizes: "You been to see a specialist".

This is followed by the already mentioned hit single, 'Cindy Incidentally', all catchy melody lines, but getting the tempo down a bit in order to save some breath for the kind of energy a whole album needs – well, just. At thirty minutes, this LP managed two thirds of their *Long Player* – a mini album in the 1990s... On the subject of length, 'Flags And Banners' by Lane and Stewart is a gorgeous gem, barely two minutes long, sung by Ronnie in his inimitable style. Deeply melancholic, this song is about a nightmare. By the way, Ronnie is heard on electric bouzouki, while the equally amplified guitar comes courtesy of Rod Stewart.

Woody and Rod deliver the mid tempo rocker 'My Fault' as a nice but ultimately irrelevant duet before the band really let loose again on 'Borstal Boys'. There is a nasty, howling siren, and it's down to some hard rocking, with a few lyrical surprises. Mac, Woody and Rod relate the situation in an approved 'reformatory' school with sharp criticism: ("See the years roll on by/Such a senseless waste of time/What a way to reform/Call out your number who's a non-conformer, not me baby oh yeah").

You can't follow contentious lyrics like that and 'Fly In The Ointment' doesn't try. A dynamic instrumental piece, it spotlights Woody's slide guitar, and features an appearance by guest percussionist Neemoi 'Speedy' Acquaye (from Georgie Fame's Blue Flames, whose brass section had toured with The Small Faces: the Soho-based Ghana man died in 1993). This is still filler material, as Rod is of course 'out for lunch'.

More substantial is 'If I'm On The Late Side', a reflective love song with melody supplied by Ronnie Lane, text by Stewart. Woody and Laney try and keep things varied by swapping instruments, the guitarist plonking the bass, whereas Laney shines on his acoustic. Rod sings this title with marked ease. The atmosphere remains sad for the next number, implied by its title: 'Glad And Sorry'. Here Ronnie shares vocals with Woody, while in the lyrics it's pretty much Lane's fragile state of mind oozing out of every single line. The decision to leave The Faces for a new path seems to be taking shape: "Glad and sorry, happy or sad/When all is done and spoken/You're up or I'm down".

The tension within the band continues in 'Just Another Honky', a swinging ballad with Mac's honky tonk piano. The writing's already on the wall with this composition by Ronnie Lane. If it's not only taken at face value – a song of failed love – this number only makes (ambivalent) sense if sung by Rod, the undisputed band leader, himself. The chorus of "You can go if you want to/I don't own you, go be wild/Leave my hand it's wide open, so's the door forever more", is directly aimed at Ronnie, surely.

After all the worry and melancholy tinged songs, the album at least closes with its amusing title song. A smart and witty number with a catchy melody, solidly strumming acoustic guitars by Ron and Ronnie (who abandoned his bass one more time) with Mac's honky tonk and unusual harmonium sounds in the background. Woody puts all his vocal energy in 'Ooh La La' although it was originally meant to be sung by Rod. The text is about grandad, who had his fair share of troubles with "the ladies", and passed his experiences on to his grandson, who didn't really take it to heart: "I wish I knew what I know now, when I was younger". Listening to this relaxed item, it's hard to believe that the recording cost the band a lot of heartaches: it was recorded four times, Stewart neither liked the arrangement nor the key it was in, which wouldn't suit Laney's voice either and in the end Woody had a go and it worked okay. Ron Wood as well as Ronnie Lane later integrated this joint composition in their respective solo sets.

Fast as *Ooh La La* shot to the top of the British album charts, it plummeted out of the listings. Rod plainly kept his distance from the record, dismissing it in the press: "A bloody mess", he told *Melody*

Maker, and indeed it was everything but a joint effort, as Kenney Jones criticised with hindsight: "Nobody went to the studio with a song. It was like get there and write it on the spot. Not being a songwriter I always wanted to go in the studio with a definite idea: that's what I was used to with The Small Faces – here's a song, it's all together, all we've got to do is maybe change the arrangement. And we used to knock them off like that, all good ones. But to go to the studio and have to write a song...and the lyrics weren't even written! The riff was there and we had to write the whole backing thing, arrange it, write words to it. It was mostly like that."

Ronnie Lane had long since had enough. Over the years, he'd been degraded from the original founder of the band to simply playing bass in some rock star's backing band. He still managed to place his songs on the albums, but ever since 1971 – when The Faces had all but invented party rock – his numbers did not play their part in the live repertoire. And he felt abandoned by his mates whenever he put his foot down and protested, getting into hot arguments with Rod. Kenney, Mac and Woody refused to be drawn in, not daring to risk their lucrative jobs.

On 26 May, 1973, Ronnie left The Faces at the end of another US tour – tired of life on the road just as much as band politics. New plans were already in his head. There was talk about replacing him with Andy Fraser (ex Free, Sharks) or Phil Chen, but they both declined. Finally, Rod and remaining colleagues decided to hire the Japanese bass player Tetsu Yamauchi (born 21 October, 1947), who had succeeded Fraser in Free. He eased into the group harmonically and had no further ambitions. Ian McLagan admitted quite freely: "I think the band is much better since Ronnie left. Tetsu's a different sort of bass player and he's given us a kick up the arse. Tetsu's a bass player first and foremost, whereas Ronnie wasn't."

In October 1973 – backed by the live 'I Wish It Would Rain' from the suitably wet Reading Festival – 'Pool Hall Richard' became the first Faces single to feature Tetsu on bass: a rough'n'ready rocker that only became a British chart hit (Number Eight) because of its typically English subject matter. Shortly before its release, a Rod Stewart solo single had come out – 'Oh No Not My Baby', the cover of a 1964 Manfred Mann hit. 'Baby''s B-side was 'Jodie' by the team of Wood/Stewart/McLagan: Faces band product which had obviously been recorded in a happy and 'refreshed' atmosphere, as documented on its logo: Rod And The Faces – and a bottle of Campari.

That same October 1973, the band went on another, albeit obligatory US tour, whose final gigs in Anaheim and Hollywood were scheduled to be recorded for a live LP. It's best to treat the resulting concert album, January 1974's *Coast To Coast – Overture And Beginners* with complete silence. Revealingly, it was the first long playing release sporting the tag 'Rod Stewart/Faces', and music critics as well as Faces fans took these 'works' as a slap in the face. Teja Schwaner, a reviewer in Germany's then leading rock magazine *Sounds*, was pretty much to the point: "There has been the odd concert by The Faces plus Stewart which became a failure thanks to fire water, other gigs maybe worked well with the help of the booze. But regarding the eleven titles recorded on the last American tour, the indignation of listening to its total of forty-nine minutes and forty-seven seconds is based on the alcoholic peaks all the participants stumbled about with: and that includes the sound engineers...There's some wooden rocking with too much marching band flourish, the blues has little feeling and concentration, everything is too flat, weak and fatuous." What's left as a half witty gimmick is the treatment of 'Borstal Boys' which, of all things, is interrupted by a verse of the hymn 'Amazing Grace'.

Coast To Coast closes with a failed interpretation of John Lennon's 'Jealous Guy', whereas the album's opener, 'It's All Over Now', would have been a more fitting finale. Rod's words at the end shout it all out unmasked: "Thank you for your time...and your money!" – surely the ultimate in polite robbery. Still, *Coast To Coast* became a Number Three hit album at least in Britain, supposedly because of many expectant – and unsuspecting – advance orders.

Soon, the first signs of The Faces drifting apart became visible after that long world tour which came to an end in February 1974. The fact that Rod immediately started preparing another solo LP was business as usual, but when Ron Wood also believed he had to present his own LP – *I've Got My Own Album To Do* was the fitting title – it was obvious now that Faces band releases did not have absolute priority at all. Kenney Jones let frustrated steam off in public. He hated the notion of a successful writing team – Stewart/Wood – wasting the chance of creating convincing group products. Instead, attractive and strong Faces recordings like 'I'm Losing You', 'Angel' or 'True Blue' had surfaced on Rod Stewart solo albums – without the actual band benefiting: "We've proved that we can make fucking good records by just playing on Rod's things as The Faces. 'Losing You' could have been on a Faces album, there are so many things that could have made a great Faces album already. But after everyone's done their own thing, no one wants to write songs for the band, or if they do they can't think of any ideas because they've run out."

With all that frustration Kenney did not miss the opportunity of recording his own disc, even if it was only a single – 'Ready Or Not' – which appeared on Ronnie Lane's GM label, so that link was intact. The single appeared in tow of Wood's debut album and Rod's fifth solo LP *Smiler*, in October 1974, and was a flop. Woody's record didn't fare any better, in spite of massive guest stars in attendance – among them Keith Richards and two Micks, Jagger and Taylor, courtesy of the Stones. Rod's LP became another smash: Number One in Britain, Thirteen in the US. It had its surprises – presenting a happy-go-lucky atmosphere, a wide selection of styles ranging from folk through rock'n'roll and R&B to Dixieland, and featuring not a single Faces mate on its tracks.

On the other hand, Rod and The Faces went on their high profile UK and European tour from September 1974 in – and probably also with – good spirits. It was their most successful trip this side of the Atlantic yet, and surely helped them growing together again. The production of another single, 'You Can Make Me Dance, Sing Or Anything' probably also helped band morale. During the tour, they had almost spontaneously found their way into Munich's Musicland Studios at the end of October. Inside forty-eight hours, two songs had been entirely completed: a catchy, pop-orientated and string-laden mid tempo number with the longest ever song title – 'You Can Make Me Dance, Sing Or Anything, Even Take The Dog For A Walk, Mend A Fuse, Fold Away The Ironing Board, Or Any Other Domestic Short Comings' – was coupled with a beautiful ballad – 'As Long As

You Tell Him' – sporting Woody's sensitive slide guitar. Both titles were released on one single by 14 November, 1974, which would be the last one by The Faces – and one of their most successful – at Number Twelve in the UK.

After a break of fifteen months, the United States was back on the agenda in January 1975. Spirits in the band were again riding high, and there were even plans to go into the studios during the US sojourn in order to record a new album – at long last, after a gap of two years! For breaks in their intinerary, an LA studio had already been rented. But everything would turn out completely different – at the end of this tour, the split of the band already seemed destined. In March, Rod met a Swedish actress during an LA party, and apparently became besotted. The couple stuck together like John and Yoko. A few weeks later, Rod announced that he was planning to spend at least one year in the States – primarily for tax reasons of course – and that he would also record his next solo album there.

All this meant that Rod would not be returning to England for a long while; Faces concerts were now only possible abroad while the chances of another group album dropped to zero. Ron Wood reacted to the signs first. Together with Ian McLagan, Kenney Jones and Bobby Womack – an acquaintance from the winter tour – he went into the studios to complete his second solo album, *Now Look*. There was only a handful of numbers to record, because he had usable material left over from the 1974 sessions.

Woody made another crucial decision. In December 1974, guitarist Mick Taylor had left The Rolling Stones, and Mick Jagger had asked Ron immediately if he wanted to join them. (So with a five year delay, he must have had the right Ron on the phone!) After the successful US Christmas tour Ron saw no reason to let his band down. What he did offer Jagger was helping the Stones out should the need arise: "Look, if you ever get desperate, give me a call." And Jagger did make that call. The Stones were booked to tour the States from 3 June, 1975, but still hadn't agreed on a lead guitarist – in spite of discussing other candidates in The Faces camp like Peter Frampton and Steve Marriott. In early April Wood finally agreed to help out as a guest musician. With some neat timing, he could then jump the Stones ship and criss-cross the same stadium venues on the imminent second 1975 US tour by The Faces, which was due to start in August.

Meanwhile, Rod Stewart had completed his sessions for *Atlantic Crossing*, the crucial album which was destined to change his solo career substantially. It came out in time for a massive US tour stopping in sixty cities. Stewart's excellently produced, but decidedly pop orientated solo outing presented a giant problem: armies of string and brass players had featured on the lavish *Atlantic Crossing* as prominently as numerous studio cracks, like Jesse Ed Davis and half The Blues Brothers Band with Steve Cropper and Duck Dunn. How on earth would a band like The Faces translate this sound for the live stage? Did anyone hear the distant shouts of "Ogdens' Nut Gone Flake"? Rod himself was more than sceptical regarding the musical possibilities of his well-worn combo. The first rehearsals had not gone too smoothly, and he insisted on an additional string ensemble and requested Steve Cropper as second guitarist.

The Faces tried hard to talk their big time over-achiever out of this strategy – after all, this was a Faces tour and not some *Atlantic Crossing* promo glamour. McLagan offered to simulate the necessary romantic Atlantic sounds with the help of a string synthesiser – this was the age before samples. But Rod dismissed this alternative and insisted on his show. The prima donna's only exception: Wood got his way with a second guitarist, *Crossing* session cat Jesse Ed Davis. The band mates ground their teeth and accepted Rod's rule, but felt at the same time that a split was due at the end of this tour. All this came in the face of McLagan's full-blown comments on the band's future: "We're going into the studio in November, and if Rod isn't going to sing the numbers we'll do them ourselves...If Rod does decide to leave, we'll carry on by ourselves."

Contrary to expectations, Rod and The Faces managed to move closer together than of late – soon it seemed like the old days. This was partly due to a kind of 'scandal' that was typical for the fun and practical jokes in The Faces: this had caused their chaotic reputation and the panic in hotel managers' eyes the world over! Out of sheer boredom they had often 're-arranged' their hotel rooms. And based on such pertinent experiences, the complete Holiday Inn chain pronounced a Faces ban!

On the tour itinerary, The Faces were now scheduled to play two concerts in Hawaii. Ron Wood, who joined the band directly from his tour with the Stones, remembers: "We were sitting on the beach in Honolulu...Rod and Britt Ekland got up to go back to the hotel, and when they got there, they were told that they were being evicted from their room. Helen Reddy [the Australian pop chanteuse] and her manager husband Jeff Wald had just blown into town and demanded their usual room, which was occupied by Rod and Britt. Coward that I am, I stayed on the beach, sipping pina coladas.

"But when Mac – Ian McLagan – got wind of it, he went running up to the hotel cursing. He punched Helen Reddy's husband, knocking him against a wall, and a big painting of John Constable's 'Haywain' fell right on his head. It was like a scene from a cartoon. Nevertheless, the hotel management didn't change its mind. But we made them suffer for it. While Rod and Britt were packing, we stopped up the toilets so they would flood as soon as you flushed them. We put booby traps above the doors, sawed the legs off the bed and put them back under it, and clogged up the mouth piece of the phone so no one could hear the person calling out. I wish I had been there to see them walk in the door and have things fall of their heads. Then, flush the toilet and have the bathroom flood. And finally, sit on the bed to complain to reception, only to have their bed collapse while they scream their lungs out over the phone without being heard."

Suddenly, The Faces were having fun together again, and at the end of September, Rod surprisingly confirmed these renewed vibes of friendship – and that his mates' ambition had improved the quality of the band: "At first it seemed like we would break up. But we're playing better, it sounds tighter. I'll be honest...I think we'll stay together."

Very soon he came over even more enthusiastic and even mentioned another Faces album, which could be recorded in Australia during December. So when the successful tour ended in the Nassau Coliseum on Long Island on 12 October, 1975, The Faces' future looked bright again. The five mates agreed to stay in close contact to contemplate the next move.

Under the circumstances, then, the *Daily Mirror* headline "Why

Rock Star Rod Is Quitting The Faces" must have come as a complete blow. On 19 December, 1975, the British million-selling tabloid revealed that Rod was going to give them the sack after all. As his reason, Rod quoted his friend Woody's indecision of all things – complaining that Ron was being rented out to The Rolling Stones all the time and that contacts had been cut off. Wood saw it completely the other way round, while the other Faces were sulking in the background. They would not accept Rod's split in this manner.

The remaining quartet were intent – in all seriousness – on recording another Faces album and started work on new songs. Tetsu and roadie Chuch Magee flew to Paris in January 1976 in order to choose the right studio. Woody, involved in working with the Stones on the *Black And Blue* album, was the first to realise that this project didn't have a chance in the world. After their record company – initially in favour of another Faces LP – backed out, Ron Wood said goodbye too, lighting the touchpaper for the final Faces countdown.

CHAPTER FIVE
Ronnie Lane
The Lovable Outsider

When Ronnie Lane quit The Faces immediately after the US tour in May 1973, this came as anything but a surprise. It was Ronnie who had fought for continuing The (Small) Faces, so feeling pushed aside by Rod Stewart hit him hardest. For a long time, he had had no influence whatsoever on the fate of the band and he found the constant touring gruelling, especially after having started a family with his second wife, Kate.

In an interview with *Melody Maker*, he explained: "We've been working together for eight years, and the whole thing seemed like a never-ending story. Then one morning I woke up and I asked myself why I went along with all these hectic schedules. Then I thought of singing my own songs, and I drove around Ireland in my Land Rover and sang my songs in pubs, and I had a lot of fun with that. And these experiences also made me realise that my songs weren't suitable for The Faces anymore, and that was when we split."

At least his years with The Faces had been lucrative financially and in that respect Ronnie was able to fulfil two of his great dreams: he bought a farm on the Welsh border near Shrewsbury – The Fishpool – and a mobile recording studio called Lane's Mobile Studio (LMS). Ronnie had purchased a streamlined mobile home/truck in the United States (he probably remembered the first Ry Cooder album; also, spot the LMS on Ronnie's album *One For The Road*) and had it transferred to England to re-equip it with the help of sound engineer Ron Nevison (who later came to fame as producer of Jefferson Starship, UFO, Survivor etc). In British musicians' circles the LMS was soon in demand. Not just Ronnie's own productions, but also The Who's *Quadrophenia*, Bad Company's and Chilli Willi's debut albums as well as Eric Clapton's *Rainbow Concert* were produced with the LMS, in part or in their entirety.

But Ronnie had more projects and ideas going at the time. For one thing, there was his own new band that could assist him in playing his own songs again at long last. On top of that, there was a special kind of enterprise unseen and unheard of on the scene. It was meant to be something extraordinary: a synthesis between live concert and variety show, but without falling into the traps of grandeur and perfectionism. It was the birth of the Passing Show, a kind of rock'n'roll circus with clowns and fire eaters who travel the land in gypsy coaches.

In September 1973, Ronnie presented his complete seven-piece backing band, who he could finally call Slim Chance – instead of, as intended, the earlier Faces: Kevin Westlake (guitar, vocals), Billy Livsey (keys), Bruce Rowland (drums), Jimmy Jewel (sax, an old school tie, by the way, of Hollie Bob Elliott's – both Jimmy and Bobby were termed "musically hopeless" by their old lady teacher!), Chrissy Stewart (bass), Benny Gallagher (guitar, accordion) and Graham Lyle (guitar, banjo, mandolin, vocals).

While Ronnie's brother Stan and roadie Russel Schlagbaum (a Faces 'token') organised the setting-up and co-ordination of The Passing Show, Slim Chance were busy rehearsing on Ronnie's Welsh farm. On 5 November, 1973 – Guy Fawkes' Day – the 'Penny For The Guy' festival on London's Clapham Common saw the debut concert, including the premiere of the first single. 'How Come' came out on 16 November, backed by 'Tell Everyone', a ballad once interpreted by Rod Stewart (the British EP version also contains the title 'Done This One Before').

During the same month, the band's first TV appearance materialised in the *Russell Harty Show*, as well as an invitation to a session in the BBC Studios. Everything was going brilliantly: 'How Come', a swinging vaudeville number with humorous lyrics about superstition, managed the British charts with surprising ease, reaching a respectable Number Eleven on 12 January, 1974 (according to other sources even Number Three).

Ronnie was the talk of the town again. Roy Harper invited him to a notable session, which took place on 14 February – St Valentine's Day – in London's Rainbow Theatre with, among others, Jimmy Page and Keith Moon. In mid March, Ronnie went on a tentative tour with Slim Chance, featuring Biddy Wright on bass instead of Chrissy Stewart, who had only been 'borrowed' from Spooky Tooth. The Passing Show programme, meanwhile, was complete. The risky project, in which Ronnie had invested almost all his financial resources, was due to start at the end of May with a summer tour, and just in time, a second single 'The Poacher' was lifted from the previously announced debut album.

Things were going so well that something had to give and, a fortnight before the first gig in Marlow, Buckinghamshire on 27 May, 1974, Gallagher and Lyle left. At short notice, folk duo Robin Lucas and Drew McCullouch with several singles to their credit, who had been engaged for the Passing Show in their own right, joined Slim Chance.

Still, after only two months on the road, Ronnie was forced to cancel the circus project, in spite of some enthusiastic reaction by a provincial audience which was far from spoilt by entertainment. And it wasn't just a stormy summer that was to blame for its failure: "I couldn't hold it up...because I didn't have any more money. It was as simple as that. We were flogging everything in the end just to buy enough diesel to move the show...and I had to worry about the toilets and the firemen coming round and saying 'This ain't right'..."

Ronnie also had some bad luck with the second single, 'The Poacher'. Until mid June, the song just about managed a chart position for a few weeks and only reached Number Thirty-Six (15 June, 1974). Ronnie blamed this disappointment on a BBC strike which had led to the cancellation of the crucial, sales-boosting *Top Of The Pops*, for which 'The Poacher' had already been nominated. Meanwhile bass player Biddy Wright, who had come in in time to record the album, left during the tour and was replaced by Steve Bingham.

After a lot of effort had been put into it, the album *Anymore For Anymore* (London bus conductors' old ticket sales slogan) appeared in July 1974. Like all of Ronnie's solo albums, it was recorded at The Fishpool with his own mobile studio. And you can actually hear the relaxed country atmosphere, as a note on the back cover points out: "Any rumble on *Anymore For Anymore* is wind in the microphone, please do not adjust your set. Ta all."

The LP met with good reviews throughout. It certainly got off to a good start with 'Careless Love', a country blues classic, mostly viewed as a traditional, but sometimes credited to WC Handy. There are countless lyrical variations, almost all of them about lost love. Ronnie's version comes over as swingy and optimistic. Accordion, honky tonk piano and a snappy sax solo by Jimmy Jewel at the end give the slightly over-used classic its necessary drive. At a more relaxed pace the Passing Show goes on with 'Don't You Cry For Me', a decidedly melancholic ballad which almost offsets the optimistic atmosphere of the opener. The song fades out after yet another Jim Jewell sax solo with an acoustic guitar instrumental passage, which serves as a bridge for 'Bye And Bye (Gonna See The King)' where again the collection picks up speed. Graham Lyle comes in with a bottleneck guitar and puts his brilliant stamp on the entire song. This Lane composition has a religious touch highlighted by gospel elements, but there are also hints of skiffle.

Next, 'Silk Stockings' is a lively, simple, almost nursery rhyme-type number which Ronnie wrote with Kevin Westlake. This leads into 'The Poacher', the second single. Jimmy Horowitz, courtesy of Long John Baldry's studio and stage gang, fitted this song with a comparatively complicated arrangement of oboes and strings. His help seemed crucial for the song's impact, but as a follow-up to 'How Come', it bombed, much to Ronnie's disappointment.

A wonderful love song from the pen of American Folk singer Derrol Adams follows. Adams is rumoured to have custom-made 'Roll On Babe' exclusively for Ronnie. It's a real 'train song' with an addictive fiddle-banjo-Dobro rhythm that causes the wheels rolling over tracks effect, nicely delivering passengers to 'Tell Everyone', the ballad first interpreted by Rod Stewart on The Faces' *Long Player* album. Lane's version isn't necessarily better; it's Jewell's saxophone which easily steals the show.

'Amelia Earheart's Last Flight', which comes next, is black comedy about "the first lady in the sky", a female American pilot who presumably crashed and drowned in the Atlantic Ocean in 1937 while trying to fly around the world. Ian Matthews' band, Plainsong, had put this track down on record in 1972, but Ronnie's arrangement, a country waltz with soppy background vocals and Jewell's cool soprano sax, stresses the cheeky humour missing from the earlier version.

Maintaining the upbeat and flying themes, the title track is an airy happy-go-lucky number, very folky and with a catchy melody. Apart from Gallagher's accordion, it's the acoustic guitars and the seriously sweet background vocals that fascinate.

Acting as a bridge towards the final number, is 'Only A Bird In A

Gilded Cage'. This Tin Pan Alley standard – written by legendary composer Harry Von Tilzer – is barely a minute long here. Ronnie only borrows the (unchanged) chorus, accompanied solely by subtle piano, just long enough to build expectations for 'Chicken Wire', the rousing finale by the complete Slim Chance. Ronnie, who meanwhile worked as a part-time farmer, sings about crazy chickens in his courtyard – at first glance. He also possibly hints at 'chicks' on two legs used for background vocal and other 'services'.

With this album, Ronnie continued the path he had tried to pursue in The Faces of British country rock, catchy but independent of any trends. But the initial success of 'How Come' (which understandably did not appear on the LP) now seemed like a one hit wonder and Slim Chance broke up after the premature end of the Passing Show tour (their last gig went ahead on 1 July in Newcastle).

Ronnie left the mini-label GM Records for Chris Blackwell's Island Records, and till October 1974 he recruited an entirely new Slim Chance, whose members predominantly had a pub rock background: Steve Simpson (guitar, mandolin, fiddle; ex-Tumbleweeds), Charlie Hart (keyboards, violin; ex-Kilburn And The High Roads featuring Ian Dury), Ruan O'Lochlainn (sax, keyboards; ex-Bees Make Honey), Brian Belshaw (bass, ex-Blossom Toes) and Jim Frank (drums). At the turn of 1974/75, this line-up once again embarked on a UK tour, ending up in Ronnie's farm for recording sessions. The resulting album – simply titled *Ronnie Lane's Slim Chance* – was released on 28 February, 1975. A promotional tour and a further appearance on BBC television followed. Meanwhile, Glen le Fleur occupied the drums, but was replaced by Colin Daves as early as March.

Like its predecessor, this second album got rave reviews. In the German *Sounds*, Teja Schwaner found a fitting characterisation of what Ronnie's music was all about: "Unpretentious beyond belief, as uncommercial as 'not for sale', likable like 'I'm lost for words' and as stress-relieving as 'more relaxation is unheard of'." Schwaner was right, too, at least as far as one point went. The LP, which in terms of the players' inventiveness and musical diversity was superior to their debut, almost bombed. But Ronnie had again written some excellent songs.

An ingratiating little song, 'Little Piece Of Nothing' shows off Charlie Hart's precise fiddle for the intro. The 'little piece' it is aimed at is

Ronnie's young daughter.

'Stone' follows, the third version of Ronnie's philosophical views of reincarnation, arranged in a very folky style. Among its highlights are Steve Simpson's mandolin and again the fiddle of Charlie Hart. This is more dynamic – but still more pleasant than the rough Faces version.

A real drinking anthem, 'Bottle Of Brandy' was originally by the little known Isaacs Family. Ronnie's singing is unusually strained – the stars are his drinking mates in the background – so perhaps it's fitting that 'Street Gang' is an instrumental which rests his voice. A charming bossa nova, penned by Laney and Ruan O'Lochlainn, it is packed with a lot of drive and fun-conscious passion.

Back to normality briefly, 'Anniversary' is a mid tempo rocker characterised by Brian Belshaw's elastic bass lines, although the finale is dominated by fiddle and organ. Then it's old-time rhythms once more in 'I'm Gonna Sit Right Down And Write Myself A Letter', a swing classic sporting a Dixie clarinet, fiddle and honky tonk piano, all matching the humourous lyrics. As a pointed contrast to Ronnie's tribute to his great idol Fats Waller, it's followed by 'I'm Just A Country Boy', a song performed by Harry Belafonte as early as 1954, and countrified later in the Don Williams version. The legendary Band also interpreted this on their 1993 comeback album *Jericho*, but here Ronnie treats the song with tons of charm and feeling and without ever drifting off into the depths of Nashville schlock.

Another style change comes in 'Ain't No Lady', a sort of relationship rockabilly, with racing sax solos by co-author O'Lochlainn, which stands as further proof of Ronnie's tongue-in-cheek humour. From rockabilly it's now the turn of 'Blue Monday' to get the Laney treatment, this time as a competent, Cajun-influenced interpretation. Fats Domino's smash is another departure compared to the Georgie Fame EP version Ronnie so admired.

Back on familiar territory style-wise, 'Give Me A Penny' features a catchy melody that would be applied again by Ronnie for the song 'Annie' on *Rough Mix*. Steve Simpson's mandolin dominates proceedings, while piano and organ provide a matching sound foundation.

Yet another cover version follows, and yet another Chuck Berry rock'n'roller. In a Louisiana groove not unlike Emmylou Harris's version, 'You Never Can Tell' offers finger-snapping joys driven by Glen le Fleur's drumming until the next track, 'Tin And Tambourine', kills the pace. It starts as a brooding love lament, with mandolin and a harmonica which speeds the song up, only to slow it down again before the final fast verse.

Finally, a children's song, 'Single Saddle', is chosen as the closing number, sung by Ronnie with his lady. Snatches of country life open the track, probably recorded right at the front door of The Fishpool – then hand-clapping, mandolin, accordion, a little mumbling, someone whistles. All this is simple yet effective, and a strangely touching climax.

The US version of the album has a different track listing. For instance, Ronnie's new arrangement of 'Brother Can You Spare Me A Dime', composed by Gorney and Harburg and made popular by Bing Crosby, was commissioned for the 1974 British Hollywood documentary of the same name, displaying movie sequences ranging from 1929 to World War II.

Sales were not great but Ronnie refused to get depressed over yet another disappointment and tried third time lucky. In the autumn of 1975, Slim Chance – now down to a six-piece as O'Lochlainn had left – retreated to Ronnie's farm for rehearsals. While the recording sessions for the new album *One For The Road* were in full swing, news of Immediate's reissue of The Small Faces' classic 'Itchycoo Park' hit the farm. The single stayed in the charts for eleven weeks and, quite unexpectedly, even reached the Top Ten (Number Nine on 13 December, 1975).

Kenney Jones, who like Ian McLagan was looking for new musical perspectives, had daydreams about a reunion of the original band. Steve Marriott, who had ended his Humble Pie era in the meantime and pursued solo projects with only modest success, was quite taken with this idea. Only Ronnie couldn't get used to the thought of re-uniting The Small Faces, but agreed to the production of video clips for both 'Itchycoo Park' and 'Lazy Sunday' (which was about to be re-issued too), as well as taking part in playing a few gigs, just for fun and for old times' sake: "And then they started producing contracts and things, and I didn't want to know about that. Remember that The Small Faces left me, not the other way round."

Anyhow, much to the chagrin of the others, Ronnie preferred to concentrate all his energies on Slim Chance. For him, The Small Faces era was definitely gone, although there would be one song on the first reunion album co-written by him: 'Find It'.

On 9 January, 1976, *One For The Road* was released at long last, the first album to consist entirely of Lane material. It was met with sympathy rather than excitement and brilliant ideas and witty arrangements were few and far between, even though the quality of the songs left nothing to be desired.

'Don't Try And Change My Mind', an incredibly catchy mid tempo rock song, opens the collection, with a confident Ronnie singing, solid fiddle and mandolin backing, fitting breaks and an easy flow that Slim Chance rarely matched so perfectly, yet effortlessly

'Thirty-Second Street' slows things down, but this cheeky, funny number gains momentum with a dominant harmonica and a wailing chorus, with occasional laughter in the background. Likewise, the title for 'Snake' also seems to appear from way back in the farm scenery, only to develop into a lively folk'n'roll, displaying honky tonk piano off-set with acoustic guitars.

By comparison, 'Burnin' Summer' is maudlin, a touching ballad with fitting, sparse instrumentation. Ronnie gives it all he's got, almost suffering through to its peaceful fade-out. But then the title song puts the foot down with a hot mandolin, solid rhythm section and tumultuous chorus singing. A thrilling melody urges listeners irresistibly to join in, and the pace is maintained throughout, even continuing in 'Steppin' An' Reelin' (The Wedding)'. This cunning song is a declaration of love, aimed at Ronnie's wife of the time, Kate, most probably. Sadly, six minutes is too long to hold the attention of the audience.

Continuing the romantic strain, 'Harvest Home' is a lovers' instrumental featuring songbirds, dreamy strings and subdued accordion, all designed to convey self-contained life in the country musically. You can almost smell the fresh hay on the fields around The Fishpool.

Staying with the idea of hay and barns, 'Nobody's Listening' is glum country rock with unintended thematic relevance courtesy of Slim Chance's ongoing absence from the charts. There's the welcome, overdue sound of electric guitars and drummer Colin Davey gets a chance to let loose before the mood goes Cajun again in 'G' Morning'. An up-tempo number, it sees a return to farm sounds, but would also fit the swamps of Louisiana. It's an optimistic end to the album, religiously faithful with flutes, a mandolin and the inevitable accordion.

The whole record isn't bad at all, but in spite of a lengthy promotional tour in the spring of 1976, it shipped only very limited amounts, much to Ronnie's disappointment: "Oh, that was disastrous for me. It wasn't for them [Island Records]. When I had *One For The Road* out we were on tour and we had good houses and a lot of people were interested. Then at the end of the show all these kids would come round and say, 'We're trying to get your album.' I got on to the record company and back comes the answer: 'We can't make the shops order the album until it's in the charts.' But how could the record get into the charts if people couldn't buy it anywhere?"

In any case, Ronnie's financial situation deteriorated dramatically. Money being tight, the release of the soundtrack album for the Canadian movie *Mahoney's Last Stand* was more than welcome – Ronnie had recorded it during his Faces period around 1972, with Ron Wood and numerous stars of the British rock scene. Apart from Pete Townshend and Family/Blind Faith's Rick Grech among others, long standing band buddies like Kenney Jones, Ian McLagan and later Slim Chance sidemen Bruce Rowland, Benny Gallagher and sixth Stone Ian Stewart took part.

The melodrama, starring Sam Waterston and Alexis Kanner, who doubled as director, was only shown in North America. Apart from the obviously required instrumentals, there are some songs on the album which undeniably carry Ronnie's stamp: 'From The Late To The Early', 'Just For A Moment' and a rocking version of 'Chicken Wired', which later – somehow more restrained – appeared on Ronnie's first solo album.

In the interim, Pete Townshend had heard about Ronnie's financial troubles and suggested a joint LP production. Ronnie had been Pete's pal since the days of The Small Faces and had of course supplied his song 'Evolution' (a lyrically extended version of 'Stone') to his friend's first solo album *Who Came First*. Furthermore, both shared a mutual interest in Indian philosophy and were active disciples of the guru Meher Baba (who died in 1969).

The resulting duo album *Rough Mix* was recorded during the winter of 1976 and spring 1977 with a hand-picked cast of session musicians, among others Stones drummer Charlie Watts, Ian Stewart (piano) and Eric Clapton. At long last, Pete Townshend was able to let go with some songs unsuited for or untypical of The Who. As for Ronnie, whose chances of getting his Island contract renewed after the commercial disappointments were more than grim, he was banking on a new beginning. Five out of eleven songs had been penned by Townshend, Ronnie composed four. 'Till The Rivers All Run Dry' is a venerable Don Williams classic, and the only joint effort was the instrumental title track. The autobiographical 'April Fool' and the newly arranged version of 'Give Me A Penny' which received a new set of lyrics and was now called 'Annie' – all breathed that warmth typical of Ronnie's ballads. In his vehemently positive *Sounds* review, Peter Urban concluded: "Light the fire, baby, with Townshend and Lane you'll get through the coldest winter night."

Even while the *Rough Mix* sessions continued, Ronnie's newly linked contacts with Eric Clapton led to a definite musical partnership (apart from that, Ronnie acted as best man for Clapton and Patti Harrison's wedding). Initially this collaboration was limited to pub gigs in Shropshire (unannounced of course), which was the neighbouring county to Ronnie's Welsh residence.

On 15 February, 1977, Eric and Ronnie's Slim Chance got together for a benefit concert in Cranleigh Village – under the mystic, unassuming pseudonym of Eddie Earthquake And The Tremors. Eric returned the compliment at the end of April during his Hammersmith Odeon gig when he asked Ronnie onto the stage for a final jam session. Subsequently, Slim Chance played the (thankless) support slot on Eric's European tour during June and July that year. Ronnie and his band weren't quite booed off stage by the Clapton fans – who apparently knew very little about their idol's love of country rock – but the audience weren't exactly open-minded towards Slim Chance's comparatively 'good time' ramblings.

Back home in England, Ronnie underwent a medical check-up. For some time, peculiar complaints had plagued him, especially short-time paralysis symptoms. The doctors came up with a shattering diagnosis: suspected MS (multiple sclerosis), an as yet incurable disease of the nervous system, which is known to be terminal sooner or later. The shock had a deep effect on Ronnie. He disbanded Slim Chance, retreated from the music business and proceeded to breed sheep on his farm.

Meanwhile, *Rough Mix* had appeared at long last (16 September,

1977), as had Roy Harper's *Bullinamingvase* for which Ronnie had contributed vocals to 'Watford Gap'. *Rough Mix* didn't exactly storm the charts, but sold excellently in the United States. After that, little was heard of Ronnie for two years. He was only spotted once as a guest at Alexis Korner's fiftieth birthday party (19 April, 1978). During the party session, which was filmed by the German WDR TV *Rockpalast* team, Ronnie also met old acquaintances like Eric Clapton, Ian Stewart and Chris Farlowe.

Dealing with chickens and sheep in the Welsh provinces, away from rock's metropolis of London seemed far from boring and frustrating to Ronnie, and he used his time for writing songs. Quite how long this (re)creational break was going to last was partly beyond his control, as was to be expected. The bad luck that seemed to stick to his feet, cursed Ronnie further during the ice cold winter of 1978/9. Many of his animals died and he was forced to sell a substantial part of his estate. Fed up with his ecologically sound country life for the time being, London beckoned. Numerous friends encouraged Ronnie to attempt a comeback and the small record company GEM Records, which he had a share in, made it possible for him to produce an album. *Melody Maker* also remembered Ronnie and presented a tribute dedicated to him.

A tentative single – 'Kuschty Rye' – co-produced with Pete Townshend, was released in October 1979 and received positive reviews, not just in *Melody Maker*. Further song material for the album *See Me* (originally scheduled to be titled *True Stories*) was subsequently recorded with numerous friends and ex-Slim Chance mates (among them Bruce Rowland, Charlie Hart, Bill Livsey and Steve Simpson). Again, the trusted mobile studio came into use, mainly at The Fishpool. Newcomers at the sessions were the ex-guitarist in Cat Stevens' backing group, Alun Davies (who also co-wrote), and Henry McCullough (guitar, keyboards, mandolin), who Ronnie had met via Roy Harper. And of course, the proceedings weren't complete without Eric Clapton.

A relaxed mid tempo starter in the form of 'One Step' reassures us that nothing much has changed since *One For The Road*. The sprightly lead guitar courtesy of Cal Batchelor lifts the old verse-chorus routine up a bit, while the sweet female background vocals sound like an eco-friendly Moulin Rouge ensemble of Ronnie's old tent circus, the

Passing Show – long legs in sheep's wool suspenders.

'Good Ol' Boys Boogie' may be less catchy than the warm-hearted 'One Step', but it more than makes up for it with an unusual rhythm structure and an array of breaks. Certainly worth getting into, weird arrangement gems like Charlie Hart's rocking accordion and Batchelor's cutting guitar grow on the listener with a strange fascination. Drummer and fellow farmer Bruce Rowland drums with the panache which made him a first choice for the era's new traditionalists like Joan Armatrading.

A sad, waltzy ballad follows. Ronnie interprets 'Lad's Got Money' in all its necessary melancholia. Eric Clapton shines here with some brilliant lead guitar, and you can hear London's eternally underrated R&B lady Carol Grimes growl in the background, setting the mood for the next track, 'She's Leaving'. Another one on the rather sad side, it features massive fiddle presence for which Charlie Hart is joined by old Slim Chance buddy Steve Simpson (who plays with Micky Moody and Roger Chapman these days). Mel Collins' saxophone is a fitting symbol of utter loneliness – whoever the lamented lady is, she may not come back and there's a heartbreaking fade-out.

By a long stretch, the best song on this album is 'Barcelona', a joint composition by Ronnie and Eric Clapton, who picks with the tenderness shown on his much later *Unplugged*. An exquisite melody sticks in the mind right away, Ronnie sings with feeling, while Carol Grimes tackles the duet's second voice with sensitivity. With its elaborate string arrangement, this reminds us of 'The Poacher'.

'Kuschty Rye' – Romany for 'good fellow' – had been selected as the seven inch taster in 1979. Its catchy tune is characterised by Lane's singing as well as Hart's trademark squeeze box. The female background vocals mean serious business here – contrary to 'One Step' these are slick city chicks, as Ronnie's old pal Marriott would have concluded with a mean chuckle.

Next is 'Don't Tell Me Now', a strangely structured song with an ever so laid back rhythm – JJ Cale on valium – but extremely atmospheric indeed. There's nice vocal backing for Ronnie's fragile singing, enhanced again by the characteristic accordion sounds of Charlie Hart before the altogether perkier B-side to 'Kuschty Rye' arrives. 'You're So Right' comes as a short, unassuming up-tempo number, sporting Bill Livsey's nice little Floyd Cramer piano theme for

BBC2's playlist.

'Only You' follows, an unyielding, rolling New Orleans ballad that owes more than its title to The Platters' number: similarities in rhythm'n'romance evoke memories of their old soft soul classic. Lane doesn't just work on guitar and vocals this time. Via overdubs he also took over the drumming chores. Mel Collins reliably adds his tender saxophone playing, Fats Domino is acted out by the rather slimmer Charlie Hart on the ebonies and ivories.

An attractive sequel to 'Don't Try And Change My Mind', which opened *One For The Road*, the boogie bass on 'Winning With Women' is identical, but gets new adrenalin from a cheeky acoustic guitar off-beat, courtesy of Alun Davies. Davies even holds his own on the album's finale when he is joined by Eric Clapton. 'Way Up Yonder' is a little known traditional track with happy lyrics and a catchy melody calling for Chas'n'Dave-type pub singalongs. Bill Livsey and Ian Stewart tinker away on their respective pianos.

See Me is a conscious link to the Slim Chance tradition: British country rock with fiddle and accordion – what an absolute anachronism at the height of the New Wave movement. Altogether though, the album didn't have the tunes to activate the faithful.

But elsewhere in music the happy-go-lucky vein of the majority of songs had long been missed – it was a sentiment largely ignored by rock's pretentious acts as well as the safety pin revolution, and the New Romantics with their tinny synths. For their mood, 'Kuschty Rye', 'Barcelona' and 'Good Ol' Boys Boogie' are real departures which rock traditionalists should have absorbed with fascination.

Still, a release all over Europe – originally planned by the distributor, RCA – was cancelled. In England, where the album appeared in spring 1980, it was hardly noticed, or bought for that matter. At the turn of the new year, Ronnie had once again picked up his bass: as a member of Paul McCartney's all-star Rockestra conglomeration he showed his goodwill for sensible benefit gigs during the finale of Concerts For The People Of Kampuchea at London's Hammersmith Odeon (now the Labatts Apollo), on 29 December, 1979.

Undeterred by the modest commercial success of his *See Me* album, Ronnie put together yet another band for club gigs in and around London. Even the German *Rockpalast* assisted Laney's comeback attempt and invited him to Cologne for a studio session. The concert on 19 March, 1980, was hampered slightly by technical problems, but has since been resurrected and repeated on the German network. The Ronnie Lane Band consisted of Ian Stewart, Henry McCullough, Bruce Rowland, Charlie Hart and Chrissie Stewart as well as two black sax players, Mick Carless senior and junior. For several months, the line-up appeared all over the UK. After that, Ronnie was forced to lie low.

It turned out later that the suspected MS diagnosis seemed was confirmed as the symptoms intensified. Often he had trouble moving his hands and playing the guitar. Nevertheless, Ronnie played further gigs as far as his physical state would allow. On 29 July that year he appeared in London's famous Marquee Club with the following line-up: Chrissie Stewart, Charlie Hart, Big Dot, Mick Weaver, Bruce Rowland and veterans Brian Knight and Ian 'Stu' Stewart. "It was Brian and Stu who started the Stones. I used to go and watch them when I was in knee-pants", was how he introduced his old idols.

"Quite a big band," Ronnie would comment in his nonchalant way after the show. "You know I'm doing a better job than the Musicians' Union keeping musicians in employment!" During March 1981 he had a one-week club residency in Berlin, after which his health deteriorated periodically.

Then, in September 1981, his path crossed that of an old colleague he had left fighting and arguing: Steve Marriott (who since the split of the Small Faces Mark II in 1978 had mainly lived in Atlanta, Georgia) suddenly came to London. His second Humble Pie project had also been put on hold, but Steve was restless after a forced holiday following serious health problems (see Chapter 7). The idea for a joint album brought Steve and Ronnie together for the time being. With Jim Leverton (bass) and Dave Hines (drums) – both Marriott partners in the short-lived Blind Drunk and Firm projects of 1978 and 79 – Mick Weaver (keys) as well as Mick Green of Pirates fame, they recorded a classic low budget album in the Corbett Theatre in Loughton, Essex.

As Ronnie told us in 1989: "They weren't demos, we made a real tape with the mobile. But it's all lost, so there you go!" The proposed title *The Midgets Strike Back* revealed it all. But there was no record company in sight willing to release the tapes, and what's more, the old quarrels between Steve and Ronnie soon flared up again.

And Ronnie's state of health was worsening. Bill Wyman, who visited him at home, was devastated. He and his Rolling Stones decided to support their mate financially and cover the cost of a therapeutic stay in Florida. Ronnie could stay in Bill's business associate Fred Sessler's Miami Venom Institute (where Keith Richards' aunt had been treated previously) – though for only a few months, by which time the venom injections had at least stopped his physical deterioration. Unfortunately the US Food and Drug Administration closed the private clinic at short notice on account of an unlicensed diluted snake venom therapy.

Embittered, Ronnie returned to London, where he found refuge at the house of his partner at the time, Boo Oldfield. He was completely depressed and helpless, having to cope with two failed marriages, and financially all but finished, partly because of tax debts. His treasured sixteen-track mobile studio had been taken apart (again) and looted by punks, under the ironic suspicion that Ronnie belonged to the big profiteers of the rock-biz. On top of all these mounting problems there was the painful, hopeless disease. At last, Ronnie's misery found its way into the public consciousness when the American journalist Kurt Loder conducted a moving interview with him, which was published in *Rolling Stone* on 5 August, 1982: "How can I describe it? Can you imagine the strands of your hair hurting? That's what happens. And when you blink, it's like your eyelids are made of sandpaper. I was quite prepared to feel bad, like with the flu or mumps. But I've never had anything like this. This is like hell itself."

Ronnie blamed the wild, hedonistic lifestyle he had pursued during the (Small) Faces era for his disease: drugs, alcohol and the road stress of a working live band – groupies included. But his mother used to suffer from MS too, so it seemed obvious to him as well as to his doctors that he wasn't immune to this wicked illness. He found comfort in reading the Bible during these hard times. A musicians' reception in EMI's Abbey Road Studios was – for the time being – his last public showing. After 22 September, 1982, he disappeared for almost an entire year.

Nevertheless, his mates from happier days had not forgotten Ronnie, and the *Rolling Stone* interview must have made them realise they had to do something for him. The fact that in London expensive technology existed for the treatment of MS (for example, hyper oxygenation), gave Ronnie's girl friend Boo the idea of staging a benefit concert. Bill Wyman and Eric Clapton offered to organise the project.

Meanwhile, Ronnie had established contact with the self-help organisation Action For Research Into Multiple Sclerosis (ARMS), which was supposed to benefit from the proceeds of the concert. Still, first and foremost this became a concert for Ronnie. After months of preparations under the direction of the tried and tested producer Glyn Johns, things were finally ready by September 1983. The Ronnie Lane Appeal For ARMS – that was the official title – went ahead on 20 September, 1983 in the legendary Royal Albert Hall in London – in front of six thousand excited fans.

The list of appearing artists was indeed impressive: Steve Winwood, Bill Wyman, Charlie Watts, Kenney Jones, Andy Fairweather-Low, Chris Stainton, Ray Cooper and many more. For the first time ever, the three Yardbirds lead guitarists (who in the Sixties had succeeded each other) appeared together: Eric Clapton, Jeff Beck and Jimmy Page. As a roaring finale there was a tremendous jam session, at the end of which Ronnie (restricted by a wheelchair) was helped onto the stage to sing a moving version of the Leadbelly classic 'Goodnight Irene'.

The following night saw a second edition of the concert due to public demand and because the Prince of Wales had kindly requested it! And that wasn't going to be the end of it. During December 1983, a complete charity tour went ahead through the United States, organised at short notice by the promoter Bill Graham, with nine appearances in Dallas, San Francisco, Los Angeles and New York. Instead of a preoccupied Steve Winwood, Joe Cocker and Paul Rodgers took over lead vocals. (Incidentally, during the tour Rodgers and Page discussed the basic idea for the formation of The Firm, pinching the name from Lane's buddy Marriott in the process.)

Again, Ronnie was part of the team. *Rolling Stone*, running a cover story on the ARMS tour, called it simply "Concert Of The Year". By autumn 1984, the video recording of the Royal Albert Hall concert at long last appeared in the shops. At the end of that year, Ronnie was able to present a one million dollar cheque of video and concert profits to the newly founded US section of the charity. For the time being, he remained in the States to help getting the US leg of the organisation off the ground. Apart from these activities, he underwent treatment in Houston, Texas and was able to work at the local radio station – KLOL – as the presenter of a special MS programme.

In the meantime, Bill Wyman had initiated the gathering of a bunch of half-forgotten British rock musicians to continue as an ARMS charity band named Willie And The Poor Boys. A debut album was released in 1985, featuring many friends and band mates from better times: apart from Wyman, there were Mickey Gee and Geraint Watkins (from Dave Edmunds' band), Andy Fairweather-Low, Kenney Jones, Paul Rodgers and Chris Rea. Ronnie was scheduled to be involved in the production of a second LP.

But that was to remain wishful thinking. Without warning, Ronnie was absorbed in a scandal that almost ruined his good reputation. The US section of ARMS was forced to wind up after the accounts were reportedly run incorrectly. On the grounds of alleged embezzlement Ronnie was under suspicion as well. Mae Nacol, the former manager of ARMS USA, had accused him of premeditated advantage. Ronnie was actually in the position to disprove these charges, but the scandal deeply affected him. The very fact that he himself – as the initiator and victim – had been massively and falsely accused, hit him hard.

For several months, Ronnie again stayed in London, but he didn't like the atmosphere there anymore and soon headed for Texas again. "I found that Texas was kind of happier, a happier place for me to live in my condition. Even though it's hot, as long as I stay in air conditioning, it's okay. England is so dreary, you know – we have twenty-four hours of summer, that's all we get in England. And in Texas, you see a lot of sunshine!"

What he didn't want though, was to move back to Houston, the hectic metropolis with its hot and humid climate. He felt this time drawn to Austin, the centre of the Texan music scene. Soon, in spring 1986, he met a bunch of interesting people, among them Radio KLBJ's DJ Jody Denberg. His new friends were proud to have a member of the still legendary Faces in their city and Ronnie's general well-being suddenly began to improve. Once again he felt like making a little music again, if only for the fun of it. Together with Denberg and a few friends, he formed the Seven Samurai, who were less a band than a loose conglomeration, covering standards and Lane songs on acoustic instruments.

Ronnie ardently watched the musical activities in and around Austin, and before long he was part of the local music scene. One day he happened to enter a studio complex where young musicians were busy rehearsing: "I walked into this studio, and there was a bunch of kids there. When they saw me walk in, the lead guitarist played the introduction to 'Itchycoo Park', and it kind of chuffed me, I suppose. Anyway, I got to know them, and they became my band. As Bobby Keys was not in The Rolling Stones, and Keith Richards was yet to put his finger up, he was able to come and play with me, which was a really good experience. And I love Bobby Keys!"

The new enterprise happened under the heading Ronnie Lane And The Tremors, and as early as spring 1987 they pursued a club tour through the United States which was received extremely well and was appreciated by the national press as well. Physically, Ronnie felt better than he had for some considerable time, but still had to be careful not to overdo things. He used to cover half a gig, singing 'British Beat' standards like 'Shakin' All Over' or The Kinks' 'Tired Of Waiting For You', his own old songs – 'Ooh La La'', 'April Fool' – and newly penned numbers like 'Across The Rio Grande', done in 1981 for Midgets Strike Back.

But the Tremors project wasn't quite his cup of tea. They played too rock'n'roll orientated for his liking. As early as his Slim Chance days Ronnie had had a soft spot for Cajun music, especially the black, Zydeco variety and its protagonist Clifton Chenier. Now firmly based in his chosen exile, he got into Tex Mex – to know it is to love it – the rockabilly-influenced dance music of the tejanos – Mexicans living in Texas. Both Cajun and Tex Mex music put the accordion way up front, and thus Ronnie went looking for an accordion player and other musicians for yet another band.

Those he found after the March 1988 Austin Award Music Show, a locally important talent contest. Ronnie had joined young rock band The True Believers on stage and presented 'Ooh La La', accompanied by ex-Television guitarist Richard Wright. Two of The True Believers, Alejandro Escovedo (guitar, vocals) and JD Foster (bass) wanted to take part in Ronnie's new project, and further local heroes joined, among them accordion player and singer/songwriter Randy Banks. Ronnie Lane's Tex Mex Slim Chance was complete.

The first gigs were promising, but Ronnie didn't appear satisfied, he wanted the ensemble sound more 'traditional' and folk orientated. With Irish folk aficionado Rich Brotherton (mandolin, guitar) and the fiddle queen Susan Voelz plus ex-Tremors bassman Ronnie Johnson, he was convinced he had found the right bunch of people. As The Ronnie Lane Band he resumed his East Coast club circuit, and at long last the recording side of things began to get hot. Ronnie had sufficient new material, and what's more he had established contacts with producer Ian Horn (Ian

Dury, among others), but didn't want to act under pressure: "Personally, I'm very critical of everything I have already done and I don't know how long it's gonna be before I'm satisfied to release anything, but something will be released. But it's gotta be good I think. I can't put a lukewarm album out after all this, you know? I'm not going to play that stupid record company game of 'You got three months to make an album, man…'."

With good intentions, recording plans for a new album remained on the shelf. As small consolation, the first three solo (or rather) Slim Chance albums got a CD release, if only in Japan. But this presented a sufficient cause for a promotional tour of the land of the rising sun. For this purpose, Ronnie formed yet another backing group, including accordion ace Ponty Bone (with several solo albums to his credit as well as collaborations with Joe Ely and Timbuk 3), guitarist Daniel Castro, drummer Lance Womack and Scott Garber on bass.

Following his spring 1991 tours of Japan and the American north east and midwest, Ronnie finally found his way back into the studios. His agent Paul Swick had acquainted Ronnie with John Lombardo, founder member of the new folk outfit 10,000 Maniacs and now going out as John And Mary with Mary Ramsey. John liked Ronnie's songs as well as his voice. So Laney ended up singing backing vocals for the ballad 'We Have Nothing'.

The album *Victory Gardens* containing this track was issued on the Rykodisc label in the summer of 1991, which also showed an interest in releasing a *Best Of Ronnie Lane* compilation CD as well as a collection of live recordings from the BBC archives, but so far this has not materialised, unfortunately.

Recently, Ronnie (with his wife Susan – they got married in 1989) has gone into hibernation again and has obviously retired from all musical activities. England and the British Press, who have ignored him since the ARMS project, he doesn't want to know about. He was especially hurt by an article in the *News Of The World*, who had warmed up the alleged fraud case and portrayed him as a broken hero, an impoverished, diseased vegetable.

Ronnie himself only mentions the subject of his MS disease very reluctantly in his rare interviews, and tries to live with it as best he can. According to a certainly well-meant statement by Bill Wyman, Ronnie's surprising if momentary recovery at the end of the Eighties had been due to the renewal of all Ronnie's tooth fillings. Indeed, dental work on MS patients has led to speculation that perhaps a few MS sufferers had contracted mercury poisoning – from the mercury contained in their dental fillings.

But Ronnie didn't improve any further after his dental work was done. Friends and fans had been hoping that the medical findings Bill had reported would lead to fact and final recovery. But the news that Ronnie had to seek treatment in a Houston hospital in February 1993 sadly seemed to confirm his suffering from MS once more. His general state of health had deteriorated, and in Houston he received hyperbaric oxygen treatment which is specific for MS.

Since then, he seems okay bearing in mind the circumstances. He began to resume songwriting, for instance collaborating with the singer/songwriter Brad Brobisky, who had founded The Keepers in Austin, with Ponty Bone and other Texas rock hot shots in the beginning of 1994. Two songs from these sessions finally found their way onto that band's debut album *Looking For A Sign*, with Ronnie supplying a modest part as a background singer.

After from the hot climate in Texas, Ronnie relocated to the small town of Trinidad in Colorado down by the Rocky Mountains, a move initiated by his wife in mid 1994. Since then, he's been hiding out there as a virtual recluse, with spectacular musical activities allegedly out of the question. This was where Ronnie, frail and probably never going to pick up his work again, celebrated his fiftieth birthday on 1 April. His long-awaited autobiography, which he has been busy writing on and off, is apparently on ice.

CHAPTER SIX
Steve Marriott
All Stars And Studio Parties

A&M might have thought that work in Steve Marriott's Clear Sound Studios was meant for a *Thunderbox* follow-up, but Marriott was in no particular hurry to release a record – "the fun is making them," he quipped. He wasn't even working with all of Pie backing him, but jamming through wild all-nighters for all sorts of projects. From the end of 1974, he preferred Snape's drummer Ian Wallace, who would re-appear later with The Steve Marriott All Stars. Of the *Thunderbox* line-up, Mel Collins (sax), The Blackberries' Venetta Fields and Clydie King and Pie mate Clem Clempson remained. Further guests were Alexis Korner, Boz Burrell (soon to be Bad Company's bass), Tim Hinkley (piano),and also BJ Cole who, after 1970's *Humble Pie III/Salomé*, had also graced *Rock On* and *Eat It* with his pedal steel guitar.

A brief flashback: Ian 'Wally' Wallace, Boz Burrell and Mel Collins had left King Crimson after a Pie-supporting 1973 tour and joined Alexis Korner and Peter Thorup, whose blues duo opened for Humble Pie, calling themselves Snape as the new five-piece. Steve had enjoyed the gigs, mutual jams and subsequent studio sessions for the band's LP as guesting pianist and backing singer so much that he now persuaded the threesome to join him in his own studios. Ian, Boz and Mel were free after studio and concert dates with Alvin Lee, so they happily agreed. Alvin Lee and his wife Susanne would then become frequent visitors.

While Steve Marriott later insisted that the countless night and day sessions were meant to result in material for an album with Greg Ridley as well as a solo LP, Tim Hinkley remembers the twenty recorded tracks aimed at one particular Marriott project with the provisional title *The Scrubbers*. Probably because of Steve's lyrical hints at the business, or, as Hinkley put it, "to those he felt were controlling his life and career", the

LP tapes as handed over in 1975 were rejected. Steve does sing about "legal eagles" he wants to rot in hell in 'Bluegrass Interval', sure, although that song could have been left off. It seems more likely that A&M's bosses, instead of promoting erratic solo LPs, simply wanted a new Humble Pie album for a contracted tour (which the band in their own chapter described as their most easy-going time together and which was going to be their farewell).

However cynical the music industry always tends to be portrayed, A&M had a point: still looking for a follow-up to *Smokin'*, the last Pie album to be solidly commercial, they were missing a certain coherence on these tapes. How do you sell Phil Spector's soft girl group oldie 'Be My Baby', combined with Muddy Waters' tragic 'Louisiana Blues'? But for the hardcore fans and blues enthusiasts, these tapes – which did not make marketing sense in the age of Glam Rock – are a treasure of styles, moods and pleasures from a twenty-years-on perspective. Cover versions never heard in Steve's or Greg's voice, new songs which re-appeared later in different arrangements as well as genuinely new gems make up an amazing kaleidoscope.

Except for the mentioned guest appearances, Steve, Greg and Tim took complete care of putting the guitars, keyboards, bass and even the drums on tape. Jerry Shirley became a studio zombie via Steve's assembly of tape loops, eternally providing pre-recorded drum grooves for session work whenever Steve didn't feel like supplying his own drum overdubs. Steve had to be that inventive in a period when studios didn't possess all those gadgets like drum computers, as he remembered with a little contempt in some of our Eighties interviews.

The recordings only saw the light of day at the end of 1991 when Greg Ridley and Tim Hinkley had founded their tiny Elastic Cat label, with Kris Gray of Vinyl Village in Barkingside, Essex. Historic as the collection truly was, Elastic Cat soon became annoyingly irregular in supplying all the CDs they had been paid for, and in 1992 the sloppy Indie enterprise disappeared from the British trade registers. Barsa in Spain and Repertoire in Germany have released the album in the meantime.

Steve's long time friend – and trustworthy administrator of the Marriott music heritage – Jim Leverton, had this comment: "Never trust a recording that only exists on a simple cassette copy!" The Elastic Cat certainly did not use, let alone own, the master tapes. Still, the document is pure pleasure, and compared to a lot of vintage Hendrix it's also pure high fidelity!

'Shake', by Sam Cooke, had already been in the early Small Faces set, returning here mid tempo in a dry, slightly heavy blues rock arrangement which Steve later tended to overdo with his DTs. The extremely echoed voice is a little distorted, but this version is short and precise, a kind of slow son of 'Natural Born Bugie'.

Track two was 'Mona'. A typical Bo Diddley beat can be found on this number which The Pretty Things also made famous. This is surely welcome in a collection of Marriott's R&B favourites, like 'Shake', but it could have come in a more structured guise, as Steve's shouts for more "organising" here suggest, too.

'Lend Us A Quid' should be re-named 'The Never-Ending Echo' since by the third track, this gadget is a touch repetitive. On the other hand, Steve's two vocal tracks on this chaotic acoustic ballad result in an interesting delay effect which was most probably not even intended. If Hinkley and Ridley had had the master tapes, they might have gone for one vocal, but then it does give the song a one-off touch. One of the guitars is played with a mandolin touch, Steve's harmonica playing is heartfelt as always, and in terms of the recording, this kind of splicing job was what Macca McCartney got away with in 1970. The lyrics on this remind us that Steve was always complaining that there was never any ready cash coming from US manager Dee Anthony.

At last on 'Send Me Some Lovin'' we get a clean bass-guitar-drums basis for a twelve-bar blues underneath Ridley's wonderfully warm, sorely missed voice. He delivers Lloyd Price's southern lament, a standard which Allan Clarke decided to cover that same year – 1974 – for his eponymous EMI solo album. Hammond and piano are added for maximum effect here, while 'She Moves Me, Man' opts for songbirds and hand-clapping to lead into this John Lee Hooker-type blues stomping. As spontaneous as it is chaotic, the song features Steve's voice as if fed through a telephone.

'Street Rats': some of the multi-tracks in this *Scrubbers* mix are identical with the title song of 1975's Humble Pie LP, which is hardly surprising, as tapes like this were scattered round Steve's Clear Sound Studios when A&M scouts 'confiscated' suitable album material. This mix – again with plenty of echo – has a more prominent and more carefully sung vocal. (Steve: "Andrew [Oldham] did use the wrong vocal on the title track.") Ian Wallace's drums are also more dominant. He plays with precision to Steve's distorted guitar; Hinkley's rock'n'roll piano and Greg's thundering bass add to the general feeling of energy and bite. No reason to hide from 1975's up-coming punks on this one.

'Captain Goatcabin's Balancing Stallions', a grotesque song title if there ever was one, comes as a toe-tapper reminiscent of the 'Universal' days of The Small Faces. Just a few months prior to their 'Itchycoo Park'-fed reunion, Steve saw this kind of song as one reason for leaving Pie: "There are songs which I couldn't give Humble Pie. Who the hell wants to sing about 'Balancing Stallions'. I do!" Maybe this was also a hint on that nasty 1975 silly season/summertime rumour of a drunken night spent grilling and eating a horse on Steve's farm (*NME* 16/8/75). Marriott sings double-tracked, his deep voice reminding us of Ronnie Lane. Its honky tonk piano also seems a remnant of Ronnie's Slim Chance Passing Show.

Marriott would re-record 'High And Happy' two years later for The Small Faces' comeback album, but the rendition here is straight and relaxed, with a slow, sensitive appendix of twelve-bar blues which they should have retained for the later version. Truly great stuff.

Finally a version of 'Be My Baby' makes it onto disc. (The Small Faces recorded the song in late 1968 for the follow-up to *Ogdens' Nut Gone Flake*, but the track didn't surface on *Autumn Stone*. According to Kenney Jones it's in the Immediate archives; Repertoire in Hamburg might also have it in their vaults.) Steve's incomparable vocal phrasing can turn this much-covered Ronettes standard once again into an emotional adventure. All the Phil Spector wall of sound ingredients like backing vocals and echoey drum-breaks are put to use, but Steve's voice is the energy factor.

For 'It's All Over', Steve shares vocal duties with Greg, once again demonstrating the three-dimensional trademark they had perfected with Peter Frampton on Pie's debut – most impressively on 'One-Eyed Trouser Snake Rumba'. Sharp breaks dominate this down-to-earth rocker.

'Bluegrass Interval' also sounds like the early Seventies with BJ Cole's unmistakable steel guitar, plus finger-picking delights by Steve aimed at lawyers, wheelers and dealers. Nothing so subtle follows in 'Don't Take But A Few Minutes', where studio drinking-party ramblings open this slightly fatigued funk shouter. Numbers like these did not belong to Pie's more entertaining ideas, but dynamics are more in evidence here than for instance on 'Funky To The Bone' on *Street Rats*. There is a certain groove, but recording it seems like more fun than simply listening in.

Steve "learnt from Muddy Waters" he assures us in the spoken intro to 'Louisiana Blues'. This begins guitar and harmonica dominated and could have pleasantly continued in that vein, but Marriott, Ridley, Hinkley and Wallace (or Shirley?) rev it up with 4/4 breaks, Steve goes to the hilt with his voice. The country-type wooden drum beats at the end seem a bit out of place, but otherwise this is a raw gem in the collection.

Elsewhere in the Mississippi Delta, Steve sings Elvis on 'You're A Heartbreaker'. This time, those country drums fit the occasion – a fast, tender love lament in Presley's early Memphis Sun Studio days, which makes the idea of a complete Marriott country album more than desirable. Maybe a witty A&M A&R person will one day combine *Eat It*'s side three with selected acoustics since 'Alabama 69'!

'I Need A Star In My Life' eventually saw the light of the music industry on Marriott's solo-album in 1976, more polished of course by the US West coast session mafia. Steve looking back: "It was a pressure situation A&M had put me in. I'd given them songs done by me at my studio, but they said, 'No, it's not good enough quality, we use Dolbys these days,' and all that crap." Surely, this version has all it ever needs, with Mel Collins' tender soprano sax and brass work and a great gospel feeling.

'Cocaine (Round My Brain)' presents more funk sounds, similar to 'Groovin' With Jesus' on *Thunderbox* but – even with a possible lack of master tapes – much better produced, with fantastic Hammond, pedal steel guitar and string passages, set off by the always inventive Marriott guitar sounds.

After that comes 'I'll Find You' – not the Small Faces reunion song with the same title, but the cheekily changed *Another Side Of Bob Dylan* country waltz 'To Ramona' (1964). With acoustic guitars, harmonica and tambourine, it is complemented further with piano, bass and drums.

That Marriott was also a canny compiler is shown by the fact that the last three songs on this album cover different styles. 'Lord Help Me Hold Out' features a warm Hammond leading into this fast yet dreamy gospel song. Its Christian lyrics are a new departure for Steve, the chorus is pure magic, and you can spot a few interesting 'quoted' Small Faces chord sequences – answers to the publisher please. The piano work is reminiscent of *Rock On*'s 'Strange Days'.

Style two comes in 'Hambone', another mid tempo country song, US-style with fiddles and a tough drum beat. Steve's tone is as nasal as in 'The Universal'. The song is spat out in no time at all, but it holds its own special atmosphere, as does the final style change, 'Signed Sealed'. This is slower, solid blues rock again with typical talking vocals and romantic Ridley passages, an almost beseeching chorus and a sharp, faded-out lead guitar.

Conclusion: at least sixteen songs in this collection could have made for an absolute masterpiece, maybe with less vocal echo on the initial tracks and Glyn Johns on the mixing board. After the lack of coherence on *Eat It*, which would have made a great single album without the half-hearted live side, and the flat and shrill *Thunderbox* with some magic moments, such an inspired album, presenting stage-bound material and inventive production, could have secured Marriott's or Humble Pie's career for quite a while yet. What's more, Jerry Shirley was the only Pie missing from these early All Stars sessions! *Scrubbers* is certainly richer and more entertaining than the merely solid *Street Rats* which, in turn, sounds much better than slaggings in the Pie camp gave it credit for. There is a lot more of Steve's real feelings in here than on the 'official' 1976 solo album *Marriott*, which Steve himself considers over-produced.

Meanwhile, money was scarce all round. Although Humble Pie had "been doing great business everywhere" on their last US tour, nobody knew where the money had gone. More bad luck was in the wings for Clem: "At the end of the American Pie farewell tour I was asked to play for Deep Purple when they were looking for a guitarist. By the time I got back from LA it was all over!"

Jerry Shirley then quickly left the Pie camp to move to America, where he joined the band Natural Gas with Colosseum's ex-bass player Mark Clarke, an ex-mate of Clem's. Clempson and Ridley, close friends especially after the mutual rescue operation for *Street Rats*, formed a heavy trio called Strange Brew together with Jeff Beck's Schwarzenegger-type drummer Cozy Powell, whose band Hammer had just broken up. But this fresh combination immediately had to face the 'supergroup' tag – high expectations based on name dropping bogged down early rehearsals which were meant to have been informal. They hadn't even found a lead singer.

Greg Ridley was full of enthusiasm regarding the new horizons, but delayed their move into the recording studios, because he was not able to see through his jungle of contracts: "I found out that nobody could find out how long I was contracted for." In any case, Greg still seemed to 'belong' to Humble Pie agent Dee Anthony's US stable. Soon, Ridley abandoned Strange Brew, who vowed to continue without him, and found himself back in Steve Marriott's country cottage and studios.

Steve continued with recordings featuring his *Scrubbers* crew, and there was talk of a more permanent band taking shape. BP Fallon, Marriott's Irish press agent, spoke of the involvement of ex-Fleetwood Mac guitarist Bob Weston, who Mac had thrown out because of his liaison with John McVie's wife, Christine, after which he'd started Paris.

Blues daddy Alexis Korner was also still part of Marriott's sessions at Clear Sound. The Greek-Austrian Father of British White Blues also invited the little cockney with the black voice into CBS Studios for recording of a new Korner and All Stars solo album, after Marriott had interrupted the *Scrubbers* sessions to join Alexis on a Scottish tour, as a replacement for his Snape partner Peter Thorup. While the Korner tracks 'Strange'N'Deranged' and 'Tree Top Fever' were being put on tape, Steve had renewed his friendship with ex-Cochise (whom he had produced) and Frampton's Camel bass player Rick Wills. The next day, Steve could hardly believe his tiny hungover eyes – behind the thick glass of the control room he discovered Rick's old boss, Pie brother Peter! After four solo years, Peter was still broke and took every paid session opportunity and so got booked for Alexis. The collaboration became an emotional reunion, and as if to prove it, Peter presented himself with a Marriott T-shirt on the cover of his fourth solo album *Frampton*, which came out a few months later.

Two further surprise Korner All Stars could be detected in the cigarette smoke of CBS Studios: pianist and honorary Stone Nicky Hopkins (he sadly died of heart failure in September 1994) – who was a Marriott cohort from the mutual 1967 recordings for Bill Wyman's 'satanic' song 'In Another Land', and secret Stones leader Keith Richards himself. With this line-up, a witty, laid-back version of the old Stones title 'Get Off Of My Cloud' was cut, and Keith once again enquired if Steve felt like joining the 'strolling rocks', seven years after his offer during the final Small Faces days, this time for the missing Mick Taylor and because candidate Ron Wood was still committed to The Faces. Smiling, Steve once again declined – even in the face of melting financial fortunes he rated his freedom more than superstardom. Marriott: "Keith always wanted to have me in. It was, 'My mate Steve's got a great voice, plays a bit of guitar.' And I spoke to Mick about it, and I played with Keith for a while, and I thought it was great. Keith would have liked me with them, playing second guitar and singing backing vocals, but Mick didn't want to play ball, and I don't blame him, he was absolutely right, ha ha."

Alexis Korner had also been asked to join by Keith, but he felt even less suitable, although – or may be because – he thought the Stones were a great live band. Alexis had "various reasons. I'm much too independent, I couldn't do it, I'm not a good enough player anyway, not a sufficiently good all-round player that I could fit in. Image-wise I should think I'm totally wrong for them…Steve would have been a better bet than me for it, but I don't think that would have been a practical proposition either."

And summarising his feelings as a kind of godfather, as well as observations over the years, live and in many studios, Korner added: "I think Steve is one of the most exciting stage performers I've ever seen in my life. He's an incredibly intense blues player and his whole life is really what happens to him on stage and when he's recording. Music is his whole life." And this intensity was naturally something Mick Jagger wouldn't want next to him.

But it was Alexis Korner himself who brought some welcome live atmosphere after the studio winter of 1975. After a six week promotional radio US tour for his *Get Off Of My Cloud* album, he needed a guitarist for Scandinavian and German concert tours, and he'd thought of Steve's involvement even while in the studio, as he told *Melody Maker*: "Oh, I could work with Steve. Actually, he depped for Peter Thorup, who was the regular lead guitarist I worked with when I had a band called Snape for a short time and we took him on tour in Scotland. He was surprised because he suddenly found out he could play lead guitar, as he'd always had other lead guitarists working with him."

Steve still felt full of power, and what's more, while at home in the studios, he was always reminded of his recent divorce from wife Jenny.

Their eventual separation had been tour-inflicted in itself, but now Steve felt restless and accepted gratefully. Nick South was the bass player in Alexis' band, and he'd been the one to accompany both Korner and Marriott during The Small Faces split gig on New Year's Eve 1968! Anyway, the German tour got well documented via a German television programme from a Berlin media exhibition, the annual Berlin Funkausstellung.

For the Bremen-based *Beat Club* series, director Mike Leckebusch filmed a Korner live feature underneath Berlin's telecom transmission tower. Although the smallest on stage – as always – Steve stood out with his sheer temperament, during the big finale, and when folk singer Bill Clifton and Pete 'Wyoming' Bender's German band joined Korner's group on stage, Steve was at the top of his voice – and everyone else's – singing gospel tunes as if possessed, an inspirational sight and sound. After the end of filming procedures, the band felt lonely, which meant they were groupie-bound, so Alexis persuaded them all to retreat to the Folk Pub in Berlin's Leibnizstrasse, promising some "Mongolian ladies" and a bottle of tequila! But apart from that Mexican stimulant, the band only discovered Pete Bender in the pub. The session still took place – in the highest of spirits.

But could the uncomplicated party atmosphere in Korner's quarters have been a new band home for the Pie-frustrated Steve? Alexis commented at the time: "We had a ball, he loved it. But I couldn't work with him on a regular basis any more than he could work with me on a regular basis. I don't think he's at the point anymore where he could happily be a member of a band." Indeed, being a second league group member had not worked out in Humble Pie either, so Alexis had a point.

Instead, back in Essex, Steve shared his cottage with a new lady, Jan, who was expecting his child, and the line-up of a band which Steve would lead as undisputed front man took shape: 'Scrubber' Ian Wallace would be on drums, Greg Ridley had returned from Strange Brew to become permanent bass player, and a certain Mickey Finn was on second guitar – behind Steve's lead championed by Alexis Korner. Contrary to press reports, Mick wasn't the Mickey Finn who had played bongos for T Rex, but Mickey Waller of The Heavy Metal Kids and Phil May's Fallen Angels. Meanwhile, Clem Clempson, whatever his plans with the stagnant Strange Brew, broke his right hand playing football.

When, at the end of September 1975, Steve Marriott returned from studio recordings in Los Angeles, all the disappointments, hang-ups and quarrels seemed a thing of the past. He had a promising single in the can which looked set to propel him back into the charts: 'Soldier' written by Steve's cockney and rock'n'roll mentor Joe Brown – he of The Bruvvers and husband of long-time Pie backing vocalist, the late Vicki Brown. Joe, apart from his current country and R&B band Brown's Home Brew, was usually more Pop orientated than the increasingly 'black' Steve. 'Soldier' had been recorded with arranger David Foster, the LA Philharmonic Orchestra plus The Blackberries, but twenty-two years later it's still in the vaults – so whoever's got it, release the damn thing!

The first British tour without Humble Pie was scheduled to take Steve via Hemel Hempstead, Cardiff, Leicester and Birmingham to London, presenting music which, according to Steve, wouldn't be much different from Humble Pie's. But which Humble Pie was Steve talking about? Marriott: "The All Stars are going to the States. I'm going to take out The Blackberries again. And hopefully also David Foster on keyboards. So if we play England, it's only to rehearse the basic rhythm section, of which I'm one. It'll be augmented in the States and if it's successful I'll bring it back here. I'll do a six week tour and then cool it."

In London's Roundhouse – "much loved oasis of the freak community" (*Time Out,* 1973) – a huge refurbished hall originally built over a rail turntable, Steve presented his new band Steve Marriott's All Stars. In a pleasant mood, full of energy and boasting the very qualities on lead guitar which old man Korner had detected, Marriott got the audience's love and respect. Since August 1974, when we'd seen him perform at Dortmund's Westfalen Halle with Humble Pie, his voice had become richer, his stage talk was more considerate, and the overall presentation much more careful.

Steve with Mickey Finn, Greg Ridley and Ian Wallace comprised the line-up which had put new songs down for a group album recently, after *Scrubbers* had been rejected six months earlier. Towards the end of the Roundhouse gig, an additional All Star appeared: Clem Clempson, recuperated from his broken wrist and equally broken Strange Brew dreams. Steve had told *Melody Maker* journalist Chris Welch the secret only days before: "He wasn't supposed to be there, but he came in one day when we were rehearsing and said, 'I'm bored, can I play?' Sure."

A few days after the Roundhouse concert, Steve flew back to Los Angeles, taking his new band with him this time. The tapes laid down in Essex with The All Stars were to be re-mixed, and he was also booked to record more big budget solo tracks with arranger and keyboard wizard David Foster, featuring LA sessioners and The Blackberries. Foster was also scheduled for augmenting The All Stars on an up-coming US tour. Recording and living in LA didn't run too smoothly. Steve was kicked out of two hotels, once because of obscene behaviour – which he denied, and he'd be the first to admit it if it was true, reputed raver that he was. The other time, he had taken a stray dog into his suite, found in a Hollywood dog pound. So he'd wrecked hotel staff's nerves again – 'Big Black Dog Revisited'! In the end, the animal found a new home with one of The Blackberries.

Meanwhile, Marriott possessions were getting kicked out of the LA Record Plant Studios as well: practically all The All Stars' tapes had to go! Everything had to be newly recorded, and that included the group material as well as Steve's rejected *Scrubbers* solo stuff, which he had over-dubbed and improved in recent months. Then, to make matters worse, A&M suddenly decided that two albums, solo and band, were "too much product". Instead they now planned a single album, *Marriott*,which was to feature one British group side and one American session cat side with more 'US' All Stars like legendary sax player Ernie Watts, guitarist David Spinozza and Red Rhodes, the pedal steel man working for Mike Nesmith (ex-Monkees).

Steve was devastated: "My solo album, as it came out, wasn't my concept. It was a pressure situation A&M had put me in. I'd given them songs done by me in my studio, but they said, 'No, it's not good enough quality.' It cost me three hundred thousand dollars to have the same songs sound like an LA clinic, but I didn't really have a choice. They brought in Kenny Kerner and Richie Wise to produce it; they're nice people but let's face it, the album's no great shakes. They didn't know how to produce English rock musicians, guys used to thrashing it out. It sounds like they put a limiter on everything and squashed it into a can. The other side is too clinical – they said my version sounded too black, but the LA side came out sounding blacker – or rather more contrived 'black'. They're mostly my songs, but they didn't come out as I'd visualised them – or as I'd already *done* them."

In spite of this criticism by Steve himself, the album did sound a lot more compact and powerful than anything he had put out since *Smokin'*, even if it couldn't touch Glyn Johns' mixes. Glyn was the man Steve had wanted for LA anyway. The loose jamming character of Marriott's studio parties in Clear Sounds was missing, though, as documented by comparing the two versions of 'A Star In My Life'. But A&M wanted sales-compatible sounds – just like all the majors. In terms of variation, the collection wasn't as rich as *Eat It*, but its sound was more coherent. Looking back, it remains an impressive journey through Steve's talents as a soul shouter, ballad and rock singer plus, of course, as a remarkable lead guitarist. So Alexis Korner had not been exaggerating in his anecdote about the mutual Scottish tour.

The British All Stars side begins with 'East Side Struttin''. Here, mid tempo means it's slower still than 'Street Rat', but the band sounds like Humble Pie when they're fresh and keen and after they've bought new equipment, so whatever Dolby A&M applied, this bites. Steve tells his story by singing instead of the mumbled talking blues of late. His solo comes effect-laden, but not as a gimmick, and the rhythm section is rock solid.

'Lookin' For A Love' is an R&B standard by Zelda Samuels and JW Alexander (the latter assisting The Rolling Stones when they recorded *Out Of Our Heads* in Chicago), and an old love of Steve's. It had already been covered by Bobby Womack as well as The J Geils Band who often shared the bill with Pie. After this take, Steve would record the song again for The Small Faces' *Playmates*, but this LA version with The Blackberries remains definitive.

Sparse Fender Rhodes piano leads into 'Help Me Through The Day', a blues ballad by Leon Russell, with an intensity Steve would rarely reach again, with 'My Lover's Prayer' on Humble Pie's *On To Victory* and the live 'Five Long Years' on Marriott's live *Dingwalls* possible contenders.

A rocker in 'Natural Born Woman' vein, 'Midnight Rollin'' is done with verve and acts as a showcase for Marriott's prolific lead guitar work. His runs were stunning by now – this way he needed neither Frampton nor the returned Clem Clempson.

And on the subject of former colleagues, on the remake of The Small Faces' 'Wham Bam Thank You Mam' Ian McLagan's Hammond organ is missing, but the take is convincing due to its speed and energy – Ian

Wallace's driving drums, Steve's singing is much clearer than on the original, and an inventive break leading onto another exciting guitar solo. Steve himself often insisted he found producing records more interesting than having to flog them, but A&M's commercial gloss certainly did no detectable harm to this All Stars hard rock side.

By comparison, the LA session side does not start with complete success. The *Scrubbers* version of 'Star In My Life' had been rejected in spite of its coherent gospel feel, only to have been replaced here by a conglomerate of styles: the keyboard intro and solo passage uneasily wail between Stevie Wonder-style ghetto funk and *Saturday Night Fever*. Suddenly there's Red's pedal steel, completely out of place, and the wonderful Blackberries chorus is ruined by far too much brass.

'Are You Lonely For Me Baby' is more convincing as funk satire. Rhythm and brass arrangements are of one founding, and you can feel all the fun Steve was having with his beloved Blackberries (at the time Venetta Fields, Carlena Williams and Maxayn Lewis).

The centre piece of the LA side was 'You Don't Know Me', a twilight blues ballad, this time in a Ray Charles style and therefore introduced via a touching gospel grand piano. The brass is a bit on the Las Vegas side – which explains how David Foster spent Steve's budget – but vocals and Watts' sax are great though.

More tongue-in-cheek funk follows, in the form of 'Late Night Lady', this record's second gem in the ongoing Marriott-Blackberries love story. Wah-wah pedal and period piece Seventies disco toms out of the Donna Summer cookbook lead into Steve's search for his mistress for the night. Amusingly, his enquiry "Has anybody seen my late night lady?" is answered by Venetta, Carlena and Maxayn's "Has anybody seen Steve's late night lady?" The truly electrifying vibes are dressed up by the reliable saxophone of Ernie Watts.

From ladies of the night to 'Early Evening Light', for the romantic finale, David Foster got thinking of his Phil Spector and Andrew Oldham ambitions and hired the LA Philharmonic Orchestra (again, for Steve's money). It's unusually attractive though to hear Steve with symphonic backing and nothing else during this intro. His equally done up 'Soldier'" single – never released – would surely have worked sensationally this way. On 'Light', the romantic verses are set off with double speed choruses, a nice idea but still not making up an entirely convincing number.

Ultimately the LA side is okay as well, and Steve could hardly have wished for a better calling card as the frontman of a US-bound big All Stars and Blackberries line-up.

When *Marriott* was finally released in April 1976, its sales were not impressive. To a certain extent, this was surely due to Steve's half-hearted live promotion during the only All Stars American tour. Wally, Greg, Mickey and Clem and The Blackberries had been complemented by keyboard player Damon Butcher, who Clem had recommended. Steve remembers: "I'd been touring *Marriott* but stopped shortly after. I was disillusioned by the whole thing."

But what was the real reason behind that? How about a look at the British charts. Even during the American tour, Steve talked about reactivating The Small Faces, who had been successful during the winter of 1975/6 with the reissue of 'Itchycoo Park'. Anyway, apparently without any set plans for the future, Steve abandoned his All Stars in California and flew back to Britain in May, with Mickey Finn, who was able to join Pretty Things singer Phil May and his new band, The Fallen Angels. Clempson, Butcher and Wallace remained in Los Angeles, with plans for their own band. When nothing serious developed, Ian Wallace joined Bob Dylan's road band, and via the connection with David Lindley found his way into the LA session elite.

Dave Clempson and Damon Butcher eventually returned to London, where they got a welcome call from Uriah Heep's thrown out, stranded singer David 'Lord' Byron. With him and Wings drummer Geoff Britton they started a band called Rough Diamond, immediately recording an album but gigging rarely.

After David Byron's decline and split (he later died of alcohol abuse), Diamond recruited new lead singer Gary Bell and replaced Britton with future Climax Blues Band and Status Quo drummer Jeff Rich, going out as Champion. But like many of the more traditional rock bands, they became victims of the punk era and disbanded after only one album, Clem Clempson reverting to session work before he joined The Jack Bruce Band in 1979.

CHAPTER SEVEN
Small Faces II
Playmates Again

Steve Marriott's lack of direction was hardly the only reason for abandoning the All Stars project – it was not even the main factor behind it. 'The Black Humble Pie Story' could easily have continued quite successfully, with the returned Blackberries and the assistance of Pie and Frampton manager Dee Anthony. There was also a new British agent (Dave Clark, not the beat drummer of Dave Clark Five and astute business man behind the *Ready Steady Go* archives).

But Steve had long ago stopped trusting Fat Anthony, who would start estate deals in the West Indies but never really pay Pie or the All Stars substantial sums of touring money. And what's more, before the American tour started, a look at the British charts must have got Steve thinking when he returned from his LA sessions on 13 December, 1975: 'Itchycoo Park', the 1967 hippy success by The Small Faces, was one of the first reissues by publishers NEMS Enterprises, who had bought the old Immediate copyrights, and climbed up Britain's Top Ten. For the transaction, the ex-Stones/Small Faces/Humble Pie mentor Andrew Loog Oldham had taken the trouble to come to London from his Columbian exile. Except for a few Caribbean sessions with Jimmy Cliff, little had been heard of Andrew. A first, tentative meeting between the four protagonists on 'Itchycoo Park' took place in Steve's house before Christmas – "We shouted at each other for a few hours and then made friends again" – talking about the old times and even playing a bit.

In January, Steve and Ronnie Lane celebrated the news about charting by jamming together during a Lane and Slim Chance gig at Essex University. A second jamming night at Brunel University,

Uxbridge, was only prevented because it was on 30 January, 1976: Steve's twenty-ninth birthday was celebrated in such high spirits that he missed the gig! But a few days later, he met with Ronnie, Kenney Jones and Ian McLagan (freshly 'left behind' as The Faces by Rod Stewart) – as The Small Faces! Laney had arrived with a whole entourage: he brought his current Island label's A&R man David Betteridge, EG's management partner David Enthoven (the 'E' in EG) as well as his complete family. The four little ex-Mods came together only for (still) down-to-earth purposes: discussing the current royalty situation and producing *Top Of The Pops* promotional material for the single.

After the BBC had pioneered little pop promo films in their chart show *Top Of The Pops* with 1967's 'Strawberry Fields Forever' clip, or of course The Small Faces' 1968 'Lazy Sunday', the video age was in full swing by 1975 – and so the surprised little hitmen were asked into Island Record's Hammersmith film studios for a miming session. As well as 'Itchycoo Park', the follow-up 'Lazy Sunday' was also filmed, because the old promo clip was deemed out of date. Steve's antics and his request to Ronnie to form a Status Quo-type boogie front had even the veteran BBC cameramen collapse with laughter. "See you in five years, then we'll do it on ice!" Steve winked when it was over.

In the end, 'Itchycoo Park' narrowly missed *Top Of The Pops*, but was screened in the more serious *Old Grey Whistle Test* hosted by 'Whispering' Bob Harris. But the little reunion of sorts was documented (and still is: on a moderately priced Small Faces video called *Big Hits*, see Discography). Celebratory drinks went over the counter of the little bar next to Hammersmith Studios – characteristically without Ronnie, whose family "needed sleep".

And although Steve's "See you in five years" was ringing in each of the four ex-stars' ears, fans and Faces began to think about a real reunion. Marriott especially spoke of The Small Faces with unhidden affection, though he was still contractually tied to his All Stars, whose American tour with The Blackberries in tow would begin a few days later in mid February. Steve had played the other midgets a song from his *Scrubbers* tapes while the videos were produced – namely 'Captain Goatcabin's Balancing Stallions': "I wrote stuff I could never have done with Pie. Just a few days ago I played it to them [Ronnie, Mac and Kenney] and they loved it. So you never know..."

Asked in late January 1976 whether a new Small Faces project would play big summer open airs that summer, Steve told the *NME*'s Steve Clarke: "We have talked about playing together but as yet there's nothing definite...Like the other night we did the films and we said 'Wouldn't it be nice to play somewhere?' I think there's a definite possibility of something. But what annoys me is that someone puts it in the paper – which could be wrong and makes everybody look an asshole!" So reunion plans were denied heavily, especially because of Steve's ongoing ties to Pie manager Dee Anthony. ("The media almost messed the whole thing up," Steve would tell Penny Valentine in 1977 when they *had* reformed.) Meanwhile, Ian McLagan was seen catching a number of dates with Ronnie's Slim Chance, so two Small Faces on stage together was a start.

As for Steve's All Stars: after a gig at Croydon's Fairfield Halls in the south of London, they went through the States with the black singing trio The Blackberries. Following the rather sudden end of that project after only one six week tour, Steve remembered the real Mod veterans' get together like this: "After that tour I started talking to the rest of The Small Faces about a reunion. It wasn't my idea. I'd had no plans. [Why the break-up of The All Stars then?] Kenney Jones, I think, rang me up; he and Ian McLagan knew Rod Stewart was splitting from The Faces, and they'd been talking about getting back together for a couple of gigs and a live album from them." Indeed, in spring 1976 Kenney as well as Mac could remember only too well how they'd been left out in the rain after that first Small Faces split. This time, they were determined to stick to their hard earned money, or at least invest it – not as businessmen but music career minded. Ronnie, on the other hand, was mildly nostalgic and keen enough for a few little things, but ultimately happy with Slim Chance.

Kenney would confirm only as much as, "I phoned them up. We were just trying to get a couple of gigs". Right from the first meeting in December 1975 he had made it clear that his ambition was not long-term. All he wanted to prove was that his band of yore were now able to play his favourite album *Ogdens' Nut Gone Flake*! He stuck to this view in a *Trouser Press* interview almost four years later: "I didn't want to reform The Small Faces permanently. But we got together and instead of playing the old stuff, everybody was writing new songs and some of them were good. And then they got fucked up and things got out of hand when a lot of people began to say we should stay together permanently. That frightened me, but I thought, 'Well, I'm not doing anything else.' And it frightened Ronnie Lane. He didn't want to do it, though he loved the idea of the reunion gig."

Mac saw Ronnie's lack of commitment with less tolerance: "We had a play. [That was still a secret project, in Steve's cottage.] It was great with the four of us. So we thought, get in the studio so we could get to know each other again and put down some songs. But after one night, Ronnie was talking about going back to Wales. We'd ditched our projects [Kenney, for instance, could still have done the US tour with Rod Stewart for good money], but he wanted to keep on with Slim Chance. We even agreed to go with his management company. We'd bend with the wind." In all the turmoil, it certainly didn't help matters when some old animosities flared up between Lane and Marriott, who had this to say: "But there was an insult given out and I still take it as one today. At which point I whacked him, and Ronnie said goodbye. It was a minor fracas but it was heavy. It'll obviously turn out to be all my fault."

Whatever, they needed a successor for Ronnie, and quick. Steve still had Rick Wills, ex-bassist with Cochise, Frampton's Camel and Roxy Music – he'd stumbled on him during Pie's *Smokin'* sessions, where he sang, and during Alexis Korner's recording of his *Cloud* album only a year ago: "I had him up my sleeve all along but I didn't know if he was free." Steve duly called Rick in the middle of the night, and the situation was: Rick wasn't just free, he was in such dire straits that he worked building sites to pay the rent. Roxy were on a sabbatical, and all other offers he considered redundant. Steve hated to get turned down – so he'd pretend it was all about a mutual gig with his cockney Bruvver Joe Brown. But when Rick arrived at the cottage and saw his three little teenage idols sitting side by side, the dimensions of his new engagement began to dawn on him.

Love of playing as well as 'camaraderie' (one of Steve's key words at the time) were cruelly put to the test during the spring and summer of 1976. Marriott's contracts were pending, and without an official reunion there would be no live gigs – and certainly not a single advance paid out. And so, there was no regular income for the band. In a heart-breaking and creatively crippling move, Steve sold his particular pride – Clear Sound Studios. Mac and Kenney ransacked their bank accounts. Happy boys happy?

Subsequently, recording sessions were held to a very low budget in Joe Brown's Grange Sound home studio in Chigwell, Essex, which ironically was situated very near Steve's ex-complex. Anyway, this way Marriott, McLagan, Jones and Wills had valuable assistance at hand: Bruvver Joe's mandolin work as well as his wife Vicki Brown's fab voice. Other vocal guests calling in included Greg Ridley, Dave Hynes from Joe's Band (he'd been with a 1968-9 edition of the Spencer Davis Group and will continue to play his part) as well as PP Arnold, coming full circle after her work for The Small Faces and Humble Pie. Mel Collins on brass also stuck to Steve, who remembers their Grange Sound sessions with affection:

"We fell in love with *Playmates* while recording in the studio. It was very light and laid back, just right for that time; you didn't have to push for anything." With this newly found happy-go-lucky atmosphere and countless 'refreshed' allnighters in Chigwell – just the way Steve used to love things going back in Clear Sounds – they had enough songs in the can for two albums by July. Mac remembers not without amusement: "We thought that it would come over as pretentious if we came out with an initial double album, but there was enough material." Kenney Jones, on the other hand, couldn't disagree more with wild Steve's attitude of not pushing for anything. "The ideas on some of the songs were great," he told *Trouser Press*. "If we'd have used a producer and acted professionally it might have been really good. I'd do the tracks and go home, because I refuse to work through the night and always have. If they want to stay up all night and blow their brains out they can. So I'd go home and when I came back they'd finished it and it wasn't very good."

Steve got him for that: "Don't say, 'Well I think I'll go to bed, have a listen tomorrow.' I hate that attitude…We did stay up for a couple of days, but that's nothing. I mean, what am I, fucking Mother Reilly, have I got to go to bed at ten? Mow the lawn in the morning? If you're onto something – you're with a sound and you want to finish it – then go for it!"

After six long months of sitting around penniless, all the contractual hassles of the old Small Faces had finally been solved in December 1976. Mel Bush, the influential British rock promoter, had more than his fair input in these proceedings. He really seemed keen on the band and set an ambitious goal for himself: "If I don't succeed in getting [especially] Steve out of his contracts, I am not worthy to be your manager." Marriott confirmed this: "They all wanted the band so bad, but were not able to get to grips with Dee Anthony, the record company [A&M] and the publishers. He [Mel] was the only one who had the guts to go out and get me out of my commitments."

It was then that Kenney and Rick had to have a car accident, and the release of their album was postponed yet again. "Two months wasted," was Steve's bitter comment, because it took them till March 1977 to announce the official reunion of The Small Faces to the press. They had sat around for months on end, hardly enough money around to buy the odd cable, guitar string or, of course, the next round.

Now the band were keen to see their posters on the walls again, but also weary about what the public would make of them – after all these years and new product not in the shops yet. Perhaps Steve had a notion of what was in store for the band. Asked by the British *Sounds* about his feelings in the face of up-coming shows and – afterwards – a new album (in the can for yonks), Steve readily admitted: "I'm nervous. It's like having assembled a model plane, wondering if it's going to fly."

It was exactly this fear of flying which characterised at least the first of the eleven spring gigs The Small Faces played in England that year, with a Ricky Wills who wasn't quite Small enough, but a welcome singing aid in their trusted, heartful Pat Arnold. There were good vibes, and the music, though tentative and shaky at first, became better and better, as John Pidgeon, 'Playmates' co-writer with Mac, remembered: "I saw the first and last nights of the tour.

The first night in Sheffield was chaos, everything went wrong. Steve dropped his guitar, Mac's electric pianos (all three of 'em) went out of tune. It was a night I'd rather forget.

"But the last night at the Rainbow was great. The whole band, including Pat Arnold, who they were taking with them again, had fun and communicated it to the audience. Marriott did his whole Jack the Lad bit, getting the crowd to say 'all right, guv'nor' instead of 'yeah'... and it was a total gas hearing 'All Or Nothing' done how it should be done. The new songs I wasn't quite so sure about. By the time you read this the album will be out anyway; it's going to be called *Playmates*. Whether they'll ever be as good as...well, I don't know, nor do I much care. They've given me enough great memories already. To expect more would seem greedy."

When the album *Playmates* and counterpart single 'Lookin' For A Love' (its only cover song) finally did hit the shops in August 1977, almost a year had passed since it was recorded. At least it seemed like something of a wedding present for Steve and his Southern (Atlanta) Belle Pam Stephens – mother of his son Toby Joe.

Right from the start, the new outfit rocks out its message – they don't want to appear as a nostalgia combo. This song chosen to announce their return is 'High And Happy', lifted from Steve's *Scrubbers* repertoire. Very R&B orientated, with Mac's Booker T Hammond and Mel Collins brass pattern led by Steve's roaring voice, it is reminiscent more of Humble Pie than the just re-charted Sixties memories of 'Itchycoo Park' and 'Lazy Sunday'. But then, rougher sounds had dominated The Small Faces' Frampton gig, so here's some history revisited. The production was tackled by the boys themselves with sound engineer John Wright. It's not spectacular, but more clean and dynamic than anything since the *Rock On* album.

'Never Too Late' follows, proving the band's charm is intact. This first of four joint compositions by Marriott and McLagan is a slow rocker with solid drums and romantic harmony singing – a brilliant showcase for the female voices of host Vicki Brown and Pat Arnold, the original 'Tin Soldier' lady. Repeating the chorus after the fade-out is an old DJ trap from the Sixties – but it's nice to have it around once more.

Mac's unusual solo venture, 'Tonight', comes across with a

country feel. His soft voice helps to make up for Ronnie's sorely missed vocals and the song is one of the most charming on the entire album, thanks to the two background ladies, Mac's own acoustic guitar work and Steve's delicate, almost pedal steel orientated guitar licks.

The guitar in 'Saylarvee' is of the Carl Perkins ilk and therefore keeps up the country flavour. That aside, Steve leads the listener into the pub – or rather saloon – world of Pie's 'Red Neck Jump' on *Rock On*. It's at this point at least that the very range of styles points to the band's aim: this is music for Marriott friends or fans of relaxed ensemble playing. It is not meant to be the soundtrack for a Mod revival by old Small Faces fans! Kemastri – KE-nney, MA-c, ST-eve and RI-ck – are bound to look into the future creatively.

And on the subject of creativity, the group's versatile attitude is confirmed by the six minute soul jam 'Find It'. This Memphis groove was developed during the early – December 1975 – session by Steve and Ronnie. It's as prolific as it is relaxed, but especially with the vocals by PP and Vicki there are clear associations to Humble Pie's era with The Blackberries. Why did Steve have to change the name of his firm when the sound didn't get altered? On the other hand, early Small Faces numbers were R&B laden – and they failed live only when later studio gems couldn't be reproduced. Surely this couldn't happen here.

On with some black repertoire in 'Lookin' For A Love', taken directly from The All Stars' set this time, although the rhythm section on this Shel Talmy production is more easy-going. "This won't do shit!" was how Steve Marriott introduced this single release live in Dortmund, Germany in September and in front of ten thousand people, he angrily kicked his mike stand over. Backstage, he explained his Ally Pally reminder: "Without asking us, they chose 'Lookin' For Love' as our single, without the slightest chances chartwise anyway – and without promotion!" He had a point, for in spite of his solid harmonica work and the band's exciting arrangement, why do this standard again – and release a cover version as the first comeback single of a renowned writing band?

'Playmates' is next. The title track's reflective walking blues is again Memphis bound – a rhythm guitar with regards from Steve

Cropper – but Mac's Hammond makes sure there is a Small Faces element in there, too. Steve's lyrics seem autobiographical: "We're playmates of the millionaires" seems like the bitter truth behind all his contractual confusion that preceded the release of these recordings.

The 6/8 time drinking blues of 'This Song's Just For You', about the ale-assisted end of a love affair, begins exactly like 'Love In Vain' on the Stones' *Let It Bleed*. This intro then leads into an original melody presented via some great harmony singing – lost love gets credibility here. The overall result is solid, and for once probably matches the public's expectations.

The 'Find It' riff gets repeated in quicker speed on 'Drive-In Romance'. The tune is more melodic, but the element which can rescue this song from mediocrity is the psychedelic middle eight – a continuation of old Small Faces virtues like Mac's organ work, set to another of those songs about life on the road making love impossible, the 'rock'n'roll as a marriage breaker' theme, written by McLagan and Pidgeon.

'Smiling In Tune' completes the reunion. Another walking blues, its pub piano and an equally bar-bound melody are supplied by Steve from the same old cockney collection which also produced 'Queens And Nuns' on *Street Rats*. Reminiscing, he sings about the good and bad times of the old Small Faces, quoting old hits – "I've been looking for a bookin' on this 'Lazy Sunday' afternoon" or "It's bin light, it got dark, gates were locked in 'Itchycoo Park'", arriving at some wishful thinking: "Now we're all back where we all belong, and the four of us can't be wrong", when there were really only three old Faces left. Anyway, his blues harmonica work, Joe Brown's mandolin and Kenney's last minute snare fills make this a relaxed and amusing affair. Looking back in 1982, Kenney would still say: "I'm proud of my mistakes." On the other hand, he was the one who rarely got the chance to overdub drums, because by the time he'd arrive the morning after all night sessions, a certain number would have been finished. There is something exciting about a few drum lapses here, but much of it must be due to 'drinking in tune'.

The album still remains a solid and well played piece of, well, pub rock. In the best sense of the term, it would have gone down well if promoted on the up-market club circuit. Unfortunately, it was released in the summer of 1977, in the face of punk still making the headlines, and with high expectation towards these Small Faces as a cult band whose great hymns belonged to a quite different musical era. Bands like The Who or The Rolling Stones had been able to grow slowly into the growing festival and stadium market, like the little ones' predecessors, Humble Pie and Faces.

So the big time stage experience was certainly there. But then, crowd pleasers like 'I Don't Need No Doctor', 'Had Me A Real Good Time', or 'Maggie May' for that matter, could not be replaced easily – perhaps by playing all the old Small Faces hits, but certainly not with the *Playmates* set, which, pleasant as it is, belonged in the clubs. Steve and the boys realised that only too well, but economics and the IRS dictated a different career move. Steve: "Too many of us had too many tax and other financial pressures to do what we'd've had to do – take it street level and play all the clubs and support gigs."

Instead, the concert halls Mel Bush had booked had been too big to a certain extent, and the audience, while raving about the old Top Ten smashes, of which there weren't too many in the set, applauded the new songs politely but also at a loss. So the new wing of Steve's toy plane didn't quite support the band. The little cockney was devastated, and this could still be felt years later. In a 1984 interview with Chris Welch, he revealed with a lump in his throat: "If it had been an exact copy [of the old Small Faces] it might have lasted longer, but the stuff we were doing was nothing like the old days. And it was not accepted at all."

In Germany, Holland and Austria, the band fared better doing the festival circuit – for instance second on the bill to The Doobie Brothers – but the basic reaction was the same: the old hits still went down a storm compared to new stuff. Back from Europe, *Playmates* was promoted with a second British tour in September. The Small Faces had been augmented to a six-piece now: Pat Arnold was back after they'd done Europe as a four-piece, and Steve had his way now with a second guitarist.

While he had not been able to get Peter Frampton in The Small Faces back in 1968, Steve now recruited Jimmy McCulloch (born 4

June, 1953), the Scottish whizz-kid who had stepped into the limelight as a sort of teenage veteran (like Steve and Peter) when he replaced Stone The Crows leader Les Harvey after he had tragically been electrocuted on stage in 1972. After the Crows, who with Maggie Bell sported a female Steve Marriott link, Jimmy then found more early fame with John Mayall, only to join Paul McCartney's Wings in 1974.

The six-piece Small Faces presented a much better oiled, more inspired band version during that autumn of 1977. Their set would begin in shameless party mood with the vintage 'What'cha Gonna Do About It' and then mix old Sixties gems like 'Itchycoo Park' or 'All Or Nothing' with *Playmates* R&B, for instance 'High And Happy'. Steve had picked Bob Seger's 'The Fire Down Below' as an additional cover standard: the song would have suited Humble Pie too and demonstrated again that a real identity had not yet been found for the new Faces. 'Lazy Sunday' usually was the rousing finale.

Atlantic Records toyed with the idea of releasing the recordings from the tour as a double live album, but whatever the label's strategy, The Small Faces again disappeared behind studio doors. As during the summer of the Peter Frampton contract jungle in 1969, enough material for two albums had accumulated in Joe Brown's Grange Sound in between 1976-7, which were now complemented and also overdubbed, partly with a more focused R&B feeling, and with the assistance of their new permanent member Jimmy McCulloch, who was expected to supply a fuller sound picture. Steve: "*Seventy-Eight In The Shade* was the prophetic album title – the LP was supposed to be in the shops early 1978, and from then on the band really led its existence in the shadows."

During the late 1977 sessions, six female singers graced the studios: Lavinia Rodgers, Helen Chapelle, Liza Strike, Madeline Bell as well as Vicki Brown and her fourteen-year-old daughter Sam(antha) Brown. "We broke her in during those days," Steve reminisced in 1990, and as Madeline Bell recalled during our August 1994 interview: "Whenever more than two singers were needed, Vicki would call me, 'Mind if Sam comes along?' Of course I didn't, and thus Sam had the best in service training you could dream of!" (In 1988, Sam would begin her solo career with the smash 'Stop!', and she's still in demand as a hired backing voice, shining for Pink Floyd on their *Division Bell* album and tour during 1994.)

John Elijah Wright twiddled the crucial knobs for the second time around for the project which everybody calls "that difficult second album" that was *Seventy-Eight In The Shade*.

With clean, relaxed electric guitar chords, the album's opener 'Over Too Soon' begins things on a much more rhythmically inclined note than anything on *Playmates*. A catchy chorus with female backing and a lively and inspired band supply exactly the sort of punch many had missed on the first comeback album.

The tempo drops on 'Too Many Crossroads' – amidst over subdued electric piano, Steve wonders what to do at the crossroads having been left by his wife and child, until his sister goes to the circus and advises him to leave, too. Meanwhile, Kenney and friends have paved a comforting mid tempo groove, which unfortunately is over too soon. At least two minutes more would have been necessary to let this coherent number develop its atmosphere.

On 'Let Me Down Gently' the loose harmony singing continues the tradition of 'Thirty Days In The Hole' from *Smokin'*, which also featured Miss Bell. The song gets going in no time. Its quiet, reflective middle eight section – with truly inventive patterns by Kenney, a pleasure to listen to on its own – is reminiscent of yet another Marriott number, 'Drive-In Romance' on *Playmates*. For the chorus, the loose female backing becomes more disciplined to supply a romantic gospel feeling.

Back to a more relaxed atmosphere, here's that Memphis Steve Cropper guitar again, on 'Thinking 'Bout Love', which was omnipresent on *Playmates*. The girls' assisted chorus is a bit too much like 'Gently', but attractive organ and guitar parts more than make up for that, and those voices are beyond moaning, including Steve's of course.

'Stand By Me (Stand By You)': the tempo is even more slowed down here, but accelerates before the chorus, which has a truly tremendous, radio friendly impact. This Marriott composition became the single, and quite rightly so. But again, it wasn't promoted properly by Atlantic, prompting Steve to ask bitterly: "Have you heard it? Have you really heard it on the air?"

In 'Brown Man Do', Mac's electric piano leads into some mid tempo meditation by Steve, this time about the exploitation of black – well, brown – people. There's nothing wrong with social criticism and vocal acrobatics, but again the number needs more time to develop; these three minute snatches are little more than a sketch.

McLagan and Pidgeon supply 'Real Sour', a relaxed number, whose chorus is too close to 'Thinking 'Bout Love' for comfort or real excitement. The pattern is simplistic: subdued verses, more tempo for the hookline and a romantic middle eight for variation – solidly played but tame. Kenney takes exciting risks during the breaks, but we're not sure whether he wouldn't have preferred to try and overdub again.

At long last, the song Steve was raving about in 1975 – when he recorded the orchestral version with the Los Angeles Philharmonic Orchestra lead by David Foster – appears on record. The solo single of 'Soldier' never saw the light of day – come on, A&M! – but this new band version is still the standout track on the album, probably even the absolute highlight of the whole Small Faces reunion, and it works although the formula described in 'Real Sour' was not even abandoned. The band plays with enough energy, but Steve and the ladies work themselves into such a convincing gospel feeling that there remains the desire for a complete collection of gems like this.

'You Ain't Seen Nothing Yet' is rhythmically and instrumentally another reminder of 'Thinking 'Bout Love' and 'Real Sour'. Steve of course belts his guts out again, but the band just play along too nicely.

For the last number, Steve makes up for any weak points with some cheeky cockney humour. He doesn't touch his pub piano this time, but belches his dirty story about the 'Filthy Rich' over Mac's vulgar Farfisa organ sounds. It's hardly more than an exercise to get the crowds roaring along in the chorus. Like in 'Seventy-Ninth And Sunset', Steve gets to sing about the female bust – this time it's Jayne Mansfield's. In these politically correct 1990s, 'Parental Information' would again announce some 'offensive language', but so far, Repertoire's 1992 CD has escaped without one.

Even with its shortcomings, this is a real charmer which would certainly grow on its small audience. But questions had to be asked.

If there was such a wealth of material to choose from even before McCulloch joined, why did this album contain three fairly similar numbers, and why did it clock in at even less time than *Playmates*. That LP was considerably shorter than Humble Pie's albums, and at thirty-two minutes, *Shade* was hardly a real long player, even in the days before compact discs.

In early 1978, all the small print hassles left over from the original Small Faces and from ties to Pie eater Dee Anthony still didn't appear completely solved. The corporate headaches seemed especially hard on Steve. He had sacrificed his adored Clear Sound Studios to keep his new band going through the hard times, and now that The Small Faces hardly made a tiny profit, Inland Revenue bills crammed his cottage post box. The man hadn't seen any real money, and now they reminded him of a Sixties career that had left him almost penniless as well. Tour plans for America – crucial for their financial survival – also got stuck, and so a frustrated Ahmed Ertegun, music-loving Atlantic boss since the Fifties, still sat on a good but nicely unobtrusive album of a disillusioned band.

With little hope for a career resurrection, and still without new studio product, four Small Faces went on another tour of Germany – without Jimmy McCulloch or PP Arnold. The quartet's inspired cocktail hours before and after the shows began to evolve into a non-stop party, juicily reported by the music and gutter press. "Small Faces Only Just Avoid Scandal", was the headline in *Hamburger Abendblatt* (Hamburg Evening News) about the little hotel monsters. On their second tour stop in Kassel, Steve had enacted a sequel to his 1968 horror serial 'In New Zealand With The Who', kicking his tiny two-tone boots into a television set – frustration about once again poor promotion, bad advance sales and half empty halls. Promoter Mel Bush, who made a point of travelling with the band – just as Dee Anthony had done in the old Pie days – and apparently still believed in The Small Faces, tried to lift their spirits as best he could. And so in spite of refreshments, the band did deliver a dynamic sixty-minutes-plus every single night. Incidentally, during the German venture, Steve wore the long, yellow Mod jacket he'd pose in three years later on Pie II's album *Go For The Throat*.

Back in England, *Seventy-Eight In The Shade* finally appeared in

August, reaching the shops through the back door without a publicity campaign, and that meant the corresponding, really strong single 'Stand By Me (Stand By You)' wasn't pushed either. 1978 in the shadows – irony had become bitter sarcasm by now. Finally, some dreaded money matters would defeat a band that had gone out to prove they could stay together at long last.

Right now, The Small Faces were simply not allowed to exist as a company – for in spite of advance payments, the band's and also Mel Bush's investments, the IRS bills were simply too high – yeah, I'm the taxman, as Joe Brown's neighbour George Harrison had sung in 1966. Steve realised the pecuniary truth as well: "The reunion wasn't financially viable…We all had to run away; it was a case of 'scramble!'" Ian McLagan scrambled first – and he soon earned some real money, too: on tour with The Rolling Stones and reunited at the same time with his old Faces mate Ronnie Wood.

Rick and Kenney survived with sessions. Wills, after jamming with Steve for a while, played on David Gilmour's solo album *About Face*, later joining Foreigner, the band lead by Mick Jones, he who had produced the Johnny Hallyday sessions with Marriott, Frampton and Lane.

Kenney Jones got work via (Small) Faces producer Glyn Johns – drumming for Joan Armatrading – before he got the big offer by those other kings of Mod. He seemed the only imaginable successor of the sadly deceased Who drummer Keith Moon. Jimmy McCulloch joined forces with Miller Anderson, renowned guitarist, songwriter and singer for The Keef Hartley Band, Savoy Brown and Hemlock (featuring Mick Weaver and Jim Leverton, both future Official Receivers for Steve). McCulloch and Miller had steered their new band project The Dukes through a debut studio album, when Jimmy died of a heroin overdose on 27 September, 1979 – only days before the band's first gig.

But what had happened to Steve Marriott, who – after initial hesitation – had invested most in The Small Faces reunion, in terms of money and emotion?

The exact text of a small ad in the back pages of *Melody Maker* read: "Is Matt Vinyl A Small Face?" The ad was announcing a gig in a pub called the Canning Town Bridge House, situated in a suburb in

London's East End, only a stone's throw from Steve's birth place Stepney. And indeed, it was Marriott's new pick-up band, sporting All Star guitarist Mickey Finn, Dave Hynes and Jimmy Leverton! Drummer and *Playmates* backing singer Hynes had been Pete York's successor in 1969's Spencer Davis Group and Tony Williams' dep in Joe Brown's Home Brew; bass player Jim Leverton was in the ex-Hendrix spin-off Fat Mattress and had served alongside Miller Anderson in Hemlock and Savoy Brown. Steve paid compliments to Jim, with a brandy in his hand: "That's one of my weaknesses, always pushing other mates in the spotlight, whether it's Rod Stewart or Jimmy Leverton here – but this boy's really got a smashing voice!"

Then old 'Matt Vinyl' got a lump in his throat: "Have you heard 'Stand By Me (Stand By You)'?" he enquired, and when we nodded our heads vehemently, he insisted, "I mean have you really heard it, every single fucking day on the radio? I'll tell you, there is an audience for The Small Faces, and Atlantic Records will do nothing about it. All I want now is to have some fun!" And fun he had, with his new wife Pam in tow, little Toby Joe on her arms, he tried another brandy before he took the Bridge House stage.

Opening with Lonnie Mack's instrumental version of 'Memphis', he immediately lost the back panel of his Hammond organ. His new 'protegé', Jim Leverton, did turn out to be a really good singer – though there was no contest with the master of these East End ceremonies. Apart from a few Humble Pie numbers, for instance a *Thunderbox* gospel tune, 'Groovin' With Jesus', deliriously renamed 'Boozing With Jesus', there were numerous standards from the endless American R&B catalogue.

After a few more of these half official pub gigs, Steve already had another big project in his mind – apart from his vow to have fun – but he'd be forced by the taxman to try his on the other side of the Atlantic. Blind Drunk bass player Jim Leverton gave us his memories in numerous talks over the years:

"Steve had to leave the United Kingdom for tax reasons, and originally he wanted to take The Small Faces' recent bass player, Rick Wills, with him. 'I'll give him one more chance,' Steve would say, 'see if he plays things my way this time.' But nothing came of it, so in the end I got a US ticket, me and Dave Hynes went to Boulder Creek near Santa Cruz, California, to work on songs for a new band project The Firm – before Jimmy Page and Paul Rodgers nicked the name later. You know, for Steve it was, forget The Small Faces and Pie-connected past and start afresh."

The shaping of the new band seemed boosted by the arrival of an American: Leslie West (ex-Mountain) is the guitarist who immortalised his Seventies looks with his solo album title *The Great Fatsby*, and together with Marriott he could have complemented a kind of rock'n'roll Laurel And Hardy act. The combination looked promising and sounded great in the recording studios. Steve: "We carved out nigh on twelve tunes, which will eventually see the light of day…" (Jim Leverton started to remix and overdub several Steve Marriott US-recordings in 1993.)

But no matter what the rock press made of the line-up, problems arose via Leslie before The Firm even got started: "He only came in as the last member of the band, and he was the real beginning of the end. He's so greedy. Leslie wasn't even asked to join, but he phoned Steve one day and said he was keen to be part of it and all that. And Steve didn't know what to do about it. He gave in then, and five minutes after Leslie joined, he claimed he had to have fifty per cent of the publishing rights. Steve called a bluff – 'We haven't written anything' – but Leslie insisted on fifty per cent of any takings there were going to be, and the other two band members (Dave and Jim himself) were to be put on a wage. Can you believe that? That's where the rot set in."

Drummer Dave must have felt it first. Jim: "Dave Hynes didn't like the American way of doing things, so he returned home to England. We tried BJ Wilson of Procol Harum and The Joe Cocker Band – who sadly died in 1991 – and Ian Wallace from Marriott's All Stars. But America and especially his Los Angeles session scene had him well established, so he saw no point in joining."

So down and out in Santa Cruz, The Firm were quarrelling and crumbling at the same time. Stuck with Leslie West but blessed with old cohort Jim Leverton, the final blow for the band came from US immigration officials. The long arms of the law which had destroyed Steve's activities in Britain now ruined his Stateside ambitions just as the industry was getting interested in Marriott matters again. As Jim recalled not without bitterness: "There was a big CBS contract in the pipeline, but in the end I could not get a proper work permit in the States. A clever lawyer we hired suggested that I pop over to Canada to apply for an extension of my visa. I did that, but it didn't work out."

With hindsight, it's not difficult to see how Steve just about kept his lovely humour but got increasingly dependent on mental uppers, like alcohol. In five years, four albums were doomed to stay in the archives: *Scrubbers*, *The Blackberries*, *Marriott And Ridley* and currently *The Firm*, while the two Small Faces albums hardly sold. Patience and money were now running out fast.

CHAPTER EIGHT
Humble Pie II
On To Victory?

So Steve Marriott seemed haunted by bad luck: "After that (the crumbling of The Firm) I was just pissing around, and I got fed up with it. I hate to see a good name get passed over, so I thought about getting Humble Pie back together." But his Blind Drunk and The Firm bass player Jim Leverton knew a much less romantic reason for this plan: "Steve would never have considered that if The Firm had worked out. It was a financial necessity: the sponsored money that backed the project was getting tight!"

In fact it was Jerry Shirley and his manager David Krebs who had the idea first. Jerry had joined Natural Gas in 1975 after Pie I split, with Pete Woods (ex-Sutherland Brothers and Quiver), Joe Molland of Badfinger and Clem Clempson's old Colosseum partner, bassman Mark Clarke. Later on, Natural Gas became Magnet. Steve: "David Krebs sent Jerry out to get me, I think. He said, 'Will you come and talk about getting back?' I said, 'Okay, as long as you pay the air fares!' went to New York and sat there, and it's going nowhere, quite frankly...Then I rang Greg Ridley. He's selling antiques in Gloucester – retired, officially. He said, 'My old lady don't want me to do that stuff no more. I'm quite happy in the antiques business.'" During our conversation in Canning Town's Bridge House pub in late 1978, Steve had also been complaining about Greg's dependence on ladies 'rolling in it'.

Clem Clempson at least promised to fly out from England, but for the moment there was only Steve and Jerry. Shirley then suggested Magnet bass player Anthony 'Sooty' Jones, also from New York, as their new member. Jerry put Sooty in touch with Stevie, so Humble Pie II could start life as a power trio, a format Marriott had championed before when Frampton had left.

Jim Leverton, who would have liked to be part of Pie II, had to play England now because of immigration authorities, but Steve kept him informed. Jim: "Jerry, whose bands Natural Gas and Magnet were managed by David Krebs, had the idea for a Humble Pie reunion. So David flew over to Santa Cruz to present Steve with a fifteen page contract, which Steve duly tore in pieces! But they did sit down to talk things over, and eventually a contract was drawn up and signed – on a napkin from a Denny's hamburger restaurant – and in very simple terms, sort of 'If you pay dis, I'll do dat!' As a test, Steve, Jerry and Magnet bass player Anthony Jones – as I still couldn't get a work permit for the States – cut 'Fool For A Pretty Face' in New York."

Steve: "At the end of this meeting we said, 'We'll go our way, write a hit song over the weekend and record it ten o'clock Monday morning in a shoebox [small studio]. A friend from Santa Cruz who is used to me being arrogant signalled to me 'Tell them to fuck off'. And the best way to tell them to fuck off is to do it. So we went – bang! – wrote 'Fool For A Pretty Face' over the weekend!"

Steve had no idea whether the new number would have any public impact: "We recorded it Monday morning, waited for a reaction, it freaked and then I split...I went back to California and thought no more of it than 'Maybe, who knows?' But we got such a violent reaction on it – airplay in New York, stuff like that – that we said, 'Okay, let's make a go of it!'"

Johnny Wright, The Small Faces II producer of *Playmates*, got the three-piece a fair deal with a little studio of his friend, engineer Akili Walker, at Villa Recorders in Modesto, near Boulder Creek and Santa Cruz. While a new album was being cut, they were still looking for a fourth band member. As promised, Pie guitarist Clempson flew in for the sessions.

Steve: "Clem and Bobby Tench came out to California." (Bob Tench is a singer/guitarist with a prolific background from The Jeff Beck Group, its Beck-less studio version Hummingbird as well as Roger Chapman's Streetwalkers and Shortlist.) "Clem was 'artin and 'fartin; he didn't know what he was going to do, the Jack Bruce thing or whatever." So, after only twelve days of recording over-dubs on the trio's stuff, Clem finally decided to join The Jack Bruce Band. The renowned Cream bass player was due to start another supergroup with jazz rock drummer Billy Cobham and keyboard ace David Sancious.

So in autumn 1979, Humble Pie II chose Bob Tench. Steve: "I've known Bob for years. He was knocking around in bands like The Gass in the mid Sixties. Bobby and I aren't great guitarists, but we're good ones, and with the vocals we've got we don't want no flash guitar, Van Halen can cover that sphere." In any case, both Bob and Steve now finished Clem's guitar overdubs, just like Clem had started his Pie career on *Smokin'* eight years ago. But Bob, apart from his guitar duties a tremendous vocalist in his own right, also got the chance to sing on two tracks which he co-wrote.

Apart from Bob's vocal assistance, Steve negotiated more budget from manager David Krebs and producer Johnny Wright – in order to get some new Blackberries-type 'chicks' to Modesto: Cheryl Ashley, Lisa Zimmerman and Marge Raymond sang behind Steve like in the old days, even if they didn't use the other trio's name. The resulting album came out in April 1980. True to its title, *On To Victory* sported the most dubious cover illustration in Steve's entire career – a World War II air combat scene probably reminiscent of the Pie live volume, and a band picture on the back that makes Guns N'Roses look like some vacuum cleaner salesmen! What the hell, the stranded Small Face had new product on the market.

And what product. 'Fool For A Pretty Face' was a genuine style defining comeback. In fact 'Fool' is almost the prototype for everything that ever made Humble Pie popular in the United States: dynamic R&B, a chorus to shout along to, a memorable riff, interesting guitar sounds, supplied here with a clear and heavy production that the old Pie had never really cracked without either of the Johns brothers. A success in US singles charts which would have deserved a much higher placing, Steve would keep this Marriott-Shirley number in his live set for the rest of his career!

'You Silly Prat' has the task of following the hit. A collaboration of the basic trio, this solid slow rock makes it easy to see why Steve regarded some of the album's elements as "groping for ideas". The static theme only comes alive with Jerry's energetic drumming and

Steve's Hammond organ, and the gospel helpings of the 'new Blackberries', Cheryl, Lisa and Marge.

Marriott's up-tempo vehicle for stage antics, the accent for 'Infatuation' is on his soul revue of 1973 again, with Steve and girls doing their call and response like in the old days, assisted by Gary US Bonds and Werewolves sax player Joey Stann, who Shirley had met during recordings for singer Benny Mardones in 1978.

'Take It From Here' is more slow rock like 'Prat', but salvaged by versatile guitar chops, most possibly by Dave Clempson during his working holiday in Modesto.

Then comes 'Savin' It', a fascinating jazz funk cooperation of Steve's with new recruit Bob Tench, composed and arranged by the duo. The marked contrast between the two great soul voices is presented to great effect. Joey Stann's sax plays a major part in the overall sound. The groove is irresistible, and those who like more of the same should check out *Eat It* and Bob Tench's three LPs with Hummingbird 1975-7.

Unlike The Small Faces Mk II, where 'Lookin' For A Love' was reluctantly repeated, Steve never shied away from re-vamping old Mod oldies in the All Stars or several Pie line-ups. Marriott sang 'Baby Don't You Do It' with The Small Faces Mk I as early as 1966. With a more experienced band and three black girl singers – who assist Jerry's drumming with hand-claps – this one sounds more energetic than ever before. A gospel/soul happening as they'd have said in the Sixties.

'Get It In The End' is another trio number. Steve's melancholic intro promises more than this formula song can give, but groove and the integration of the backing singers are more coherent than on *Eat It*.

'My Lover's Prayer' is a highlight: Otis Redding's ballad belongs to the three blues gems which Marriott's interpretations turned to classics: in line with 'Five Long Years' and 'Help Me Through The Day'. Steve accompanies himself on E-piano, and the band get in dynamically without ever getting in the way.

Professional and memorable riff rock is delivered in 'Further Down The Road', composed and executed by all four with routine panache. This could have benefited from audience participation.

Many fans who only knew Steve's happy-go-lucky party character didn't realise his profound knowledge of the American R&B songbook. 'Over You' had originally been released as a 1966 single by falsetto fetishist Aaron Neville – of The Neville Brothers – as the follow-up to his solo hit 'Tell It Like It Is'. Steve derives obvious fun out of browsing through his old record collection, and so this song is the most relaxed performance on the entire album, and a fitting finale.

On To Victory on the whole deserved much more promotion. In the States, it came out on Atlantic's subsidiary Atco which also owned the imminent solo album *Empty Glass* by Marriott's fellow (ex-)Mod Pete Townshend, whose brandy glass in those days was often as well-filled as Steve's. Back home in England, *Victory*'s release got the former Small Face back into the claws of his erstwhile slave driver, without him realising what sort of deal had been made. Steve: "When I reformed Humble Pie, I ended up with [Don and Dave] Arden's label without my knowledge. It was just a case of David Krebs telling me he'd done a deal with Jet Records and I said, 'Isn't that Ardens' label?' I don't mind…"

Even on a small label, *On To Victory* meant new product which enabled them to start touring, and Humble Pie could be spotted in various support slots, for example for Ted Nugent, and in mid size clubs with reassuring regularity. On the East and West Coast, Chicago the Mid West and the Southern States, it was 'hard slog' the way Pie Mk I had started their US career in 1969. Steve and Jerry were happy to be back on the road. Jerry: "Where I sit as a drummer, I get to scope out – if I pick up on a thirteen year old mouthing the words to 'I Don't Need No Doctor' If that's not a big compliment…"

Steve, after a two year absence from touring, missing it ever since that ill-fated European Small Faces tour in early 1978: "I'm amazed as to the amount of people who still remember your voice, your songs…I did Humble Pie from scratch when I was twenty-four years old, and that was ten years ago, and I haven't got another ten years to build and build, so what I'm hoping is we'll score pretty soon. We could have called this band The Black Hole Of Calcutta, but that would have had a harder time going on tour with people like Ted. We actually use the name Humble Pie to our advantage…it doesn't really have a lot to do with the old Humble Pie."

That of course was wishful thinking, because the mixture was the same, just better produced – but who'd blame Steve for a bit of hustle of a new era. On to victory indeed. In the meantime, Steve, Pam and their four year old boy Toby Joe had moved from California to Atlanta, Georgia, the home of 'Southern Belle' Stephens-Marriott. But most of Steve's time was spent 'further down the road', and Jerry, Bob and Sooty began to wonder if their little boss didn't overdo the non-stop partying bit in hotels and backstage – excited by live work, disappointed with meagre sales of the album.

In order to make sure of the success of a follow-up, manager David Krebs and his partner Steve Leber were now looking for a well-known mainstream producer, who would be expected to put his heavy but ultimately commercial stamp on Pie II, whose potential was undoubted. They chose Foreigner's mainman Gary Lyons, who would later work for The Scorpions. And so another studio album, mostly recorded between live gigs during 1980, was another giant step forward in terms of sound clarity, panache, song selection and togetherness – and its release in May 1981 could have been the basis of many more Humble Pie II years...

Go For The Throat begins with 'All Shook Up' and the listener gets left breathless right from the start. This really is the old Presley number, but with monster riffs and breakneck breaks it goes for the metal kill, quite a departure as Elvis covers go – Steve had interpreted the early 'You're A Heartbreaker' faithful to the original seven years earlier on *Scrubbers*. Even at full speed, he doesn't forget to stay tongue-in-cheek. For variety, Bob takes over for a great vocal break, a nice continuation of the old Marriott-Ridley-Frampton tradition. Like 'Fool For A Pretty Face', this number was to stay in Steve's live set for good.

With 'Teenage Anxiety' we get a change of scene, and the guv'nor at his acoustic piano. From time to time, Marriott surprised everybody with his sensitive, heartfelt ballads. This lament was the last number to be added to the collection, and Steve sings about the hard life in the limelight of rock'n'roll: "It's rough out there, it's tough out there – I believe I had enough out there!" – "I wrote these words because I didn't like to do 'nuthin' no more'!" Fighting back his tears, Steve revealed on release that he wrote the song in memory of John Lennon shortly after he was killed in December 1980: "It always chokes me up to talk about it. It's more about my attitude than what actually happened. It just sickened me! What is it worth?" And so he sang: "They shot my hero in the streets, and as I said, the world still weeps. It stands to serve my memory, 'cause he meant so much to me!" The melodramatic atmosphere Marriott and the band create here stuns in every second – excellent guitar work, everything kept together by Jerry's drums.

Another Small Faces oldie follows. After 'Wham Bam' on *Marriott* and 'Baby' on *Victory* this remake of 'Tin Soldier' adds odd detail like a nice guitar line to the 1967 version, but it generally excels with sheer recording quality, and a comparison proves that Steve has lost nothing of his charisma since his early hit successes.

For 'Keep It On The Island', the drum sound is among the best ever recorded by Jerry, and yet another set of fresh 'Blackberries' are show-cased to good effect. For the sessions, they consisted of the future Coca-Cola singer Robyn Beck as well as Maxine Dickson and Dana Kral. Cheekily, Steve and Bob's guitars quote Cream's 'Strange Brew' theme, maybe as a little hello to Pie's deserter Clem Clempson, now working with Jack Bruce.

'Driver' sees R&B illustrating the most dangerous corners of Chicago's ghetto district. This is about a bloke who is on a rather bad acid flashback. Steve: "A true story – he looked like Charles Manson! 'Cocaine hair' means no hair. His terrible eyes and bald head, he was frightening. He was the worst driver, he would never let me in the bus, where my little studio equipment bits were to write the songs! That's why it was called 'Waiting For The driver', because he always locked me out." A quiet but speedy boogie turns to an absolute blues rock orgy, but in contrast to some of the *Thunderbox* tracks, it is delivered with absolute discipline.

Marriott had met Richard Supa via the real Blackberries in LA during the All Stars period. Richie's solo-LP *Supas Jamboree* was already a decade old at the time, after which he worked sessions for BJ Thomas and Frankie Miller. He wrote 'Restless Blood' for Pie and assists the girls on backing vocals – rhythm and soul with Bobby Tench's welcome, all too rarely used solo voice.

For the title track, a Marriott/Tench joint composition, an elegant subdued groove, skillfully set twin guitar lines, unusual chords and hot vocal passages mean that every detail sounds perfect. It contains all the ingredients Steve wanted for his Pie; the guitar licks quote blues standards as well as *Abbey Road* sounds, much more creatively than on the Fab Four covers Pie I delivered for *Street Rats*. Jerry's never-ending drum fills are a further joy, and the number should have gone on for twice its actual length.

'Chip Away The Stone' is the other Richie Supa number on the LP, maybe a bit too similar to 'Blood' to make real impact, but the type of formula rock for stadiums Steve might have thought necessary for growing audiences. Things would turn out quite differently...

Even the often extremely self-critical Steve was completely over the moon with the songs, playing and production on this one: "I'm very proud of the new album. Gary Lyons is a great producer; I want to use him forever. He says it's the best album and he's worked on a few. The drive on it is insane, and there's not one cut I can point to as weak – which I can do on nigh all the other albums I've done. *On To Victory* was groping for ideas, like *As Safe As Yesterday Is*, but Gary sifted through all our songs and chose some things that maybe I wouldn't have picked – and they all turned out to be spot on. It took us almost a year to get this one out, but no complaints at all."

Atco Records followed the Humble Pie II career with growing attention. The band certainly worked hard, for instance as a support act for the Big Marathon Tour 1980-1 with the old snorting champions Aerosmith. Bad company probably, because Pie were forced to cancel a few dates due to a stoned Steve breaking his right hand in a hotel door. Hotels were a favourite place for going mad for him. For instance he remembered the Hollywood Hiatt Regency, known to rock bands as the 'Continental Riot House', with affection: "I'm one of the original boys that stayed there doing nasty things!" Or how about another hotel in Salt Lake City? Friends and groupies were in Steve's room, one of them would throw a chair out of the window, and Steve had the cheek to go down to reception and complain about it: "He attacked first!" Rioting went on, and when there was a knock on the door, Marriott asked the girls for love noises – 'Make them jealous' – which they duly supplied. What Steve couldn't have guessed was that in front of his door, fifteen policemen were waiting to escort him from the premises!

But when on duty, Pie delivered, and received encouraging audience reaction, even if they had to stick to their standards for optimum crowd reaction and got little chance of promoting the album. Steve: "In major halls as a support it's a bit of a blow because they know 'Fool For A Pretty Face'…and definitely know 'Thirty Days In The Hole' and 'I Don't Need No Doctor', but when it comes to promoting this one [*Throat*], playing two or three off of this, it kind of puts a dip in your set, but it's gotta be done!"

Still, their latest album had captured the live atmosphere as much as seemed possible behind studio doors. But someone must have remembered *Rockin' The Fillmore*'s impact. For Humble Pie II's summer tour of England, the recording of another live album was discussed – sort of 'Fillmore – ten years after', to be recorded during two nights at London's Marquee. Even when most tour dates were scrapped in favour of an even bigger British headlining tour during the autumn, the live date remained on the agenda. Now, an Americanised band would play a legendary British venue, while in 1971 at New York's Fillmore East, it had been the other way round.

Pie II's British comeback was going to be celebrated at London's Rainbow Theatre, where Pie I had triumphed on several occasions, including the summer of 1974. But a week before the scheduled concert date of 29 July 1981, the most dramatic cancellation came via Texas, USA.

While on tour, Pie boss Steve Marriott had been rushed into the intensive care ward of a Dallas hospital with inner bleeding injuries – his life was at risk. Steve himself had felt this coming but ignored the symptoms: "Silly boy, you see. Wouldn't listen. Wouldn't be told. I had a split in the duodenal tract. I would rather have had an ulcer because you can take things for that. A split can open up and start all over again." But how had it come thus far when he seemed happy enough fronting his band? "It was a sign of unhappiness. It had nothing to do with the group itself, it was a management thing. It was being put on a wage. Here is your sixpence. It didn't make sense to me. That's when I started boozing, and taking drugs. And obviously it took its toll because intensive care is serious. I came out of it thinking a lot. I curbed everything and gradually got better."

In fact, the abuse had begun seven years before, around 1974, when Steve was put on a wage for the first time, not by his current manager David Krebs, but by Dee Anthony. Back then, it wasn't only Humble Pie who slid into a crisis; Marriott's first marriage with his wife Jenny failed. Steve felt left alone by the industry: "That pisses me off about record companies. To them it's another number, to you it's your history, you've got to live with it, you've got to go to bed with it, good or bad, forever. And if I have to get drunk to go to sleep…"

CHAPTER NINE
Kenney Jones & Ian McLagan
Separate Ways

Just as The Faces were drifting into their separate ways, the reissued Small Faces single 'Itchycoo Park' reached the Top Ten of the UK charts – in December 1975 – and McLagan and Jones spotted the chance of a reunion, especially since as early as June 1976, a second edition of The Small Faces had (re)formed.

Rod Stewart drew a complete line between himself and his old cohorts, slagging their musical abilities in interviews and – for the time being – was unwilling to be reminded of his life and times with The Faces. Their spontaneous, happy-go-lucky approach, both on stage and in the studios, apparently got on his nerves. He also realised that – with the looming punk age – he couldn't impress anybody with the still likable, yet visibly anachronistic Faces-type party rock. Consequently, he polished and streamlined his music and turned it in the direction of AOR – Adult Orientated Rock. This immediately turned out to be exactly the right move, with excellent production courtesy of Tom Dowd and the studio elite from LA, Memphis and Muscle Shoals, Alabama. But Rod's enigmatic solo career needn't be pursued here, as numerous American, British and German authors have written about it – more or less critically (see Bibliography).

Ron Wood stayed true to the spirit of The Faces – as the eternal new guy with The Rolling Stones. Indeed, there were clear stylistic parallels between the two bands, and a substantial number of music critics had seen The Faces as a kind of ersatz Rolling Stones. Woody's solo albums, far from revealing musical genius, sound like a mixture of The Faces and The Rolling Stones. This comes as even less of a surprise when one realises that Ian McLagan and Kenney Jones, as well as Keith Richards, Mick Jagger and Charlie Watts, almost always lent a hand as session musicians and songwriters. But the fun side always sees Woody through: bass veteran Andy Pyle (Blodwyn Pig, Savoy Brown, Chicken Shack, Kinks, Gary Moore and many more) told us that back home in Surrey from long, gruelling tours, a Woody album is what he invariably plays.

The Faces remained in the public eye for two or three years after the split, but always – as was to be expected – with a dig at Rod in bold print. In 1976, the movie *Rod Stewart's Farewell Concert*, directed by Mike Mansfield, hit the cinemas. This turned out to be the recording of a Faces concert that took place in London's Kilburn State Theatre on 23 December, 1974. Rod treats the audience to a boring, 'raving fairy' glamour rock show. His colleagues, augmented by Keith Richards, are allowed to relish their parts of star-assisting extras.

Also in 1976, the compilation *Snakes And Ladders/The Best Of Faces* appeared, followed by the double album *The Best Of The Faces*, which in May 1977 still reached a modest Number Twenty-Four in the British album charts. In June, the band even cracked the singles listings once again: with their EP 'Memphis', including their three biggest hits. But that was as much as they could milk from that creative cow called The Faces.

Meanwhile, the revived Small Faces tried in vain to pick up the sounds and impact of their most glamorous period. By May 1978, this chapter was finished irrevocably. Kenney Jones and Ian McLagan had never exactly been in the limelight, neither in The Small Faces nor Faces line-ups, and had always been content with their positions near the back line. Over the years, they had trained and sophisticated their musical skills, so now they were able to relax and face their professional future as in-demand session/studio guns. Ever since their Faces days, they had been active as guest musicians, individually or together; for Marsha Hunt's *Woman Child* (also featuring Ron Wood) and Chuck Berry's *London Sessions* (1972).

Kenney Jones soon played for artists related to (Small) Faces producer Glyn Johns, like the underrated singer/guitarist Andy Fairweather-Low, and Joan Armatrading. He then took up the drum seat behind Cactus lead singer Pete French's new band project Ducks In Flight (featuring Marriott's men Joe Brown and Tim Hinkley). But management hassles prevented their live appearance and so the band name became Pete's solo album title. But Kenney, who'd had his fair share of business problems in The Small Faces II, soon got a much more attractive offer.

Three months after the sudden, but hardly surprising death of Keith Moon, The Who offered their fellow ex-Mod their vacant drum stool. Kenney in *Modern Drummer*: "Their manager Bill Curbishley told me, 'The Who...haven't considered, and will not consider, anybody else. They want you to join as an equal member.'" On 22 December, 1978, Kenney agreed – and remained a Who member till the end of 1982, with extra concerts, like Live Aid in 1985 and the BPI Awards in 1988. Obviously, the rather introverted Jones was never able (or willing) to replace Keith Moon as the chaotic clown. Consequently, his drumming turned out very much according to his own rules, but rock solid as usual: on the two studio albums *Face Dances* (1981) and *It's Hard* (1982) as well as the live double *Who's Last* (also recorded in 1982 but released in 1984).

After The Who's 'final' split in 1982 (till 1989), Jones slightly retreated from the music scene. As a drummer, he only appeared sporadically, like during the ARMS concerts for Ronnie Lane in 1983, Bill Wyman's related Willie And The Poor Boys project in 1984-5 and Bo Diddley's thirtieth anniversary gathering in 1985, where he got together with Woody and Ronnie Lane again.

In 1989, Kenney ran into ex-Free singer Paul Rodgers by chance in a night club. He had known Paul well since the later Small Faces days around 1968, and had worked with him during the ARMS tour through the United States. Rodgers invited him into his studio, where the idea for the duo project The Law took shape. Finally, the eponymous debut album (featuring Bryan Adams and Pink Floyd's David Gilmour) appeared on the shelves, and pretty much stayed there. The sound just didn't impress: the record company's (Atlantic's) politics had dictated mainstream AOR without rough edges, and so good songs and faultless musicianship appeared uninspired and powerless. A second Law album was nevertheless finished, but remains unreleased due to a business disagreement between Rodgers and Jones.

After this disappointment, Kenney once again resumed the private pleasures of country life. He owns an estate in rural Surrey with his wife Jan, who – surprise, surprise – comes from a very musical family. She's the daughter of the well-known orchestra leader Tom Osbourne and sister of Gary Osbourne, an in-demand session singer (for Elton John, Kiki Dee and Jeff Wayne among others), for whose duo Vigrass And Osbourne Kenney had played drums in 1974. The dedicated horse addict and polo player at least picks up the sticks in his home studio from time to time.

In February 1993, his latest project crystallised: a re-recording, including songs, and animated cartoon film of *Ogdens' Nut Gone Flake*. Stanley Unwin's scheduled successor as narrator of the wonderfully weird story line was none other than Robin Williams. But three years after starting on this ambitious immortalisation of his little band, the finishing and release dates for Kenney's 'Mod Darlings Go Disney' feature are absolutely uncertain.

Comparatively, good old Ian McLagan leads a much hotter musical life these days – for many years now he has been among the most busy session keyboard players in the USA. After The Faces split, Mac joined Ronnie Lane's Slim Chance for a short time and subsequently took part in the new Small Faces till the summer of 1978. When their Mark II incarnation had stuffed their gear and IRS bills forever, he was hired by the new wave outfit The Rich Kids, a Sex Pistols sideline. Negotiated by Ron Wood, he soon joined The Rolling Stones as a tour and studio musician (*Some Girls*). At the end of 1978, he moved to the United States with his second wife Kim, the former Mrs Keith Moon: "In punk terms, I'd had it, but over there, I was suddenly a big deal!"

The close contact to The Rolling Stones, especially his old cohort Ron Wood, continued to smooth his path. But a rather sad coincidence led to the appearance of a new band, which was also destined to put Mac's first solo album on the map. In October 1978, Keith Richards was charged and found guilty with possession of heroin in Toronto, Canada. Rather then getting imprisoned (that fear had led to hectic recordings much beyond *Some Girls*) he luckily got away with being sentenced to two benefit concerts for the Canadian National Institute for the Blind. These he was supposed to have staged in the course of six months. Keith put together a session band at short notice, with substantial help from Ron Wood: the New Barbarians. Apart from Keith and Woody, Ian McLagan, Meters drummer Ziggy Modeliste, sax man Bobby Keys and bass ace Stanley Clarke joined the ranks. Having delivered the charity concerts, the Barbarians went on a well-received four-week tour of the States in April 1979. The cheerful live atmosphere is documented on the bootleg double album *Buried Alive* which, in spite of technical deficiencies, is superior to Mac's solo LP. That appeared as *Troublemaker* at the end of 1979. The album confirms the old insight that an all star line-up (among others, there were Keith Richards, Ron Wood, Ringo Starr, Jim Keltner, Stanley Clarke, Bobby Keys) does by no means guarantee a good album. The song material, almost entirely Ian's own compositions, is pedestrian – except for the title track and 'Hold On' – and the production is professional, but still sterile and without that certain kick.

Shortly after The New Barbarians had disbanded at the beginning of 1980, Mac founded his own Bump Band, a more or less loose project with varying members, with whom he eventually cut his second solo album *Bump In The Night*. This turned out to be a much more accessible achievement than his debut. Ian presented better songs – including 'Little Girl', which he co-wrote with Woody – and the production was sparse, as to leave more rough edges to the individual tracks. Unfortunately, it was only released in the USA, where it soon appeared in the bargain racks.

Mac then joined Bonnie Raitt's backing band for three years, and from the mid Eighties he toured with Bob Dylan, Jackson Browne and the reconciled Everly Brothers. In between, he attempted another solo trip with a band called Loco, and also recorded the EP/mini album *Last Chance To Dance*, with an appearance by ex-Rod Stewart Band bass player Phil Chen on the title track. The four songs have a definitely powerful rock appeal, with sparse but appealing arrangements. For example, Mac plays the accordion on 'You're My Girl'.

After a few Texas sessions with Austin's new citizen Ronnie Lane, the two little British expatriates had definite recording plans. But when these didn't materialise, McLagan accepted David Lindley's invitation to join his backing group El Rayo-X in 1987. For one year he hit the road with the guitar wizard, and since then Mac has been predominantly busy in the studios; the list of artists who require his mastery of the keyboards is still growing, but to name but a few: Bruce Springsteen, The Stray Cats, Melissa Etheridge, Bonnie Raitt, Arc Angels featuring Charlie Sexton and Joe Cocker. On top of those, Ian had tremendous fun collaborating with the party and sleaze rockers of Dogs D'Amour, and Faces descendants Georgia Satellites, both of them bands who made no secret of their admiration of The (Small) Faces.

From his long-term base in Pasadena, LA, Mac also took care of keen young newcomers like Miracle Legion, and as far as his studio schedule allowed, he also worked with The Bump Band, ably cutting 'Pictures Of Lily' for the *Who Covers Who* tribute, for instance.

A Faces reunion concert, which was widely advertised in the UK, remained almost unnoticed by the European and especially German press. After a lot of hassles, it finally took place at Wembley Stadium on 5 July, 1986. After Rod Stewart had not taken part in Ronnie Lane's ARMS concert and subsequent tour in 1983, he had suggested this renewed benefit concert with a Faces reunion custom-built for the occasion. (There was also a rumour in insiders' circles that Rod had been banned from the 1983 Albert Hall stage that first night because the other musicians involved had threatened to let the gig fall through should he appear.)

Anyway, Rod the Mod certainly lived up to his reputation by milking this media event for his own purposes. In the end the half-hour Faces gig was little more than an encore following Rod's own two-hour show.

The Faces had hardly had any rehearsal time, and as a result, the sound and vision Rod, Woody, Mac, Kenney and Bill Wyman presented was suitably chaotic and rough. Bill acted as a substitute for the ill Ronnie Lane; originally, Duran Duran bass player John Taylor had been pencilled in for the part. Ronnie was also helped onto the stage and bravely joined in on vocals – in pain. The Faces were allowed a mere four titles on their own: '(I Know) I'm Losing You', 'Twisting The Night Away', 'Stay With Me' and 'We'll Meet Again'; Stewart's band 'assisted' during two further numbers, 'Sweet Little Rock'N'Roller' and 'Here We Go'. The British Press covered the concert in a rather subdued way. Still, they pronounced The Faces' contribution more entertaining than the usual, perfectionist Stewart show. Further concerts – Rod had even talked of a reunion tour – didn't materialise; the remaining Faces had seen through the promotion stunt and were quick about leaving the locality of the crime. For many years, contact between Rod and the others was pretty icy.

The 'others', though, retained their friendships, especially Ron Wood and Ian McLagan, whose studio paths met frequently, for example at Buddy Guy's comeback sessions for the *Damn Right, I've Got The Blues* LP. The recording dates for *Slide On This*, Woody's first studio album in ten years, were so much fun for the pair that Mac didn't need much persuasion to join Ron's newly formed backing band. In October 1992, Wood and friends, also featuring Stones sax man Bobby Keys, started a tour of North America lasting several weeks, in order to promote the solo album which had been received rather positively by the music critics.

On 13 November, the entourage also stopped in Austin, where – hardly unexpected – a sort of Faces mini-reunion took place. At the end of the concert,Ronnie Lane was pushed onto the stage of the Terrace Club in his wheelchair, where he joined in the vocals for 'Ooh La La'. Meanwhile, MTV had enquired whether Rod Stewart was interested in appearing as part of the *Unplugged* acoustic concert series. For sheer prestige alone Rod could not have declined and so he asked his old buddy Woody, who he had lost sight of for such a long time. Ron didn't hesitate, and after they had agreed on mainly presenting tried and tested material from The Faces' era, the MTV recording on 8 February, 1993, could be tackled without hassle.

For the scheduled honour of Rod Stewart in connection with the British Phonographic Industry Awards, The Faces were about to be considered, too. With the exception of Ronnie Lane, who could not make the trip to London because of his illness, Rod and Ron were joined by the other two 'small' Faces, only days after the *Unplugged* sessions: Mac had flown home with the two acoustic ramblers, and in London Kenney Jones met them, with ex-Stone Bill Wyman in tow. On 14 February, 1983, this line-up played the Town And Country Club (which is now called The Forum) in London's Kentish Town. This gig was screened by British television. Two days later, the 'Brit Awards' presentation followed. Rod received an honour for his lifetime achievement, and as The Faces played an undeniably crucial part in his (solo) career, the contribution of the band was also honoured.

The fact that of all the members, Ronnie Lane as the true Faces initiator couldn't be present, made Rod sad, too: "Really, he was the heart and soul of the band, not me or Woody..." Rod knew, from Ronnie and Mac, that Ronnie's health had deteriorated lately. Anyway, with two tasters from the good old times, 'Stay With Me' and 'Sweet Little Rock'N'Roller', Rod and co (featuring Bill Wyman) thanked the jury and the audience for having been honoured. The good vibes between the five players led to Rod's proposal for a renewal of the 1986 Faces reunion. On 23 February he announced a single 1993 charity concert for Ronnie Lane. The occasion guaranteed publicity: Rod spoke in Hamburg, where he mainly presented his new album *Lead Vocalist*, a compilation of old and new songs, including Faces numbers. But for the time being, this didn't work out, allegedly because of Ronnie Wood's tour commitments with The

Rolling Stones.

Still, Ian McLagan had free dates, and in 1994, Rod took him in his tour band. At the same time, Mac and his wife Kim decided to relocate from LA to Austin, Texas. Ironically this move happened just as Ronnie was moving away from the place to live in the Rocky Mountains. What a waste: for years, the two had dreamed of resuming their partnership via projects in the hot Texan music metropolis. Mac revealed the motives behind his move to Austin for the *Austin Chronicle*: "We finally escaped from LA. We've been talking about leaving for some time because we were very tired of the smog and the violence. The last earthquake was the catalyst."

Hyperactive as ever – but never hectic – Mac became an integral part of the Austin music scene in next to no time, thanks mainly to numerous calls as a session player. He also started another new backing band named Monkey Jump. His autobiography is scheduled for 1997.

About two years later, December 1995, there was a Faces reunion after all: in Dublin during the Rod Stewart sojourn, Ronnie Lane being replaced by Carmine Rojas. It looks like Rod will not leave his beloved Faces era untouched, as he proceeded to announce more concerts – and indeed there was talk of an album – for the autumn of 1996…

CHAPTER TEN

Peter Frampton
Where I Should Be

Peter Frampton, born on 22 April, 1950 in London, was raised in its South Eastern suburb of Beckenham, Kent. He went to Beckenham Grammar School, where one of his school mates was one David Jones – aka David Bowie – who was taught Arts by Mr Frampton senior. Peter played guitar from the age of eight. In the process, he joined local bands like The Truebeats, soon picking up lead vocals: Cliff Richard's 'A Girl Like You' and Adam Faith's 'Poor Me' were his debut solo spots on a school gig.

With school friends Gary Taylor on guitar and vocals – later to turn to bass – and keyboard player Andy Bown (27 March, 1947), at nineteen both veterans by comparison, as well as singer Terry Clark and original Stones drummer Tony Chapman, Peter was in the 1965 version of The Preachers. Chapman had started their first incarnation in 1963 with singer Steve Carroll, who died in 1966. The Preachers Mark II issued the Bill Wyman-produced single 'Hole In My Soul'. In his autobiography *Stone Alone*, Bill juicily points out that he taught Peter, already a dab hand at pulling guitar strings, how to do similar things with young ladies on the London club scene.

At the end of 1965, The Preachers turned into The Herd, featuring Frampton, Bown, Taylor and new drummer, Andrew Steele. The R&B quartet commanded impressive audiences at London's Marquee Club and gigged with star guests like US blues veteran Jimmy Reed or, predictably, Bill Wyman. A record deal with Parlophone was lost when the first three singles, 'Goodbye Baby', 'She Was Really Saying Something' and 'Too Much In Love' did not chart. Soon after parting ways with their agent Billy Gaff, The Herd landed a deal with Fontana via the Dave Dee, Dozy, Beaky, Mick And Tich-

composers/producers/managers Ken Howard and Alan Blaikley. The
Fontana debut single 'I Can Fly' did not do so but flopped – in spite of
a giant campaign in *NME*.

But then – with the Flower Power year 1967 in full flight – the
psychedelically-pompous 'From The Underworld' – adapted from
Orpheus In The Underworld replaced the Herd stage sound with lots
of brass and strings – and hit the British Top Ten, peaking at Number
Six. It was followed by 'Paradise Lost', equally attractive in orchestration
and combining symphonic rock with a big band strip show intro. The
Herd's monumental sound pushed the single towards the fifteenth UK
chart position around Christmas, with the help of pirate radio stations.
Incidentally, its catchy vocal background theme was later pinched by
The Hollies for the 1976 song 'Be With You' on their *Russian Roulette*
album – "Pure coincidence though," was Hollie Tony Hicks' comment
in 1995...

With a slight lack of adventure, the Herd LP, which followed hot on
the heals of the second singles chart success, was also titled *Paradise
Lost (Paradise And Underworld* in Germany). In addition to the
singles, it featured some happy beat, but little in terms of their original
R&B music. A versatile array of numbers, partly self-penned by
Frampton/Bown, contained anything from cocktail jazz – with some of
Pete's delicate Wes Montgomery chords – plus gospel, Henry Mancini
sounds and Walker Brothers leanings via Gary Taylor's pleasant
baritone, taking turns with Frampton's lead singing.

But in spring 1968, producer Steve Rowland accepted a more rocky
group sound: Howard/Blaikley's 'I Don't Want Our Lovin' To Die'
presented infectious 'power pop', ages before the term was coined and
became a deserved Top Five smash for the actual band – as opposed to
the orchestra-backed vocal group. Then, just as Peter Frampton could
actually recognise his underrated electric guitar playing on pirate
airwaves – as well as the newly founded BBC counterpart Radio One –
the hysterical pop media paid him an extremely dubious service. *Rave*,
a long extinct teen magazine for screaming young ladies, voted him
'The Face Of 68' – amidst Frampton's hopes that his Gibson Les Paul
guitar counted more than his sunny smile at long last. As if that wasn't
enough, Peter's girly fame caused envy and irritation within the band.

Next to the hype-inflicted emotional low, The Herd had to suffer

Andrew Steele's exit, for health reasons – the drummer just couldn't face the emotional pressures and touring commitments of the popular music profession any longer. Steele was replaced by drummer Henry Spinetti – kid brother of nationally known actor Victor. More changes followed before 1968 was through. Herd's mentors Howard and Blaikley were replaced by Stones agent Andrew Oldham who had a reputation of granting his acts – like The Small Faces – more artistic freedom. Consequently, Andy Bown and Peter Frampton wrote the next single A-side themselves. 'Sunshine Cottage', an excellent, psychedelic as well as guitar orientated song, was coupled with the stage compatible R&B number 'Miss Jones', and released with high hopes. It bombed, leading to the big bang.

In the winter of 1968-9, two grown-up whizz-kids realised that they shared similar problems. Both Frampton and Steve Marriott desperately wanted to replace their endlessly quoted, full colour 'pop files' with a new rock credibility. Hadn't Eric Clapton left The Yardbirds, hadn't young Stevie Winwood flown the cosy nest of The Spencer Davis Group? On top of these thoughts, both angry young men wondered where all their concert fees and record royalties, amounting to several thousands of pounds, had gone.

Frampton had been made aware of potentially dubious accounts by his equally suffering friend Graham Nash, who was about to leave his Hollies and was also motivated artistically and financially. Disgusted by recent dives into contract small print, Peter announced his split.

The Herd carried on as a trio for a while but gave up after a final forty-five, 'The Game', which they had acquired from the Hammond/Hazlewood catalogue and coupled with 'Beauty Queen', tough Frampton/Bown rock based on The Kinks' 'You Really Got Me' riff!

Subsequently, Gary Taylor became a radio DJ. Frampton in 1995: "Hank Marvin told me that Gary now lives in Perth and uses his studio complex for radio commercials." Andrew Bown and Henry Spinetti formed Judas Jump with a Welsh singer, Adrian Williams and Amen Corner's saxmen Mike Smith and Alan Jones. Taylor and Steele would collaborate one more time in 1971, recording 'You Got Me Hanging From Your Loving Tree', without success. After Judas Jump, Andy Bown, who was to cross Frampton's musical path again before long, stayed in the Amen Corner camp and worked in Andy Fairweather-Low's band. Henry Spinetti reverted to sessions and established a long and stable drumming career, behind Eric Clapton, Tina Turner, in Roger Chapman's band Shortlist and Gary Brooker's Procol Harum among others.

The following years are Humble Pie history – and thoroughly covered in the respective chapters. But it all started like this: still a Herd member, Peter Frampton had guested with The Small Faces on stage and had even accompanied them to Paris for sessions with French Rock idol Johnny Hallyday. Thus, he was rumoured to have joined the band. Steve Marriott had actually tried to persuade his cohorts Lane, Jones and McLagan to accept Peter as a valid hand in the guitar department, which The Small Faces leader himself didn't want entirely on his shoulders. But when Ronnie, Kenney and Mac vetoed this, Steve found a rhythm section for Peter's own band project Humble Pie.

They were Spooky Tooth's Greg Ridley on bass and the drummer in Apostolic Intervention (a Faces studio brainchild): Jerry Shirley, two years the junior of still only eighteen-year-old Frampton. When Steve Marriott left his Small Faces in early 69 and asked whether he could join the trio that was meant to be Peter's own, the press smelled a supergroup – when all the two frustrated teen idols had finally wanted was to be listened to properly. Frampton ended up growing a beard to escape the 'pin up' tag!

For the next two years, Humble Pie's career carried Peter's considerable stamp in terms of compositions, lead and acoustic guitar work and vocals, with prolific appearances behind drums and keyboards for good measure. But from their start with experimental studio work and versatile concerts of Springsteen proportions, Humble Pie had become an American good-time R&B road attraction. Peter felt it was time for a change on the day he heard the tapes recorded in New York's Fillmore East venue for a projected live LP. He had to accept raving shouter Steve Marriott's absolute dominance, the almost entirely hard-boogie-on-down Pie weren't Frampton's band at all. Steve tended to agree:

"As soon as I started throwing my balls a bit Peter realised that I was gonna take over. It scared him a bit, and he split. I don't blame him. I would have done the same thing. When you see someone coming on stronger than you can, the jealousies start creeping in and there's no more feeling of being a unit."

And so, only days before the double album *Performance/Rockin' The Fillmore* was released to thrilled reviews and a Number Twenty-One position in *Billboard*, Peter made the decision to leave and produce his own solo album. But he had a tough time witnessing the runaway success of the live document from the outside: "I then watched *Rockin' The Fillmore* zoom up the US charts, and this gave me the feeling I had made a big mistake!"

For a while, Frampton lived on recording sessions, for jazzer Ben Sidran, late blueser Duster Bennett, late boozer Harry Nilsson as well as Ringo Starr and George Harrison. "You play lead," the quiet Beatle guitarist had told a starstruck young Frampton during the sessions for Peter's very first date as a hired hand – for Doris Troy's 'Ain't That Cute'.

Now the two ex-Beatles gave Peter the honour of guest appearances on his first solo album *Wind Of Change* (US Number One-Hundred-And-Seventy-Nine), together with their clan members, organ grinder Billy Preston and *Revolver* designing bass player Klaus Voorman as well as Greg Ridley's Spooky Tooth drummer Mike Kellie and Andy Bown from The Herd. Behind the recording console, Pie producer Glyn Johns' assistant Chris Kimsey directed proceedings for his first time, doubling as debutant with Peter. Later, even The Rolling Stones would use the fast learning Kimsey's services.

During these studio days, Frampton proved that his first class melodic ballads, which had only survived on the fringes of Pie's latter-day sound, could well shine side by side with more furious fast numbers. And so, the old McCartney-type 'soft' tag did not stick: 'Frampton The Face' could rock out very well whenever he wanted. His inventive version of 'Jumpin' Jack Flash' – "'Wes Montgomery'-style in octaves" he called it – stands the test of time well. When Keith Richards met Peter during sessions for Alexis Korner, he told Peter he liked the number and added, "Thanks for that house of mine in Upstate New York, I got it for your fucking nice royalties!" Indeed, Peter's 'Flash' wouldn't have been out of place in Steve Marriott's tougher and more soulful Humble Pie catalogue – as the band proved with their version of 'Honky Tonk Woman', albeit with far less love of detail.

Towards the end of the sessions, things got slightly less relaxed. Peter: "Someone took my words book; I'd finished the words to songs I hadn't sung yet. It was in the studio, I knew where it was. I left it there over night – when I came back it had gone!" The last song for the album proved to be a minor nightmare. Frampton was suffering from severe writer's block, and on the night before called Kimsey in desperate two-hour intervals.

Chris told him to persevere, and in the early hours he managed to structure the chords that would become 'All I Wanna Be (Is By Your Side)', "still scribbling the words at five am. In the end, I didn't even put it on a cassette, just played it to the boys in the control booth and off we went!"

For live work, Peter soon assembled Frampton's Camel, featuring Marriott protegé and ex-Cochise bass player Rick Wills, the rather eccentric drummer Mike Kellie from Spooky Tooth and Peter's *Wind Of Change* sessions as well as keyboard player Mickey Gallagher, who would later join Ian Dury And The Blockheads. The trio had just left the singer-songwriters Parrish and Gurvitz. As their 'very special guests', they opened for Humble Pie's big 1972 autumn tour of the United Kingdom, in the face of media claims Marriott and Frampton would not even talk.

Pie and Camel manager Dee Anthony then sent them on never-ending tours of the United States, two hundred gigs a year and losing Frampton money in the process. Frampton's Camel would support any act with a name and a half sizeable auditorium: ZZ Top, Edgar Winter Band, The J Geils Band (also handled by Anthony), Steve Miller Band, Santana and – time and again – Humble Pie. In order to keep his rising debts down and financial wolves from hotel and dressing room doors, Peter had to accept further studio work in between tours, for Tim Hardin and, as he did within The Small Faces camp, Johnny Hallyday. Mere club-status for home gigs certainly didn't help Frampton's career fortunes either.

For the next four years, Peter would use his respective three off-road months for writing and recording. Three further albums appeared without much impact. There was the follow-up to *Wind Of Change*, the eponymous *Frampton's Camel* (US Number One-Hundred-And-Ten), tracks of which Peter graced with his Pie-trained drumming: "I was trying to be a jack-of-all-trades, but I really enjoy drumming!" During only eight days the album developed, under the direction of Hendrix's sound man Eddie Kramer in Jimi's New York Electric Ladyland Studios. Camel drummer Mike Kellie's pre-punk tour conduct had become intolerable even for Frampton's Marriott-induced standards and Peter replaced him (he later joined the suitably punky Only Ones) with John Siomos from Todd Rundgren's Utopia: "Eddie Kramer had given me three phone numbers of drummers and John was the only one in when I called. He joined the band that week."

They had to give up the band's name soon though, in order not to be confused with Peter Barden's group of the same name. What's more, the Them veteran had Camel registered in early 1973. The following year saw the trio album *Something's Happening* (US Number Twenty-Five) with Rick Wills and drummer John Headley-Down. Chris Kimsey was back behind the console knobs, the Stones' studio-pianist Nicky Hopkins guested on 'Waterfall' and 'Sail Away'.

Peter would later see this album as the result of his Motown period, experimenting with ambient drum sounds and not necessarily writing on guitar. The title track, for instance, Peter had composed on piano, "adding a slide guitar orchestra later on".

After more gruelling tours, Peter relocated to the Caribbean to write another set of songs in desperate need of peace and quiet. As he revealed in the US radio programme *Up Close* in 1994, "the *Frampton* album was written in eight days. I went down to the Bahamas. I didn't have a place there at the time, but Humble Pie had four cottages, I stayed in Steve Marriott's cottage. He had a piano there and I brought a couple of guitars. Alvin Lee was staying at my manager [Dee Anthony]'s house. Instead of writing, I would go down there. I stayed for three weeks, not working at anything. Then they left, the second week I still didn't write, but come the weekend, it just kicked in, and I would write so much stuff. I'd write a verse and a chorus lyrically as well, then I would go home and I'd know where I was – everything came very quickly!"

In 1975, the album *Frampton* (US Number Thirty-Two) showcased this stronger song material. On its cover, Peter sports a Marriott T-shirt – supposedly a hint to mutual and hatchet-burying Alexis Korner sessions for the bluesman's *Get Off Of My Cloud* LP during the early summer. For the recording of *Frampton*, John Siomos had returned from his stint with The Rick Derringer Band, Herd friend Andy Bown rejoined on bass as Rick Wills had answered Roxy Music's call in November 74. Frampton left the world of downtown studios for this collection and went towards the romantic Welsh border, the Ronnie Lane mobile recording truck in tow: "I decided to record the *Frampton* album on location at Clearwell Castle, Gloucestershire," Peter recalls in the notes for his *Shine On* compilation.

He would call *Frampton* his sad album, because some of the songs reflected his separation from his wife Mary Frampton, nee Lovett. Mary later came to minor prominence as a role model for Linda McCartney. Long before Mrs Macca became the British veggieburger queen, Mary Frampton & Friends published their *Rock'N'Roll Recipes* (Anchor Books, New York, 1980). In between lines of coke and southern comfort, the Framptons' old mate Steve Marriott must have had a soft spot for Italian cuisine, maybe because he attended the Italia Conti Drama School as a youngster. Anyway, according to old Steve, Mary recommended 'Fettucini A Stephano': simply melt two spoons full of butter in a skillet, add a clove of chopped garlic, a quarter pound of chopped mushrooms and cook, then add a half pint of fresh cream and stir in an ounce of grated romano cheese. The fettucini, cooked in lightly salted water, gets a blob of butter plus the cream sauce, and amounts to a fine basis for further drinking sessions...

Back to the recording site of *Frampton*: Clearwell Castle seemed sufficiently interesting to pay the venue a visit – even years after the event. "Up until the Eighties, its running costs were financed by regular leases to rock bands. Led Zeppelin for instance recorded part of their *Physical Graffiti* here", the Lord of the castle told us when we had a look around in 1979. As soon as we felt the rooms' atmosphere, we saw Peter's point for a new sound experience: "The natural, ambient sounds of the different rooms were not as restricting as the studio and made for a myriad of different sounds for each instrument. The drums were either in the kitchen, the entrance hall or the huge living room area. The guitars were wherever they sounded best for each track." At Olympic Sound in Barnes by the River Thames, familiar to Peter since his Pie days, the album was mixed.

As far as Frampton's general career moves were concerned, his financial status dictated great expectations all around. During the sessions with Alexis Korner, Stones guitarist Keith Richards was as involved as he was impressed with the guitar work Peter presented. His erstwhile mentor and Stones bassist Bill Wyman even saw him as a replacement for the recently Stone-free Mick Taylor: "Peter was among many guitarists considered in 1975 on the departure of Mick Taylor, but we signed Ron Wood instead," he muses in his autobiography in 1990. Another Frampton friend who was about to see real money was bass and keyboard wizard Andy Bown, who joined the indestructible boogie muppets Status Quo.

Disillusioned by the still relatively low-key response to his albums, Peter nevertheless persevered, helped by his new girl friend, model and soon self-confessed Frampton career coach. With 'her outdoors' in tow, Peter continued to build up a brilliant, reliable live image, in spite of rising costs – and debts. When he finally reached headliner status at the end of 1975, he was two hundred and fifty thousand dollars in the red. He was desperate, but still not ready yet to give up the long struggle, and dead keen to document his new level of stage acceptance. Peter recalls the events: "The first time we headlined a show in San Francisco was also the night we recorded the majority of *Frampton Comes Alive*. Some night! The event of headlining was so much more nerve-racking than recording, that I think we almost forgot there was a mobile recording truck outside. It was just one of those all-around great nights when you usually say, 'I wish we'd recorded tonight!' Well, thank God, we did! When I first heard a playback a few days later with Bob [Mayo, Peter's new keyboard and guitar player], Stanley [Sheldon on bass] and John, the energy coming off the tape just knocked us back against the wall. I'll never forget it. The original plan was for just a one record, live album. But when Jerry Moss [then president and co-owner of A&M Records] heard the one disc, he asked, 'Where's the rest?' I guess he was right. The one album did not include 'Show Me The Way' or 'Baby I Love Your Way'. We then went ahead and recorded a few more nights to get more from which to choose."

After finishing the final mix, Peter spent a few days' well deserved rest in the Bahamas. At the beginning of the spring 76 tour which at one point could have been the last one he and Dee Anthony were able and willing to afford, *Frampton Comes Alive* sold continuously, then sensationally! By June three million copies had been sold (US Number One, UK Number Six). Almost everywhere the band went, Dee had to arrange a second show. After three Top Ten singles from the album – 'Show Me The Way', 'Baby I Love Your Way' and 'Do You Feel Like We Do?', Peter's songs as well as his 'voice box', a mouth piece for bending his guitar tone, were the sound of the season. Nineteen years after its initial release, this concert record is still the best-selling live album of all times, sixteen million gone and a thousand still shipped per week in 1994!

Instead of thinking about quitting life on the road and reverting to mere session work, Peter headlined stadium events in front of up to a hundred thousand fans: mega stars like Stephen Stills or Carlos Santana honoured their new buddy in fame by jamming with him on stage.

In addition to Frampton's on-going tour commitments, which had been colossal ever since 1972 and grew even more intense through the *Comes Alive* craze, Dee Anthony arranged an avalanche of chat show dates. With the ever-present fashion model/girl friend Penny McCall, Peter mutated to a TV personality, and became The Face and pin-up all over again. *Rolling Stone* and *People* magazines managed to capture him with make-up and shirt-free: "Peter Frampton Industries!"

With all those autumn '76 hassles, Dee Anthony's golden media boy was of course expected to find the peace and concentration for his next, eagerly awaited studio album. When Peter learned of three million advance orders for recordings that didn't even exist yet, nerves – and alcoholic refreshments – went beyond control, and he fled to Mexico for a short holiday. There, he lost the demo cassettes with his entire musical sketches since his fourth album *Frampton*: "All my ideas, recorded with pilot vocals and acoustic guitar, I left those tapes lying around. Later, in New York, I tried to remember all the things I had composed, it was very frustrating!" Peter's only treasure was the home-recorded ballad 'I'm In You'.

This demo tape eventually found its way onto the twenty-four-track master for the album of the same name, and the single became a US Number Two (UK Number Forty-One). But with all the other demos Peter had lost his remaining self-confidence. Yet, in spite of constant hangovers and late studio arrivals, the new album sounded remarkably strong, refined with guest appearances by Stevie Wonder and Little Feat's wonderfully groovy drummer Ritchie Hayward. But out of three and a half million sold copies, the cruel pop media constructed a flop, cynically comparing it to the runaway success of the live album.

On top of unfair reviews, fatigue and general disillusion, Frampton agreed with svengali Anthony's further tour plans. During his 1977 sojourn, some days would see two complete shows, ninety minutes instead of the Sixties package tour standard of half an hour, when two gigs a night weren't frowned upon. It was grotesque. Flower bouquets courtesy of Elvis Presley and exquisite cognacs would greet him in hotel rooms. Would Peter end up like a king of Vegas? "Let's just say I was exploited!"

In September, his tiring *I'm In You* tour came to its end, but instead of a well-deserved time for reassessment, Hollywood was waiting for his part in the Frampton-Bee Gees rock spectacular of The Beatles' *Sgt Pepper*. Peter's only consolation was the fact that the Fab Four's producer George Martin, one of his heroes, had been contracted to supervise the music production. Still, he smelled the quick buck. Gossip about Frampton's separation from Penny McCall – and her sensational alimony attacks, claiming she had given up her career for Peter's – cost him inspiration and strength. The critical onslaught which the movie suffered even before the Gibb-Frampton-Mop Tops were released on the big screen certainly didn't help his feelings.

The summer of 1978 saw the almost final, almost fatal crash, both realistically and symbolically. Peter had wanted a few quiet days in his holiday cottage in the Bahamas, to get away from frustrating reviews and ongoing media gossip about his private life. As always with good intentions, friends related that his beloved Penny was hanging out with whoever in their apartment there, partying like mad. A furious Frampton booked a flight, rented a jeep and headed there – but apparently he'd fallen asleep at the wheel and ended up against a palm tree. He broke six ribs, his left foot and right hand, and suffered cuts in 'The Face' – honoured exactly one decade ago! His recovery was painfully slow and for a number of weeks he thought depressingly about possibly never playing the guitar again. After special treatment in New York's Lemox Hill Hospital, Peter retreated to his chosen home state of Florida.

Time for reflection and regaining consciousness had been long overdue, and four months' vacation had been out of reach for Peter ever since childhood! "I'd been in bands since I was ten, became a professional musician at sixteen, and really, I went straight from The Herd into Humble Pie, into my solo thing. When the live album came out, I'd been working for fifteen years – six to nine months touring a year, which doubled when *Comes Alive* hit! What I didn't realise was that you cannot turn on the creative juices, face the pressures for a follow-up and then the next one and so on. What I should have done – after a hit that big – was stop, and take time out to go right back and look at new ways of writing. And I never took time off, because of the greed of people around me. No one thought of Peter the person."

By November though, incredibly fit, he was back on tour, but booked studio time would probably never again be spent as relaxed as in pre-superstar days. It took Frampton months before his next album, produced with a light soul and funk touch by guitarist Steve Cropper, was arranged and recorded in Los Angeles! *Where I Should Be* was the confident album title, and the overall sound and song material was memorable and contemporary enough to reach the US position of Number Fourteen – the single 'I Can't Stand It No More' even went Top Ten!

On the strength of those records, Peter continued to tour – in smaller halls this time instead of arenas, but with a vengeance. How literally Frampton threw himself into work he related to us, reminiscing with a smile in late 1995: "At the time it was not funny at all. This was the late Seventies and what happened was we'd been playing all daytime shows, with a white stage, white equipment and no lights, coloured outfits so that you could see everybody. There's no problem, I come on, wave to the crowd and used to start with the acoustic. But in Hartford, Connecticut, we switched to an all-black stage, lights, black equipment and six super troopers. So I walked on, waving and I couldn't see where the front of the stage and the pit was. Forty thousand people. So I went 'Heyyyyyyyy' – off the front of the stage – and disappeared! And every time I play there now, all the DJs on the radio go 'Do you remember...?' So someone pulled me by the hand – but I had my very tight satin trousers on, and they got ripped all the way – forty thousand people went 'Uuuugh'! I broke a rib actually, but

210

I changed and played the show – completely numb!"

A tougher band sound was about to be documented with an unusual live-in-the-studio project. An energetic Frampton hired the Charlie Chaplin Sound Stage in Hollywood and cast Toto's session veterans Steve Lukather – some strong guitar competition for him – and drumming legend Jeff Porcaro (who unfortunately died in 1992). Peter himself came over as self-assured in his singing (you could feel the fun doing his cover of 'Friday On My Mind'), guitar playing, keyboards as well as guitar synth work.

Breaking All The Rules (US Number Forty-Seven) didn't break any rules or chart statistics, but at least a once irritatingly marketed pop star was able to reclaim his solid rock reputation of the mid Seventies. For his 1982 album, the lively, hard-rocking and crystal clear sounding *The Art Of Control*, Frampton enlisted his new friend, guitarist and writing partner Mark Goldenberg who later worked with Linda Ronstadt and Aaron Neville. But its undeservedly low chart placing (US Number One-Hundred-And-Seventy-Four) made A&M drop its one-time biggest earner – surely an astounding exercise in business-like thanklessness.

Following that, Peter went into a rather pleasant period of semi-retirement, idly taking care of home, marrying his long-time partner Barbara Gold and raising their daughter Jade. After session work with Chris Spedding – the sophisticated 'Work' on the Thelonius Monk-tribute *That's The Way I Feel Now* – Frampton hired a new manager, Genesis' Tony Smith, and took his time recording a new album, *Premonition* (US Number Eighty), an attractive song collection which was made a bit bland by one synthesiser too many. Session experts like Steve Ferrone (ex-Average White Band) and Omar Hakim, both on drums, and bassman Tony Levin contributed exquisite tracks, but the overall result sounded less inspired than the clear *Art Of Control*. Relaxed as he now was, Peter could accept his second league status on the concert circuit and readily welcomed a support slot on Fleetwood Mac elf Stevie Nicks' summer 1986 solo tour.

In 1987, still musically curious, Peter honoured the invitation of an old school tie. As lead guitarist for his Beckenham mate David Bowie, he recorded the album *Never Let Me Down* and took part in the Glass Spider world tour. Its over-sized stage pomp may have distracted fans from the music, but they surely felt the excited rapport between the two friends. Back in his residence and home studio in North Hollywood, Peter spent the best part of 1988 and 1989 working on songs for his *When All The Pieces Fit* collection, collaborating amongst others with Scottish singer-songwriter BA Robertson and a couple of sound-alike Steve Winwood's mates: lyricist Will Jennings and producer Chris Lord-Alge, who would also work for Joe Cocker and Robert Palmer in 1994.

Seasoned pros like John Robinson (drums), Lenny Castro (percussion) and bassist John Regan became the rhythm section for a melodic mainstream direction that had really started with 'I Don't Want Our Lovin' To Die', but was kept at a contemporary sound level with Robbie Nevil-type grooves – 'My Heart Goes Out To You' and, again, too many synthesisers to keep album rock fans interested. As far as a new audience went, Atlantic quietly sat on the album, keeping the 'Hiding From A Heartache' single and its follow-up off the airwaves as well. In spite of his relative financial security ("Though it's not as much as you'd think," he told reporters in 1992) and his solid family life, Peter was bitterly disappointed by the lack of promotion, as he was keen and felt he still had things to pursue and prove in his career. Maybe there was a symbolic meaning in Will To Power's 1989 chart smash with a medley of 'Baby I Love Your Way' and Lynyrd Skynyrd's 'Freebird' – it was not too late yet for the Peter Frampton sound!

Peter remained an in-demand session guitarist: together with old hand Mark Goldenberg he recorded for Linda Ronstadt's songwriter Karla Bonoff in 1988, helped Julian Lennon with his album *Mr Jordan* and recorded a distinctive solo for his old friend and 'financial advisor' Graham Nash on CSN's *Live It Up* in 1990: "Joe Vitali was producing that, and had played drums for me. So he invited me down, and I met Graham Nash again. So I was just sitting there very quietly, watching the three working – a dream of mine, it's a great learning experience. David Crosby was joking he'd split and start a band with me, a lot of fun. Then Graham goes, 'You wanna try playing a solo on 'Straight Line'?'

"But Steve [Stephen Stills, their solo man!] was right there, so I said 'Excuse me?' But he told me to go ahead – 'cause I know Stephen, he's jammed with me. So I went home, did it on my multi-track tape recorder, and worked out this harmony solo, and then got back and played it to them. They asked me to play one note and that was it – one of those special moments!"

But the relative leisure was against his nature, and by the end of that year Peter was ready to form another road band, and he felt the time was right for getting in another lead singer. When nobody fitted his acquired taste, Frampton flew over to London in December 1990 and visited an old Humble Pie cohort: "I was looking through tapes, and I found that nobody sounded as good as Steve Marriott, who was my point of reference as a singer."

Several days were spent jamming, writing and demoing, and the two Pies, who twenty years ago got on like chalk and cheese, even appeared together on stage. The commercially long-gone Marriott had recently abandoned his recent Next Band and resurrected his Eighties club trio Packet Of Three with the indestructible 'Uncle' Jim Leverton on bass and Alan 'Sticky' Wickett from his DTs days, and this outfit appeared in West London's Putney, in the Half Moon pub (which counts R&B legends like Chicken Shack and The Steve Gibbons Band as regulars, in front of the bar as well as on the boards). When Peter and Steve had finished a rousing 'Natural Born Woman', a rare live rendition indeed, Steve Marriott's rather ill-informed father-in-law must have thought the gig was a kind of audition: he nudged Peter and quipped, "Did you get the job, boy?"

It was rather a question of the newly wed cockney getting a job on the other side of the Atlantic. Steve had even promised softer *Town And Country* reminiscences when he talked to German DJ Ulli Kniep in the studios of Hannover's Radio ffn, only days before he went to the US in January 1991: "That's why I'm interested in doing this thing with Peter, because I have all these songs, and they're not at all like what I'm doing on stage now – they're more piano-based, things in the tradition of 'Red Neck Jump' or 'Strange Days' [from their 1971 *Rock On* LP].

"'Phone Call Away' from the *Thirty Seconds To Midnite* album, co-written with Jim Leverton, is only one of them. Now there's the chance to get them out, because Peter knows all these people who want to pay me for doing them. And if that means Peter and I will do them together, well, what could be better? That's another one out of the bag. But of course I wouldn't mind going on working like I've done in the past."

That was exactly what he did: "He told me he couldn't come out straight away, because he had this tour of Germany to do," recalls Peter. But in March 1991, studio sessions down at Peter's in LA got under way and resulted in five tracks. Indeed, the songs which surfaced showed a lot of promise.

'The Bigger They Come', for instance, was soon scheduled for the soundtrack of *Harley Davidson And The Marlboro Man*. It was later re-mixed and fitted with real drums, courtesy of Anton Fig, for Frampton's *Shine On* compilation.

Another track was the romantic 'I Won't Let You Down', which also appeared on *Shine On*. There was also 'Out Of The Blue', a slow soul number in the Smokey Robinson 'My Girl' tradition: "We had already written 'Out Of The Blue' in Stevie's country cottage, and recorded it onto a cheap cassette player. Later, it became a labour of love. It took a week to transfer the vocal track onto digital tape – and the rest we recorded the way we thought Steve would have liked the arrangement."

These three songs illustrate the different characters of the midget, bluesy, soulful, spitting Marriott and the jazzy, dreamy, but also rocking Frampton. 'Beauty and The Beast' were still able to induce a mutual thrill that could lift up both. Of course, the strain of the business side was not altogether absent in the studio, but in retrospect Frampton reckons they could have overcome those.

In our 1995 interview in Cologne, Peter remembered their tensions as positive: "We knew we were writing great stuff, and we knew it would get a look-in because of the two people involved. There was tension between us, there always was, but the tension pushed us to our limits. The thing I will always remember is that we sat in my makeshift studio in Los Angeles, just the two of us. We were there every day, he got a place in Santa Monica, and we started writing. It was quick, and then we started to make little demos. We were doing the vocals to 'I Won't Let You Down', just the two of us singing into this mike. And if you solo the vocal track, you hear us laughing in between each line, because it just sounded so good and we were having such a great time being back together. And right after we did that, we sat on this dirty old couch. Steve looked at me and said, 'I never would have believed that you and I would be working together – this is so great, Pete, I'm having such a great time!' I said, 'You know, I'll remind you of that one day!'"

Whatever. After six weeks of writing and sessions Peter was getting worried. Looking round an LA conference table one morning, the contrast between the two artists who were about to sign a record contract couldn't have been more significant. A keen and concentrated, charming Frampton sat on one side, facing an unkempt, hungover Steve, who ended up grabbing an unnamed industry person by his tie to belt out his "You can't bend the midget with a contract that lasts for bloody years!" For the time being, they had to send him home. Peter remembers: "A bit of sour grapes crept into that, but when you're upset, you say things you don't really mean. It wasn't the best of circumstances, but to be honest, I'm sure we would have picked it up again. He did call me right before he left to go to England. I got the feeling he was coming around. He was on a different plane unfortunately, because – I don't drink or smoke – I'm no angel, but I've been through all that!" There, fate struck and the interruption became final.

Alone in his country house in Arkesden, Essex, after celebrating the return to England with wife Toni and friends, Steve Marriott fell asleep in bed with a cigarette in his hand – not unheard of in his recent years, but this time burning him to death on the upper floor of his house. It was 20 April: two days before his renewed partner in rock, Peter Frampton, could – and now wouldn't – celebrate his birthday. Instead he flew to Steve's funeral: "Some hurtful things have been said by his friends – they had picked him up from the airport – and they weren't very truthful. When Steve got home, he was just trying to justify the fact that it hadn't worked. Not that it didn't work – it did. I figured we'd get one album and one tour, I didn't see it going any longer than that."

Instead, back in LA and on his own, Peter was devastated. His half-hearted attempts to rescue all the tapes as well as their new band, with Denny Fongheiser on drums and Vito San Philipo on bass, who played with Billy Idol, was given up soon. He didn't really listen to any music until October 1991: "Lynyrd Skynyrd played the Universal Amphitheatre and got me up to play a song. And the fantastic audience reaction gave me the road fever again. I thought, 'I'm the guy who did the big live record.' Now, I was without a recording contract. And I wasn't touring!"

And so in February 1992, after a six year break, Peter embarked on one of the longest tours of the States and Canada in his career. He had originally planned on seven weeks of fun in prestigious clubs, but ended up playing seven sold-out months, including bigger venues as well, and all that without a new product in tow, not even selling a book. His old *Comes Alive* member Bob Mayo was on keyboards and John Regan played bass. Both had played with Hall And Oates and The Robin Trower Band in the Eighties. Peter's drumming was supplied by long time Eric Clapton Ludwig skin beater Jamie Oldaker. In turn, Eric used Frampton's long-standing drummer Steve Ferrone in 1992, so the rock'n'roll circus isn't unlike the football league...

Peter's only compact disc that was in US shops at the time of the new tour was *Frampton Comes Alive*. Subsequently, a big contingent in the repertoire of this keen and precise band came from that legendary collection, sounding better than ever before, as a Westwood One live radio show from the Ventura Theatre proved. During the tour, the compilation *Shine On – A Collection* appeared: "It was my personal Best Of, and it should have been called 'A Selection' instead of collection. I would have liked three CDs, but two is fine!"

Before the gigs, 'The Bigger They Come' came over the PA, and for the encore, at least in the Variety Theatre in Downtown Los Angeles on 17 April 1992 where we encountered Peter, he recalled the history of a famous Fillmore East riff, three days before the date of Steve's death the previous year: "This riff is for Steve. When he heard it, he ran to the front of the stage, quite excited. That took a while, 'cause Steve was a small bloke. The riff goes like this..." – and with these words he started 'I Don't Need No Doctor'.

In early 1993, Peter signed his new record contract with the small but ambitious Relativity label, to be distributed by Sony. "I never went into the studios so well prepared," he proudly announced, "with enough songs that had actually been well worked out beforehand." Still, he would not be drawn into the dreaded deadlines of the past, which for instance had made his *I'm In You* sessions such a nightmare. Consequently, Frampton spent all of 1993 recording at his own pace, and the resulting album, marking a new start with its eponymous title *Peter Frampton*, proved he'd used the time well.

"It was like a combination of all my old solo records," he mused.

Attractive melodies, excitingly played with stylistic journeys from the sweet Caribbean instrumental 'Young Island' to Beatles harmonies and chord changes on 'You Can Be Sure', even Humble Pie rock in 'Off The Hook', complete with a cheeky Shadows quote which was acknowledged by Hank B Marvin himself, as Peter happily recalls: "It was one of the highest points in my career to have him backstage in London in 1995. He made me pick up the guitar, and now he's asking for my talk box. I made damn sure that one was sent out to him from America."

On *Peter Frampton*, there was also the sad but beautiful reminder of Peter's work with old Pie mate Steve Marriott, with their resurrected mutual demo of 'Out Of The Blue'. Peter hadn't promised too much. With the new band members, the result was breath-taking soul music, which Peter had shied away from in the early Seventies – leaving Steve – but ultimately came to grips with on his Memphis-influenced album *Where I Should Be*.

The album came out with – initially – considerable promotion efforts by Sony. But while the single, 'Day In The Sun', got considerable airplay in the US AOR stations, the album just about dented the Hot Hundred in the States and in Germany. Peter toured the US through spring with The Robin Trower Band as support, only interrupting the schedule for radio promotion in Europe and Japan.

In Europe, the album stalled at Number Eighty-Seven, and so he postponed live plans there, knowing full well why his stuff stalled everywhere: "At Relativity, I worked with really nice people. The owner was Barry Coburn, and their A&R man was Cliff Cultreri, and we worked together very closely. But when we released the second single ('You Can Be Sure'), Sony came in and bordered up. It was as if I didn't have a record out at all."

On the other hand, Frampton had not planned his first LP in five years as a make or break affair at all. His contract with the young Relativity crew was designed long term: "I had asked them if this doesn't sell, does it mean bye bye and they said 'no no!'" So Peter would continue to have product for tours, and everything seemed fine for his new lease of life.

"And then Relativity were swallowed by their distributor Sony," Peter remembers, "and Barry Coburn was bought out; he went. There were new people in there who didn't see the picture – and hadn't made a promise to me. Obviously, it wasn't making money at that particular time – well they didn't even say goodbye. All I got was a pre-printed piece of paper – they sacked me!"

It was not as if Peter was on the streets – but almost, as his marriage with Barbara broke up roughly the same time and he then relocated to Nashville with his new fiancée Lisa – but the treatment surely hurt. "Still, I was convinced of my successful live work, that's where I always functioned best," Peter continued in our long interview in the winter of 1995, "and I was so sure I wanted another live album I would even have paid for it myself. And if I could also write new material for it, it would be old and new, from *I'm In You* onwards. But then Miles Copeland and the IRS went for it, and this really is long-term – in terms of labels I've got a home now! When Miles heard about *Frampton Comes Alive II*, he went '*Bat Out Of Hell II*? – The Sequel?' – but then he got excited, he did go for it!" What certainly helps is that Copeland has an office in Nashville and "so have Rondor, my publishers, so it's becoming like a satellite of LA now".

So in June 1995, Peter Frampton returned to the original *Comes Alive* hunting ground, San Francisco, and recorded his stage set yet again, at the newly founded Fillmore West this time, instead of the demolished Winterland. He made sure nothing overlapped – relegating all the old favourites to a limited edition bonus CD, and recorded fairly recent album tracks plus his all-time Tim Hardin favourite, 'Hang On To A Dream': "I recently found my Sixties albums *Tim Hardin I & II* on CD, and later I met Hardin, played on 'Painted Head' and 'Nine'. He was not a well man, he was on methadone at the time, he'd been through the mill, but 'Hang On To A Dream' had always been my favourite track. Then my bass player John Regan thought we should do it for the live album."

Peter's next studio move would be an instrumental album, to be recorded with the help of his old mate – and new rehearsal studio neighbour in Nashville – Stevie Winwood!

Indeed, collaborations and new challenges seem a matter dear to Peter's heart, as a recent Miles Copeland Songwriter's Workshop in the South of France testified: "I was part writer of five things, two for me, one for Dennis Greaves of Nine Below Zero – they just cut that, 'I

Never Needed You Anyway'. There was one I wrote with Gary Burr, who writes Number One country singles in Nashville. One more that I did was a real rocker. It's very nerve wracking when you get there. You sit at a table like this, everybody's down for breakfast, then somebody comes by and says, 'Okay Peter, you're writing with Pat McDonald from Timbuk 3 and Steve Saskin!' It's 'Hi' and off you go!" I call it forced collaboration, but it works great. You're very heightened, you want it to work, want to get in a creative mood. The whole vibe, everybody sings and plays each other's songs at night."

Soon, the relative sedateness of Cote D'Azur castle life was once again replaced by months of touring the United States, Europe and also South America. But after half a year of solid, well received road work, *Comes Alive II* had not even dented the Top Two Hundred on either side of the Atlantic by Christmas 1995. A desperate showing, especially when all the so far displayed copies sported the mentioned bonus CD with classic repertoire: the limited edition circulation had not even been sold out.

Disappointed as Frampton was by this utter ignorance, he cut his ties with the Miles Copeland management. The deal which he'd celebrated as "I've got a home!" now seemed a mere stopover. The already booked second European tour was cancelled in the semi retirement process, postponed until sometime in 1997 – not a good move, after the disappointment of the 1994 dates he had called off. But in the face of slumping record sales, family matters seemingly counted more: awaiting a baby with Lisa, now his third wife. In terms of his songs, 'Barbara's Vacation' would now be followed by 'Lisa's Vacation'!

Little Mia arrived in February, and Peter enjoyed doting on his second daughter. Music seemed a relaxing hobby; country picking on the veranda with Chet Atkins was one of the pastimes Frampton enjoyed so much that it made the press.

In May 1996, the creators of *The Simpsons* cartoon series announced they were going to feature Young Peter in one of their June episodes. Peter, who was going to spend all summer enjoying his third honeymoon and waiting for a new baby before resuming live work in the autumn, happily agreed to supply the necessary recording of dialogues. Didn't that voice box sound like vintage Woody Woodpecker anyway?

But soon after Peter left the cartoon studios, the honeymoon was over, and the musician's gypsy soul got the better of him. After just four months of staying home, he called his new manager, Charles Brusco in Atlanta, to talk tours – and quick! The result was a forty-three date cross US sojourn called 'Can't Stop Rocking'. Apart from The Peter Frampton Band it featured Seventies contenders Foreigner and REO Speedwagon, all summer long and was an obviously incurable case of 'Where I Should Be'!

CHAPTER ELEVEN
Packet Of Three
Don't Need No Doctor

By August 1981, when at long last Steve Marriott was able to leave his hospital bed in Dallas, Texas, his life seemed to have gone to pieces. For a start, there was the rocky part time marriage with his second wife Pam, the Southern Belle whose home town Atlanta, Georgia, Steve had willingly made his own. Steve, Pam and little Toby Joe were hardly ever indoors together. But Marriott wasn't on the road either, for his excellent band – Jerry, Sooty and Bob – had deserted him. There just hadn't been the financial backing for such a long waiting period. On top of that, Steve's record company Atco, an Atlantic subsidiary, had not renewed contracts after his two highly acclaimed flops *Victory* and *Throat*. The only rescue would have been the literally ill-fated live-album: "I had a lean period for a while. I wasn't touring or recording or anything and my wife even left me when the money ran out – if it'd been me, I would have left me, too – and there's always the chance she'll come back if things work out!" Steve remembered in 1982 one night before he went on stage in Atlanta.

Bass player Sooty Jones had returned to his hunting ground, New York City. Bob Tench secured a short-term recording contract in London, but only cut Sam Cooke's 'Chain Gang' for a single, and gigged sporadically with Hinkley's Heroes, a loose pub outfit organised by Marriott's and Humble Pie's mid Seventies keyboard player, Tim Hinkley. Apart from Bobby, Tim recruited Roger Chapman, Bad Company and *Scrubbers* bass picker Boz Burrell, drummer Mitch Mitchell and Grease Band guitarist Henry McCullough, a close friend of Steve's mate Jim Leverton. Jerry Shirley bumped into Motorhead's Eddie Clarke, forming the hard rockers

Fastway, and after his Atlantic crossing back to the UK he lived on session work in the British metropolis like Clem Clempson.

Meanwhile, back in that Indian summer of 1981, Steve was at least still on a little retainer from his Leber/Krebs management and thus escaped from his marital Atlanta mansion into a nice little apartment in Manhattan's creative capital, Greenwich Village – after another New York City spell in intensive care due to his split duodenal tract.

But Steve just didn't have time for an unlimited period of recuperation. He was dying to play again, and he had to, as well. The lay-off inflicted debts hurt – in the States, a hospital stretch like Steve's, with no social security, doesn't just ruin artists. And for Steve, the stage was his thread of life. Marriott remembered his British home, London's East End, his parents, and – Ronnie Lane! Ronnie had felt his energies dwindle via his cruel suffering of MS, but had still cut another solo album in late 1979 – this time with the assistance of Pete Townshend's buddy Eric Clapton – and promoted it in a rather lacklustre way in 1980 and 1981 with gigs in the British provinces for instance, and a week in Berlin.

Steve went up to jam with him in Loughton. For the audience, it was a moving picture to spot the two struggling former Mods on stage, together. For the old Marriott/Lane partnership, it was a slow motion approach after their attempted reunion in 1976 had failed so thoroughly.

This time, the feeling seemed just right on both sides, and as Ronnie still owned his Mobile Studio – and star clients like the Stones were not renting it at the time – it was decided on the spot to record demo tapes for a mutual album. Hence, the mobile truck moved to Essex, and they rented the local Corbett Theatre. With Steve and Ronnie's nods and winks still intact, the project was christened 'The Midgets Strike Back', although another comeback option was 'The Return Of The Two Midgets'.

Bass mate Jim Leverton was part of the deal again: "Steve came to England in September 1981, and we cut this album on a tight shoestring, Steve paid for the sessions himself. It was recorded mainly with Steve and Ronnie, plus Mick Weaver on keyboards, Dave Hynes on drums again, myself on bass and Mick Green of The Pirates on guitar."

During the studio recordings, Steve didn't miss the chance for another appearance in his beloved East London homeground. Exactly three years after their last gig he presented Blind Drunk in the same East End pub that saw their debut: the Bridge House in Canning Town. The rhythm section again consisted of Jim and Dave, while Marriott, alias Matt Vinyl, presented R&B legend Zoot Money on keyboards as well as ace saxman Mel Collins, who had accompanied Steve from Pie days, all along his solo ventures and up to The Small Faces II.

Also, some new blood from the Mark II *Seventy-Eight In The Shade* sessions became the darling of the audience that night: young Sam Brown, daughter of Pie backing singer Vicki Brown and skiffle man Joe Brown, gave her stage debut with Blind Drunk, stone cold sober and charming. Her father, old Joe himself, had wanted to be part of the Bridge House proceedings, but couldn't make it due to prior commitments.

Steve led the band with his customary vigour – and humorous hints towards Ronnie's 'Reels On Wheels' mobile that was running along outside – through Small Faces classics like the hard and riffy 'What'cha Gonna Do About It', 'All Or Nothing' and 'Tin Soldier'. Thrown in for good measure, the crowd was treated to rarely played Pie-stuff like 'I Can't Stand The Rain' (which Tina Turner picked as one of her own comeback numbers a very short time later). Ronnie himself quietly sat in the audience most of the time; for his short singing spot he had to be helped on stage, his disease had already weakened him considerably.

When shortly afterwards the industry turned down the prepared studio-takes, along the lines of Ronnie and Steve losing their vital energy and optimism, Steve said: "Ronnie had been over to the States for a while and we were taking it to all the record companies. But if one person passes on it it's like a chain reaction. I was under the impression that Keith Richards wanted to buy it, but at the last minute he said no as well. I don't think he wanted to be responsible for anything."

While the two Midgets were trying to sell their album, Steve's David Krebs management were getting restless about Steve neither touring nor getting Pie product ready in order to be worth any of his still ongoing monthly retainer. Steve: "So I had no income at all – they just stopped my income right there, like they can do."

A visibly weakened Marriott (the provisionally healed duodenal tract could open up any time due to stress, malnutrition or substance abuse) appeared to be at the end of his tether. In terms of his long time friend Jim Leverton, his situation seemed like down and out in New York City. Jim: "During the period when *Midgets* was recorded, I lived down in Fulham, West London, and Steve came round and said, 'Come back with me to America, I need some friends around!' Well, I wasn't that desperate money-wise, but couldn't afford a ticket just like that, so Steve shrugged and went, 'I'll get you a ticket', which he did, and we spent about three weeks in Greenwich Village, writing and recording some nice songs there. But things were really tight! I can honestly remember us throwing small change together to get some groceries into his apartment, it really was as bad as that!" (Tabloid accounts of collecting empty bottles and living on the deposit money were nastily exaggerated though!)

Finally, in 1982, Steve picked himself up again. He had no option but to go on the road around the States and do "some hard slog", gigging without a record deal: "So I borrowed some money from Keith Richards to do it. Otherwise I don't know what I would have done. Guess run home to England with my tail between my legs which I didn't wanna do!"

Jim Leverton stuck with him. They found Chicago-based drummer Fallon Williams III (Steve: "Brilliant, a negro chap"), who had been recommended by ex-Pie II bass player Sooty Jones, and Steppenwolf's keyboarder Goldy McJohn, who had at least one potential stage number in common with his future boss Steve ('Desperation' graced his band's debut as well as Humble Pie's first album).

Rehearsals took place in the piece and quiet of rural Georgia, where Steve still shared a part time home with his wife Pam Stephens. A solid Pie/Faces/R&B set took shape in the little village of Stone Mountain. With the help of a new Manhattan-based promoter, Martin Druyan, and the nimble, but reliable Empire Agency in Marietta, an Atlanta suburb, Steve was soon a regular in the clubs of the entire United States.

Ronnie Lane fronting Slim Chance, 1974, before the Passing Show became too expensive

"Bloody Comfort- able..."

Steve Marriott, founding member of the original Small Faces and leader of Steve Marriott's Allstars, has never been one to lay back on stage. His music is strong, gutsy and demanding of his equipment. Here's what Steve has to say about his Ovation Deacon:

"Like my Ovation here. I was an Ovation fan before I had an Ovation electric. I've had the Ovation twelve string for years. That's how I knew the electric was going to be good."

"And in fact I've found it's one of the most versatile electric guitars I've ever played. With the tone controls and phased pick-ups you can get any guitar sound you want."

"Then there's the bridge — it's great for harmonics. And the machine heads, the pick-ups, the cutaway, the adjustable string-heights — well, all those things speak for themselves."

"The whole shape and weight of the guitar is well thought out and very comfortable to play."

Strength and versatility make the Ovation Solid Body more than just another guitar with an unusual shape. Quality workmanship, sound technology and balanced design are the things professionals like Steve Marriott look for in electric guitars. You'll find them in Ovation.

For a catalog and Steve Marriott poster, send 50¢ (to cover postage and handling) to Ovation Instruments, Dept. GP, New Hartford, CT 06057.

Ovation® A Kaman Music Product

Steve posing for an Ovation advert, early 1976

To dispel rumours of a rift,
Peter's 1975 solo album,
Frampton, featured the
guitarist wearing a Steve
Marriott T-shirt

Peter Frampton live at the height of his career, 1976/7

No atlantic crossing: the enlarged Small Faces Mk II (top l-r: Kenney Jones, Rick Wills, Ian McLagan; bottom l-r: Steve Marriott and Jimmy McCulloch)

The Small Faces Mk II live on stage in 1978 (l-r: Jimmy, Rick, Kenney, Steve and Mac)

The appropriately named Blind Drunk before a 1981 gig (l-r: Dave Hynes, Steve and Jim Leverton)

Humble Pie, 1974

This promo pic for Steve's solo A&M career was actually taken during his Humble Pie days in 1975

Packet Of Three in 1986, featuring Jerry Shirley, Steve and Jim Leverton

Risky business – hard times for Steve and his Pie as a US club entity in 1982 (l-r: Steve, Fallon Williams II, Jim Leverton and ex-Steppenwolf organist Goldy McJohn)

Jim Leverton, left-handed bass player and Steve Marriott's long-time mate

Steve live in Germany in the late Eighties

Steve Marriott and the Birmingham-based blues band The DTs in 1988 (l-r: Steve Walwyn, Greg Rhind, Simon Hickling, Steve and Chess Chaplin)

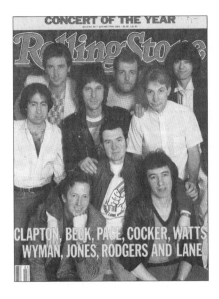

Ronnie Lane's ARMS tour of 1983 attracted more than a couple of famous friends as this *Rolling Stone* cover shows

Ronnie Lane's Tex Mex Slim Chance at the Continental Club in Austin, Texas, in 1988 (l-r: Susan Voelz (vi), Randy Banks (g, acc), Daren Hess (dr), Ronnie (voc), JD Foster (b) and Rich Brotherton (mand))

The Ronnie Lane Band in 1988 (l-r: Randy Banks, Ronnie, Daren Hess, JD Foster and Rich Brotherton)

A Ronnie Lane promo shot from 1980

Top: The Midgets strike back – Ronnie Lane and a homecoming Steve Marriott on stage at London's Corbett Theatre, October 1981
Left: Steve's last European tour, January 1991
Right: Ronnie Lane retiring at the Continental Club in Austin, Texas, 1988

It was around this time that Steve meant to call his band Official Receiver, but commercial aspects made the team go for Steve Marriott And The Pie. Wasting no time, the promoters often went ahead and billed them as Humble Pie. Steve took that in his stride, as he remembered in a pub conversation in 1984: "I couldn't stop the club owners putting it up. Then I got threatened. I was amazed people would even think I wanted that name, and annoyed as well. After all, I had thought up the name. If anybody had a right to use it, it should have been me. But I wanted to call us the Official Receivers. [These captains of bankruptcy he was to start in the UK at the end of 1986.] As soon as we went out, we were billed as Humble Pie!" For seven months Steve Marriott And The Pie toured the United States and Canada like that.

During a catastrophic tour of Australia in October 1982, the boys, who had now been down to a trio without Goldy for quite a while, were not only eating Humble Pie, but had to be content with getting billed as Small Faces. Steve reminisced with Small Faces fan Chris Welch in the summer of 1984: "They expected us to play 'Itchycoo Park' and it was like guns held to our heads. It was like the old days. Guns out, contracts torn up and we have to work to pay off Canned Heat's bill. It was awful. They had lost money on Canned Heat [on a previous tour down under], so our fees were non-existent. We survived." The stand-up cockney also complained about hired equipment which was scarcely up to standard and told Aussie magazine *After Dark* after a gig in a club called The Sundowner: "Please don't judge us on that!"

Instead of giving up, Marriott saw the tour through with fond thoughts about his still existing home in the Deep South, where he was a bit of a local lad. Between tours he found himself adored quite a bit by Atlanta's local pub regulars: "I think some of them like the idea that I'm living there. I get around the clubs in town, occasionally get up and play with somebody when I've had a few...it's nice to be part of a place that's growing and maturing, rather than somewhere fully developed and static," he said about 'the city too busy to hate'. And it was also Down South that record company interest flared up again due to the solid touring image Steve had done 'hard slog' for in the recent months.

Capricorn Records in Macon, Georgia, reputed for their high profile output of Allman Brothers records, were in the process of signing the band. And while in 1982, the only Marriott release had been A&M's *Best Of Humble Pie* compilation – the one with the fat tart-throwing tart – Steve now raved about an up-coming new long-player: "The planned album will include nine original songs, and 'Sweet Nothin's', a song that was a hit for Atlanta native Brenda Lee in the Sixties. It's one of those good songs nobody's ever covered [The Inmates then did in 1989] her voice at the time she recorded was just as raw as mine is today!"

Jim Leverton recounts the hopeful beginning of 1983: "There were definite and big plans with The Allmans' company, Capricorn Records. They were keen on working with us, sessions had been lined up for January 1983, with a nationwide tour to follow. I flew in with high hopes, but – they wouldn't even let me out of the airport: no work permit! So it had happened to me for the second time. I can tell you, it put a lot of people out of work – the roadies had all been hired for a start. Steve eventually played some of the bass parts himself, but the project died."

While that album never saw the light of day (after *Scrubbers, Blackberries, Marriott & Ridley, The Firm* and *The Midgets Strike Back*, Steve's sixth album to stay in the vaults!), Jim is happy to report that Capricorn Records have kindly deposited the master tapes with him. Back in London, Uncle Jim has put them on twenty-four-track, with all of Steve's contributions on vocals, guitar and bass intact. Together with Blodwyn Pig's drummer Graham Walker (also renowned for his work with Gary Moore), Leverton hopes to add these songs – including a truly fantastic 'Sweet Nothin's' to others he's cleaned up – for a solid Steve Marriott album of pearls that should have come out while he was alive, kicking and deserving that big break.

Meanwhile, all that seemed left to Steve was the winding, endless schlepp through the club circuit, with several pick-up bands: "The career's doing okay in the States," he consoled himself, "but it's a case of relying on the past...thank God there's one there, otherwise I'd have no living at all. You have to do it a bit like homework...the whole thing is like a machine. Empire in Atlanta's a great agency. I do anything from a thousand upwards, like little theatres and stuff."

In the summer of 1983, apart from Fallon, the line-up featured Tommy Johnson or later Phil Dicks on second guitar – so Steve could branch out on keyboards again – and bass player Keith Christopher from Atlanta's band Brains was also part of the new four-piece: "The two guitars, bass and drums is like sort of Humble Pie-ish, so most clubs want to use that name. I don't mind because I'm playing those songs there in the set, they can call it Jack Shit if it works!"

But back in England, Jim Leverton knew too well that Steve wasn't altogether happy with that constellation and the homework was getting to him. Jim: "He wasn't happy with that band; he used to call me from Chicago or Memphis and complain about a shitty gig he had just done." But Steve patiently stayed on the road, with few breaks in Atlanta at Pam's. One day in late 1983, returning from a long bar session celebrating the completion of another hard sojourn, he was cruelly reminded of that old blues standard 'Someone Changed The Lock': he couldn't get into his own house. No one could be seen, everything he owned was locked up – including his complete, treasured guitar collection (see Guitarography). With the last dollars he could gather, Steve returned to England, with the clothes he was wearing his only possessions.

Back in Essex, Steve would camp out at his sister's, chased by the taxman within days of arriving, the final humiliation after years of disappointments. Hats off to Steve for keeping his stamina in those days. What confidence Marriott had left, he invested in calling Jim in order start his non-existing career from scratch. The one time fate struck well towards the end of 1983 was when Steve met his teenage sweetheart Manon Pearcey again one evening. They struck a chord again, and soon she presented him with a lovely Gibson ES335 guitar.

That treasured axe, which always seemed far too big for the little midget, was the basis for "taking it steppa by steppa", as Stanley Unwin had called it on Steve's triumph *Ogdens' Nut Gone Flake*. His sister was able to persuade a local priest to organise a local hall for rehearsals, Jim and Blind Drunk cohort Dave Hynes formed a trio with Steve, and he even remembered someone to get work.

Above Soho's Ronnie Scott's, Steve had an old friend in manager – and ex-Georgie Fame sax player – Mick Eve, who over a pint was asked to organise some gigs. Soon, Dave Hynes left the trio on friendly terms, wanting to concentrate on his other career, painting. Steve was in the position of buying the air fare for his Stateside drummer Fallon, and he was now stable enough to give the press a less pitiful story of events: "I was living in America and I came back in 1983 because my dad was ill. So I came back to see him but he turned out to be all right...I sort of got side tracked into staying here by Jim Leverton who plays bass for me and a couple of other people said, 'Why don't you hang about and play a bit over here again. I thought about it, found myself a new old lady – she was my girlfriend when I was sixteen – and it all felt good. So I decided to stay."

Very quickly, Steve, Jim and Fallon managed to get established as one of the hottest things on the pub circuits of Greater London – and soon the rest of the Britain – not without getting a name which could make you blush even in Margaret Thatcher's punk-rattled kingdom. Packet Of Three are of course those 'Red Balloons' (Small Faces title) you get out of the slot machine, and this naughty school boy humour wasn't even by an all-male band. During the summer of 1984, Marriott continued the good tradition of those old Humble Pie And The Blackberries times and presented two girl singers for a number of gigs: The Li-Lettes! Really, Steve.

He was in top form throughout, and British audiences noted his severely improved guitar playing as well as an energy level that never suffered from partying. Jim saw working back home as the best therapy to get Marriott back on his feet: "To be honest, America was never good for Steve. You know the States' reputation for musicians, everything was all too readily available for people in the rock business – drugs, ladies and Steve had a reputation of living life to the full. In England, things were much more down to earth."

Steve also enjoyed his new career because he and Mick Eve kept the band business absolutely ground level, with no arty big projects in sight. Pub rock with foreseeable financial rewards seemed much more healthy than being put on a retainer, and the 'supergroup' imaginations by his former manager – who is now successful worldwide with The Scorpions – had made Marriott sceptical "all the time. Especially David Krebs. They wanted me to put a blues All Stars together, but I don't like that idea. It's so short-lived. I don't mind playing the clubs with my little group.

"There was talk of Jimmy Page wanting me to sing with his new band. But I don't think I could do it," he told Chris Welch. Ironically, Jimmy's band, soon with Paul Rodgers, proceeded to use Steve's name from his 1979 Leslie West era: The Firm. Steve preferred his street level, and also declined an offer by Dave Dee to appear in a TV spot about Carnaby Street. The pay would have been fantastic, but Marriott would have had to interrupt his new residency at London's Half Moon Putney for that week – no way!

The next record project was also as down-to-earth as one could get. In North London's seedy Dingwalls, a rock, punk and beer joint situated in Madness quarters Camden Town, the Packet recorded a live concert which was also transmitted by Capital Radio. The resulting album was released at the end of 1984 on the tiny Aura label of Aaron Sixx, who also dealt with the solo output by Hollies lead singer Allan Clarke at the time. Like the old days – after all The Small Faces had always been a singles band – Aura even issued an accompanying seven inch: the old Mod soul number 'What'cha Gonna Do About It' was coupled with the Humble Pie II metal arrangement of 'All Shook Up'. The album gave a rough and dirty impression of Steve's preferences – in an incredibly full sound: "I chose a couple of tunes from my Small Faces days, a couple from Humble Pie days and some Jimmy Reed and Muddy Waters. I don't think you can escape your history and I don't even want to. But I don't want to get sunk in nostalgia either. It seems to work very nicely. We enjoy it anyway."

One reviewer from the British music mag *Sounds* did not really seem to share his enjoyment, and Steve saw no point in this kind of slamming: "It was, 'He's over the hill, can't sing any more, and shouldn't be in the business!' I thought fucking hell! Total paranoia. I thought, where's me knife? I'll slit me wrists for him. I'd forgotten what that sort of violent, hateful criticism was like. It's not meant to be constructive, just hate – aimed at an individual. The funny thing is, on the back of the album is a *Sounds* review of the live show!"

Clocking in at forty-six minutes with only seven tracks chosen, the LP (with two more tracks on the cassette) was a mere appetiser for the concert programme – after all The Packet Of Three usually played sets of between seventy and ninety minutes: "If you want more, go and see fucking Bruce Springsteen and get bored for three hours," Steve told Hannover's Radio ffn DJ Ulli Kniep. Marriott had come a long way since Belgium 1969, where it had been Humble Pie themselves who delivered a three hour gig.

Finally, the complete concert was released as a compact disc in 1991, with its new title *Dingwalls 6/7/84*. With almost eighty minutes of steaming R&B it remains *the* legacy of Marriott's live repertoire during the mid Eighties.

'What'cha Gonna Do About It' opens. Drummer Fallon rolls excitedly into this old Small Faces track which sounds more compact than ever before: apart from the solid rhythm section, Steve is obviously a better guitarist than he ever got credit for, combining solo and rhythm chops in a way that you'd never take it for a single guitarist in the band.

'Fool For A Pretty Pace' (only on *Dingwalls*) follows. After thanking his father for "not noticing the hole in his Packet Of Three", the musical journey goes back to 1980. The New York radio hit 'Fool' by the half-black Pie II was originally cut as a three-piece, but sounds even fuller here, remaining loose and melodic at the same time.

For 'Shame Shame Shame' (only on *Dingwalls*) the ever reliable Uncle Jim takes over on lead vocals, in this harmless little up-tempo toe-tapper which still became one of the trademarks in Steve's Eighties gigs.

The chords of the Stones-covered 'Love In Vain' lead into the old Creedence Clearwater Revival standard 'Bad Moon Rising'. This is not easily recognised here, fitted into an unusual but moving slow blues, which serves its beautiful melody ever so well. The prototype of a successful cover treatment.

'The Cockney Rhyme' (only on *Dingwalls*) is Steve's tribute to his home in East London: "My aunt's name is Eloisa Waterbucket, she lives down in Burton-on-Trent. When she goes out shopping on a bicycle, she always gets her handle-bars bent."

Then it's back to Humble Pie's repertoire for the metal 'All Shook Up'. This Elvis Presley tribute was fed through a heavy blues mill for *Go For The Throat*. Bobby Tench's voice had been an integral part, but Jim takes over adequately here. Attractive riffs and breaks dominate which would have brought a smile to the original burger king.

This collection's first journey to the Seventies comes with 'The Fixer', when Steve was on the threshold to worldwide fame. The memory of *Smokin'* sounds pleasant, its familiar, heavy riff sounds less formulaic here, the experienced trio obviously enjoying more freedom. And talking of freedom, like Steve said about the Packet set choices, he does not want to get sunk in nostalgia, so 'All Or Nothing' is the only chart hit on the agenda; no cabaret circuits in sight. Still, Steve charmingly gets the crowd to sing along to his classic: "We're on the radio" (Capital Radio) and "You're doing good" he would quip to encourage them – a great atmosphere!

Next is 'Five Long Years', Steve's rendition of the Eddie Boyd classic. This must be one of the most emotional blues recordings ever achieved by a singer, black or white. Even Buddy Guy didn't match this version when he recorded his own in 1991 with Mick Weaver from Steve's Official Receivers. Likewise, Eric Clapton's version on his celebrated *From The Cradle* blues album pales in contrast with the intensity displayed by Marriott – almost eight minutes of lost love, suffered with that great voice and matching brilliant Gibson ES335 guitar work. Towards its end though, Steve takes the edge off by introducing himself as a fat, balding motherfucker. Magic!

Following that (only on *Dingwalls*) is the job of 'Thirty Days In The Hole'. A return to the *Smokin'* period, one of Steve's favourite periods before Humble Pie lost direction a bit – here he presents eleven minutes of versatile classic rock, the highlight of this album in terms of band interplay and invention. It's got the epic length of Seventies rock indulgence, but The Packet Of Three never let go here – the jamming joint sessions of 1969 being replaced by hard work, not least Steve's breath-taking blues harp wailing.

The next onslaught is even longer, and here, nostalgia alone couldn't possibly carry a classic like 'Don't Need No Doctor'. The punters just had to compare this trio's workout with the legendary 1971 *Fillmore* version. But it passes, because it cooks.

The first encore, taken from 1984's Aura cassette version, is a R&B original written by Marriott and Leverton called 'Big Train Stop At Memphis'. It proves again how Steve and Jim manage to sound like a four-piece supplying a simply dual-voiced chorus – backed by the unobtrusive but lively rhythm section of Fallon and Jim's own solid bass, the fundamental quality control basis of the whole Packet sound.

'Walkin' The Dog', the popular Rufus Thomas theme from the old Memphis Sun Studio era, favoured by the Stones two decades ago, is here simply served up again to close procedures. Steve couldn't care less about royalties when he selected his numbers; on the other hand he didn't even possess the publishing rights to his own Sixties hits. Here, we get the feeling that the fans as well as the Packet are in the mood for 'last orders', as there is neither marketing nor corporate strategy behind the entire venture.

So how far was Steve going to take this band then? "As far as it leads," was his reply. "I think that the respect that we get from punters is enough. If it gets any further than that we'll try and control it. But I can't really see us appealing en masse. Frankly we're not looking for that anyway. We want a nice little niche for ourselves, and a bigger van for when we go abroad. I can't see big success happening again. We aren't exactly image bound, not old tossers like us! But it's true, I am happy and it comes across."

The one about the bigger van was an understandable Christmas 84 wish one would hope could come true, for the old Portobello Road roaring Sixties Transit we found parked on German venue car parks would have looked pitiful even in the Bronx.

So the band surely didn't rest on any financial laurels. Still, the tour, or 'European Earner 84' – as Packet Of Three's T-shirts advertised – proceeded happy enough. They went down well everywhere they appeared. In Amsterdam's stoned Paradiso – home of Humble Pie's second only gig – Steve even presented a guest saxophone player. But the 'Earner' developed into a commercial flop: Marriott and his easy-going Packet had become the victims of some dubious German concert promoter.

On the other hand, the Empire Agency in Atlanta, Georgia was one enterprise Steve knew he could rely on, so straight after New Year's Day 1985, The Packet Of Three were back in America. In spite of Steve's vow to stay away from those endless highways, the band toured there all through spring, billed as Humble Pie as often as not.

The strain of one-nighters, as always, took its toll: "New Year, New Band, New Company", John Mayall had sung in the Seventies – true to his attitude as rock's major 'hire and fire' employer. Now that great midget among the blues daddies would work according to those lines in the Eighties. Towards the end of the American Packet tour, Fallon Williams II got the sack and returned to Chicago. Steve replaced him with a Stateside exile: young Jerry Shirley, who was tired of touring with Fastway.

Jim Leverton had seen that coming: "Fallon thrived on the popularity of the band, but that also made him try out the odd 'refreshment', and he overplayed on stage. Steve gave him a fair warning to play team orientated, but in the end he had to replace him because he appeared a show-off."

Back home in the UK, Steve presented the new band on 19 July, 1985, in a popular London West End club, the Cottonwood Cafe. A midnight gig, ear-thrashing as always, showed the band's optimism intact. To boost their energy, audiences over in Europe became bigger. On 7 September, 1985, Steve and his new Packet became festival headliners at long last – at a big Open Air in Tegelen near Venlo, Holland. After an All Star band with members of national groups like Golden Earring and Muskee (ex Cuby and Blizzards), The Packet Of Three delivered a convincing set. "Welcome to the gig, wherever the fuck we are," a geographically challenged Marriott quipped, and he got the audience raving with his energy, charm and all the band's musical wit. This line-up, which was soon hitting faithful and growing audiences in Scandinavia and the USA, is excellently documented on a live video from London's Camden Palace, where the *Dingwalls* set is complemented by a rousing 'Tin Soldier'.

With the promising turn of events in Europe, 1985 seemed like a rewarding, happy year for the band. Steve lived harmonically with his girlfriend Manon Pearcey, "my new old lady who I knew as a nipper in the East End", and their little daughter – Molly Mae. Steve's musical children, namely Eighties Mod bands like The Purple Hearts and The Lambrettas, paid their Godfather Steve a tribute, done as a charity for a mutual dear old friend.

The London-based Phoenix Modernist Society was able to gather many young bands as well as an impressive guard of Sixties stars for a Band Aid Trust – and Ronnie Lane's ARMS Trust. The producer, singer and Small Faces insider Kenny Lynch managed to assemble Steve Marriott, his old singer friend PP Arnold, R&B veteran and Immediate recording artist Chris Farlowe (who Steve had produced in the Sixties), and Creation guitarist Eddie Phillips. Together, they recorded a thrilling version of 'All Or Nothing', which was released on seven and twelve-inch under the project name Spectrum. Appearing in Britain and Germany, it didn't get the necessary promotion, unfortunately.

Apart from band commitments and charity work, Steve found time for studio dates as a guest singer during 1985 and 1986. He sang the duet 'Young Savages' on Jim Capaldi's solo album *One Man Mission*, while James Leverton supplied bass on 'Ancient Highway' (Steve had guested with Capaldi's Traffic as early as 1968 on *Mr Fantasy*, singing on 'Berkshire Poppies'). Other acts Marriott lent his voice to included Mother's Finest spin-off Illusion and Scorpions drummer Herman 'Ze German' Rarebell, a contact from their joint 'Marathon Tour' 81. The organisational link had once been David Krebs, of course. But there were plans to record Packet Of Three for a studio follow-up, too. At least Steve announced a new album early 1986 in Münster and Hamburg on tour, claiming it was "almost in the can".

Well, nothing came off it, instead, the Packet embarked on their second American tour, with a young Californian agency named Risky Business, which according to Jim Leverton certainly lived up to its name. "The tour schedule was ridiculous. We had to criss-cross the States in long, gruesome night journeys that sometimes took more than fourteen hours. So you arrived knackered, did the gig and off you went. I was ready to go home after just two weeks running. The bus they gave us was pure luxury, but the driver was a nut-case! [He must have heard Pie's 'Driver' anthem.] He seemed full of coke – so instead of getting some welcome sleep, I ended up on the co -driver's seat talking him out of his stupor. And when someone took over and I'd nodded off, here came Steve with his cassette player to play me the latest sounds. After five weeks of this, we realised Risky Business were losing us money, our money. Steve had had enough by now and we returned home."

Back in Europe, Marriott's Packet jumped at the chance of another Scandinavian tour, where one of his indulgent phases put his backside in prison. From the lands of the midnight sun, here's our 'reporter', the ex-John Mayall's Bluesbreakers guitarist Walter Trout, who used to share agencies with Packet Of Three:

"My promoter in Denmark also promoted Steve Marriott for many years in all of his Scandinavian tours. His name is Thomas, and one night he got a call from a town in Sweden – and Steve Marriott was in jail! It turns out that what had happened was Steve had played in a club in Sweden and after the gig he had decided that he wanted to play more, that he hadn't had enough of playing, and that he was not satisfied. He was very drunk, and he got his amplifier and he set it up on the roof of the hotel – and plugged it in, got his guitar and started playing to the whole town – at four o'clock in the morning with the amplifier all the way up (no doubt up to eleven!). The police came and arrested him and put him in jail – the promoter had to go down there and bail him out of jail. That's one of my favourite stories about Steve Marriott, like: 'I wanna play more – I didn't get enough. So I'll just set up and play to whoever can hear it!'"

The postponed studio work was probably due to lack of funds, as he hinted at in late 1986: "What I'm doing at the moment – I've got a little portastudio set up in my bedroom – is pile up all the new songs till we have the time and the money to go into a studio and put it all down. But for the moment, we haven't got the time or the money to do it!" But time and money didn't seem too pressing when a big-scale German tour with twenty-five scheduled gigs bombed all of three times, including TV spots on a prime time family quiz and music show called *Na sowas* (ZDF-TV) and a popular live in the studio night spot *Ohne Filter* ('Without Filters') on SWF-TV. Apparently, one cancellation was due to Jim Leverton's broken arm, while the trio was sighted playing the London club circuit rather happily. But on home turf the Packet remained inspired. That same year, Steve presented a dear old friend on the stage of Putney's Half Moon – one of the blues legends who seemed as underrated as Steve himself was: 'Bumble Bee' Bob Nowak, a harmonica player from Chicago who must have given Steve ideas about an augmented line-up.

Business as usual then for Marriott Inc? Since the Packet's start in

1984, Steve had suffered from bad agencies in Germany, and now that more reliable enterprises wanted him, there were excuses or absolutely unrealistic ideas about the money charged. Sure, Steve wanted to be in control and on ground level, but now everything seemed so haphazard that promoters and fans on the continent became frustrated. On top of failed tour commitments, the only new album to appear in German shops by the end of 86 did present new Packet Of Three artwork – but inside was the two-year-old *Dingwalls* recording. Great stuff, but most of the fans owned a copy.

Steve's thoughts were miles away from commercial points of view, he wanted improved sound possibilities. In the trio, the little berserker missed the opportunity to put his big Gibson ES335 down from time to time for a little harmonica set, and he also longed for the warm Hammond of his idols Booker T that Ian McLagan had often supplied for him. With Mick Weaver (solo pseudonym Wynder K Frog) he introduced a first rate R&B session man into the band.

Jerry Shirley didn't like the change of sound and left the band. For him, a real musicians' kid joined up: Richard Newman was the foster-son of Marriott's long-time studio backing singer Vicki Brown and her husband, cockney star Joe Brown, Steve's drinking partner. The Browns had taken young Richie in as a kind of step brother to their daughter Sam, as his real mother had felt overwhelmed with raising a child and Richard's father was touring non-stop (he's Tony Newman, who apart from Joe's own band Home Brew had played with Sounds Incorporated, Long John Baldry, The Jeff Beck Group, Joan Armatrading, David Bowie, The Hollies' Allan Clarke and Chrystal Gayle in the States). With his son, 'little' Richard Newman, Marriott's band now featured a member of the next R&B generation. Richie's stepmother Vicki Brown, Margo Buchanan and, again, PP Arnold soon helped with studio recordings, which really hinted at that Booker T sound – and got the German EMI interested.

After the burst dreams and plans of the previous year, it seemed typical for Steve that he was looking for new horizons, but still hinted at bygone disasters in the name for the new band. Based on his 1981 idea, he now settled for Official Receivers at long last. He presented the band live in early 1987, and on his own birthday, 30 January in the Red Lion in Brentford (Dave Edmunds' and this book's authors' local in the Eighties). "Of course I'm pissed, it's my birthday," he confirmed to enquiries on the state he was in. Grinning, he recalled those events during our conversation in Hereford, Germany in January 1990: "Of course I remember the gig. I played rather badly, it was one of those days you start with a lager and you lose track."

"Considering, he played astonishingly well!" Jim admired his stamina. We both hadn't forgotten that he'd started the day with a lager, but that was 29 January, and "no sleep till Red Lion!"

So the sound and tightness of the new band came over excellently in spite of party times. More than ever, Steve relied on his beloved R&B standards from the American Fifties and Sixties. The new titles in the set told the black blues story of the States: 'Some Kinda Wonderful', 'Can I Get A Witness', 'Don't You Lie To Me', 'My Girl'. The group kept all its promises on two German tours during the spring and autumn of 1987, but unfortunately didn't get any promotion to speak of, certainly not via the television.

Meanwhile, EMI had remixed tapes for a scheduled, up-coming Official Receivers album. There was talk of a collaboration with the Dutch studio wizards Bolland and Bolland, who'd made their fortune with Falco and had just ruined a Roger Chapman album by running him through sequencers and a drum machine jungle. A group album was to be preceded by an already finished single, the beautiful 'If You Find What You're Looking For', written by Jim Leverton. All that was needed was Steve's signature on the EMI contract.

Understandably there was maximum irritation when Steve didn't catch that plane to Cologne. What had happened? Jim Leverton: "We'd arrived at Heathrow, and instead of checking in, Steve simply announced, 'Let's book a room in a hotel nearby and relax!' There was nothing I could do, he just didn't feel like going. It was probably fear of flying, too, but he just couldn't be bothered. I've heard claims about EMI Cologne insisting on a solo contract, and Steve not wanting to let the band down, but what's the sense behind that? We would all have benefited from a record deal, surely!"

But Marriott had no comments. He worked at home in Britain, and the four Official Receivers continued to play their club gigs. Steve seemed content. His royalty income from old records was a far cry from the fortunes other Sixties legends reaped in, but it must have been enough to refuse any compromise in the studios and cabaret-type oldies shows. Instead, Steve preferred to roam the R&B club scene in Britain and check out other underdog bands, just like he had done in Atlanta. One of Marriott's comments about his superstar friends of yore: "They move in a different circle. I'm playing the clubs and I'm enjoying myself on that level. I think they're still trying to pay off their mortgages. I'm more modest, don't want to make disco records. I stay with what I've been doing for twenty years – it's still basic, loud rock'n'roll. When you're looking for something better than the clubs, you might be in for a disappointment. I'm not looking for anything. The big stadium gigs are all blown up. Everything has to be shown larger than life for the people in the back. In a club that's different. Here the sweat on your forehead tells the whole story!"

CHAPTER TWELVE
The DTs And Beyond
You Soppy Prat

One of the blues bands Steve jammed with during his tours was the reliable team of The DTs (the apt, abbreviated 'Delirium Tremens') from Birmingham: Simon Hickling, vocals and harmonica; Steve Walwyn, guitar and vocals; Greg Rhind on bass and Chess Chaplin on drums. When Chess couldn't make the dates for a German tour, The DTs replaced him with Alan 'Sticky' Wickett, ex-Chris Barber and The Steve Gibbons Band. Sticky speaks fluent German from his Top Forty band days in Heidelberg and so he seemed perfect for the job on top of his drum chops.

Anyway, Steve couldn't stop raving about this band. So one day, his Soho agent Mick Eve (as a short reminder: he's the ex-Blue Flames and Gonzales saxophonist) said aloud what Steve must have been contemplating: "Steve, you won't shut up until you've actually joined them, so why don't you just do it?" So that's what he did, and suddenly there was Steve Marriott And The DTs.

There had been tensions in the Official Receivers camp anyway, because Steve had 'missed' that plane for his EMI Electrola contract. Steve had given them a half-arsed story about not wanting to go solo, and had another lecture ready that was hardly convincing: "Record companies would rather have a sixteen-year-old that said 'Yes, sir – no, sir' than have someone like me that would tell them to fuck off!" So the Receivers sat on five finished tracks (which Jim Leverton is currently editing), with no advances due for finishing a whole album's worth of material, and of course, the atmosphere between Steve and the rest of the band suffered, not helped by a shift in Marriott's private company. His new girlfriend, Judy 'Toni' Poulton tended to shelter Steve backstage, widening the rift. So when The DTs cropped up, the end of the band as it was had been in sight for a while.

The remaining Receivers counted their blessings and joined Mick Weaver and Jim's friend, the Irish guitarist and singer Henry McCullough. Henry, ex-Joe Cocker's Grease Band and McCartney's Wings, had used Weaver, Leverton and Marriott as early as 1975 on his solo album *Mind Your Own Business*, and now they quickly made a patchy live album, *Get In The Hole*, in Folkestone, Kent, a benefit for the Shepway Muscular Dystrophy Group (not unlike Ronnie Lane's ARMS appeal) released by Line Records in Hamburg. Subsequently, Richard Newman joined his step sister's Sam Brown Band; Mick and Jim formed The Breadheads featuring drummer Mark Sagdon and ex-Procol Harum and Cochise guitarist Mick Grabham – but they didn't make too much bread during their short life span.

Steve was not too fortunate with his Delirium Tremens bluesers either. In tiny clubs like the wild, legendary Dingwalls his Packet Of Three might have recorded their live album four years ago, but now, come 1988, Steve's DTs were reduced to playing support for Dr Feelgood (who'd catch DT Steve Walwyn a year later). Bigger opening slots, like playing before Chuck Berry at London's Hammersmith Odeon, remained an exception.

The DTs' repertoire was R&B based like the Receivers' set, but routine gigs with often heard standards and sometimes lacklustre playing didn't reach the heights and energy level of Steve's former band. Wasn't it time to feature some more Marriott compositions, instead of appearing as the fiftieth band to recycle 'Let's Work Together'?

But in 1988, Steve saw that attitude as dangerous: "I could go on the road and play 'Sha La La La Lee', 'Lazy Sunday', 'Tin Soldier', 'Itchycoo Park', 'All Or Nothing', 'Hey Girl', but it wouldn't be any good, it would be a con, it would be cabaret. I have to be very careful at my age not to be cabaret…there are some obscure Humble Pie and Faces numbers that are good to play live – but you need horns, you need chicks, black singers. To do that, you'd have to augment – that would be another thing altogether. Maybe next year…"

His agent Mick Eve would comment in 1989: "Surely, Steve is just treading water at the moment, but he genuinely likes the repertoire, it gives him the feeling that he's a contemporary artist instead of jumping on the oldies bandwagon. He wants to be independent and play whatever he likes, nothing else!" And that was exactly what Steve continued to do in Britain, Scandinavia and – often postponed – in Germany.

Apart from Europe, Eve had worked intensively on organising a Japanese tour, but – like beat mate Paul McCartney back in 1980 – he couldn't crack Nippon's rather hypocritical attitude to the consumption of dope refreshments. In 1992, Mick recalled events in the *Ogdens'* fanzine: "In 71 Steve got his one and only conviction for drugs; smoking a joint on a park bench, for which he got a twenty pound fine. In 1989, eighteen years on, I set up a nice little tour for him in Japan, knowing that he'd already been in and out of Japan, with Humble Pie. All of a sudden, the day before he was due to go, he was refused entry, due to his conviction. The promoter in Japan was devastated, as he'd got a beer company to promote the gigs..."

On top of such disappointments, the record side of things would remain unsatisfactory for a while. The solo or rather Receivers project had been put on ice, and the latest attempt for some CD or vinyl material in the shops was the recording of a DTs live album in Hannover's Capitol Club in Germany. Local station Radio ffn was head of productions. It turned out that the equipment the promoter had hired for the band was rotten and the tapes were of inferior quality. So the concert album couldn't get out as planned on SPV Records. All that was left for fans was an avalanche of CD reissues and compilations (see Discography). The only new studio productions Steve seemed to do were single songs, put down on tape sporadically.

One such project Steve enjoyed was for re-cutting the old Humble Pie/Blackberries classic 'Black Coffee' – as a commercial jingle for Nescafé's new roast Blend 37. The session, together with Pie's Clem Clempson, got the team a Gold Medal Award for the top Commercial 1989! Clem remembers: "I'd been booked for a coffee advert, and the producer called me the night before to cue me about the track – he wanted to get as close to the original as possible. He went, 'I don't know if you heard it, it's an old Humble Pie number called 'Black Coffee'...that was fantastic, because I had to go into the studio and copy myself. And Steve Marriott was part of it; it was the first time I'd seen him in a couple of years, and he was in really good shape. We did it in one take, with Steve singing his heart out like he always did. I loved it. And that'd be the last time I saw him."

Steve also wrote and sang 'Law Of The Jungle' for Puma trainers; and for the horror movie *Food Of The Gods II* he recorded a new version of 'Shakin' All Over'. Apart from that, Bon Jovi wanted him in the studios, and there were even rumours Guns N'Roses had an interest in a collaboration, but both projects were never heard of again.

Producer Stephen Parsons must have had the knack – both in terms of studio technique and psychology – in order to collaborate with Steve Marriott who was notorious for being relaxed to the point of laziness, and disillusioned with the world of studios anyway. In any case, the recording of 'Shakin' All Over' was such a lot of fun for Steve that he was willing to do more takes, especially as Stephen reassured him that he could drop in the studios whenever he felt like it. In August 1989, a little ball started rolling with the release of a seven-inch Sixties oldie. 'The Um Um Um Um Song' had been a US hit for its composer Curtis Mayfield and now scored in Britain courtesy of Wayne Fontana And The Mindbenders from Manchester (with 10cc's Eric Stewart on guitar and backing vocals). According to his wife Toni, Marriott wanted this one as the single because the fans then had to enter the shops in order to stutter away "um um um um". The old cockney cheek was shining through again.

There were pre-conditions for the majority of the considered tracks though. Parsons wanted titles which his little Trax Music Ltd – sideline of the corporate Film Trax plc – was able to lease on the cheap because of existing publishing rights. But a follow-up album was supposed to be fifty per cent vintage Steve. Meanwhile, the Trax team left it at one old and one new Marriott composition – a modern version of The Small Faces' 'All Or Nothing' (revived on record for the third time after Packet Of Three and Spectrum), and the romantic 'Phone Call Away' which Jim Leverton had written with Steve. Apart from those, Stephen and Steve still managed to pick suitable titles, as well as a studio crew that was astounding in terms of ability and pedigree. They were, among others: PP Arnold on backing vocals;

Steve Walwyn, guitarist with The DTs, who joined Dr Feelgood in August 1989, played rhythm guitar on the backing tracks; Simon Hickling: blues harmonica player with The DTs, and with Steve's next band, The Next Band; Jim Leverton, who sings, obviously not bearing a grudge about Steve having joined The DTs; Mick Weaver, the Official Receiver is on keyboards and backing vocals; James Litherland, the ex-Colosseum member is on rhythm guitar (ironically he was Clem Clempson's predecessor in that band); Frank Ricotti, a percussion specialist who had been rattling away on Peter Frampton's first 1972 solo album, *Wind Of Change*; Chris White, a saxophone player courtesy of Dire Straits and Justin Hayward; and finally Neil Sidwell, trumpeter with Georgie Fame.

The list could be continued, though, and old Master Marriott himself, who was not always present during the proceedings, was taken aback with the line-up, insisting in our conversation in January 1990 that it was him who played all the lead guitar parts, in spite of the other present musos. Jim Leverton could confirm this – Walwyn and Litherland only contributed rhythm tracks. In spite of an overall technical feel due to programming, the album was still exciting, full of life and desperately overdue. Steve himself soon didn't rate the album much, though. In terms of production and sound, he dismissed it as too modern, especially irritated with the drum computer.

His long-standing brother of the road, Jim Leverton, was surprised that Steve had been open to such techno attitudes in the first place: "He was almost a session singer on this album, wasn't he? Almost all the songs are cover versions, apart from 'Phone Call Away', which I wrote with him. I never thought he would make an album with drum computers and lots of keyboards, because he always complained how the technical side had taken over in the rock world. I didn't play with him when this was recorded, and I only do backing vocals."

Even with all these misgivings, Steve still fires away with all his vocal and guitar playing talent on *Thirty Seconds To Midnite* – very truly thrilling after eight almost studio-free years.

'Knockin' On Your Door' opens with vicious bite, digital snare drum sounds and a genuine saxophone doing credit to this John Fogerty up-tempo rocker. Steve had already used and bluesed 'Bad

Moon Rising' by the Creedence Clearwater shouter in Packet Of Three, but here he presents the great Bayou man in a Memphis arrangement.

The hit compromise follows. In terms of a Marriott marketing exercise 'All Or Nothing' is not bad, but with its banks of keyboards it remains nothing more than an interesting alternative version, no contender for the original or the Packet and Spectrum re-runs.

'One More Heartache' belongs to the best attempts Steve ever made in the soul idiom. With Marvin Gaye and The Artwoods he had high class role models, who he defeats with aplomb. This has been cruelly overlooked by DJs so far.

Curtis Mayfield has always been one of Steve's favourites and British fans remember the Wayne Fontana version of 'The Um Um Um Um Song'. But the Booker T And The MGs/Stax backing is pleasant in the best sense of the word, and an attractive contrast to Steve's sandpaper voice.

Marriott's breathing organs are surely tortured to the nth degree on the fittingly titled 'Superlung'. Steve re-vamps this hippy ode by Donovan into a R&B orgy, and propels it to share the high point acclaim with 'Heartache'. It's another energy monster – with dancefloor credentials still due.

Steve never had any time for reggae which makes 'Get Up, Stand Up' seem an odd choice, so Parsons refurbishes this Wailers track with a Temptations arrangement. But for all its groove, brass and congas, it still sounds electronic. Steve's voice, Gibson guitar and the piano theme just about rescue the song.

The original of 'Rascal You' was made famous by Louis Armstrong, still featuring in the funeral repertoire of many New Orleans bands, although ironically, its lyrics were supplied by local comedian Spodie Odie. This could have become a declaration of love to Steve's second/Eighties home, Louisiana, but via this dramatic keyboard overkill it sounds more like his day of reckoning.

Marriott and ex-Talking Head David Byrne go together amazingly well on 'Life During Wartime'. Steve roars Byrne's critical and cynical lyrics with a nonchalant conviction as if they were his own. The whole thing has a perfect bite, groove and credibility.

As already stated, the ballad 'Phone Call Away' is the only new composition in the whole collection, but it's got class. Jim Leverton recalls: "'Phone Call Away' I wrote together with Steve. The melody line 'Why Don't You Call Me' for instance is by me. The song thankfully exists in our mutual, more sensitive version!" Steve and Jim had worked together on compositions ever since their Greenwich Village days in 1981, and the catchy hooklines presented here showed they had certainly not lost their touch since. Their quiet qualities were hardly recognised live with the Packet. Here, with PP Arnold's assistance, romance ruled, and more gems of this kind would soon be promised by Steve for a Frampton/Marriott project in LA at the beginning of 1991.

Shirley Ellis had been in the charts during the era of 'Sha La La La Lee' with a version of Lincoln Chase's 'The Clapping Song' about, er, "rubbers dollies" and Steve must have seen the thematic Packet Of Three connection. The ex-couple Marriott and Arnold surely deliver this one with charm and tongue firmly in cheek.

'Shakin' All Over' follows. Recorded for the horror film *Food Of The Gods II*, this was the track with which Stephen Parsons had started his collaboration with Steve. The old R&B standard, unforgotten in its Johnny Kidd And The Pirates version, was re-heated with suitable drama, Steve shouts his head off, but studio technique puts too much metallic rust over it. Similarly, the closing track, 'Gypsy Woman' also suffers from its sheer weight of keyboards. Steve's phrasing can still let his love for Curtis Mayfield shine through, and ultimately his vocal cords prove stronger than all the studio gadgetry he came to criticise more and more during his pub rock days.

With this collection, fans finally had their chance to discover new Marriott music, and the CD also got Steve into the digital era – as one of the last contenders and with a miserable BMG distribution. In fact fans on both sides of the Channel were frustrated from trying to get hold of it, and an American release only got going in 1994.

Steve Marriott had stopped appearing with The DTs in the meantime, but hand-picked Simon Hickling as his harmonica player. Although a likable and talented player, it was still a strange choice as Steve himself blew the harp so well himself and counted as one of the best in the trade. But then he never did fear for his profile, true to his statement to us during that Blind Drunk gig in 1978: "I'm always

pushing other people!" At the time, this referred to the vocal artistry
of Rod Stewart and Jim Leverton. The latter now served as Steve's
bass player again for the group Steve shruggingly called The Next
Band.

After the Official Receivers' Richard Newman, Steve's drummer
for this venture, Kofi Baker, also came from the 'next generation' – he
was the son of Peter 'Ginger' Baker (his exotic Christian name is fairly
common in Kofi's birthplace Lagos, Nigeria – where Ginger ran
recording studios in the Seventies). Asked in January 1990 how the
band ran into Kofi, Steve would answer charmingly, "He fell off the
back of a lorry!" He was quite sensational loot anyway. The young
man left a great impression on the Half Moon in Putney and on the
subsequent German tour – with sensitivity and energy he was the
motor of a band who played with a conviction not heard since
Humble Pie in 1972. Unfortunately, Kofi went less traditional paths
soon after the tour, playing in younger bands.

Before Marriott, Leverton and Hickling found the time to look for
a replacement, they were faced with another small but highly unusual
recording project. The Georgia Satellites of all people, hailing from
Steve's second home Atlanta, Georgia, were on tour in England and
combined with the trio for a musical comment on the highly
controversial British 'poll tax' – a local community charge which – in
short terms – collects less money from the well-off, single Yuppie in
a trendy suburban semi than from a family of five in a run-down East
London council house.

Eastender Steve was all for making a politically correct noise
about it, but how it all started is best related by Kevin Jennings, then
the Satellites' manager, who told us in February 1991: "It was about a
year ago, we were on tour in England during the 'peak of chaos' over
the new and very unpopular tax law. Rick Richards, aka Dickey Lee,
decided one hot'n'sweaty night at the Mayfair Club in Newcastle-
upon-Tyne to voice the opinion of the masses by way of a song.

"He churned out a dirty, greasy blues riff through his Marshall
amp, then sang, 'I ain't gonna pay no poll tax no more' – everybody
immediately sang along and when the band kicked in the place just
about exploded. It was completely spontaneous and a good time was
had by all. The following night in Glasgow was a repeat

performance..."

This called for an immortalisation in the studios. Kevin: "Although the whole thing was a novelty anyway, for me personally it was a great triumph and thrill to record with one of 'the all time greats', Steve 'Matt Vinyl' Marriott, and the other world class players. Jim Leverton and Simon Hickling are both regulars in Steve's band, Dicky Lee Richards is from the Satellites and Dick Young is an old friend of mine, who is a very established session man, and a member of a fine British rock group called Buster James!" (With that last name dropped, Kevin could have mentioned that the "fine British rock group" is The Searchers – Buster replaced Mike Pender in 1985.)

Soon after the sessions, harmonica player Simon Hickling joined R&B tough guys Nine Below Zero, depping for an ill Mark Feltham. Steve reverted to a trio format as well as to that tried and trusted band name of the Eighties: Packet Of Three. As well as Jim Leverton, in came yet another remnant of Steve's DTs days: Alan 'Sticky' Wickett. Another welcome guest towards the end of 1990 was none other than Peter Frampton, ex-superstar and former Marriott cohort in Humble Pie. Soon, there were joint recording projects on the agenda (reported in Chapter 10).

Steve's German tour with Packet Of Three in early 1991 seemed to be under a falling star. Steve appeared haphazard, "treading water" more than ever, his wife Toni would accept nobody backstage with him anymore, the sound (for example in Hannover's Capitol) could be diabolical, and Steve would comment shruggingly: "Sure, I've got a terrible hangover, but then I'll always be hungover!" He was not the only band member who felt the tension on that tour. Jim Leverton remembers those days with regret: "That was a very, very difficult tour for me. Up till a few days before we went, I was inclined on not doing it. All he'd say when I asked him about the future of the band was 'What do you mean?'"

When, after a London gig in March 1991, Steve flew to Los Angeles for studio sessions with Peter Frampton, Leverton didn't like the sound of it as he recalled in 1992: "Personally, I didn't like him recording in LA, because me and him had collaborated on songs, which are now safely stored on multi-tracks and will come out as soon as I find the time to finish them. [They still haven't come out.]

I think they [Peter and Steve] got on well enough musically, and managed to record four songs in little more than a week. But then Peter's management made the old mistake: presenting Steve with a big contract about reforming the original Humble Pie. You guessed it, Steve didn't want to know and he and his wife Toni flew home. He didn't trust anybody anymore. Towards the end, I was about the only one allowed to step into his house!"

Leverton blames the incidents after the return from Los Angeles to Arkesden, the little village near Saffron Walden, on the strain of a transatlantic flight: "Well, he was totally jetlagged, hated flying anyway. Both Steve and I had developed quite a fear of flying during the 1980s, when terrorist threats increased. And Steve wanted to be in his own house, you see…"

But before an eventual return there, Steve and Toni went out to a local restaurant, together with a friend, 40-year-old garage owner Ray Newbrook. On 21 April, 1991, he described what had happened in the early morning hours of the night before last: "We were celebrating his trip. Steve had been working on a record deal with Peter Frampton. At the end of the evening the pair were dead on their feet from jetlag. They came back to my house and I put them both to bed. But a few minutes later Steve got up and said he wanted to sleep in his own bed. I called him a cab and he went home alone. Toni stayed where she was."

In the early hours of that morning of 20 April, neighbours had witnessed the wonderful, thatched cottage, The Sextons, go up in flames – it had no fire alarm. The Marriotts had rented the house about two years ago, which had become quite famous via the TV series *Lovejoy*. When the fire brigade arrived, the roof was on fire, and the window frames had turned to charcoal.

As soon as they entered the ground floor, the firemen realised what kind of personality the inhabitant of the little villa was. Assistant Divisional Officer Keith Dunatis reported in the *News Of The World*, 21 April: "There was memorabilia everywhere. When we got in the house we could see tons of pictures of rock stars on the wall. I especially noticed a print of guitarist Ronnie Wood. All those Sixties people on the wall – they were his colleagues in the business, and my idols. I deal with many fires but this one was like walking down memory lane. You knew you were in a pop star's house immediately…"

But Keith and his fellow fire fighters hardly had time for reminiscing: "When we arrived there was smoke pouring out of the building and the flames were really fierce. We had to break in through the back door. It was a tough fight getting upstairs. We searched the bedroom areas and it was very hot – we knew immediately that no one could have survived the fire. We began to feel our way around the walls and discovered him lying on the floor in between the bed and the wall. I would say he had been in bed and tried to escape. As soon as I saw the body clearly I knew who it was. It was Steve Marriott!" This was confirmed on the following Monday via dental records and fingerprints.

Fire fighter Keith: "I used to be a fan. It's difficult to put my feelings into words. The scene was horrific in that corner of the room. I saw him lying there and thought what a pity it all was. It was lucky he was still a person and we could preserve his dignity. We managed to salvage all his guitars and musical equipment. I feel a bit upset – all the firemen did. It was like seeing part of our lives gone forever."

These documented statements formed the more harmonic, well-meant part of an uproar in the British gutter press. With glee, those million selling tabloids quoted trippy tales by fellow musicians and friends – drawing horror pictures of Steve's – undeniable – love of alcohol and also inhalable drugs. This flew in the face of the increased stability those around him had witnessed during the last decade. Steve had seemed to calm down in the company of Manon Pearcey from 1984 to 1988, who had given birth to their daughter Molly Mae, as well as his third wife Toni, who by her own account, had been able to get Steve down to earth.

Finally, the autopsy confirmed that Steve had in fact become a victim of his desire to get "high and happy". On 19 July, 1991, Britain's tabloid *Daily Mirror* reported: "Sixties rocker Steve Marriott was knocked out by booze and drugs when he died in a blaze, an inquest heard yesterday. Cocaine, valium and alcohol had put him in a coma – and might have killed him. But the forty-four-year-old Small Faces singer breathed in lethal fumes from the fire – which was probably started by a cigarette as he slept alone in his rented luxury cottage in Arkesden, Essex. He had flown back from a recording date in America earlier that day. The Epping inquest was told he may have taken valium to offset the effects of cocaine and misjudged the dose because he had drunk so much. Verdict: accident."

The broadsheet *Guardian* put it more exactly the same day: "Rock singer Steve Marriott consumed a lethal cocktail of drink and drugs on the night he died in a fire at his home, an inquest heard yesterday. The body of Mr Marriott, aged forty-four, was found in the wreckage of his sixteenth century thatched house at Arkesden, Essex, on 20 April. The inquest in Epping was told that an examination of his blood showed he had taken a large quantity of valium as well as alcohol and there were traces of cocaine. But the Essex coroner, Dr Malcolm Weir, said there was no evidence that Mr Marriott – who had a string of hits with The Small Faces in the Sixties – had tried to take his own life. A verdict of accidental death was recorded.

"A postmortem examination found the cause of death to be carbon monoxide poisoning due to smoke inhalation. Dr Weir said that the effects of the valium and alcohol would have put Mr Marriott into a deep sleep, although the sedative effect would have been lessened by the cocaine. The valium, alcohol and cocaine together 'probably would have been lethal on its own'.

"PC Ian O'Sullivan said that the smoke from the fire was so thick it had filled the main street of Arkesden. The cause of the fire appeared to be a cigarette end or possibly a candle, which Mr Marriott used to read by in bed. After the hearing Mr Marriott's widow, Toni, said her husband had taken valium because he had flown back from America that day and was 'terrified of flying'. She said the trip had been a success, with Mr Marriott completing a recording session with Peter Frampton, his former colleague in Humble Pie. Mrs Marriott added: 'He was not into drugs in a big way. He liked to drink more than anything else.'"

But the most tragic part of Steve's accidental death, the little detail which suggested he could have escaped had fate struck in a milder way, hardly anybody dared to mention. *The Sun* did, one day after initial reports, on 22 April: "The charred body of Sixties pop legend Steve Marriott was found in an *airing cupboard*, police revealed yesterday. They believe the forty-three-[*sic*] year-old Small Faces star dived through the wrong door in a desperate attempt to escape the blaze that gutted his country home. Inspector Martin Reed said: 'There were doors on either side of the bed. He opened the cupboard by mistake.'"

This smallest lack of orientation, due most probably to several weeks in a hotel bed away from home, made Steve's death all the more unnecessary, useless and way before time. Whatever a final outcome of Steve and Peter's collaboration, the little midget had actually stopped "treading water", he had started to create again. The legacy of this is small but impressive. The completed album would probably have received its working title *Chalk And Cheese*, a hint on Frampton/Marriott's stormy relationship, and it's worth looking at the four available tracks of what could have been the greatest hard rock comeback of the Nineties.

'The Bigger They Come' is energetic, riffy rock which had all the ingredients of a working, traditional yet forward-looking Humble Pie comeback. Even the treasured trademark of taking turns in the lead vocals was being used again to great effect. Peter Frampton and Steve Marriott were commissioned to record this initially for the film *Harley Davidson And The Marlboro Man* accompanied by drum computers, but after Steve's death Frampton had Anton Fig supply real drums for his underrated anthology *Shine On*. Classic.

Steve had not merely been boasting when he announced more reflective tracks for the reunion with Peter. The ballad 'I Won't Let You Down' was a welcome return to the melodic richness of 'All Or Nothing' which had all too often given way to a majority of 'bashing tracks'. Steve lets Peter take the lead here, but his presence is felt the second he's let loose himself! Again, this was eventually released on the 1992 Peter Frampton anthology *Shine On*.

There was only a demo tape of 'Out Of The Blue' when Steve died, but the vocal track was sufficiently intact to be sampled onto a new recording for the 1994 album *Peter Frampton*. This is Memphis soul with touches of Smokey Robinson's 'My Girl' – a beautiful melody, impeccably phrased by a sensitive Steve. It's interesting to note that Peter seemed to accept Marriott's *Eat It* phase where successor Clempson had been all too sceptical.

And finally to 'So Hard To Believe'. Frampton and his bass player John Regan had finished the guitar and bass parts of this mid tempo lament the day before the recordings with Marriott were due to start. Peter: "The first day we got together, I went back to the hotel and wrote most of the lyrics, except for the last verse, which was written after he died." So this was meant as part of the new Humble Pie set, even if Steve narrowly missed it. Instead, Frampton now sings it with more than enough soul to make his partner proud. It also was released on Peter's 1994 *Peter Frampton* album.

Frampton may have been the last person to work with Steve, but in his too-short life he touched a lot of people more than he could ever know. It seems only fitting that we end with the memories of him held by others.

Toni Marriott: "It's all very tragic and sad. We will all miss him very much – and we'll play his records and think of Steve and his music."

Kenney Jones: "I always held Steve in high esteem. He was a wonderful, lovely man who had a great voice and was a brilliant guitarist. I can't believe he's dead. I'd heard he was on the wagon and was really together. Steve was so happy. He'd been working with Peter Frampton and everyone was looking forward to their new album. He was a ball of talent and I couldn't wait to hear the new stuff he'd written. I hadn't seen him for a couple of years but I was delighted when I heard about him reforming Humble Pie. Now I suppose the album will be a big hit. But I'd rather have Steve alive than have a tribute like that to him."

John Peel (British DJ since 'day one'): "He was hardly an enviable character. An everyday, cheeky London boy who'd done well. But after he'd gone to the top in the Sixties, he simply sank. Lately I heard he was doing the rounds with a band called Packet Of Three, kind of back to the roots. It's hard to understand for normal people how terrible it is to be a star who suddenly loses everything – only a few survive this. He didn't."

Alexis Korner, Steve's musical mentor, had died before him as early as 1984, but a decade before that he commented on Steve in timeless words, quoted from *Melody Maker,* March 1975: "I think Steve is one of the most exciting stage performers I've ever seen in my life. He's an incredibly intense blues player and his whole life is really what happens to him on stage and when he's recording. Music is his whole life."

Ozzy Osbourne: "Somewhere in the world someone has this one drink too many and dies...just look at Steve Marriott. It was in a club in Los Angeles, I hadn't seen him for six or maybe even seven years. So I went to this Rainbow Club, where I met him. And he told me he was going to form another band to go on the road. He wanted to do that together with Peter Frampton. And the next day he went on a drinking tour; at home he went to sleep with a cigarette in his hand...his house burnt down with him in it. That's another one."

Roger Daltrey: "I think he was one of the greatest British soul singers of all times. The tragic thing is, he was just getting back on his feet."

Jim Leverton: "To imagine the ordeal he must have gone through that night, it makes me sad. In a way, the almost thirteen years, on and off, that I played with Steve were the best, certainly the most enjoyable part of my musical career. I loved his attitude, and I loved going on stage with him – just plug in and go for it!"

Clem Clempson: "Well I'm really glad I was part of it. It was a great time and I learned a lot of stuff from Steve, about playing rock'n'roll. Steve was one of the few genuine talents in the business...the vast majority of people in this business are just kinda talented, but not really gifted the way Steve was – and it's just a shame that we won't see him again."

Jerry Shirley: "We lost in my view probably one of the truly greatest white blues singers in the entire world, way better than almost all of them out there. We lost one of the absolute best songwriters we ever had. We lost a much better guitar player than anybody ever gave him credit for, in particular a rhythm player. We lost a fabulous piano player. We lost one of the naturally most witty people I've ever known. As far as live performer in terms of working a stage, working an audience, he helped invent a lot of what is taken for granted as a rock'n'roll performance of today."

Steve Walwyn: "Steve was a total eccentric. That means on many nights he was fantastic, but he had his off-nights, too. Let's remember the good ones!"

Andrew Loog Oldham, who tends to stick to the advice of ex-US chat show host Johnny Carson that "people smoking in bed should keep one foot on the floor": "Marriott might have lived if he hadn't had to whore himself going to America entertaining the idea of redoing Humble Pie. I know nothing bored him like the past. Money would have made a difference in that man's life."

Mick Eve confirms Oldham's views: "Steve was lured out to the US by Peter Frampton, and although he is a nice man, he's a different animal altogether compared to Steve. Frampton went back a long way with him, although I probably knew Steve better than he did, by now. He wanted to get Steve involved in a film theme he was working on, which he could earn a substantial amount by doing. However, the lawyers and record company then started talking about a three-year recording contract etcetera…which would virtually mean Steve committing himself to a reformed Humble Pie. He always said, 'I'll never go backwards again. I'm doing The Packet Of Three, The Official Receivers, and that's what I'm happy doing.'"

But to try and reconstruct the useless American trip as cause of death would really go over the top. Performers with Steve's talent and charisma always die too young; and on the other hand, Steve has left a true treasure of songs and recordings, which we should be grateful for – maybe this would have been added to substantially. maybe not. In any case, we would have loved to been able to enjoy him several times a year, screaming his head off. To put it straight: "We miss you, Steve!"

POSTSCRIPT
Yesterday, Today & Tomorrow

When the German edition of *Happy Boys Happy!* appeared in the summer of 1993, it was a case of 'At long last somebody's taking care of them' – people without a word of German since their O level history lapped it up for the pictures and the sheer feeling of owning a book on the almost forgotten Faces. Hardcore fans were rumoured to marry German, Swiss and Austrian spouses for a chance to get our stories read at bedtime.

Now the band is well and truly re-established. *The Darlings Of Wapping Wharf Launderette E1* is one of the most lovingly assembled fanzines on the market, and they've even succeeded in putting a Small Faces calendar back in the marketplace, up on the shelf with household Sixties legends like The Beatles, The Stones and their ilk.

Steve Marriott probably didn't know how to write the word Internet, but here we are with Martin Payne from Ealing, West London, supplying his 'Room For Ravers' homepage under the heading http://ourworld.compuserve.com/homepages/Martin_Payne/ surely one of *the* sources of information for younger generations growing up without teen mags on glossy paper.

And continuing the legend in another manner, after The Bootleg Beatles and Brown Sugar there's now a Small Faces revival group, Mustn't Grumble, who spread decent versions of the band's repertoire in the south of England.

In 1996, The Small Faces were awarded an Ivor Novello Award for their "outstanding contribution to British music". Ian McLagan flew over to London from his home in Austin, Texas to accept the award with Kenney Jones. Sadly, Ronnie Lane was unable to travel as his health had once again deteriorated, so instead his brother Stan stepped in to accept the award.

On 10 August, 1996, there was a high profile British radio documentary on BBC Radio 2. Apart from excellent research and presentation, it contained one of the last interviews with Steve Marriott as well as the remainder of the band, including their former keyboard player Jimmy Winston. Producer Glyn Johns, disciple Paul Weller, svengali Don Arden and other ardent followers were also included.

After more than one year of preparations, the new generation of BritPop bands succeeded in releasing an excellent tribute album, *Long Agos And Worlds Apart*, hot on the heels of dancefloor ravers M People's version of 'Itchycoo Park'. New versions like these continue to point out the strength and relevance of Small Faces material, and what's more, the bands' enthusiasm and inventiveness makes it clear that there's more to BritPop than Blur and Oasis. Those two outfits helped bring that across by staying away from the album roster.

Last but by no means least, *Happy Boys Happy!* will be in very good company on the high street book shelves, with a biography planned by Ian McLagan for summer 1997. And those who want to relive the whole exciting era of The Small Faces (Mk I) will be in for a treat from the *Darlings Of Wapping Wharf*. Their spiritual leader John Hellier has been labouring on a day by day time machine which is going to be published in early spring 1997. Yesterday, today and tomorrow indeed!

APPENDIX
Quotes

Mick Jagger:
"If you don't like The Small Faces, you're getting old!"

Ray Davies:
"When Steve Marriott and Peter Frampton...started Humble Pie and scored a great hit with 'Natural Born Bugie', many people immediately started talking about a supergroup. The first two LPs were not super successes, though. And then the sceptics could laugh cynically and say: 'Just having a name won't do!' But with this third album [*Humble Pie*] they have...proved at long last that they really are a supergroup!"

Chris Farlowe:
"When I read that a good band is on somewhere – like Humble Pie – I just have to go and see them. Most of the time I end up in the dressing room – just to say 'hello' – and a little later I find myself on stage and singing with Humble Pie."

Paul Rodgers:
"Really, though, there's so many good singers it's hard to put one above the other. I think people like Steve Marriott and Rod Stewart are incredible. I liked The Small Faces when they were in their heyday."

Ozzy Osbourne:
"The bands I dig are people like Humble Pie. How can you get more basic than Humble Pie? But what a band. They're absolutely incredible on stage."

Midge Ure:
"In my younger days, Steve Marriott with his Small Faces was one of my favourites." (He calls 'Itchycoo Park' his favourite record.)

Mark Hollis (Talk Talk):

"People who impress you leave their tracks. I'm thinking of the Sixties, of The Small Faces and Steve Marriott, who used to sing in the highest registers of his voice. At the time I was thinking, 'God, his singing is fantastic. That's what I want to do one day.'"

Paul Weller:

"It was The Small Faces who brought me to the Mods as a source of inspiration. I bought a Rickenbacker guitar, a Lambretta GPT, and I had a haircut like Steve Marriott around 1966." (PS *Ogdens' Nut Gone Flake* belongs to the six LPs which Weller would take on that famous desert island.)

Rick Springfield:

"I've always liked the songs by The Small Faces, and this song ('If You Think You're Groovy') comes from that period of rock history I treasure the most. I'm not losing my self esteem when I admit that other people also wrote great songs."

Chris Robinson (The Black Crowes):

"To me, it's so obvious I'm a Steve Marriott rip-off that I never think about Rod. I admit it. Steve Marriott is *the* guy – him and Paul Rodgers and Greg Allman."

Rory Gallagher (about Steve Marriott):

"He's a very talented guy, he could play keyboards, he could play drums – a brilliant voice, a fantastic guitarist, great songwriter."

Brian May:

"I've always loved it ('Rollin' Over'), I loved the album it came from, the *Ogdens' Nut Gone Flake* album. I was a big fan of The Small Faces, really, they seemed such young boys, you know. I was a young guy at the time, but I think they were younger than I was. They were certainly smaller, and in the beginning you didn't want to take them seriously. They seemed like a pop band, but then they majored very quickly and wrote some wonderful material. And he [Steve] was definitely a great singer, and I loved the feel!"

GUITAROGRAPHY

Steve Marriott's Guitars

Whoever spotted the tiny rhythm'n'blueser in his recent years – in his comfortable overalls and holding his treasured, huge Gibson 335 – couldn't help a smile: upright, the instrument looks about as high up as the chord thrashing Marriott. Having got used to an axe, Steve could be faithful to the model all through his career (we're still talking about guitars). As he told us: "I'm terrible. On stage I always use one guitar until it's completely worn out. I don't like putting one down to strap on the next one – it's difficult enough staying in tune with the keyboard [back in 1987, he was referring to Mick Weaver, Official Receivers]. With two spare guitars and possibly a few acoustics as well I'd be tuning up all the time!"

In spite of stage comfort, Steve had been an avid collector of guitars all through his career. Up to his sudden departure from Atlanta, Georgia in late 1983, and afterwards back in Britain, he would gather a treasured range of guitar gems, which are worth a chapter in themselves.

ELECTRIC GUITARS (in alphabetical order)

DWIGHT

In the summer of 1971, Steve got this unusual, licensed reproduction in the USA. The Dwight is similar to the Epiphone Crestwood, "a strange mixture," he told us in December 71, "of an Epiphone body and a Gibson pickup. The way the pickup is wired gives it extra volume and tone. It is an older pickup which they have discontinued owing to the hum level, but for rock'n'roll bands, it's one of the best pickups you can get."

EPIPHONE CRESTWOOD

This small, flat model Steve used in the early days of Humble Pie. According to him, it was Epiphone's answer to the Gibson Les Paul Junior. Steve got one of the makes with the white, flat pickup: "It didn't have as much 'poke' as the Dwight. Now I use it as a spare," he'd claim in the Fillmore.

FENDER ESQUIRE 1955

Steve bought this model, which was never really popular in general, around 1972 as another spare for Humble Pie gigs, paying eighty dollars for it in Chicago. But because of its extremely clean sound, he only started using it on stage with The Small Faces in 1977. He liked the sound of its simple pickup, especially when compared to the treble pickup of his Telecaster. He used numerous mid range sounds but didn't like its bass range. Steve played the Esquire with Ernie Ball strings and connected the guitar to a Fender Twin Reverb – what a contrast to the "lager than Steve" Marshall stacks of the early Small Faces and Humble Pie days!

FENDER STRATOCASTER No 62 1953

A rare find that the Fender company was taken with so much that they actually tried to buy it back from Steve. But for him it had exactly the right noise to hold on to. He loved its neck, which at the time used to be more rounded at the back. Steve still didn't use it on stage, because the sounds were "too syrupy" for him. In the end he screwed its neck off and had it assembled to his Telecaster.

FENDER TELECASTER

This one had been bought in 1965 for Ian McLagan to get him to mime to the TV playback of 'I Got Mine', which had been recorded with his predecessor Jimmy Winston. Once *Top Of The Pops* was done, Marriott used it himself, applying humbucker pickups.

GIBSON LES PAUL JUNIOR 1956

Steve was given this flat guitar as a present by a generous fan in San Francisco on a Pie tour – Steve called the phenomenon "love, peace and guitars" – but on stage he played it very rarely.

GIBSON LES PAUL ORIGINAL

This wasn't a flat model, but a fat, cello-type guitar with a cutaway for reaching high-pitch notes and a beautifully ornate scratch plate. Steve rather regretted that he'd given this guitar to Alexis Korner in the mid Seventies.

GIBSON LES PAUL CUSTOM 1957

Steve's famous black one from the Humble Pie days, bought in Cleveland, Ohio. He took out the central pickup of the three it came with, because it was in his way when picking. Later, this beauty with mother-of-pearl inlays in its neck was offered with just two pickups, exactly the way Steve had altered it.

GIBSON MELODY MAKER

A completely symmetrical, flat guitar which Steve had used as a spare for his Epiphone Crestwood before he got his Dwight.

GIBSON ES335

Another big, cello-type guitar which Steve used to play on all his numerous tours from 1983 with Packet Of Three – a present from his childhood sweetheart and then girlfriend Manon Pearcey. In the Eighties, Steve would only take this and his Ibanez Artist on the road with him. Unlike the Gretsch Eddie Cochran, the ES335 has two cutaways, and in that respect resembles the Ibanez Artist again.

GRETSCH EDDIE COCHRAN

This collector's item Steve was able to purchase in St Louis, Missouri, for only three-hundred dollars. The dealer called Steve after he had seen a picture of him with The Small Faces and kept it for a year before Steve was able to pick it up, stopping over on tour. It's an orange hollow body with a 'G' brand mark – burnt in. The only other known copy is owned by Jimmy Page. Orange Eddie Cochrans aren't so rare, it's the brand mark that counts. The real Eddie Cochran had flat, black Gibson pickups built in his 'G', but Steve kept the original Gretsch ones. He was very proud of the guitar, but never used it live because of its feedback.

IBANEZ ARTIST

A kind of Ibanez answer to the Gibson ES335, even if the neck top and the bridge have their own design. Steve used to rate Ibanez guitars because you hardly had to break them in. On the other hand he missed its top/treble presence, but raved about its out of phase position. In any case, he was sufficiently over the moon with the company that he posed for a commercial Ibanez poster in 1982-3.

IBANEZ HOWARD ROBERTS

Towards the end of the Seventies, Marriott preferred Ibanez guitars to Gibson makes, because he realised that its constructors had the necessary know-how and on top of that had bought huge supplies of Gibson wood. Steve had used the Howard Roberts as early as 1967 for 'Itchycoo Park', with very light strings.

IBANEZ 'LES PAUL' BLONDE

What Steve loved most about this copy was that a solid body guitar had a maple neck. But the pickups he found too dirty for Small Faces Mk II purposes, so he meant to replace them with double-pole Fender pickups. Who knows if he ever did?

OVATION BREADWINNER

For this designer's wet dream – in subtle 'Starship Enterprise' style – Steve also posed in musicians' trade magazines, during his All Stars phase in 1976. For Marriott, the Breadwinner was the perfect studio guitar, because he was able to get every (im)possible sound out of it, "messing with tones and boosts". The neck is flat and wide, but feels surprisingly comfortable according to Steve, similar to a Dan Armstrong.

ACOUSTIC GUITARS (in alphabetical order)

CRISPIAN MELLOR CUSTOM 1970

A Western guitar in the style of a Gibson Gospel but without the Cutaways, with a heart shaped hole. This collector's dream was handmade for Steve's first wife Jenny. Steve played quite a few bottleneck numbers on it because "it's action is very high", for example on the acoustic side of the *Eat It* album in 1973. It's got a beautiful, bassy sound, as on 'Summer Song'. Crispian Mellor had just started out; he later got famous with the crazy guitar creations for Gary Glitter.

EPIPHONE FRONTIER

Steve treated this acoustic strictly as a collector's item, at least until he got his beloved Martin.

GIBSON BANJO

For completists, we mention that Steve as well as Clem purchased banjos in 1972 and played them regularly for three years, by which time they'd lost interest.

GIBSON GOSPEL

Steve loved to play this Western guitar without cutaways, but he had difficulties in adjusting the bridge.

MARTIN 00018, 1937

"Extremely loud – like a piano – but light as a feather" is how Steve felt about this acoustic guitar when he bought it from an American family he used to jam with in 1972, for about three-hundred-and-fifty dollars. Steve used this model frequently in the studio – with ultra light strings in order to frighten sound engineers with its volume.

OVATION TWELVE-STRING

This twelve-string has a fibreglass body that's rounded at the back. Steve also used this guitar for bottleneck playing with open tuning. For a special swirling sound, Steve would send this through rotating Leslie speakers.

OVATION SIX-STRING

Steve rated the six-string version for the majority of his songs in the studio. With a split stereo lead, he'd feed it directly into the mixing board. For miking acoustics up, he alternatively used Neumann 87 and 47 microphones. Little pickup bugs he didn't rate at all, because they wouldn't get the wood tone across properly.

UKELELE

The little Marilyn Monroe-type mini guitar was bought by Steve in Hawaii in 1973, possibly in memory of his busking days as a kid in London's East End. According to Steve it sounds "like a classical guitar with a capo".

Peter Frampton's Guitars

GIBSON LES PAUL 1957

The same generous "love, peace and guitars" gentleman who had given

Steve his Gibson Les Paul Junior had this one in store as a present for Peter while he was in Humble Pie in 1970. This was made up of three different guitars. Apparently, in the States there was a craze about assembling different necks to guitars. Unlike Steve, Peter used a custom three-pickup.

FENDER STRATOCASTERS

Peter has always occupied more of the jazz end of the guitar range – ever since his days in The Herd. This is why the softer, clear Strat suited his needs better than Steve's. It would frequently accompany him in the studio when he didn't have to rock out on his Les Paul.

SCHECTER

The slim black wonder Peter first presented on *Premonition* at first looked like a Yuppie's design for a new Telecaster. Peter soon felt at home with it.

VOICE BOX

Ironically, Peter Frampton's guitar chops didn't get famous first and foremost via his expert chord playing and his soloing – which, on a Les Paul or Strat, was in turns melodically tender or aggressively attacking. Peter got into the headlines rather by some special 'word of mouth', a special gadget with the look of a giant Asthma inhaler – the Voice Box or Talk Box.

On stage, this guitar effect looks like the oxygen supply system for Mick Jagger or Michael Jackson: a plastic hose carries the guitar sound from the amp into Peter's mouth, where he can alter it with vocalising vowel movements like "a-e-i-o-u" and also via a connected foot pedal. Through the vocal mike, the sounds can reach the PA system, demonstrated in 'Show Me The Way'. The 'Heil Talk Box' is distributed in the USA by Jim Dunlop and costs about three-hundred dollars. In Europe, Frampton effects addicts (who include Jeff Beck and Richie Sambora) can get the item via Rhodes Music in London W1.

Clem Clempson's Guitars (Excerpt)

GIBSON LES PAUL

This had been Clem's trademark even back in Colosseum. In Humble Pie he played it over three Marshall hundred watt amps, and two centre cabinets.

GIBSON FLYING V

This visually exciting model was Clem's spare – Jimi Hendrix had used one but its most prominent client has always been Wishbone Ash's Andrew Powell.

Greg Ridley on Bass

Solid Greg played a Fender Precision bass guitar over four Acoustic bass cabinets fed off one Acoustic amplifier.

DISCOGRAPHY

How to use this discography:

Generally, we only consider the original releases (in Germany, Britain and USA) as well as later CD versions. Regarding Small Faces compilations, we present excerpts, as the range is now endless, while the tracks on offer do not reveal any interesting stuff not previously available. The Rod Stewart discography is limited to his early, Faces accompanied period. Those interested in later solo work find information in the literature section, ie detailed biographies about his career. Session work by the individual musicians has been limited to the relevant work (in our view anyway), especially regarding Kenney Jones and Ian McLagan. Otherwise, our bibliography would have gone beyond the limits of a volume like this. We also stayed away from listing the countless live tapes, but these will be featured in fanzines *Wapping Wharf* and *Itchycoo*.

STEPHEN/STEVE MARRIOTT (1960-65)

OLIVER!
LP: *World Record Club TP 151* – *UK 1960*

SINGLES

Give Her My Regards/Imaginary Love
Decca F 11619 – *UK 1963*

WITH THE MOMENTS

You Really Got Me/Money, Money
World Artists 1032 – *US 1964*

Tell Me/Maybe
Decca F 121 (Test Pressing) – *UK 1965*

THE SMALL FACES (1965-69; 1976-78)

LPS/CDS

SMALL FACES
Shake/Come On Children/You Better Believe It/It's Too Late/One Night Stand/What'cha Gonna Do About It/Sorry She's Mine/Own Up/You Need Lovin'/Don't

Stop What You're Doing/E To D/Sha-La-La-La-Lee
Decca LK 4790 – UK 1966
Decca BLK 16425 – Germany 1966
CD: London 8200 572-2 – UK 1988
CD: Deram 844 634-2 – UK 1996

FROM THE BEGINNING
Runaway/My Mind's Eye/Yesterday, Today And Tomorrow/That Man/My Way Of Giving/Hey Girl/(Tell Me) Have You Ever Seen Me/Come Back And Take This Hurt Off Me/All Or Nothing/Baby Don't Do It/Plum Nellie/Sha-La-La-La-Lee/You've Got A Hold On Me/What'cha Gonna Do About It
Decca LK 4879 – UK 1967
Decca ND 153 – Ger 1967
CD: London 820 766-2 – UK 1988
CD: Deram 844633-2 – UK 1996

SMALL FACES
Have You Ever Seen Me/Something I Want To Tell You/Feeling Lonely/Happy Boys Happy/Things Are Going To Get Better/My Way Of Giving/Green Circles/Become Like You/Get Yourself Together/All Our Yesterdays/Talk To You/Show Me The Way/Up The Wooden Hills To Bedfordshire/Eddie's Dreaming
Immediate IMSP 008 – UK 1967
Columbia SMC 74292 – Ger 1967
(see CD: Green Circles/1991)

THERE ARE BUT FOUR SMALL FACES
Itchycoo Park/Talk To You/Up The Wooden Hills To Bedfordshire/My Way Of Giving/I'm Only Dreaming/I Feel Much Better/Tin Soldier/Get Yourself Together/Show Me The Way/Here Come The Nice/Green Circles/Have You Ever Seen Me
Immediate Z-12 52 002 – US 1968

OGDENS' NUT GONE FLAKE
Ogdens' Nut Gone Flake/Afterglow/Long

Agos And Worlds Apart/Song Of A Baker/Rene/Lazy Sunday/Happiness Stan/Rollin' Over/The Hungry Intruder/The Journey/Mad John/Happydaystoytown
Immediate IMLP 012 – UK 1968
Immediate SMIM 74 442 – Ger 1968
Immediate Z-12 52 008 – US 1968
Virgin V 2159 (reissue) – UK 1980
Castle Communications CLALP 116 – UK 1986
CD: Immediate IMLCD 012 – UK 1986
CD: Castle Communications CLACD 116 – UK 1986
CD: Castle Communications CLACT 016 (in tobacco tin) – UK 1989
(with bonus track Tin Soldier (live))

THE AUTUMN STONE
Here Come The Nice/The Autumn Stone/Collibosher/All Or Nothing/Red Balloon/Lazy Sunday/Rollin'Over (live)/If I Were A Carpenter (live)/Every Little Bit Hurts (live)/My Mind's Eye/Tin Soldier/Just Passing/Call It Something Nice/I Can't Make It/Afterglow Of Your Love/Sha-La-La-La-Lee/The Universal/Itchycoo Park/Hey Girl/Wide Eyed Girl On The Wall/What'cha Gonna Do About It/Wham Bam Thank You Mam
Immediate IMA 101/2 – UK 1969
Immediate SMIMM 2107/8 – Ger 1969
Immediate IMLD 01 (reissue) – UK 1984
Castle Communications CLALP 114 – UK 1986
CD: Castle Communications CLACD 114 – UK 1986

IN MEMORIAM
Rollin' Over (live)/If I Were A Carpenter (live)/Every Little Bit Hurts (live)/All Or Nothing (live)/Tin Soldier (live)/Collibosher/Call It Something Nice/Red Balloon/Wide Eyed Girl On The Wall/The Autumn Stone
Immediate IMSP 035 – UK 1969

EMI Immediate 1C048-90201 – Ger   1969
*Line/Outline OLLP 5270 AS * – Ger   1982*
(1982 reissued under the same title and*
with identical live numbers; but different
studio tracks: Red Balloon/Just
Passing/Wide Eyed Girl On The Wall/Wham
Bam Thank You Mam/I'm Only Dreaming/I
Feel Much Better/Donkey Rides, A Penny, A
Glass/Don't Burst My Bubble)

SMALL FACES
Hey Girl/What's A Matter Baby/Come Back
And Take This Hurt Off Me/You Better
Believe It/Shake/Own Up/My Way Of
Giving/What'cha Gonna Do About It/Baby
Don't Do It/Do You See Me/Come On
Children
Disc AZ STEC 112 – F   1972
Bellaphon STEC 112 – Ger   1972
(Demo recordings from 1965/66, partly
with different mixes and arrangements)

THE SINGLES ALBUM: ALL THE DECCA A + B SIDES
What'cha Gonna Do About It/What's A
Matter Baby/I've Got Mine/Sha-La-La-La-
Lee/Grow Your Own/Hey Girl/Almost
Grown/All Or Nothing/Understanding/My
Mind's Eye/I Can't Dance With You/I Can't
Make It/Just Passing/Patterns/E To D
Decca ROOTS 5 – UK   1976
See For Miles SEE 193 (reissue – UK   1990
CD: See For Miles SEECD 293 – UK   1990

RARITIES – 14 RARE TRACKS...HAVE FUN
Come Back And Take This Hurt Off
Me/Yesterday, Today And Tomorrow/That
Man/Baby Don't Do It/Plum Nellie/You've
Really Got A Hold On Me/Wham Bam,
Thank You Mam/Collibosher/Donkey Rides,
A Penny, A Glass/The Hungry Intruder/Red
Ballon/Tin Soldier/The Autumn Stone/Wide-
Eyed Girl On The Wall
(tracks 1-6 are off From The Beginning,

tracks 7-14 from a 1975 Rod Stewart
cheapo compilation with misleading
credits; the recordings are alternative and
instrumental versions as well as raw
mixes for the planned album 1862)
Line/Outline LMLP 5283 AS – Ger   1984

BIG MUSIC – A COMPLEAT COLLECTION
Don't Burst My Bubble/My Mind's Eye/Sha-
La-La-La-Lee/What'cha Gonna Do About
It/I'm Only Dreaming/The Live Side: Rollin'-
If I Were A Carpenter-Every Little Bit Hurts-
All Or Nothing-Tin Soldier/Rarities: Wham
Bam Thank You Mam-The Hungry Intruder-
Tin Soldier-Wide-Eyed Girl on The Wall-Red
Balloon/Picaninny/Yesterday, Today And
Tomorrow/I Feel Much Better/Have You
Ever Seen Me/I Can't Make It
(Picaninny is an instrumental studio
outtake, like the song Don't Burst My
Bubble dating from early 1967 Immediate
sessions; the well known live recordings
were re-mixed at the correct speed: the
'Rarities' correspond with the similar
German compilation on Line)
Compleat Records 672004-1 – US   1984

QUITE NATURALLY RARE
Rollin' Over/Song Of A Baker/I Feel Much
Better/Talk To You/Tin Soldier/Autumn
Stone/Become Like You/I Can't Make
It/Donkey Rides, A Penny, A Glass/Rene'/I'm
Only Dreaming/The Hungry Intruder/Red
Balloon/Just Passing
(Tin Soldier and The Hungry Intruder are
instrumentals or alternative versions of
the originals; see also 'Rarities')
Showcase LP: SHLP 145 – UK   1986
CD: Showcase SHCD 145 – UK   1988
CD: Sound Solutions 3010502 – Ger   1992

25 GREATEST HITS
Lazy Sunday/Here Come The Nice/Tin
Soldier/Itchycoo Park/Afterglow/The
Universal/Sha-La-La-La-Lee/Talk To You/All

Or Nothing/Rollin' Over/My Mind's Eye/I
Feel Much Better/Hey Girl/Donkey Rides, A
Penny A Glass/I Can't Make It/Wham Bam
Thank You Mam/Patterns/I'm Only
Dreaming/What'cha Gonna Do About It/Tell
Me Have You Ever Seen Me/Green
Circles/Don't Burst My Bubbles/Every Little
Bit Hurts (studio version)/Wide Eyed Girl
On The Wall/Call It Something Nice
CD: Repertoire 4255 – Ger 1992

ALL OR NOTHING
Autumn Stone/Every Little Bit Hurts/Happy
Boys Happy/Don't Burst My Bubble/Wham
Bam Thank You Mam/Wide Eyed Girl On
The Wall/Eddie's Dreaming/Red Balloon/Tin
Soldier (instr)/Things Are Gonna Get
Better/Just Passing/Something I Want To
Tell You/Become Like You/The
Universal/Just Passing/Feeling
Lonely/Collibosher/Call It Something
Nice/Donkey Rides, A Penny, A Glass/All
Our Yesterdays/Live: All Or Nothing-If I
Were A Carpenter-Tin Soldier-Every Little
Bit Hurts
CD: Sony 52427 – US 1992

PLAYMATES (SMALL FACES MkII)
High And Happy/Never Too
Late/Tonight/Saylarvee/Find It/Lookin' For A
Love/Playmates/This Song's Just For
You/Drive-In Romance/Smilin' In Tune
Atlantic K 50375 – UK 1977
Atlantic ATL 50375 – Ger 1977
Atlantic 19113 – US 1977
Repertoire 4276 – Ger 1992

78 IN THE SHADE (SMALL FACES MkII)
Over Too Soon/Too Many Crossroads/Let
Me Down Gently/Thinkin' About
Love/Stand By Me (Stand By You)/Brown
Man Do/Real Sour/Soldier/You Ain't Seen
Nothin' Yet/Filthy Rich
Atlantic ATL 50468 – UK/D 1978
Atlantic 19171 – US 1978

CD: Repertoire 4392 – Ger 1993

**THE DEFINITIVE ANTHOLOGY OF THE
SMALL FACES**
I: What'cha Gonna Do About It/What's A
Matter Baby/I've Got Mine/It's Too Late/Sha-
La-La-La-Lee/Grow Your Own/Hey
Girl/Almost Grown/All Or
Nothing/Understanding/My Mind's Eye/I
Can't Dance With You/I Can't Make It/Just
Passing/Patterns/E To D/Here Come The
Nice/Talk To You/Itchycoo Park/I'm Only
Dreaming/Tin Soldier/I Feel Much
Better/Lazy Sunday/Rollin' Over/The
Universal/Donkey Rides, A Penny, A
Glass/Afterglow Of Your Love/Wham Bam
Thank You Mam
II: Give Her My Regards
(Marriott)/Imaginary Love (Marriott)/You
Really Got Me (Moments)/Money Money
(Moments)/Sorry She's Mine (Jimmy
Winston)/It's Not What You Do (Jimmy
Winston)/Real Crazy Apartment (Jimmy
Winston)/Snow White(Jimmy
Winston)/Every Little Bit Hurts/Something I
Want To Tell You */I Can't Make It */Just
Passing*/Things Are Gonna Get
Better*/Take My
Time/Collibosher*/Groovy/Rollin' Over +/If
I Were A Carpenter +/Every Little Bit
Hurts+/All Or Nothing+/Tin Soldier+ (*=
Alternative take, += live)
*2-CD Repertoire REP 4429-WO (plus 48
page booklet) – Ger 1995*

THE DECCA ANTHOLOGY
What'cha Gonna Do About It/What's A
Matter Baby/I've Got Mine/It's Too Late/Sha-
La-La-La-Lee/Grow Your Own/Hey
Girl/Almost Grown/Shake/Come On
Children/You Better Believe It/One Night
Stand/Sorry She's Mine/Own Up Time/You
Need Loving/Don't Stop What You're
Doing/E To D/All Or
Nothing/Understanding/My Mind's Eye/I

Can't Dance With You/Just Passing/Patterns/Runaway/Yesterday, Today & Tomorrow/That Man/My Way Of Giving/(Tell Me) Have You Ever Seen Me/Take This Hurt Off Me/Baby Don't You Do It/Plum Nellie/You've Really Got A Hold On Me/Steve Marriott: Give Her My Regards/Imaginary Love/Jimmy Winston & His Reflections: Sorry She's Mine/It's Not What You Do
2-CD Deram 844 583-2 – UK 1996

THE IMMEDIATE YEARS (Boxed set with 52 page booklet)
I: The Moments: You Really Got Me/Money Money/Small Faces: What'cha Gonna Do About It/Sha-La-La-La-Lee/Hey Girl (single + LP)/All Or Nothing/Yesterday, Today & Tomorrow/I Can't Make It mono/Just Passing m/Here Come The Nice m/Talk To You m/Itchycoo Park m/I'm Only Dreaming m/Tin Soldier m/I Feel Much Better m/Lazy Sunday m/Rollin' Over m/The Universal m/Donkey Rides m/Afterglow m/Wham Bam Thank You Mam m
II: I Can't Make It stereo/Just Passing s/Here Come The Nice s/Itchycoo Park s/I'm Only Dreaming s/Tin Soldier s/I Feel Much Better s/The Universal s/Donkey Rides s/Wham Bam s/(Tell Me) Have You Ever Seen Me Version 2/Something I Want To Tell You/Feeling Lonely/Happy Boys Happy/Things Are Going To Get Better/My Way Of Giving version 2/Green Circles version 1/Become Like You/Get Yourself Together/All Our Yesterdays/Talk To You/Show Me The Way/Up The Wooden Hills To Bedfordshire/Eddie's Dreaming
III: The complete Ogdens' Nut Gone Flake/Live: Rollin' Over/If I Were A Carpenter/Every Little Bit Hurts/All Or Nothing/Tin Soldier
IV: Call It Something Nice/The Autumn Stone/Every Little Bit Hurts/Collibosher/Red Balloon/Don't Burst My Bubble/(Tell Me)

Have You Ever Seen Me version 3/Green Circles version 2/Picaninny/The Pig Trotters/The War Of The Worlds/Wide Eyed Girl On The Wall/Tin Soldier instrumental/Green Circles USA mix/Wham Bam Thank You Mam guide vocal/Collibosher alternate mix/Donkey Rides, A Penny, A Glass alternate mix with experimental brass overdubs/The Hungry Intruder instrumental/Red Balloon alternate mix/Tin Soldier half instrumental/half vocal mix/The Autumn Stone alternate mix/Wide Eyed Girl On The Wall alternate mix
4-CD Charley Holdings IMM 1-4 – UK 1995

SINGLES/EPS/MAXIS

What'cha Gonna Do About It/What's A Matter Baby
Decca F 12208 – UK 1965
Decca F 25203 – Ger 1965
Press 9794 – US 1965

I've Got Mine/It's Too Late
Decca F 12276 – UK 1965

Sha-La-La-La-Lee/Grow Your Own
Decca F 12317 – UK 1966
Decca DL 25227 – Ger 1966
Press 9826 – US 1966
Sha-La-La-La-Lee/Grow Your Own/What'cha Gonna Do About It/What's A Matter Baby
Decca DX 2396 – Ger 1966
What'cha Gonna Do About It/What's A Matter Baby/Don't Stop What You're Doing/Come On Children
Decca 457091 – F 1966
EVA 705 (reissue) – F 1991
CD: EVA 705 – F 1991
Sha-La-La-La-Lee/Grow Your Own/It's Too Late/I've Got Mine
Decca 457106 – F 1966
EVA 706 (reissue) – F 1991

CD: EVA 706 – F 1991
All Or Nothing/Understanding/Hey Girl/Almost Grown
Decca 457123 – F 1966
EVA 707 (reissue) – F 1991
CD: EVA 707 – F 1991
Hey Girl/Almost Grown
Decca F 12393 – UK 1966
Decca DL 25243 – Ger 1966
Press 5007 – US 1966
All Or Nothing/Understanding
Decca F 12470 – UK 1966
Decca DL 25253 – Ger 1966
RCA 45-8949 – US 1966
My Mind's Eye/I Can't Dance With You
Decca F 12500 – UK 1966
Decca DL 25269 – Ger 1966
RCA 45-9055 – US 1966
My Mind's Eye/I Can't Dance With You/Shake/One Night Stand
Decca 457133 – F 1967
EVA 708 (reissue) – F 1991
CD: EVA 708 – F 1991
Just Passing/You Need Loving/I Can't Make It/You Better Believe It
Decca 457144 – F 1967
I Can't Make It/Just Passing
Decca F 12565 – UK 1967
Decca DL 25287 – Ger 1967
Pattern/E To D
Decca F 12619 – UK 1967
Decca DL 25297 – Ger 1967
(release not authorised by the group)
Have You Ever Seen Me/Madame Garcia
Immediate IM 043 (was not released) – UK 1967
Here Come The Nice/Talk To You
Immediate IM 050 – UK 1967
Columbia C 23524 – Ger 1967
Immediate 1902 – US 1967
Here Come The Nice/Become Like You/Talk To You/Get Yourself Together
Immediate ESRF 1876 – F 1967
Itchycoo Park/I'm Only Dreaming
Immediate IM 057 – UK 1967

Columbia C 23586 – Ger 1967
Immediate 5001 – US 1967
Itchycoo Park/I'm Only Dreaming/Green Circles/Eddie's Dreaming
Immediate ESRF 1882 – F 1968
Tin Soldier/I Feel Much Better
Immediate IM 062 – UK 1967
Columbia C 23672 – Ger 1967
Immediate 5003 – US 1967
Lazy Sunday/Rollin' Over
Immediate IM 064 – UK 1968
Immediate IM 23784 – Ger 1968
Immediate 5007 – US 1968
The Universal/Donkey Rides, A Penny, A Glass
Immediate IM 069 – UK 1968
Immediate IM 23586 – Ger 1968
Immediate 5009 – US 1968
Afterglow Of Your Love/Wham Bam Thank You Mam
Immediate IM 077 – UK 1969
Immediate 1C006-90104 – Ger 1969
Immediate 5014 – US 1969

Mad John/The Journey
Immediate 5012 – US 1969

Runaway/Shake
Pride 1006 – US 1974

REISSUES (SELECTION)

Itchycoo Park/My Way Of Giving
Immediate IMS 102 – UK 1976
Lazy Sunday/Have You Ever Seen Me
Immediate IMS 106 – UK 1977
All Or Nothing/Sha-La-La-La-Lee/What'cha Gonna Do About It
Decca F 13727 – UK 1977
Tin Soldier/Rene/Tin Soldier (live)
Virgin VS 367 – UK 1980
All Or Nothing/Collibosher
Charly Records BF 18494 – Ger 1980
Itchycoo Park/Lazy Sunday/Sha-La-La-La-Lee/Here Come The Nice

*Castle Communications TOF 103 – UK
1986*
**Itchycoo Park/Lazy Sunday/All Or
Nothing/Autumn Stone**
*CD: Castle Communications CD3-9 – UK
1988*

SINGLES SMALL FACES MKII

Lookin' For A Love/Kayoed (By Luv)
*Atlantic K 10983 – UK 1977
Atlantic ATL 10983*
**Stand By Me (Stand By You)/Hungry And
Looking**
Atlantic K 11043 – UK 1977
Filthy Rich/Over Too Soon
Atlantic K 11173 – UK 1978

BOOTLEGS

LIVE IN EUROPE 66
Stop Me (=Rollin' Over)/If I Were A
Carpenter/Every Little Bit Hurts/All Or
Nothing/Little Tin Soldier
*OQUISH Records 001
ISR 1979 (ca)
(EP with live recordings from* In
Memoriam; *1968!)*

SMALL FACES
*No info on label logo – US 1975 (ca)
(EP with similar recordings to* Live In
Europe 66; *All Or Nothing is called Oh No
here!)*

GUEST APPEARANCES BY THE SMALL FACES

PP ARNOLD
**(If You Think You're) Groovy/Though It
Hurts Me Badly**
*Single: Immediate IM 061 – UK 1968
(the A-side only is a Marriott/Lane song)*

BILLY NICHOLS

Would You Believe/Daytime Girl
*Single: Immediate IM 063 – UK 1968
(only A-side produced and/or composed by
Marriott/Lane, not confirmed to date!)
LP: Immediate IMCP 009 – UK 1968*

TRAFFIC: Mr Fantasy
*LP: Island ILPS 9061 – UK 1967
(backing vocals on the song "Berkshire
Poppies")*

JOHNNY HALLYDAY
*LP: Johnny Hallyday – Philips 844 971 BY
F 1969)
reissued on compact disc
CD: Je suis né dans la rue/1968-69 Philips
512472-2 F 1993
(Regarde por moi/= What You Will,
Amen/= That Man and Réclamations/=
News Report sound like Small Faces and
early Humble Pie, recorded as they were
with Marriott, Lane & Frampton)*

THE FACES (1969-75)

LPS/CDS

FIRST STEP
Wicked Messenger/Devotion/Shake Shudder
Shiver/Around The Plynth/Flying/Pineapple
And The Monkey/Nobody Knows/Looking
Out The Window/Three Button Hand Me
Down
*LP: Warner Bros K 46053 – UK 1970
CD: Warner Bros WPCP 4036 – JAP 1990*

LONG PLAYER
Bad'N'Ruin/Tell Everyone/Sweet Lady
Mary/Richmond/Maybe I'm Amazed/Had Me
A Real Good Time/On The Beach/I Feel So
Good/Jerusalem
*LP: Warner Bros K 46064 – UK 1971
CD: Warner Bros WPCP 4037 – JAP 1990*

A NOD'S AS GOOD AS A WINK ... TO A BLIND HORSE

Miss Judy's Farm/You're So Rude/Love Lived Here/Last Orders Please/Stay With Me/Debris/Memphis/Too Bad/That's All You Need

LP: Warner Bros K 56006 – UK 1971
CD: Warner Bros WPCP 4038 – JAP 1990

OOH LA LA

Silicone Grown/Cindy Incidentally/Flags And Banners/My Fault/Borstal Boys/Fly In The Ointment/If I'm On The Late Side/Glad And Sorry/Just Another Honky/Ooh La La

LP: Warner Bros. K 56011 – UK 1973
CD: Warner Bros WPCP 4039 – JAP 1990

COAST TO COAST – OVERTURE AND BEGINNERS

It's All Over Now/Cut Across Shorty/Too Bad/Every Picture Tells A Story/Angel/Stay With Me/I Wish It Would Rain/I'd Rather Go Blind/Borstal Boys/Amazing Grace/Jealous Guy

Mercury 9100 001 – UK 1973
CD: Mercury 832128-2 – Ger 1991

COMPILATIONS

SNAKES AND LADDERS/THE BEST OF FACES

Pool Hall Richard/Cindy Incidentally/Ooh La La/Sweet Lady Mary/Flying/Pineapple And The Monkey/You Can Make Me Dance, Sing Or Anything/Had Me A Real Good Time/Stay With Me/Miss Judy's Farm/Silicone Grown/Around The Plynth

Warner Bros. K 56172 – UK 1976
CD: Warner Brothers WPCP 4040 – JAP 1990

THE BEST OF THE FACES

Flying/Around The Plynth/Nobody Knows/Three Button Hand Me Down/Sweet

Lady Mary/Maybe I'm Amazed/Had Me A Real Good Time/Miss Judy's Farm/Memphis/Too Bad/Stay With Me/That's All You Need/Cindy Incidentally/Ooh La La/Flags And Banners/Borstal Boys/I Wish It Would Rain/Pool Hall Richard/You Can Make Me Dance, Sing Or Anything/It's All Over Now

Riva RVLP3 – UK 1977

MUSIC FROM THE FILM

LP: CBS – US 1976
(Promotion LP with tracks of the movie Rod Stewart's Farewell Concert; see Filmography)

READING FESTIVAL (Live compilation)

1 title: Losing You

Philips 6370 103 – Ger 1973
CD: Marquee Records MQCCD 001 – UK 1990

SINGLES/EPS

Around The Plynth/Wicked Messenger
Warner Bros WB 7393 (as SMALL FACES!) – US 1969
Flying/Three Button Hand Me Down
Warner Bros WB/K 8005 – Ger/UK 1970
Had Me A Real Good Time/Rear Wheel Skid
Warner Bros WB/K 8018 – Ger/UK 1971
Warner Bros WB 7442 – US 1971
Maybe I'm Amazed (studio)/Oh Lord I'm Browned Off
Warner Bros 16078 – Ger 1971
Warner Bros WB 7483 – US 1971
Stay With Me/Debris
Warner Bros WB/K 16136 – Ger/UK 1971
Stay With Me/Miss Judy's Farm
Warner Bros WB 7150 – US 1971

Cindy Incidentally/Skewiff (Mend The Fuse)
Warner Bros WB/K 16247 – Ger/UK 1972

Warner Bros WB 7681 – US 1972
Medley: Fly In The Ointment-My Fault-Borstal Boys-Silicone Grown-Oo-La-La/Dishevelment Blues
Warner Bros SFI 139 – UK 1973
(Flexi-disc; free supplement for NME)
Borstal Boys/Ooh La La
Warner Bros WB 16281 (Promo only) – Ger 1973
Warner Bros WB 7711 – US 1973
Pool Hall Richard/I Wish It Would Rain (live)
Warner Bros WB/K 16341 – Ger/UK 1973
Cindy Incidentally/Memphis/Stay With Me/Pool Hall Richard
Warner Bros K 16406 – UK 1974
You Can Make Me Dance, Sing Or Anything/As Long As You Tell Him
Warner Bros WB/K 16494 – Ger/UK 1974
Warner Bros WB 8102 (Rod Stewart on logo) – US 1974
Memphis/You Can Make Me Dance, Sing Or Anything/Stay With Me/Cindy Incidentally
Riva 8 – UK 1977

ART WOOD'S QUIET MELON

Diamond Joe/Engine 4444/Instrumental
12" Lost Moment LM 12051 – UK 1995
(Pre-Faces, recorded in 1969 with ex-Bird Kim Gardner, bass, replacing Ronnie Lane)

BOOTLEGS/LIVE LABELS

NET WEIGHT VERY HEAVY
Three Button Hand Me Down/Maybe I'm Amazed/Country Comfort/Love In Vain/Had Me A Real Good Time/Every Picture Tells A Story/Plynth/Did You Ever/Gasoline Alley
LP: K&S 034 – US 1971
(rec in Dayton, Ohio)

PLYNTH
Wicked Messenger/Too Much Woman For A

Henpecket Man/Love In Vain/I Don't Want To Discuss It/Country Comfort/Medley: Plynth-Honky Tonk Woman-Gasoline Alley/It's All Over Now/Flying
LP: TMOQ 71016 – US 1971/72
(rec Santa Monica, 30 October 1970)

PERFORMANCE
She Was A Hand Me Down (= Three Button Hand Me Down)/Maybe I'm Amazed/Country Comfort/It's All Over Now (= Love In Vain)/Had Me A Real Good Time/Every Picture Tells A Story/Did You Ever/Gasoline Alley/Never Knew What It Was (= Plynth)
LP: TMOQ – US 1973
(Recording of a New York Concert, 1971)

HAD ME A REAL GOOD TIME
You're My Girl/Cut Across Shortly/Love In Vain/Bad'N'Ruin/It's All Over Now/Had Me A Real Good Time/Losing You
LP: TMOQ – US 1973
(recording of a BBC programme of 1972)

AFTER HOURS
I Know I'm Losing You/Bring It On Home To Me/Sweet Little Rock'N'Roller/Fly In The Ointment/Every Picture Tells A Story/Stay With Me/Motherless Child/Gasoline Alley/Maggie Mae/Twistin' The Night Away
LP: TKRWM 1811
(live recording from 1974)

DANCING IN THE STREET
(I Know I'm) Losing You/Love In Vain/Dancing In The Street/Maybe I'm Amazed/It's All Over Now/Country Comfort
LP: TMOQ 1817 – US
(recording of a concert in Los Angeles Forum, 3 October 1971; identical to Best Of Rod Stewart & The Small Faces, ICR 11)

REAL GOOD TIME (Detroit, 1974)
(I Know) I'm Losing You/Bring It On Home

To Me/Sweet Little Rock'N'Roller/Fly In The
Ointment/Every Picture Tells A Story/Stay
With Me/Motherless Child/Gasoline
Alley/Maggie May/Twistin' The Night Away
CD: Swingin' Pig TSP-CD-039 – LUX 1989

LIVE & ALIVE
CD: imtrat imt 900.002 – Ger 1990
(live recording; identical to Real Good
Time*)*

THAT'S ALL YOU NEED (Live 1973)
Miss Judy's Farm/Too Bad/That's All You
Need/Stay With Me/Memphis/Time Blue
(=True Blue)/Twistin' The Night Away/I
Don't Wanna Discuss It/Cut Across
Shortly/Bad'N'Ruin/It's All Over Now/Had
Me A Real Good Time (I'm Losing You)
CD: Oh Boy! 1-9035 – LUX 1990

**WE BETTER GET OURSELVES BACK
HOME...**
Silicone Grown/Cindy
Incidentally/Memphis/If I'm On The Late
Side/My Fault/The Stealer/Borstal
Boy/Angel/Stay With Me/Time Blue (= True
Blue)/Twistin' The Night Away/Miss Judy's
Farm/Jealous Guy/Too Bad
CD: Oh Boy! 1-9064 – LUX 1990
*(London, 1973; probably BBC recording
from Paris Theatre)*

RHYTHM & BOOZE
I'm Losing You/Bring It On Home To
Me/Sweet Little Rock'N'Roller/Too
Bad/Every Picture Tells A Story/Stay With
Me/Motherless Children/Gasoline Alley/You
Wear It Well(Maggie May)/Twistin' The
Night Away
CD: Oh Boy! 1-9068 – LUX 1990
*(recording of concert in San Bernadino,
California; dated as 1976; but most
probably rec earlier, 1974/75; not identical
with Rod Stewart bootleg LP of the same
name)*

SUPER GOLDEN RADIO SHOWS No 029
CD: SGRS 029 – US 1991
(identical to We Better Get Ourselves Back
Home...*)*

PLYNTH (Santa Monica, 1970)
Intro/Wicked Messenger/Flying/Too Much
Women/Love In Vain/You're My
Girl/Country Comforts/Around The
Plynth/Honky Tonk Women/Gasoline
Alley/Around The Plynth Reprise/It's All
Over Now
CD: `WPOCM 1090D060-2 – IT 1990

LIVE AT PARIS THEATRE
Miss Judy's Farm/Too Bad/That's All You
Need/Stay With Me/Memphis/True
Blue/Twistin' The Night Away/Discuss It/Cut
Across Shorty/Bad'N'Ruin/It's All Over
Now/Had Me A Real Good Time/I'm Losing
You
*CD: Past (BBC recording from 1973) –
1991*

KILLER HIGHLIGHTS 1972-1973
Had Me A Real Good Time/Maybe I'm
Amazed/Love In Vain/Jealous Guy/Cut
Across Shorty/Bad'N'Ruin/It's All Over
Now/Memphis/If I'm On The Late Side/It's
My Fault/The Stealer/Borstal Boys/Too
Bad/I'm Losing You
CD: Scorpio F 90-8072 – IT? 1991
*(BBC recordings 1972-73; compiled from
material of* Had Me A Real Good Time
bootleg and the CD Live At Paris Theatre*)*

OOH LA LA SESSIONS
Empty Pockets/Fly In The Ointment/If I'm
Late (Take 1)/It's My
Fault/Instrumental/Ooh La La/I'm Just
Thinking/Silicone Grown/Cindy
Incidentally/If I'm Late (Take 2)/Borstal
Boys/Make Sure You Tell
Him/Untitled/Instrumental/You Can Make

Me Dance
CD: SIAE 92-ES-15/015- – IT 1992
(mainly instrumental studio outtakes;
titles incorrect!)

THAT'S EVIL
Wicked Messenger/Shake, Shudder,
Shiver/Devotion/That's Evil/Flying/Nobody
Knows/Pineapple And The Monkey/(Around
The) Plynth/You're My Girl/I Want To Be
Loved/Maybe I'm Amazed/Country
Comforts/Cut Across Shorty/Gasoline Alley
CD: SIAE 93-FA-17191 – IT 1993
(1-8 recorded live 27-3-1970 in Boston, 9-
14 autumn 1970 in Miami)

HUMBLE PIE (PIE Mk I 1969-1975, PIE Mk II 1980-1981)

LPS/CDS

AS SAFE AS YESTERDAY IS
Desperation/Stick Shift/Butter Milk
Boy/Growing Closer*/As Safe As
Yesterday/Bang!/Alabama 69**/I'll Go
Alone/A Nifty Little Number Like You/What
You Will/Natural Born Bugie***/Wrist Job
***
(PIE with Lyn Dobson, *fl (=flute),**fl,
sitar)
LP: Immediate – EMI 1C 062-90 270 – Ger
1969
LP: Immediate – IMOCS 101 – US 1969
LP: Immediate – IMSP 025 – label printed
pink – UK 1969
LP: Charly – K-22 P-385 different cover,
lyrics – JAP 1993
LP: Line – OLLP 5233 AS – Ger 1982
LP: Line – IDLP 4.00296J – white vinyl –
Ger 1983
CD: Line/Mainline IDCD 9.00296 0/ MLCD
9.002960 – Ger 87/89

CD: Immediate/Sony AK 47899 – US 1991
CD: Repertoire – REP 4237-WY+2 bonus
tracks *** – Ger 1992

TOWN AND COUNTRY
Take Me Back/The Sad Bag Of Shaky
Jake/The Light Of Love/Cold Lady/Down
Home Again/Ollie Ollie/Every Mother's
Son/Heartbeat/Only You Can See/Silver
Tongue/Home And Away/Wrist Job*/79th
Street Blues**/Greg's Song**
LP: Immediate/EMI – C 062-90 730 – Ger
1969
LP: Immediate – IMSP 027 – label printed
pink – UK 1969
LP: Charly/Bellaphon BBS 2513 – Ger 1975
LP: Oxford – Ox 3175 – different Cover – I
1975
LP: Line – OLLP 5243 AS – Ger 1982
LP: Line – IDLP 4.00303J white vinyl – Ger
1983
LP: DAFFODIL – SBA 16014 – CAN 1969
LP: Charly – K22P-392 – JAP 1983
CD: Line/Mainline – MLCD – 9.00303L
(*misleading: not on) – Ger 89/90
CD: Repertoire – REP 4231-WY + 2 bonus
tracks** – Ger 1992
CD: Immediate/Sony – AK 47349 – US
1991

HUMBLE PIE
Live With Me/Only A Roach/One-Eyed
Trouser Snake Rumba/Earth And Water
Song/I'm Ready/Theme From Skint/Red
Light Mamma Red Hot/Sucking On The
Sweet Wine
(4 Pie musicians with BJ Cole, pedal steel
guitar)
LP: A&M 80693 IT/AMLS 986 – Ger/UK 1970
LP: A&M ANMP 102 – Nice Price Series – NL
1970
LP: A&M SP-3127/SP-4270 – no gatefold
sleeve – US 1970
LP: A&M/Polygram 393 127-1 – no gatefold
sleeve – Ger 1980

HAPPY BOYS HAPPY!

*CD: A&M Ger 32 Y 3523/PCCY-10225 – JAP
1990*

ROCK ON
Shine On/Sour Grain/79th And
Sunset/Stone Cold Fever/Rolling Stone/A
Song For Jenny/The Light/Big
George/Strange Days/Red Neck Jump
(Pie with PP Arnold, Doris Troy, Claudia
Lennear, Alexis Korner, b-voc, Bobby Keys,
sax, BJ Cole, pedal steel guitar)
*LP: A&M 85199 IT/AMLS 2013 – Ger/UK
1971*
LP: A&M SP 4301 – US 1971
LP: A&M AMLS 2013 – ESP 1977
*CD: A&M/MFCD 847/A&M CD 4301 – US
1987*
*CD: Canyon Ger 32Y-3558/PCCY-10226 –
JAP 1986*

**PERFORMANCE – ROCKIN' THE
FILLMORE**
Four Day Creep/I'm Ready/Stone Cold
Fever/I Walk On Gilded Splinters/Rolling
Stone/Hallelujah (I Love Her So)/I Don't
Need No Doctor
*D-LP: A&M 85726 XT/AMLH 63506 – Ger/UK
1971*
*D-LP: A&M SP 3506 – label: live photo – US
1971*
*D-LP: A&M AMW 29-30 – lyrics included –
JAP 1971*
*D-LP: A&M AMLH 63506 Re-Release: new
A&M-Label – UK*
D-LP: A&M SP 6008 – US
D-LP: A&M 396 008-1 – Re-release – Ger
CD: A&M Ger 32 Y 3577 – JAP 1986
CD: A&M CD 6008 – US 1990

SMOKIN'
Hot'N'Nasty/The Fixer/You're So Good For
Me/C'mon Everybody/Old Time Feelin'/30
Days In The Hole/a.Road Runner b. Road
Runner's 'G'Jam/I Wonder/Sweet Peace And
Time

(Pie, now ft. Dave 'Clem' Clempson, g, +
Alexis Korner, Madeline Bell, Doris Troy,
Steve Stills, Ricky Wills, b-voc)
*LP: A&M/Ariola 86034 IT/A&M AMLS 6434 –
Ger/UK 1972*
LP: A&M SP 4342 – US 1972
LP: A&M SA&M 2089 – BRA 1972
*LP: A&M C19 Y 4002 – Re-release, lyrics
incl JAP 1972*
LP: A&M SP 3132 – Re-release – US 1987
CD: A&M CD 3132 – US 1987
*CD: Canyon-D 32Y-3522/PCCY-10228 – JAP
1986*

EAT IT
Get Down To It/Good Booze And Bad
Women/Is It For Love?/Drugstore
Cowboy/Black Coffee/I Believe To My
Soul/Shut Up And Don't Interrupt
Me/That's How Strong My Love Is/Say No
More/Oh Bella (Oh That's Hers)/Summer
Song/Beckton Dumps/Up Our
Sleeve/Honky Tonk Woman/Road Runner
(with Blackberries Clydie King, Venetta
Fields, Billie Barnum; Sidney George, sax,
BJ Cole, pedal steel guitar)
*D-LP: A&M/Ariola 86669 IT/A&M AMLS 6004
– Ger/UK 1973*
*D-LP: A&M SP 3701/SP 93701 – CAN/US
1973*
*D-LP: A&M AMW 41/42 – lyrics included
JAP 1973*
D-LP: A&M SLAM 268149 – I 1973
CD: A&M/PCCY-10196 91.4.21 – JAP 1990

THUNDERBOX
Thunderbox/Groovin' With Jesus/I Can't
Stand The Rain/Anna (Go To Him)/No
Way/Rally With Ali/Don't Worry, Be
Happy/Ninety-Nine Pounds/Every Single
Day/No Money Down/Drift Away/Oh La-De-
Da
*(with Blackberries Carlena Williams,
Venetta Fields, Billie Barnum; Mel Collins,
sax, horns)*

LP: A&M/Ariola 87660 IT/A&M AMLH 63611
– Ger/UK 1974
LP: A&M SP 3611 – US 1974
MC: A&M/Ariola 54857 DT – Ger 1974
CD: A&M PCCY-D20Y4026 E.3.21
JAP 1989

STREET RATS
Street Rats/Rock'N'Roll Music/We Can Work
It Out/Scored Out/Road Hog/Rain/Funky To
The Bone*/There 'Tis/Let Me Be Your Love
Maker/Countryman Stomp/Drive My
Car/Queens And Nuns
*(*US: There 'Tis replaces Funky To The
Bone, also diff mixes)*
*(with Tim Hinkley, keys; Mel Collins, sax,
horns)*
LP: A&M/Ariola 88767XOT/A&M AMLS
68282 – Ger/UK 1975
MC: A&M/Ariola 55410 GT – Ger 1975
LP: A&M California SP4514 – US 1975
CD: A&M PCCY-10197 (US tracks und
mixes) JAP 1990

ON TO VICTORY
Fool For A Pretty Face/You Soppy
Prat/Infatuation/Take It From Here/Savin'
It/Baby Don't You Do It/Get It In The
End/My Lover's Prayer/Further Down The
Road/Over You
(Marriott, Shirley, Bob Tench, Sooty Jones
with Cheryl Ashley, Lisa Zimmermann,
Marge Raymond, b-voc)
LP: JET 231 – UK 1980
LP: ATCO SD 38-122/XSD 38-122 – US/CAN
1980
CD: ATCO – 38-122-2 – US 1991

GO FOR THE THROAT
All Shook Up/Teenage Anxiety/Tin
Soldier/Keep It On The
Island/Driver/Restless Blood/Go For The
Throat/Lottie And The Charcoal
Queen/Chip Away (The Stone)
(Pie II with Maxine Dickson, Robin 'Coke'

Beck and Dana Kral)
LP: ATCO XSD 38-131 – CAN/US 1981
LP: Polydor 2480636 – N 1981
CD: ATCO – 38-131-2 – US 1991

**HUMBLE PIE & PETER FRAMPTON: LIVE
USA (LIVE & ALIVE)**
I Want You To Love Me (= Four Day
Creep)/Stone Cold Fever/C'mon
Everybody/I Don't Need No
Doctor/Something('s) Happening/It's A
Plain Shame/I'll Give You Money/Do You
Feel Like We Do
*(Live in Philadelphia, labelled as 1973,
according to Marriott's goodbye speech
und Frampton's introduction of Money rec
1975)*
*(Pie with Dave Clempson. Frampton with
Wills, Gallagher, Siomos)*
CD: IMTRAT imt 900.029 – Ger 1989
CD: OH BOY 1.9028 – LUX 1990
CD: KBFH 10.9.1990 DIR Radio Network –
US 1990
*(identical tracks, slightly better quality
commercials)*

**LIVE IN SAN FRANCISCO 1973 (SUPER
GOLDEN RADIO SHOWS No 019)**
Four Day Creep/C'Mon Everybody/Honky
Tonk Women/I Believe To My Soul/30 Days
In A Hole/I Don't Need No Doctor
*(featuring The Blackberries, without
Sidney George)*
CD: SRGS RECORDS SRGS 019 – I 1991

**IN CONCERT (KING BISCUIT FLOWER
HOUR PRESENTS)**
Up Our Sleeve/Four Day Creep/C'Mon
Everybody/Honky Tonk Woman/Stone Cold
Fever*/Blues I Believe To My Soul/30 Days
In The Hole/Road Runner/Hallelujah, I Love
Her So/I Don't Need No
Doctor/Hot'N'Nasty (* not on CD; Track 5
= Blues intro)
CD radio show 6 May 1973 Winterland San

Francisco – Ger/US 1996

**HUMBLE PIE/LITTLE CAESAR: KING
BISCUIT FLOWER HOUR**
*CD: KBFH DIR Radio Network 10.9.-
16.9.1990 – US 1990*

**HUMBLE PIE/FRAMPTON'S CAMEL:
KING BISCUIT FLOWER HOUR**
*CD: Radio Show dated 11 September 1988
– US 1988*

HUMBLE PIE: BBC ROCK HOUR
I Don't Need No Doctor/Infatuation/30
Days In The Hole/Tin Soldier/Fool For A
Pretty Face/Route 66/Tulsa Time (28 June
81)
LP: BBC 226 – UK 1981

**HUMBLE PIE/LOVER BOY (Live in New
York 26 April 1981)**
I Don't Need No Doctor/Infatuation/All
Shook Up/30 Days In The Hole
DLP: KBFH 364 – US 1981

**HUMBLE PIE/GARY US BONDS (Live in
LA)**
I Don't Need No Doctor/Fool For A Pretty
Face/30 Day In The Hole
DLP: Westwood One – US 1981

HUMBLE PIE INTERVIEW
with Steve Marriott and Jerry Shirley
LP: Series 16 Show 13 – US 1981

**IN THE STUDIO: HUMBLE PIE ROCKIN'
THE FILLMORE**
Album memories with Peter Frampton and
Jerry Shirley
*CD: Show Number 174, 21 October, 1991 –
US 1991*

COMPILATIONS (SELECTION)

THE CRUST OF HUMBLE PIE
Natural Born Woman/Wrist Job/+ Material
from *Safe* and *Town*
LP: EMIDISC C048-50 720 – Ger/NL 1975
LP: Line OLLP 5293 AS – Ger 1983

**AS SAFE AS YESTERDAY IS/TOWN AND
COUNTRY**
*D-LP: Immediate 3C 154-52121/22 – I
1974*

**GEMINI (Side 1: Peter Frampton – Side
2: Humble Pie)**
LP: Bootleg TKBWM 1810 – UK 1974

**LOST AND FOUND (SAFE & COUNTRY
as double album)**
LP: A&M SP 3513 – US 1970
LP: A&M SP 6009 – Re-release – US
LP: Charly LPDB CR 3002 – US 1975

**THE COLLECTION/CASTLE MASTERS
COLLECTION**
Bang/Natural Born Bugie/I'll Go
Alone/Buttermilk Boy/Desperation/Nifty
Little Number Like You/Wrist
Job/Stickshift/Growing Closer/As Safe As
Yesterday/Heartbeat/Down Home Again/Take
Me Back/Only You Can See/Silver
Tongue/(Extra LP tracks): Every Mother's
Son/Sad Bag Of Shaky Jake/Cold Lady/Home
And Away/Light Of Love
LP: CASTLE CCSLP 104 – UK 1985
*CD: CASTLE CCSCD 104/CMC 3021 – UK
86/90*

BACK HOME AGAIN
11 titles of LPs As Safe As Yesterday Is &
Town And Country
LP: IMMEDIATE IML 1005 – UK 1974
*LP: PYE Rec/Custom Disc Cutting Service
01-402 8114 – UK 19?*

SHINE ON (Special Club Edition)
Shine On/Big Black Dog/79th And

Sunset/Stone Cold Fever/Rolling Stone/Big
George/A Song For Jenny/The Light/Mister
Ring/Red Neck Jump
LP: A&M 92982 – Ger 1971

POP CHRONIK – HUMBLE PIE
21 Tracks from their A&M period, except
Street Rats
D-LP: A&M 88771 XCT – Ger 1975

**HUMBLE PIE – CLASSICS VOLUME 14
(Time 60:48)**
C'Mon Everybody/Stone Cold Fever/Black
Coffee/Hot'N'Nasty/Shine On/Natural Born
Woman/30 Days In The Hole/Get Down To
It/I Don't Need No Doctor/Honky Tonk
Woman/Take Me Back/I Can't Stand The
Rain/Live With Me + 2 pages of English
liner notes by Sam Graham
*CD: A&M D32Y3513 – VOLUME 13 – JAP
1987*
CD: A&M CD 2512 – VOLUME 14 – US 1987

**A SLICE OF HUMBLE PIE – A Compleat
Collection**
*LP: Compleat Records 672 009-1 – US
1985*

THE BEST OF HUMBLE PIE
I Don't Need No Doctor/Honky Tonk
Woman/30 Days In The Hole/C'Mon
Everybody/Shine On/Black Coffee/I Can't
Stand The Rain/Stone Cold
Fever/Hot'N'Nasty
LP: A&M Sp 9048 – CAN 1980
LP: A&M 393 208-1 – Ger 1987
LP: Bigtime LP 32 150 12 – NL 1987
*CD: A&M CD 393 208-2/CD 3208 – US
1987*
*CD: Bigtime CD 3415012(CD Made in
Korea,Cover Germany) – KOR 1987*

THE IMMEDIATE YEARS
*CD: F-Accord MUSIDISC 139240 – Ger
1987*

THE BEST OF BRITISH ROCK
Material from *Safe* and *Town*. Note:
According to booklet, leased from Castle,
but in fact recorded from rumbling vinyl!
'CD': US Pair SPCD 2-1152 – US 1987

GREATEST HITS
*LP: PYE Records – IML 2006/Durec SRL
410.003 – UK 1977*
LP: NEMS Immediate IML 2006 – IRL 1977
LP: JUGODISK – LPS-1072 – YUG 1984

THE GREATEST HITS
14 Tracks from *Safe* and *Town*.
*CD: WOODFORD MUSIC WMCD 5527 – NL
1990*
CD: SOUNDWINGS 101.1024-2 – AUS 1990

BEST OF HUMBLE PIE
CD: Korea Bigtime CD 3415012 – KOR 1988

RECAPTURED
Compilation from US LPs *On To Victory*
and *Go For The Throat*
CD: ATCD (test pressings) – US 1982

A PIECE OF THE PIE
Hot'N'Nasty/Black Coffee/I Believe To My
Soul/30 Days In The Hole/I Wonder/C'Mon
Everybody/Stone Cold Fever/Shine
On/Rollin' Stone/Drive My Car/I Don't Need
No Doctor/Old Time Feelin'
CD: A&M CD: USD 1994

HOT'N'NASTY: THE ANTHOLOGY
I: Natural Born Woman/Buttermilk Boy/I'll
Go Alone/As Safe As Yesterday/Take Me
Back/The Sad Bag Of Shaky Jake/Big Black
Dog/Live With Me/One-Eyed Trouser Snake
Rumba/Earth And Water Song/Red Light
Mama Red Hot!/Shine On/Stone Cold
Fever/Rollin' Stone/Strange Days
II: Four Day Creep/I'm Ready/I Don't Need
No Doctor/Hot'N'Nasty/C'Mon

Everybody/You're So Good For Me/30 Days
In The Hole/I Wonder/Black Coffee/I
Believe To My Soul/Beckton
Dumps/Thunderbox/Ninety-Nine
Pounds/Street Rat/Road Hog/Rain
2-CD: A&M Chronicles 31454 0164-2CD: –
US 1994

THE IMMEDIATE YEARS
I: LP *As Safe As Yesterday Is* + Natural Born
Bugie/Wrist Job/Greg's Song
II: LP *Town And Country*
*2-CD: IMM Box 3 (36 page booklet + Pete
Frame Tree)* – *Ger 1995*

SINGLES/EPS/MAXIS (12"S) – (SEVERAL ENTRIES: DIFFERENT SLEEVES)

HUMBLE PIE

**Natural Born Bugie (Note intentional
mis-spelling, years before Slade)/Wrist
Job**
Immediate C00690533 – *Ger 1969*
Natural Born Bugie/Wrist Job (sleeve)
Immediate C00690533 – *F 1969*
Natural Born Bugie/Wrist Job
Immediate 5C00690533 – *NL 1969*
Natural Born Bugie/Wrist Job (Clem-sl)
ImmediateIM 082 – *Ger 1982*
Natural Born Boogie/I'll Go Alone
Immediate 001/1969 – *US 1969*
Natural Born Bugie/Wrist Job
Immediate 1J00690533 – *ES 1969*
**Natural Born
Boogie/StickShift/Desperation**
Israel-EP I12006 – *ISR 1970*

**Lost And Found: Bang/Down Home
Again/Growing Closer/Heartbeat**
Israel-EP M. 082 – *ISR19?*
The Sad Bag Of Shaky Jake/Cold Lady
Immediate C00690917 – *Ger 1969*
The Sad Bag Of Shaky Jake/Cold Lady
Immediate 00690917M – *NL1969*

The Sad Bag Of Shaky Jake/Heartbeat
Immediate IMI 518 – *I 1969*
Big Black Dog/Only A Roach
A&M 14711 AT – *Ger 1970*
Big Black Dog/Strange Days (NL cover)
A&M 14711 AT – *NL1970*
Big Black Dog/Strange Days
A&M AMS 807 – *UK1970*
Big Black Dog/Strange Day (text+cover)
A&M 63 – *JAP1970*
Shine On/Mister Ring (NL cover)
A&M 10031 AT – *Ger/NL 1971*
Shine On/Mister Ring (ESP/PORT cover)
A&M N-35-28 – *ESP/PORT 1971*
I Don't Need No Doctor/Song For Jenny
A&M 10431 AT – *Ger/NL 1971*
I Don't Need No Doctor/Song For Jenny
A&M AM 1282 – *US 1971*
I Don't Need No Doctor/Big George
A&M 102 – *JAP 1971*
Hot'N'Nasty/You're So Good For Me
A&M 12183 AT – *Ger   1972*
Hot'N'Nasty/Eres Buena Para Mi (You're)
A&M SP AM HS 849 – *ESP 1972*
**Hot'N'Nasty/30 Days In The Hole/C'Mon
Everybody**
Thailand-EP MC 969 – *THA*

Hot'N'Nasty/+Take It Easy (EAGLES!)/
Thailand-EP M. 025 – *THA*
Powder Blues Mercedes Queen (Raiders)/4-
Track Current Song Hits)
Conquistador (Procol Harum)
(Humble Pie on cover)

**30 Days In The Hole/Sweet Peace &
Time**
A&M 1366 – *US 1972*
30 Days In The Hole/C'mon Everybody
A&M 152 Promo – *JAP 1972*
**30 Days In The Hole/Road
Runner/C'mon**
Thai-EP M.047 – *THA*
Get Down To It/Honky Tonk Woman
A&M 12796 AT – *Ger   1973*

Get Down To It/Honky Tonk Woman
A&M 7070   Promo – UK 1973
Shut Up Don't Interrupt/Black Coffee
A&M 12640 AT – Ger 1973
Black Coffee/Say No More
A&M AMS 7052 – US 1973
Black Coffee/Say No More (cover)
A&M 181   Promo –JAP 1973
Cafe Negro/No Lo Digas Mas (Coff/Say)
A&M SP AM HS 935 – ESP 1973
Oh La De Da/The Outcrowd
A&M 13086 AT – Ger 1973
Oh La De Da/The Outcrowd
(cover+text)
A&M 205 – JAP 1973
Oh La De Da/The Outcrowd
A&M AMS 7090 Promo – UK 1973
Ninety-Nine Pounds/Rally With Ali
A&M 13373 AT – Ger 1974
Ninety-Nine Pounds/Rally With Ali
A&M SP AM 13.373A – ESP 1974
Ninety-Nine Pounds/Rally With Ali
A&M AM-217 – JAP 1974
Ninety-Nine Pounds/Ninety-Nine Pounds
A&M 1530-S Promo – US 1974
Rock'N'Roll Music/Scored Out
A&M 13949 AT – Ger 1975
Rock'N'Roll Music/Scored Out
A&M AMS 7158 Promo – UK 1975
Rock'N'Roll Music/Road Hog
A&M 1711 – US 1975
Rock'N'Roll Music/Rock'N'Roll Music
A&M 1711S   Promo – US 1975
Natural Born Bugie/Sad Bag Of Shaky
Jake
Charly BF18512 – Ger 1975
Natural Born Woman/Heartbeat
ARIOLA 103 459 – Ger 1977
Buttermilk Boy/Only You Can See
Charly 80170 N – Ger 1978
I'll Go Alone/Alabama 69
Charly 80171 N – Ger 1978
Fool For A Pretty Face/You Soppy Prat
JET180 – UK 1980
Fool For A Pretty Face/You Soppy Prat

ATCO 7216 – US 1980
Fool For A Pretty Face/Fool For A Pretty
Face ATCO
7216 Promo – US 1980

STEVE MARRIOTT – Solo LPs, singles & guest spots (1963-92)

LPS/CDS

MARRIOTT
East Side Struttin'/Lookin' For A Love/Help
Me Make It Through The Day/Midnight
Rollin'/Wam Bam Thank You Mam/Star In
My Life/Are You Lonely For Me Baby/You
Don't Know Me/Late Night Lady/Early
Evening Light
(A-side ALL STARS: Marriott,voc, g, Mickey
Finn, g, Ian Wallace, dr, Greg Ridley, b,
Blackberries: V Fields, M Lewis, C Williams,
b-voc.)
(B-side LA Stars: David Foster, keys, Ernie
Watts, sax, see text)
LP: A&M/Ariola 27193 XOT/AMLH 64572 –
Ger/UK 1976
LP: A&M SP 4572 – US 1976
CD: A&M/PCCY-10230 91.8.21 – JAP 1990

PACKET OF THREE
What'cha Gonna Do About It/Bad Moon
Rising/All Shook Up/The Fixer/All Or
Nothing/Five Long Years/I Don't Need No
Doctor/30 Days In The Hole*
(Marriott, voc, g, Jim Leverton, b, voc,
Fallon Williams III, dr)
LP: AURA AUL 792 – UK 1984
LP: Bellaphon 255.07.006 – Ger 1986
CD Bellaphon 288.07.139 – Ger 1990
*CD: Guitar Recordings Classic Cuts ***
(bonus track) – US 1993

30 SECONDS TO MIDNITE (45:16)
Knockin' On Your Door/All Or Nothing/One
More Heartache/The Um Um Um Um Um
Song/Superlungs/Get Up, Stand Up/Rascal
You/Life During Wartime/Phone Call
Away/Clapping Song/Shakin' All Over/Gipsy
Woman
(Steve Marriott, voc, g, with several Official
Receivers, DTs and studio musicians, see
text)
LP: Trax/BMG MODEM 1037 – UK 1989
CD: Trax/BMG MODCD 1037 – UK 1989
*CD: Castle CLACD 386 (Legacy Records
licence) – UK 1993*

DINGWALLS 6.7.84*
What'cha Gonna Do About It/Fool For A
Pretty Face/Shame On You/Bad Moon
Rising/The Cockney Rhyme/All Shook
Up/The Fixer/All Or Nothing/Five Long
Years/Thirty Days In The Hole/Don't Need
No Doctor/Big Train Stop At
Memphis/Walkin' The Dog
(Line-up see Packet Of Three: Marriott,
Leverton & Williams)
(* Complete 78 minute-version of the
Packet Of Three album.)
*CD: Demon/Mau Mau MAU CD609 – UK
1991*

SCRUBBERS
Shake/Mona/Lend Us A Quid/Send Me
Some Lovin'/She Moves Me, Man/Street
Rat/Captain Goatcabin's Balancing
Stallions/High And Happy/Be My Baby/It's
All Over/Bluegrass Interval (Muttering
Interval)/Don't Take But A Few
Minutes/Louisiana Blues/You're A
Heartbreaker/I Need A Star In My
Life/Cocaine (Round My Brain)/I'll Find
You/Lord Help Me Hold
Out/Hambone/Signed Sealed
(Steve Marriott, Greg Ridley, Tim Hinkley
with Boz Burrell b, Mel Collins sax, Venetta
Fields & Clydie King b-voc, Clem Clempson

g, Ian Wallace dr, BJCole pedal steel, Alexis
Korner b-voc)
CD: Elastic Cat CDEC1 – UK 1991
*CD: Barsa Promociones Madrid CD0029 SP
1996*
*CD: Repertoire Records REP 4603-WP Ger
1996*

LIVE AT THE GEORGE ROBEY 23.10.85
Rock'n'Roll You Can Trust/What'cha Gonna
Do About It/A Fool For A Pretty Face/Shame
Shame Shame/All Or Nothing/All Shook
Up/Talkin' About You/Five Long
Years/Afterglow/I Don't Need No Doctor/Big
Train Stop At Memphis/Tin Soldier
(Similar to Dingwalls but Pie's Jerry Shirley
on drums, sound quality not up to
Dingwalls quality, but acceptable. Legal
release)
CD: Zeus/Pinnacle ZEUS CD2

THE OUTLAW RECORDINGS
Warning: These 'products' by companies
like Outlaw claim they own the rights to
recordings but they unashamedly mess
about with stuff. Eg, some Dingwalls takes
have been fitted with new applause to
appear that they have been recorded by
other Steve Marriott bands like All Stars,
Official Receivers and Blind Drunk on an
album called Live Pure Energy. Marriott And
The All Stars mixes a few Midgets Strike
Back songs with Small Faces Immediate
recordings like Red Balloon. Most retailers
and mail order companies we contacted
immediately took the stuff off their shelves.
Until the matter has been cleared legally,
we list one release for the most ardent of
collectors, although we believe the master
has not been used:

TOGETHER AGAIN
The Lost Magic Midgets Recordings
Chicken If The Cap Fits/Lonely No
More/Bombers Moon/Toe Rag/That's The

Way It Goes/All Or Nothing (live)/Last
Tango In Nato/Ruby Jack/Shut Your
Mouth/Please Be The One/Birthday Girl/Son
Of Stan/You Spent It

(recorded in 1982: SM vocals, guitar, piano;
Ronnie Lane vocals, guitar, bass; Jim
Leverton bass v, ocals; Mick Weaver keys;
Mick Green, guitar; Dave Hynes drums; Mel
Collins, sax)
CD: Outlaw Records London OTR 1100013

SINGLES/EPS/MAXIS (12"S) – (SEVERAL ENTRIES: DIFFERENT SLEEVES)

PACKET OF THREE

What'cha Gonna Do About It/All Shook Up
Aura AUS 145 – UK 1985

SPECTRUM

All Or Nothing (Part I)/All Or Nothing (Part II)
Phoenix Modernist Society 7-THE-1/Stiff – UK 1985
Stiff/Teldec 6.14495 AC – Ger 1985
(ft PP Arnold, Chris Farlowe, Eddie Phillips)

All Or Nothing(Traditional)/All Or Nothing(Contemporary)
Stiff/Teldec 6.20515 AE – Ger 1985
(line-up identical with Maxi 12" single)

STEVE MARRIOTT

Star In My Life/East Side Struttin'
A&M 17063 AT – NL 1976
Star In My Life/Star In My Life
A&M Promo 1825-S – US 1976
Star In My Life/Midnight Rollin'
A&M AMS 7230 – UK 1976
The Um Um Um Um Um Song (The Um

Um Song)/I Never Loved A Woman (The Way I Love You)
Filmtrax/BMG7TX8 – UK 1989
I Never Loved A Woman (The Way I Loved You) (different mix)/Oh Well/Stay With Me Baby
Bubblehead UK 1996

THE POLLCATS

Pollcat Blues (ft Steve Marriott, Jim
Leverton & The Georgia Satellites), both
sides identical
UK 1990

GUEST SPOTS BY STEVE MARRIOTT

THE EASYBEATS – The Easybeats Collection
CD: Line-Impact IMCD 9.00823 – Ger 1989
(SM vocals on Good Times, identical to single)

THE EASYBEATS – Gonna Have A Good Time
UA 2109 XW114 – US 1968
Friday On My Mind
Parlophone 8406 – AUS 1968

BILL WYMAN – In Another Land/The Lantern
London 45907 – US 1967
(SM backing vocals, taken from Satanic LP)

THE ROLLING STONES – Their Satanic Majesties' Request
LP: Decca Records TKS 103 – UK 1967
LP: London Records NPS 2/L20P1018J7 – US 1967
CD: London Records 820 129-2 – Ger 1986

BILLY NICHOLS (SM vocals) – Would You Believe/Daytime Girl

Immediate IM063 – UK 1967

**PP ARNOLD (SM vocals on single) –
Groovy/Though It Hurts Me Badly (+LP)**
Immediate 23703 – Ger 1967
PP ARNOLD – The Best Of PP Arnold
Immediate 5C048.90908 – NL 1968
PP ARNOLD – Greatest Hits
Immediate IML2006 – UK 1978

**COCHISE – (SM vocals on single A-side)
Why I Sing The Blues/Jed Collder**
UA/Liberty 15460 – Ger 1971
COCHISE – Swallow Tales LP
UA/Liberty LBG83428 – Ger 1971

**BLACKBERRIES – Twist & Shout/Don't
Change**
On Me A&M 12753 – US 1973
**BLACKBERRIES – Twist & Shout/Don't
Change**
Promo AMS 7067 – UK 1973

**ALEXIS KORNER & PETER THORUP –
Snape – Accidentally Born In New
Orleans**
LP: Transatlantic TRA 269 – UK 1973
*CD: Line/Transatlantic TACD 9.006379 –
UK 1990*
*(SM backing vocals; organ on Country
Shoes)*

ALEXIS KORNER – Get Off Of My Cloud
LP: CBS 69155 – UK 1975
*CD: Castle Communications/Sequel
Records ESSCD 156 – UK 1990*
*(SM vocals, guitar on Tree Top Fever,
Strange'N'Deranged and Get Off Of My
Cloud, Frampton: guitar on The Wasp, You
Are My Sunshine, Slow Down, Ain't That
Peculiar, Cloud)*

JOHNNY THUNDERS – So Alone
LP: Real/WEA RAL1 – UK 1978
CD: Sire 7599-26982 – Ger 1992

*(SM vocals, piano, harmonica on Daddy
Rolling Stone)*

JIM CAPALDI: One Man Mission
LP: WEA 251 350-1 – Ger/UK 1984
*(SM vocals on Young Savages, Leverton
bass on Ancient Highway)*

**HERMANN RAREBELL: Herman Ze
German & Friends**
LP: Capitol 2404881 – Ger 1986
(SM vocals on Having A Good Time)

ILLUSION
Geffen 24.067/CBS-Import – US 1985
(SM vocals on Weighs A Ton)

RONNIE LANE – Solo albums and guest appearances (1970-91)

LPS/CDS

**ANYMORE FOR ANYMORE (Ronnie Lane
And The Band Slim Chance)**
Careless Love/Don't You Cry For Me/Bye
And Bye (Gonna See The King)/Silk
Stockings/The Poacher/Roll On Babe/Tell
Everyone/Amelia Earheart's Last
Flight/Anymore For Anymore/Only A Bird In
A Gilded Cage
LP: GM Records GML 1013 – UK 1974
LP: GM Records GML 1017 – US 1974
LP: Philips 6370 109 – Ger 1974
CD: Wizard/Wave EVA 5006 – JAP 1990
CD: Marquee Records – UK 1990
CD: See For Miles SEECD 338 – UK 1992
*(plus bonus tracks How Come and Done
This One Before)*

RONNIE LANE & SLIM CHANCE
Little Piece Of Nothing/Stone/A Bottle Of
Brandy/Street Gang/Anniversary/I'm Gonna

Sit Right Down And Write Myself A
Letter/I'm Just A Country Boy/Ain't No
Lady/Blue Monday/Give Me A Penny/You
Never Can Tell/Tin And Tambourine/Single
Saddle
LP: Island ILPS 9321 – UK 1975
LP: A&M Records SP-3638 – US 1975
LP: Island/Ariola 88 648 IT – Ger 1975
CD: Polystar HI-1002 – JAP 1990
CD: Edsel EDCD 463 – UK 1995

RONNIE LANE & SLIM CHANCE
The Poacher/Stone/Bottle Of Brandy/Street
Gang/Anniversary/I'm Gonna Sit Right
Down And Write Myself A Letter/Little Piece
Of Nothing/Brother Can You Spare Me A
Dime/* Ain't No Lady/Blue Monday/Give Me
A Penny/You Never Can Tell/Single Saddle
*LP: A&M SP-3638 (different track list * bonus) – US 1975*

ONE FOR THE ROAD (RONNIE LANE'S SLIM CHANCE)
Don't Try'n' Change My Mind/32nd
Street/Snake/Burnin' Summer/One For The
Road/Steppin' An' Reelin' (The
Wedding)/Harvest Home/Nobody's
Listenin'/G' Morning
LP: Island ILPS 9366 – UK 1976
LP: Island/Ariola 89 862 XOT – Ger 1976
CD: Polystar HI-1003 – JAP 1990
CD: Edsel EDCD 464 – UK 1995

MAHONEY'S LAST STAND (Soundtrack; RON WOOD & RONNIE LANE)
Tonight's Number/From The Late To The
Early/Chicken Wire/Chicken
Wired/I'll Fly Away/Title One/Just For A
Moment (inst.)/Mona The Blues/Car
Radio/Hay Tumble/Woody's Thing/Rooster
Funeral/Just For A Moment
LP: Atlantic K 50 308 – UK 1976
LP: Atlantic SD 36-126 – US 1976
LP: Atlantic/WEA 50 308 – Ger 1976
LP: Thunderbolt THBL 067 – UK 1988

LP: Thunderbolt THBL 067P (Picture Disc) – UK 1989
CD: Thunderbolt CDTB 067 – UK 1989

ROUGH MIX (Pete Townshend & Ronnie Lane)
My Baby Gives It Away/Nowhere To
Run/Rough Mix/Annie/Keep Me Turning/Cat
Melody/Misunderstood/April Fool/Street In
The City/Heart To Hang Into/Till The Rivers
All Run Dry
LP: Polydor 2442 147 – UK 1977
LP: MCA Records 2295 – US 1977
LP: Polydor 2460 275 – Ger 1977
LP: Polydor 2482488 (reissue) – UK 1980
CD: ATCO 90097-2 – US 1983

SEE ME
One Step/Good Ol' Boys Boogie/Lad's Got
Money/She's Leaving/Barcelona/Kushty
Rye/Don't Tell Me Now/You're So
Right/Only You/Winning With Women/Way
Up Yonder
LP: GEM Records LP 107 – UK 1980
RCA PL 43285 (release cancelled) – F
CD: Edsel Records EDCD 492 – UK 1996

SINGLES/EPS/MAXIS

How Come/Tell Everyone/Done This One Before
GM Records GMS 011 – UK 1973
How Come/Tell Everyone
Philips 6078 104 – Ger 1973
A&M 1524 – US 1973
The Poacher/Bye And Bye (Gonna See The King)
GM Records GMS 024 – UK 1974
Anymore For Anymore/Roll On Babe
UK 1974
GM Records GMS 033
What Went Down (That Night With You)/Lovely
Island WIP 6212 – UK 1974
Island/Ariola 13778 AT – Ger 1974

Brother Can You Spare A Dime/Ain't No Lady
Island WIP 6229 – UK 1974
I'm Gonna Sit Right Down.../Brother Can You Spare A Dime
Island/Ariola 16214 AT – Ger 1975
Don't Try'n'Change My Mind/Well Well Hello (The Party)
Island WIP 6258 – UK 1976
Kuschty Rye/You're So Right
GEM Records S 12 – UK 1979
RCA Records PB 9437 – F 1980
Kuschty Rye/One Step
RCA Records PB 9530 – Ger 1980
One Step/Lad's Got Money
GEM S 19 – UK 1980

WITH PETE TOWNSHEND

Street In The City/Annie (12 inch)
Polydor 2058 944 – UK 1977
(7" version got pressed, but was never released officially)
My Baby Gives It Away/April Fool
MCA 40818 – US 1977
Keep Me Turning/Nowhere To Run
MCA 40878 – US 1978

BOOTLEGS

Rock Of Ages
(no label info) – US 1985 (ca.)
(ARMS Concert, rec 2 December 1983 in San Francisco, Ronnie sings Goodnight Irene)

Rock Gala
ETS 2542/3/4 – JAP
(filed under Clapton/Beck/Page; first ARMS concert dated 23 (not 21 as quoted) September 1983 in Royal Albert Hall; has more numbers than the official video version; Ronnie sings Goodnight Irene)

Night Of The Kings

(filed under Eric Clapton; second ARMS concert dated 24 September 1983 in Royal Albert Hall; Ronnie sings Bombers Moon)

GUEST APPEARANCES

PETE TOWNSHEND – Happy Birthday
(Universal Spiritual League USL 001; special issue)
RL: guitar, vocals on Evolution (= Stone)

ROLLING STONES – Sticky Fingers
(Rolling Stones Rec, 1971)
RL: background vocals on Wild Horses
(not confirmed; Source: Rolling Stones A – Z)

PETE TOWNSHEND – Who Came First
(Track 2408 201, 1972)
RL: Guitar, voc on Evolution (= Stone); short version of
Happy Birthday recording
(CD: Rykodisc 1992; + 6 bonus tracks by Pete Townshend)

ROY HARPER – Flashes From The Archives Of Oblivion
(Harvest/EMI SHDW 405, 1974)
RL: bass, backing vocals

ROY HARPER – Bullinamingvase
(Harvest/EMI SHSP 4040, 1977)
RL: guitar, backing vocals

WINGS – Back To The Egg
(Parlophone/EMI 257, 1979)
RL: bass

ROCKESTRA/VA – Concerts For The People Of Kampuchea
(Atlantic ATL 60 153, 1981)
RL: bass

JOHN & MARY – Victory Gardens
(Rykodisc RCD 10203, 1991)

RL: vocals on We Have Nothing

THE KEEPERS – Looking For A Sign
(CD 1994 Lizard Discs 80003)
RL: backing vocals on King Of The Lazy
World, The Boulevardier

PETER FRAMPTON

WITH THE HERD (1967-1969)

PARADISE LOST
(released in Germany as Paradise &
Underworld)
From The Underworld/On My Way Home/I
Can Fly/Goodbye Groovy/Mixed Up
Minds/Impressions Of
Oliver/ParadiseLost/Sad/SomethingStrange/
On Your Own/She Loves Me, She Loves Me
Not/Fare Thee Well +
(CD bonus tracks): Sweet William/Come
On, Believe Me/I Don't Want Our Lovin' To
Die/Our Fairy Tale
(Line-Up: Peter Frampton vocals guitar,
Andy Bown keyboards, vocals, Gary Taylor
bass, vocals, Andrew Steele drums)
*LP: Fontana/Phonogram 842 760-4 – UK
1968/1990*
*LP: Hansa/Ariola 77490 (Paradise &
Underworld) – Ger 1968*
*CD: Fontana/Phonogram 842 760-2 – UK
1990*

PARADISE AND UNDERWORLD
From The Underworld/Paradise Lost/I Can
Fly/I Don't Want Our Loving To
Die/Sunshine Cottage/The Game/Sweet
William/Come On, Believe Me/Diary Of A
Narcissist (I'm So Pretty)/Understand
Me/Our Fairy Tale/Miss Jones/Beauty
Queen/Follow The Leader/Charlie
Anderson/Bang!/Mother's Blue-Eyed
Angel/On My Way Home/Goodbye

Groovy/Mixed Up Minds/Impressions Of
Oliver/Sad/Something Strange/On Your
Own/She Loves Me, She Loves Me Not/Fare
Thee Well
CD: Repertoire Records REP 4257 WG –
Ger 1992
*(Contains all the tracks from Paradise Lost
CD plus bonus tracks made up of singles)*

PETER FRAMPTON SOLO

WIND OF CHANGE
Fig Tree Bay/Wind Of Change/Lady
Lieright/Jumpin' Jack Flash/It's A Plain
Shame/Oh For Another Day/All I Want To
Be/The Lodger/Hard/Alright
(Line-up: Peter Frampton vocals guitars
keyboards drums, Andy Bown (ex-The
Herd) keyboards, Mike Kellie (ex-Spooky
Tooth) drums, Rick Wills bass, Ringo Starr
drums, Klaus Voorman bass)
LP: A&M AMLH 68099 – GB/D 1972
*LP: A&M SP-4348/Stereo (SP 4595) 0598 –
US 1972*
CD: Pony Canyon PCCY-10231 – JAP 1989

FRAMPTON`S CAMEL
I Got My Eyes On You/All Night Long/Lines
On My Face/Which Way The Wind Blows/I
Believe (When I Fall In Love With You It
Will Be Forever)/White Sugar/Don't Fade
Away/Just The Time Of Year/Do You Feel
Like We Do
(Line-up: Pete Frampton vocals guitars bass
keyboards drums perc Rick Wills bass, John
Siomos drums, Mick Gallagher keyboards,
Frank Carillo guitar backing vocals)
LP: A&M 86766 IT – Ger 1973
CD: Pony Canyon PCCY 10232 – JAP 1989

SOMETHING'S HAPPENING
Doobie Wah/Golden Goose/Underhand/I
Wanna Go To The Sun/Baby (Something's
Happening)/Waterfall/Magic Moon(Da Da

Da Da Da)/Sail Away
(Peter Frampton vocals guitar g-synthesiser
keyboards drums perc Rick Wills bass
vocals, John Headley-Down drums
percussion, Nicky Hopkins piano on
Waterfall, Sail Away)
LP: A&M AMLH 63619 – UK 1974
CD: A&M PCCY 10233– JAP 1989

FRAMPTON
Day's Dawning/Show Me The Way/One
More Time/The Crying
Clown/Fanfare/Nowhere's Too Far (For My
Baby)/Nassau/Baby I Love Your Way/Apple
Of Your Eye/Penny For Your Thoughts/(I'll
Give You) Money
(Peter Frampton vocals guitar keyboards
bass talking box, John Siomos drums, Andy
Bown bass, Poli Palmer vibes on 'Clown')
LP: A&M AMLH 64512 – Ger/UK 1975
CD: D 32 Y 3557 – JAP 1991
CD: A&M Rebound 314 520289-2 – US 1994
*CD: A&M Rebound 314 520289-2 – US
1995**
(same number, but with included lyrics
and cover caption "features the hits Show
Me The Way and Baby I Love Your Way")*

FRAMPTON COMES ALIVE
Introduction/Something's
Happening/Doobie Wah*/Show Me The
Way/It's A Plain Shame*/All I Want To Be (Is
By Your Side)*/Wind Of Change*/Baby I
Love Your Way/I Wanna Go To The
Sun/Penny For Your Thoughts*/(I'll Give
You)Money/Shine On/Jumpin' Jack
Flash/Lines On My Face/Do You Feel Like
We Do (* not on single CD)
(Peter Frampton vocals guitars talking box,
John Siomos drums,
Bob Mayo keyboards, Stanley Sheldon bass)
2-LP: A&M AMLH 63703 – UK 1976
2-CD: A&M – US 1988
CD: A&M 396 505 2 – US/D 1989

I'M IN YOU
I'm In You/(Putting My) Heart On The
Line/St.Thomas (Don't You Know How I
Feel/Won't You Be My Friend/You Don't
Have To Worry/Tried To Love/Rocky's Hot
Club/(I'm A) Road Runner/Signed Sealed
Delivered (I'm Yours)
(Peter Frampton vocals guitar piano
synthesiser bass drums, John Siomos
drums, Bob Mayo guitar keyboards, Stanley
Sheldon bass, Ritchie Hayward drums
percussion, Stevie Wonder harmonica, Mike
Finnegan vocals)
LP: A&M AMLK 64704 – UK 1977
CD: D 32 Y 3579 – JAP 1991

WHERE I SHOULD BE
I Can't Stand It No More/Got My Feet Back
On The Ground/Where I Should Be
(Monkey's Song)/Everything I Need/May I
Baby/You Don't Know Like I Know/She
Don't Reply/We've Just Begun//Take Me By
The Hand/It's A Sad Affair
(Frampton vocals, guitar, Bob Mayo,
keyboards, Stanley Sheldon, bass, Donald
'Duck' Dunn, bass, Steve Cropper, guitar,
Gary Mallaber, drums, Jamie Oldaker,
drums, Tower Of Power Horns...)
LP: A&M AMLK 63710 – UK/Ger/NL 1979

RISE UP
(Lancamento Especial Para A Tournée No
Brasil Outobro 1980)
You Kill Me/I Don't Wanna Let You Go/Rise
Up+/Breaking All The Rules++/Wasting
The Night Away/Midland Maniac/I Can't
Stand It*/I'm In You**
(Peter Frampton vocals guitars keyboards,
John Regan bass, Jamie Oldaker + Anton
Fig drums, Billy Alessi keyboards, Elliott
Randall guitar, *live: Peter Frampton vocals
guitar, Gary Mallaber drums, Stanley
Sheldon bass, Bob Mayo keyboards, ** live
Frampton + Mayo)
LP: A&M/CBS 170006 – BRA 1980

BREAKING ALL THE RULES

Dig What I Say/I Don't Wanna Let You Go/Rise Up/Wasting The Night Away/Going To LA/You Kill Me/Friday On My Mind/Lost A Part Of You/Breaking All The Rules (Rise Up tracks newly recorded)
(Peter Frampton vocals guitar guitar-synthesiser keyboards, John Regan bass, Arthur Stead keyboards backing vocals, Jeff Porcaro drums, Steve Lukather guitar backing vocals)
LP: A&M AMLK 63722 – UK/NL1981

THE ART OF CONTROL

I Read The News/Sleepwalk/Save Me/Back To Eden/An Eye For An Eye/Don't Think About Me/Heart In The Fire/Here Comes Caroline/Barbara's Vacation
(Peter Frampton vocals guitar guitar synthesiser, Mark Goldenberg backing vocals guitar keyboards, John Regan bass, Harry Stinson drums, Ian Lloyd (ex-Stories) backing vocals)
LP: A&M AMLH 64905 – UK 1982

PREMONITION

Hiding From A Heartache/You Know So Well/Premonition/Lying/Moving A Mountain/All Eyes On You/Into View/Call Of The Wild
(Peter Frampton vocals guitar bass, keyboards drum-programming Steve Ferrone drums, Omar Hakim drums, Tony Levin bass, Richard Cottle keyboards Pete Solley keyboards, Richie Puente percussion, Johnny Sambataro + Chuck Kirkpatrick backing vocals)
LP: Virgin 207 376-630 – Ger 1985
CD: Virgin 257 376-217/CDV 2365 – UK 1986

WHEN ALL THE PIECES FIT

More Ways Than One/Holding On To You/My Heart Goes Out To You/Hold Tight/People All Over The World/Back To The Start/Mind Over Matter/Now And Again/Hard Earned Love/This Time Around
(Peter Frampton vocals guitar synthesiser bass-synth seqencer drum programming, John Robinson drums, Danny Wilde backing vocals, Rick Wills backing vocals, Nathan East bass, Chris Lord-Alge keyboards, Mark Williamson + Jean McLain, backing vocals, Lenny Castro percussion, Steve Ferrone drums, BA Robertson synth backing vocals, Alfie Silas backing vocals, Sam Riney sax)
CD: Atlantic 7 82030-2 – US 1989

SHINE ON – A COLLECTION

Wind Of Change/It's A Plain Shame/Jumpin' Jack Flash/All I Want To Be (Is By Your Side)/The Lodger/I Got My Eyes On You/All Night Long/Lines On My Face/Don't Fade Away/I Wanna Go To The Sun/Baby (Something's Happening)/Nowhere's Too Far (For My Baby)/Nassau/Baby I Love Your Way/The Crying Clown/Penny For Your Thoughts/(I'll Give You) Money/Show Me The Way/Shine On/Do You Feel Like We Do/I'm In You/(Putting My) Heart On The Line/Signed Sealed Delivered (I'm Yours)/I Can't Stand It No More/Breaking All The Rules/Theme From Nivram/Lying/More Ways Than One/Holding On To You/The Bigger They Come+/I Won't Let You Down+ (+ Steve Marriott)
CD: A&M CD MID 174 – UK 1992
CD: A&M International 540 015-2 – Ger/US 1992

IN CONCERT (Radio Show with adverts)

More Ways Than One/It's A Plain Shame/Lines On My Face/Show Me The Way/All I Want To Do/Penny For Your Thoughts/I'm In You/Nassau/Baby I Love Your Way/I Wanna Go To The Sun/Do You Feel Like I Do/Jumpin' Jack Flash/I Don't Need No Doctor

291

2-CD: Westwood One 92-44 – US 1992

PETER FRAMPTON
Day In The Sun/You Can Be Sure/It All
Comes Down To You/Can't Take That
Away/Young Island/Off The Hook/Waiting
For Your Love/Out Of The Blue/Shelter
Through The Night/Changing All The Time
(Peter Frampton vocals guitar, John Regan
+ Leland Sklar bass, Kevin Savigar +
Jonathan Cain keyboards, John Robinson +
Denny Fongheiser drums)
*CD: Relativity/Sony 475876 2 – Ger/GB/US
1994*

**FRAMPTON COMES ALIVE II (+ Limited
Edition Bonus CD)**
Introduction by Jerry Pompili/Day In The
Sun/Lying For Now/Most Of All/You/Waiting
For Your Love/I'm In You/Talk To Me/Hang
On To A Dream/Can't Take That Away/More
Ways Than One*/Almost Said Goodbye/Off
The Hook
Show Me The Way/Baby I Love Your
Way/Lines On My Face/Do You Feel Like We
Do
(Peter Frampton vocals, guitar; John Regan
bass; John Robinson and Jamie Oldaker*
drums; Bob Mayo keys; recorded at
Fillmore West, San Francisco 15/16 June
1995, except * August 1992 at the Ventura
Theatre, California)
*2-CD: Eldorado/IRS/EMI 7243 8 3598625 –
Ger/UK/US 1995*

**PACIFIC FREIGHT (Peter Frampton &
Friends)**
There's A Man/Going Home/Loving
Cup/Grits & Cornbread/Love Taker/All I
Wanna Be Is By Your Side/Madame
(in effect a Nanette Workman solo album,
rec 1973 in Canada and re-released under
the Frampton flag; Nanette Workman lead
vocals; Peter Frampton guitar; Mike Kellie
drums; Andy Bown piano; Jim Price

trumpet percussion; Lee Strike, Madeline
Bell backing vocals; Ken Kimsey drums)
*CD: Prestige CDSGP 0243 – UK 1995
CD: Javelin HADCD 199 as Love Taker – Ca
1995*

PETER FRAMPTON'S GREATEST HITS
(usual mix, digitally remastered)
CD: A&M Back Off Series 314540557-2

GUEST APPEARANCES

JOHNNY HALLYDAY – Johnny Hallyday
Philips 844 971 BY – F 1969
DORIS TROY – Ain't That Cute
Single Apple 24 – UK 1970
DORIS TROY – Doris Troy
24/EMI-CD 7987012 – UK 1970
GARY WRIGHT – Foot Print
A&M AML 64296 – UK 1971
BEN SIDRAN – Feel Your Groove
Capitol ST825 – US 1971
HARRY NILSSON – Son Of Schmilsson
RCA SF 8297 – UK 1972
TIM HARDIN – Painted Head
CBS 65209 – UK 1973
JOHNNY HALLYDAY – Insolitudes
Philips 6 325 025 – F 1973
GEORGE HARRISON – Material World
EMI-Apple 10006PAS – UK 1973
TIM HARDIN – Nine
Philips 6 370 105 – UK 1974
TERESA BREWER – In London
UK 1974
DUSTER BENNETT – Fingertips
Toadstool L 35436 – UK 1974
RINGO STARR – Rotogravure
Polydor 2302040 – UK 1976
ALEXIS KORNER – Get Off Of My Cloud
Castle SEQ ESSCD156 – UK (1975) 1990
**JOHNNY HALLYDAY – Rock'N'Roll
Attitude**
Philips 824824-1 – F 1985
STEVE MORSE – Stand Up
Elektra 960448-1 – 1985

DAVID BOWIE – Never Let Me Down
EMI CDP 7466772 – Ger/UK 1987
KARLA BONOFF – New World
Virgin CDVGC 6 – Ger/US 1988
JULIAN LENNON – Mr Jordan
Atl 756781928-2 Ger/US 1989
BURNS SISTERS – Endangered Species
CBS FC 45100 – US 1989
STEVE MORSE – High Tension Wires
MCA 6275 – US 1989
CROSBY STILLS & NASH – Live It Up
Atl 756782107-2YS – Ger/US 1990
VARIOUS ARTISTS – Tribute To Hank
Marvin
EMI ARK 21 – Ger/UK/US 1996

SINGLES (THE HERD 1965-69): (7" OR INDICATED)

Goodbye Baby/Here Comes The Fool
Parlophone R 5284 – UK 1965
She Was Really Saying Something/
It's Been A Long Time Baby
Parlophone R 5353 – UK 1965
Too Much In Love/This Boy's Always
Been True
Parlophone R 5413 – UK 1966
I Can Fly/Diary Of A Narcissist
Fontana TF 819 – UK 1967
I Can Fly/Diary Of A Narcissist
Hansa 19486 AT – Ger 1967
I Can Fly/Understand Me
Fontana 1588 – US 1967
From The Underworld/Sweet William
Fontana TF 856 – UK 1967
From The Underworld/Sweet William
Hansa 19746 AT – Ger 1967
Paradise Lost/Come On Believe Me
Fontana TF 887 – UK 1967
Paradise Lost/Come On Believe Me
Hansa 19894 AT – Ger 1967
I Don't Want Our Lovin' To Die/Our
Fairy Tale
Fontana TF 925 – UK 1968
I Don't Want Out Lovin'To Die/Our Fairy
Tale
Hansa 14017 AT – Ger 1968
Sunshine Cottage/Miss Jones
Fontana TF 975 – UK 1968
Sunshine Cottage/Miss Jones
Hansa 14153 AT – Ger 1968
The Game/Beauty Queen
Fontana 267932 TF – UK 1969
(without Peter Frampton!)

SOLO SINGLES (1972)

It's A Plain Shame/Oh For Another Day
A&M AMS 7025 – UK 1972
Jumpin' Jack Flash/Oh For Another Day
A&M AMS 12446 AT D – 1972

FRAMPTON'S CAMEL SINGLE (1973)

All Night Long/Don't Fade Away (Promo)
A&M AMS7069 – UK 1973

SOLO SINGLES (1974-1989)

Show Me The Way/The Crying Clown
A&M 16269 AT – Ger 1975
Show Me The Way (Live)/Shine On (Live)
A&M AMS 7218 – UK 1976
Show Me The Way/Baby I Love Your Way
(Live)
A&M 85955 – US 1976
Baby I Love Your Way/It's A Plain Shame
A&M AMS 7246 – UK 1976
Baby I Love Your Way/It's A Plain Shame
A&M 17097 AT – Ger 1976
Do You Feel Like We Do/Penny For Your
Thoughts
A&M AMS 7260 – UK 1976
Do You Feel Like We Do/Penny For Your
Thoughts
A&M AM 18675 – US 1976
Do You Feel Like We Do/Penny For Your
Thoughts
A&M AM 17390AT – Ger 1976
I'm In You/Do You Feel Like We Do

(Live)
A&M AMS 7298 – UK 1977
I'm In You/St Thomas
A&M AMS 5463 – Ger 1977
**Signed Sealed Delivered I'm
Yours/Rocky's Hot Club (Muster)**
A&M AMS 5607 – Ger 1977
**I'm In You/Signed Sealed Delivered
I'm Yours/Tried To Love/Putting My
Heart On The Line (EP)**
A&M AM01660940 – BRA 1977
Tried To Love/You Don't Have To Worry
A&M AMS5622Must – Ger 1977
Intente Amor/No Tienes Que Preocupato
A&M AMS 5622 – ESP 1978
=Tried To Love/You Don't Have To Worry
**The Long And Winding Road/Tried To
Love**
A&M AMS 6621 – Ger 1978
I Can't Stand It No More/May I Baby
A&M AMS – UK 1979
I Can't Stand It No More/May I Baby
A&M AMS7604Must – Ger 1979
She Don't Reply/St Thomas (D Muster)
A&M AMS 7640 – Ger/NL 1979
No La Sopor To Mas/I Puedo Nena)
A&M AMS 7604 – ESP 1979
=I Can't Stand It No More/May I Baby
Rise Up/Wasting The Night Away
A&M 47001 – BRA 1980
Dig What I Say/Lost Part Of You (Text)
A&M AMP 724 –JAP 1981
**Friday On MyMind/Wasting The Night
Away**
A&M AMS 9151 – NL 1981
**Show Me The Way/I'm In You/Baby I
Love Your Way/Wind Of Change/Penny
For Your Thoughts/Signed Sealed
Delivered (EP)**
Pickwick 7SR5039 – UK 1984
Lying/You Know So Well
Virgin 107849100 – Ger 1985
Lying/Into View
Promo Atlantic 7-89463 – US 1985
Lying (Remix)/Lying (Single Mix)/You

Know So Well
12" Virgin 602069213 – Ger 1985
Holding On To You
Virgin/Atlantic – US 1989
Hiding From A Heartache
Virgin/Atlantic – US 1990
**Days In The Sun/Diamond
Eyes/Changing All The Time (CD)**
Sony REL 6602082 – Ger/US 1994
**You Can Be Sure/Baby I Love Your
Way/Shelter Through The Night (CD)**
Sony REL 6603412 – Ger/US 1994

Kenney Jones – Ian McLagan – Jimmy Winston

KENNEY JONES: SINGLES

Ready Or Not/Woman Trouble
GMS 027 – UK 1974

THE WHO II

FACE DANCES
You Better You Bet/Don't Let Go The
Coat/Cache Cache/The Quiet One/Did You
Steal My Money/How Can You Do It
Alone/Daily Records/You/Another Tricky
Day
Polydor 2311 065 – Ger 1981
CD: MCA – US

IT'S HARD
Athena/It's Your Turn/Cooks County/It's
Hard/Dangerous/Eminence Front/I've
Known No War/One Life's Enough/One At A
Time/Why Did I Fall For That/A Man Is A
Man/Cry If You Want
Polydor 2311 180 – Ger 1982
CD: MCA – US 1982

WHO'S LAST
My Generation/I Can't

Explain/Substitute/Behind Blue Eyes/Barbra
O'Riley/Boris The Spider/Who Are
You/Pinball Wizard/See Me Feel Me/Love
Reign O'er Me/Long Live
Rock/Reprise/Won't Get Fooled Again/Dr
Jimmy/Magic Bus/Summertime Blues/Twist
And Shout
LP: MCA – Ger 1984
CD: MCA MCLD 19005 – UK 1984

THE LAW

THE LAW
A Little Ride/Miss You In A Heartbeat/Stone
Gold/Come Save Me/Laying Down The
Law/Nature Of The Beast/Stone/Anything
For You/Best Of My Love/Tough
Love/Missing You Bad Girl
LP: Atlantic – Ger 1991
CD: Atlantic 7567-82195-2 – Ger 1991
(band project with Paul Rodgers)

THE LAW PROFILED
CD: Atlantic PRCD 3880-2 – UK 1991
*(Promo interview record with Kenney
Jones and Paul Rodgers)*

TRIBUTE PROJECT

**LONG AGOS AND WORLDS APART
(A TRIBUTE TO THE SMALL FACES)**
Primal Scream ft PP Arnold:
Understanding/Dodgy: I Can't Make
It/BLOW: It's Too Late/Northern Uproar: My
Mind's Eye/Mantaray:I've Got
Mine/Changing Man ft Kenney Jones and
Mick Talbot: Afterglow/60ft Dolls: The
Universal/Granny Takes A Trip: Become
Like You/Ocean Colour Scene: Song Of A
Baker/Whiteout: Rollin' Over/Kenney Jones
All Stars: Almost Grown/Hyperglo': Talk To
You/Buzzcocks: Here Come The Nice/Ride:
That Man/Gene: Autumn Stone
LP: Nice London nyce 1/LP – UK 1996
CD: Nice London nyce 1/CD – UK 1996

KENNEY JONES GUEST APPEARANCES (SELECTION)

MARSHA HUNT – Woman Child
Polydor – 1971
JERRY LEE LEWIS – The London
Sessions
Mercury – 1972
ANDY FAIRWEATHER-LOW – La Booga
Rooga
A&M – 1975
FLASH FEARLESS – The Zorg Women
Chrysalis – 1975
JOAN ARMATRADING – Joan
Armatrading
A&M 1976
MIKE BATT – Schizophonia
Epic – 1977
JOHN LODGE – Natural Avenue
Nova – 1977
JOAN ARMATRADING – Show Some
Emotion
A&M – 1977
PETER FRENCH – Ducks In Flight
Polydor – 1978
DAVID ESSEX – Imperial Wizard
Mercury – 1979
WINGS – Back To The Egg
Parlophone – 1979
PETE TOWNSHEND – Empty Glass
Atco – 1980
ROGER DALTREY – McVicar
Polydor – 1980
KEN HENSLEY – Free Spirit
Bronze – 1981
WILLIE AND THE POOR BOYS – Willie...
Ripple – 1985

IAN MCLAGAN GUEST APPEARANCES (SELECTION)

THE MULESKINNERS

Single: Back Door Man/Need Your Lovin'
Fontana TF 527 – UK 1965

SOLO LPS

TROUBLEMAKER
La De La/Headlines/Truly/Somebody/Movin'
Out/Little Troublemaker/If It's
Alright/Sign/Hold On/Mystifies Me
LP: Mercury 9111 063 – NL 1979
CD: Mercury PHCR-4152 – US 1993

BUMP IN THE NIGHT
Little Girl/Alligator/If It's Lovin' You
Want/Casualty/Told A Tale On You/Judy Judy
Judy/So Lucky/Rebel Walk/Not Runnin'
Away/Boy's Gonna Get It
Mercury SRM-1-4007 – US 1981

LAST CHANCE TO DANCE
12" EP: All I Want Is You/Last Chance To
Dance/Big Love/You're My Girl
*Barking Dog Records GWD 90505 – US
1985*

with THE BUMP BAND
Pictures Of Lily; track on Who tribute
album Who Covers Who
CD: Humbug – UK 1993

IAN MCLAGAN GUEST APPEARANCES (SELECTION)

MARSHA HUNT – Woman Child
Polydor – 1971
JUICY LUCY – Pieces
Polydor – 1972
THIN LIZZY – Fighting
Vertigo – 1975
ROLLING STONES – Some Girls
Rolling Stones – 1978
BONNIE RAITT – Green Light
Warner Bros – 1981
RENEE GEYER – Renee Geyer
Portrait – 1982

BOB DYLAN – Real Life
CBS – 1984
**JACKSON BROWNE – Lives In The
Balance**
Elektra – 1986
FLIES ON FIRE – Outside Looking Inside
Atco – 1991
BONNIE RAITT – Luck Of The Draw
Capitol – 1991
JOE COCKER – Night Calls
Capitol – 1991
ARC ANGELS – Arc Angels
Geffen – 1992
**IZZY STRADLIN & THE JUJU HOUNDS –
Izzy Stradlin & The Juju Hounds**
Geffen – 1992
THE SEXTANTS – Lucky You
Imago – 1992
MELISSA ETHERIDGE – Never Enough
Island – 1992
BUDDY GUY – Feels Like Rain
Silvertone – 1993
IDHA – Melody Inn
Creation/Sony – 1993
RONNIE WOOD – Slide On Live
Continuum – 1993
CARLA OLSON – Reap The Whirlwind
Watermelon – 1994
BIG BLUE LEE ROCKER'S – Big Blue
Black Top – 1994
**PAT MCLAUGHLIN – Get Out And Stay
Out**
Dos (rec 1989) – 1995
CALVIN RUSSELL – Dream Of The Dog
Last Call/SPV – 1995
CHRIS GAFFNEY – Loser's Paradise
Hightone – 1995
**MICHAEL FRACASSO – When I Love In
The Wild**
Bohemia Beat – 1995
**WYCKHAM PORTEOUS – Looking For
Grand**
Bohemia Beat – 1995

JIMMY WINSTON GUEST APPEARANCES

Single: Sorry She's Mine/It's Not What You Do
Decca F 12410 – UK 1966

Winston's Fumbs
Real Crazy Apartment/Snow White
RCA 1612 – UK 1967
Sun In The Morning/Just Wanna Smile
NEMS NES 012 – UK 1976

Rod Stewart – Ron Wood (solo records)

ROD STEWART (1968-1974)

AN OLD RAINCOAT WON'T EVER LET YOU DOWN
Street Fighting Man/Man Of Constant Sorrow/Blind Prayer/Handbags And Gladrags/An Old Raincoat Won't Ever Let You Down/I Wouldn't Change A Thing/Cindy's Lament/Dirty Old Town
(ft Ian McLagan, Ron Wood, Mick Waller amongst others)
LP: Vertigo VO 4 – UK 1969
LP: Mercury SR-61237 (as The Rod Stewart Album) – US 1969

GASOLINE ALLEY
Gasoline Alley/It's All Over Now/Only A Hobo/My Way Of Giving/Country Comfort/Cut Across Shorty/Lady Day/Jo's Lament/I Don't Want To Discuss It
(ft Ronnie Lane, Ron Wood, Ian McLagan, Kenney Jones, Mick Waller amongst others)
LP: Vertigo 6333360 500 – UK 1970

EVERY PICTURE TELLS A STORY
Every Picture Tells A Story/Seems Like A Long Time/That's All Right/Amazing Grace/Tomorrow Is Such A Long Time/Maggie May/Mandolin Wind/(I Know)

I'm Losing You/Reason To Believe
(ft Ian McLagan, Ron Wood, Mick Waller; I'm Losing You is a Faces recording, not specifically credited on the cover)
LP: Mercury 6338 063 – UK 1971

NEVER A DULL MOMENT
True Blue/Lost Paraguayos/Mama You Been On My Mind/Italian Girls/Angel/Interludings/You Wear It Well/I'd Rather Go Blind/Twistin' The Night Away
(ft Ronnie Lane, Ron Wood, Ian McLagan, Kenney Jones, Mick Waller amongst others)
LP: Mercury 6499 153 – UK 1972

SING IT AGAIN ROD (Compilation))
Reason To Believe/You Wear It Well/Mandolin Wind/Pinball Wizard/Maggie May/Handbags And Gladrags/Street Fighting Man/Twistin' The Night Away/Lost Paraguayos/(I Know) I'm Losing You/Country Comfort/Gasoline Alley
LP: Mercury 6338 248 – Ger 1973

SMILER
Sweet Little Rock'N'Roller/Lochinvar/Farewell/Sailor/Bring It On Home To Me/You Send Me/Let Me Be Your Car/(You Make Me Feel Like) A Natural Man/Dixie Toot/Hard Road/I've Grown Accustomed To Her Face/Girl From The North Country/Mine For Me
LP: Mercury 6338 528 – Ger 1974

SINGLES: (1966-1975; SELECTION)

Shake/I Got Some
Columbia DB-7892 – UK 1966

Little Miss Understood/So Much To Say
Immediate IM 070 – UK 1967

It's All Over Now/Jo's Lament
Vertigo 60599 002 – UK 1970

Country Comfort/Gasoline Alley

**My Way Of Giving/My Way Of Giving
(Mono)**
Mercury 73175 (Promo) – US 1971

(I Know) I'm Losing You/Mandolin Wind
Mercury 6052 116 – UK/D 1971

You Wear It Well/True Blue
Mercury 73330 – US 1972

Angel/What Made Milwaukee Famous
Mercury 6052 198 – UK/D 1972

Oh! No Not My Baby/Jodie
Mercury 6052 371 – UK/D 1973
*(the "Jodie" label logo insists on: "Rod &
Faces and a bottle of Campari"!)*

RON WOOD: THE BIRDS

THESE BIRDS ARE DANGEROUS
You're On My Mind/You Don't Love Me
(You Don't Care)/Leaving Here/Next In
Line/No Good Without You Baby/How Can
It Be
Edsel NEST 901 – UK 1986?
*(compilation; contains tracks of the three
Birds singles)*

THE CREATION

RE-CREATION – THE BEST OF THE REST
Life Is Just Beginning/Midway Down*/The
Girls Are Naked*/Sylvette/Ostrich Man/How
Does It Feel To Feel/Bonney
Moroney*/Mercy, Mercy, Mercy*/For All
That I Am*/Uncle Bert*/I Am The Walker
Line OLLP 5242 AS – Ger 1982
*(Wood only played on * tracks)*

THE JEFF BECK GROUP (+ ROD STEWART)

TRUTH
Rock My Plimsoul/Beck's Bolero/Shapes Of
Things/Let Me Love You/Morning After/You
Shook Me/Old Man
River/Greensleeves/Blues De Luxe/I Ain't
Superstitious
Columbia SCX 6293 – UK 1968

COSA NOSTRA – BECKOLA
All Shook Up/Spanish Boots/Girl From Mill
Valley/Jailhouse Rock/Plynth (Water Down
The Drain)/Hangman's Knee/Rice Pudding
Columbia SCSX 6351 – UK 1969

WITH ROD STEWART

UNPLUGGED AND SEATED
Hot Legs/Tonight's The Night/Handbags
And Gladrags/Cut Across Shorty/Every
Picture Tells A Story/Maggie May/Reason To
Believe/People Get Ready/Have I Told You
Lately/Tom Traubert's Blues/The First Cut Is
The Deepest/Mandolin Wind/Highgate
Shuffle/Stay With Me/Having A Party
CD: WEA – Ger 1993

SOLO

I'VE GOT MY OWN ALBUM TO DO
I Can Feel The Fire/Far East Man/Mystifies
Me/Take A Look At The
Guy/Act Together/Am I Grooving
You/Shirley/Cancel Everything/Sure The
One You Need/If You Got To Make A Fool
Of Somebody/Crotch Music
WEA WB/K 56065 – Ger/UK 1974
Thunderbolt THBL 2.034 – UK 1985
(new title: Cancel Everything)
CD: Thunderbolt TB 2.034 – UK

NOW LOOK
I Got Lost When I Found You/Big
Bayou/Breathe On Me/If You Don't
Want My Love/I Can Say She's All
Right/Caribbean Boogie/Now Look/

Sweet Baby Mine/I Can't Stand The Rain/It's
Unholy/I Got A Feeling
WEA WB/K 56145 – Ger/UK 1975
CD: Thunderbolt TB 046 – UK

**MAHONEY'S LAST STAND (Soundtrack;
RON WOOD & RONNIE LANE)**
(see Ronnie Lane)

GIMME SOME NECK
Worry No More/Breakin' My
Heart/Delia/Buried Alive/Come To
Realise/Infekshun/Seven Days/We All Get
Old/FUC Her/Lost And Lonely/Don't Worry
CBS 83337 – Ger/UK 1979
CD: Columbia CK 35702 – US

1234
1234/Fountain Of Love/
Outlaws/Redeyes/Wind Howlin' Through/
Priceless/She Was Out There/Down To The
Ground/She Never Told Me
CBS 85227 – Ger/UK 1981
CD: CBS Sony 23OP 5589 – JAP

SURE THE ONE YOU NEED
Perfect Beat PB 006-2 – Ger   1989
(contains the first two LPs)

LIVE AT THE RITZ (with BO DIDDLEY)
Road Runner/I'm A Man/Crackin Up/Hey Bo
Diddley/Plynth-Water Down The Drain/Ooh
La La/They Don't Make Outlaws Like They
Used To/Honky Tonk Woman/Money To
Ronnie/Who Do You Love *
JVC VILZ-28122 – JAP 1988
CD: JVC VDPZ-1329 – JAP 1988*

SLIDE ON THIS
Somebody Else Might/Testify/Ain't
Rock'N'Roll/Josephine/Knock Yer Teeth
Out/Ragtime Annie (Lillie's Bordello)/Must
Be Love/Fear For Your Future/Show
Me/Always Wanted More/Thinkin'/Like
It/Breathe On Me

CD: Continuum 19210-2 – US 1992

**SLIDE ON LIVE – PLUGGED IN AND
STANDING**
Testify/Josephine/Pretty Beat Up/Am I
Grooving You?/Flying/Breathe On
Me/Silicon Grown/Seven Days/Show
Me/Show Me (Groove)/I Can Feel The
Fire/Slide Inst./Stay With Me
CD: Continuum CDCTUM 3 – UK/D 1993

SINGLES/12" SINGLES

I Can Feel The Fire/Breathe On Me
WEA WB/K 16463 – UK 1975

**If You Don't Want My Love/I Got A
Feeling**
WEA WB/K 16618 – UK 1975

Big Bayou/Sweet Baby Mine
Warner Bros K 16679 – UK 1976

Seven Days/Come To Realise
CBS 7785 – Ger/UK..1979

**I Can Feel The Fire/Sure The One You
Need/Am I Grooving You**
Perfect Beat PB 12.004 – Ger   1989

Show Me/Breathe On Me
Continuum 12210 – US 1992

Stay With Me (live)
Continuum 12309 – US 1993

Somebody Else Might
Continuum 14210 – US 1993

Always Wanted More
Continuum 15210 – US 1993

Cover Versions (selection)

A. SMALL FACES

+AFTERGLOW (OF YOUR LOVE):

FLO & EDDIE: Flo & Eddie
(Reprise, 1973)

QUIET RIOT: II
(Sony Japan, 1979)

QUIET RIOT: The Randy Rhoads Years
(Rhino, 1993; acoustic version – rec 1979)

GREAT WHITE: Hooked
(Capitol/EMI, 1991)

SAITENWIND (in Dusseldorf vernacular;
titled: "Endlisch alleen";
Hardcore!!!): "Band op tour"
(Vondue Records, 1988)

CHANGING MAN ft Kenney Jones:
Long Agos And Worlds Apart (see
Kenney Jones)

+ALL OR NOTHING

DOGS D'AMOUR: Maxi All Or Nothing
(China Records, 1993)

ELLIS, STEVE & LOVE AFFAIR:
Plugged In
(Double Play, 1994)

LITTLE BOB STORY: Alive Or Nothing
(live version/Musidisc, 1990)

LITTLE BOB STORY: Single
(B-side: Hot'N'Sweaty/Mercury, 1977)

LORDS OF THE NEW CHURCH: mini live
LP Rape Of The Vaults
(rec 1986 ft Ian McLagan!/Perfect Beat, 1988)

OSTBAHN-KURTI & DIE CHEFPARTIE (in
Vienna vernacular; titled "Des ollas ziht
nix"): Live
(MCA, 1985)

RIFF: Single
(B-side: Mission Love/RCA, 1989)

SPECTRUM: Single/Maxi
(A- and B-sides/Stiff, 1985)

X: Ain't Love Grand
(Elektra, 1985)

+ALMOST GROWN

MOTHER EARTH: EP Grow Your Own
(Acid Jazz, 1993)

KENNEY JONES ALL STARS: Long Agos
And Worlds Apart (see Kenney Jones)

+AUTUMN STONE

GENE: Long Agos And Worlds Apart (see
Kenney Jones)

+BECOME LIKE YOU

GRANNY TAKES A TRIP: Long Agos And
Worlds Apart (see Kenney Jones)

+DON'T BURST MY BUBBLE

THE PRISONERS: Smashing Time
(Re-elect The President, 1987)

+GET YOURSELF TOGETHER

THE JAM: Maxi B-Side
(live version/Polydor, 1978)

THE JAM: Extras
(studio version/Polydor, 1992)

+GREEN CIRCLES

TWICE AS MUCH: That's All
(Decca, 1968)

+(IF YOU THINK YOU'RE) GROOVY

(original song for PP Arnold)

PP ARNOLD: Single
*(B-side: Though It Hurts Me Badly/prod.:
Mick Jagger)*

Rick Springfield: Rock Of Life
(RCA, 1988)

+(TELL ME) HAVE YOU EVER SEEN ME

GUMBALL: CD Supertasty
(Columbia, 1993)

+HERE COME THE NICE

RICH KIDS: B-side of Marching Men
(EMI, 1978)

BUZZCOCKS:
Long Agos And Worlds Apart (see
Kenney Jones)

+HEY GIRL

UDO ARNDT & THE SAFEBREAKERS:
Single
(Ariola 1966)

THE CHORDS: B-side of Maybe
Tomorrow
(Metronome, 1980)

+I CAN'T DANCE WITH YOU

THE VALENTINES (feat Bon Scott): B-
side of Every Day I Have To Cry

*(Clarion Recods, 1967; and on compilation
The Early Years on C-Five Records, 1991)*

+I CAN'T MAKE IT

DODGY:
Long Agos And Worlds Apart (see
Kenney Jones)

+ITCHYCOO PARK

BLUE MURDER: Nothin' But Trouble
(Geffen/MCA, 1993)

QUIET RIOT: Terrified
(Concrete/Edel, 1993)

RYMES WITH ORANGE: Peel
(CS 1992)

M PEOPLE: CD single, five different
mixes
(Deconstruction/BMG 1995)

+I'VE GOT MINE

MANTARAY:
Long Agos And Worlds Apart (see
Kenney Jones)

+LAZY SUNDAY

VAN: Out In The Rain
(SPV, 1992)

SAITENWIND (in Dusseldorf vernacular;
titled "Fuule Sonndach" -
Hardcore): LP Band op tour
(Vondue Records, 1988)

TOY DOLLS: Orchestrated
(Rebel Records, 1995)

TEMPEST: CD

THUNDER: Picture CD A Better Man
(EMI, 1993)

+MY MIND'S EYE

WEBB WILDER AND THE NASHVEGANS:
Town And Country
(Watermelon, 1995)

NORTHERN UPROAR: Long Agos And
Worlds Apart (see Kenney Jones)

+MY WAY OF GIVING

CHRIS FARLOWE & THE
THUNDERBIRDS: Single A-side
(Immediate, 1967)

JOHNNY HALLYDAY (French version
titled "J'en ai jamais rien demandé"): LP
Johnny
(Philips, 1968)

ROD STEWART: Gasoline Alley
(Mercury, 1970)

+ROLLIN' OVER

DON FARDON: Lament Of The Cherokee
(only Italian pressing/Young Blood, 1968)

BRIAN MAY: Back To The Light
(Parlophone, 1992)

WHITEOUT: Long Agos And Worlds
Apart (see Kenney Jones)

+SHA-LA-LA-LA-LEE

GERMAN BLUE FLAMES: Single
(Ariola, 1966)

THE IN CROWD: Single A-side
(Star-Club-Records, 1966)

MUD: Mud Rock
(RAK, 1974)

PLASTIC BERTRAND: An 1
(Hansa, 1977)

LEINEMANN: B-side of single Mama,
Mama, Gimme Medicine
(Philips, 1978)

THE DB's: EP Christmas Time
(A&M, 1985)

THE PURPLE HELMETS: Rise Again
(Rebel Rec, 1989)

+SONG OF A BAKER

SCREAMING TREES: Sweet Oblivion
*(Sony Music, 1992; bonus track on US and
Japanese pressing)*

OCEAN COLOUR SCENE: Long Agos And
Worlds Apart (see Kenney Jones)

+SORRY SHE'S MINE

SANDY COAST: The Original Hit
Recordings
(EMI 1989, rec 1966)

+TALK TO YOU

SPEED: B-side of EP Speed
(Real Records, 1995)

HYPERGLO':
Long Agos And Worlds Apart (see
Kenney Jones)

+THAT MAN

RIDE: Long Agos And Worlds Apart (see
Kenney Jones)

+TIN SOLDIER

EARTHQUAKE: Rockin' The World
(Beserkley, 1975)

Lou Gramm: Long Hard Look
(Atlantic, 1989)

KIN PING MEH: Kin Ping Meh
(Bacillus, 1977)

QUIET RIOT: I
(Sony Japan, 1978)

TODD RUNDGREN: The Ever Popular
Tortured Artist Effect
(Lamborghini Records, 1982)

SEVEN ELEVEN: B-side
I'm In Love/Glashaus edition, 1986

URIAH HEEP: 12 inch On The Rebound
(Bronze, 1982)

PAUL WELLER MOVEMENT: Video Live At
The Brixton Academy
(Music Club, 1991)

+UNDERSTANDING

TONY JACKSON GROUP: Just Like Me
(Strange Things, 1991; rec 1966)

THE APEMEN: CD compilation Beat-O-
Mania At Its Best
(Music Maniac, 1995)

I PIRATI: I Pirati (Italian version titled
Non Scocciare)
(Destination X, 1995)

+THE UNIVERSAL

60FT DOLLS: Long Agos And Worlds

Apart (see Kenney Jones)

+WHAM BAM THANK YOU MAM

MOTHER EARTH: You Have Been
Watching
(Acid Jazz, 1995)

+WHAT'CHA GONNA DO ABOUT IT

THE BOOTS: Here Are The Boots
(Telefunken, 1966)

THE LITTER: Distortions
(Warwick, 1967)

SEX PISTOLS: The Great Rock'N'Roll
Swindle
(Virgin, 1979)

THE PRETENDERS: Flexi-Disc for
magazine Smash Hits (1979)

PRIMAL SCREAM ft PP Arnold: : Long
Agos And Worlds Apart (see Kenney
Jones)

TRIBUTE RECORDS

TRIBUTE TO STEVE MARRIOTT:
Los Covers – Get Yourself Together/The
Lazy Sundays – Afterglow/The
Runarounds – Understanding/He.Li.O –
Get Yourself Together
(Marriott Records 001, 1995)

TRIBUTE TO THE SMALL FACES
(Focus Records, UK 1996)

LONG AGOS AND WORLDS APART
A Tribute To The Small Faces
(see Kenney Jones)

B. FACES/RONNIE LANE

+CINDY INCIDENTALLY

DEL AMITRI: 12 inch Just Like A Man
(A&M, 1992)

+FLYING

LONG JOHN BALDRY: It Ain't Easy
(Warner Bros, 1971)

+GLAD AND SORRY

GOLDEN SMOG: Down By The Old
Mainstream
(Rykodisc, 1996)

+HOW COME

THE POGUES: Single
(WEA, 1995)

+NO TURNING BACK (LAST TANGO IN NATO)

THE PIRATES: From Calypso To Colapso
(with new lyrics titled Armageddon)
(Thunderbolt, 1994)

+OOH LA LA

RONNIE WOOD AND BO DIDDLEY: Live
At The Ritz
(JVC, 1988)

THE BENT BACKED TULIPS: Looking
Through
(New Rose, 1990)

SOUL ASYLUM: CD-Bootleg Runaway
Child
(Clinton Records, 1993)

IDHA: EP A Woman In A Man's World
(Creation, 1994)

+STAY WITH ME

ELKIE BROOKS: Shooting Star
(A&M, 1978)

C. HUMBLE PIE/STEVE MARRIOTT

+FOOL FOR A PRETTY FACE

MOTHER STATION: Brand New Bag
(east/west, 1994)

+HOT'N'NASTY

TONE-LOC: Cool Hand Loc (in Fatal
Attraction track)
(Island, 1991)

+PHONE CALL AWAY

SHUT UP FRANK!: Combined
(Mouse Records, 1993)

JIM LEVERTON & GEOFFREY
RICHARDSON: Follow Your Heart
(Mouse Records, 1995)

+STRANGE DAYS

JOHN NORUM: Another Destination
(Warner Bros, 1971)

+30 DAYS IN THE HOLE

KICK AXE: Soundtrack LP Up The Creek
(Epic, 1984)

MR BIG: Mr Big
(Atlantic, 1989)

FILMOGRAPHY & VIDEOGRAPHY

FILMOGRAPHY: (SELECTION)

One-song appearances are not listed. Live or playback, they ran in the usual British TV programmes like *Crackerjack, Ready Steady Go, Dee Time Show, Sounds For Saturday, Top Of The Pops* or the German TV shows *Beat, Beat, Beat* and *Beat-Club*.

SMALL FACES

DATELINE DIAMONDS
British movie from 1965 by Jeremy Summers; The Small Faces play Sha-La-La-La-Lee/Come On Children and I Got Mine *available on VHS via John Drake, 5 Hogshill Lane, Cobham, Surrey KT11 2AG*

SMALL FACES LIVE IN THE STUDIO
half hour special for Manchester's independent TV station Granada Television; was screened 28 September 1968; according to its directing assistant, Rod Taylor, it was "the most exciting show we've done since the Little Richard spot"; lost unfortunately

COLOUR ME POP
30 minute TV show serial by BBC2, for which The Small Faces had edited their Ogdens' Nut Gone Flake *album, must have been screened first on 21 June 1968; in December 1991 its only excerpt in the BBC2 series* The Sounds Of The Sixties *was* Song Of A Baker

POPCORN
American music documentary by Peter Clifton, 1969; The Small Faces play Itchycoo Park and Lazy Sunday; was only shown in US cinemas; premiered on 16 November 1969

THE FACES

SWING IN – THE FACES LIVE AT THE MARQUEE
Devotion/You're My Girl/Flying/Too Much Women/Maybe I'm Amazed/ Gasoline Alley/Plynth
30 minute film of a 1970 concert; a Dutch production for German WDR-TV; first screened 15 January 1971 in afternoon programme of German ARD-TV

FAREWELL CONCERT
It's All Over Now/Bring It On Home/Send It To Me/Sweet Little Rock'n'Roller/Angel/Twistin' The Night Away/You Wear It Well/ Maggie May/We'll Meet Again/I'd Rather Go Blind
65 minute movie concert. Direction: Mike Mansfield; document of Faces gig in London's Kilburn Theatre 1974 ; till 1982 also in catalogue of German ATLAS Film Publishing, titled Rod Stewart's Farewell Concert; *excerpts in Rod Stewart & Faces video biogr)*

RONNIE LANE

ROCKPALAST
Annie Had A Baby/How Come/Debris/I'm
Ready/Kuschty Rye/Man Smart, Woman
Smarter/One For The Road/Outro
*"small scale Rockpalast" gig, recorded 19
March 1980, first screened on Channel III
of German WDR in June 1980*

VIDEOGRAPHY

SMALL FACES

BIG HITS
Here Come The Nice/What'cha Gonna Do
About It/Hey Girl/All Or Nothing/Itchycoo
Park/Tin Soldier/Talk To Me/Lazy Sunday/
Itchycoo Park/Lazy Sunday/Here Come The
Nice/My Mind's Eye
Castle Music Pictures CMP 6066 – UK 1991

THE FACES

ROD STEWART AND THE FACES: VIDEO
BIOGRAPHY 1969-1974
Three Button Hand Me Down/It's All Over
Now/Gasoline Alley/Maggie May/(I Know)
I'm Losing You/I Feel So Good/Memphis
Tennessee/Stay With Me/Miss Judy's
Farm/That's All You Need/I'd Rather Go
Blind/True Blue/You Wear It
Well/Angel/Cindy Incidentally/Pool Hall
Richard/Sweet Little Rock'N'Roller/You Can
Make Me Dance, Sing Or Anything
CCTV Maverick VC 4053 – UK 1988

STEVE MARRIOTT

TIN SOLDIER
What'cha Gonna Do About It/Fool For A
Pretty Face/Shame Shame Shame/All Or
Nothing/Five Long Years/30 Days In The
Hole/I Don't Need No Doctor/Walking The
Dog/Tin Soldier
*The Packet Of Three; filmed and recorded
in Camden Palace, London, 1985)
Castle Hendring HEN 2 198 – UK 1990*

LIVE IN SAARBRÜCKEN
Some Kind Of Wonderful-Can I Get A
Witness?/Don't You Lie To Me/All Or
Nothing/What'cha Gonna Do About
It/Talking 'Bout You/My Girl/Fool For A
Pretty Face/Five Long Years/Tin Soldier/Run
Run Rudolph/I Know (You Don't Want Me
No More)/Slow Down
*The Official Receivers filmed and recorded
in Waldcafé, Saarbrücken, 1987
BT (professional private video; limited
edition) – D 1990*

RONNIE LANE

THE RONNIE LANE APPEAL FOR ARMS:
PARTS 1 & 2
Goodnight Irene (sung by Ronnie Lane);
other songs by Bill Wyman, Steve Winwood,
Eric Clapton, Jeff Beck, Jimmy Page,
Kenney Jones, Charlie Watts, Andy
Fairweather-Low and others
*filmed and recorded at the Royal Albert
Hall, London, 1983
Videoform VFV 16 + 17 – UK 1984
Channel Five CFV 00482 – UK 1986
(Single video with different title: ARMS –
The Complete Concert)*

BIBLIOGRAPHY

Books/Articles

Adler, Irene: *Peter Frampton*
New York: Quick Fox, 1979. 96p

Barnes, Ken: *The Small Faces*
in: Greg Shaw's *Bomp! Die Briten kommen. Aus den Kindertagen der englischen Rockmusik*. Reinbek: Rowohlt, 1983. p198-202

Benjamin, Kent/Ken Sharp/John Hellier: "For Nice Is The Music, Forever And Ever, Amen. The Story Of The Small Faces In Their Own Words"
in: *Goldmine. The Collectors Records And Compact Disc Marketplace*. Vol 22 No 13 June 21, 1996 p20-183

Burton, Peter: *Rod Stewart A Life On The Town*
London: New English Library, 1977 p120

Cromelin, Richard: *Rod Stewart A Biography In Words & Pictures*
Edited by Greg Shaw. New York: Sire Books, 1976

Daly, Marsha: *Peter Frampton*
New York: Grosset & Dunlap, 1979 p92

Du Noyer, Paul: "The most perfect group England ever made"
in: *Q* Jan 1996. p94-100

Gray, John: *Rod Stewart A Visual Documentary*
London: Omnibus Press, 1992

Hewitt, Paolo: *Small Faces – The Young Mods' Forgotten Story*
London: Acid Jazz, 1995. 160p (with a foreword by Kenney Jones)

Jasper, Tony: *Rod Stewart*
London: Octopus Books, 1977. 94p

Jones, Cliff/Andrew Martin: *All Or Nothing (Steve Marriott: The Full Unbelievable Story)*
in: *Mojo* December 1994. p56-76 (with contributions by Paul Weller and Andrew Arnhem)

Katz, Susan: *Frampton! An Unauthorised Biography*
New York: Jove Publications, 1978. 190p

Marriott, Steve/Green, Jim: *Autodiscography Part 1*
in: *Trouser Press* No 7 1981. p21-24

Marriott, Steve/Green, Jim: *Autodiscography Part 2*
in: *Trouser Press* No 8 1981. p28-31

The Mods – Part VI: Tough Kids – Small Faces
in: *Gorilla Beat* No 7 1981. (6 pages)

Moody, Paul/Paul Brannigan: *Itchycoo Parklife*
in: *Vox* March 1996. p62-66

Nelson, Paul/Bangs, Lester: *Rod Stewart*
New York: Delilah Communications, 1981. 160p

Pidgeon, John: *Rod Stewart And The Changing Faces*
Frogmore, St Albans: Panther, 1976. 144p

Rawlings, Terry: *All Our Yesterdays. A Fan's Eye View Of The Small Faces*
Edited by Paul Weller. London: Riot Stories Ltd. 1982

Rawlings, Terry: "The Small Faces"
TR talks to Small Faces drummer Kenney Jones about the band who

personified the Mod lifestyle in the Sixties.
in: *Record Collector* No 158 Oct 1992. p54-61

Reed, John: "Small Faces In Memoriam"
in: *Record Collector* No 197 Jan 1996. p30-4

Reichold, Martin: "Mods & Rockers"
in: *Oldie-Markt* No 8 1987. p5-8

Reichold, Martin: "Klein, aber oho!"
in: *Oldie-Markt* No 9 1987. p9-12

Reichold, Martin: "Rod The Mod"
in: *Oldie-Markt* No 10 1987. p5-9

Reichold, Martin: "Der zweite Start"
in: *Oldie-Markt* No 11 1987. p10-13

Reichold, Martin: "Die letzte Phase"
in: *Oldie-Markt* No 12 1987. p10-12

Reichold, Martin: "Der Aussteiger"
in: *Oldie-Markt* No 1 1988. p5-9

Röckl, Gerd/Sahner, Paul: *Rod Stewart*
Bergisch Gladbach: Bastei Luebbe, 1979. 151p

Schmitt, Roland: Ronnie Lane. "Ein liebenswerter Aussenseiter"
in: *folk-michel* No 4 1990. p32-37

Silverton, Pete: "All Or Nothing. The Small Faces Story"
in: *Trouser Press* No 10 1977. p10-15

Valentine, Penny: "Small Faces. Viergeteilt? Niemals!"
in: (German) *Sounds* No 6 1977. p36-39

Vorda, Allan: "It's All Too Beautiful. An interview with Ronnie Lane"
in: *DISCoveries* Nov 1989. p110-112

Welch, Chris: Face Values. The Story Of The Small Faces
in: *Extra Kerrang!* No 6 1985. p8-14

Wood, Ron (with Bill German): *The Works. Keith Richards, Mick Jagger, Rod Stewart, Bob Dylan, John Lennon, Jack Daniels, Jail, Fame, Sex, Art, Stars and Scars*
London: Fontana/Collins, 1988. 122p

Wright, Stuart: "The Small Faces"
in: *Music Collector* June 1991

fanzines/newsletter

Darlings Of Wapping Wharf Launderette
c/o John Hellier, 7 Waterdene Mews, Canvey Island, Essex SS8 9YP, UK

Itchycoo (newsletter)
c/o Roland Schmitt, Grüfinthalerstrasse 57a, 66130 Saarbrücken, Germany

Ogdens' (deleted newsletter)

Small Faces International
A Steel, 1 Wellington Avenue, St Ives, Cambs PE 17 6UT, UK

Internet

Room For Ravers
http://ourworld.compuserve.com/homepages/Martin_Payne/
c/o Martin Payne, 19 Freeland Road, Ealing, London W5, UK

INDEX

318

ALSO AVAILABLE FROM
SANCTUARY MUSIC LIBRARY

1-86074-160-6   **JONI MITCHELL – BOTH SIDES NOW**
by Brian Hinton   £12.99/$19.95

1-86074-174-6   **GEORGE GERSHWIN – HIS LIFE & MUSIC**
by Ean Wood   £9.99/$14.95

1-86074-184-3   **THE QUIET ONE – A LIFE OF GEORGE HARRISON**
by Alan Clayson   £9.99/$14.95

1-86074-189-4   **RINGO STARR – STRAIGHT MAN OR JOKER?**
by Alan Clayson   £9.99/$14.95

1-86074-169-X   **CELTIC CROSSROADS – THE ART OF VAN MORRISON**
by Brian Hinton   £9.99/$14.95

1-86074-130-4   **LIVING LEGEND – BO DIDDLEY**
by George R White   £9.99/$14.95

1-898141-13-4   **PETER GREEN – FOUNDER OF FLEETWOOD MAC**
by Martin Celmins   £9.99/$14.95

1-86074-136-3   **JACQUES BREL**
by Alan Clayson   £9.99/$14.95

1-86074-149-5   **WHEELS OF CONFUSION – THE STORY OF BLACK SABBATH**
by Steven Rosen   £9.99/$14.95

1-86074-182-7   **SEVENTEEN WATTS? THE FIRST 20 YEARS OF BRITISH
ROCK GUITAR, THE MUSICIANS AND THEIR STORIES**
by Mo Foster   £19.99/$34.95

1-86074-129-0   **JOHN MAYALL – BLUES BREAKER**
by Richard Newman   £9.99/$14.95

1-86074-135-5   **THE KINKS – WELL RESPECTED MEN**
by Neville Marten & Jeffrey Hudson   £9.99/$14.95

1-86074-139-8   **THE DOORS – ARTISTIC VISION**
by Doug Sundling   £9.99/$14.95

1-86074-131-2   **LADY DAY'S DIARY – THE LIFE OF BILLIE HOLIDAY 1937-59**
by Ken Vail   £12.99/$19.95

1-86074-132-0   **BIRD'S DIARY – THE LIFE OF CHARLIE PARKER 1945-55**
by Ken Vail   £12.99/$19.95

1-86074-159-2   **MILES' DIARY– THE LIFE OF MILES DAVIS 1947-61**
by Ken Vail   £12.99/$19.95

1-86074-050-2   **JAZZ MILESTONES – A PICTORIAL CHRONICLE OF JAZZ 1900-90**
by Ken Vail   £14.99/$24.95

1-86074-133-9   **RAPPERS RAPPIN' – THE STORY OF THE FRESHEST SOUND AROUND FROM RAP'S MADDEST AND BADDEST**
by Dan Goldstein   £6.99/$12.95

1-86074-134-7   **HISTORY OF HOUSE**
by Chris Kempster   £12.99/$19.95

1-86074-144-4   **GOOD VIBRATIONS – A HISTORY OF RECORD PRODUCTION**
by Mark Cunningham   £9.99/$14.95

1-86074-154-1   **BORN TO SWING – THE STORY OF THE BIG BANDS**
by Ean Wood   £14.99/$24.95

For more information on titles from Sanctuary Publishing Ltd, please contact Sanctuary Publishing Ltd, 82 Bishops Bridge Road, London W6 2BB Tel: +44 (0) 171 243 0640 Fax: +44 (0) 171 243 0470. To order a title direct, please contact our distributors: (UK only) Macmillan Distribution Ltd Tel: 01256 302659. (US & Canada) Music Sales Corporation Tel: 1 800 431 7187. (Australia & New Zealand) Bookwise International Tel: 08268 8222.